THE NORTH CAUCASUS BORDERLAND

Edinburgh Studies on the Ottoman Empire
Series Editor: Kent F. Schull

Published and forthcoming titles

Migrating Texts: Circulating Translations around the Ottoman Mediterranean
Edited by Marilyn Booth

Death and Life in the Ottoman Palace: Revelations of the Sultan Abdülhamid I Tomb
Douglas Brookes

Ottoman Sunnism: New Perspectives
Edited by Vefa Erginbaş

Jews and Palestinians in the Late Ottoman Era, 1908–1914: Claiming the Homeland
Louis A. Fishman

Spiritual Vernacular of the Early Ottoman Frontier: The Yazıcıoğlu Family
Carlos Grenier

The Politics of Armenian Migration to North America, 1885–1915: Sojourners, Smugglers and Dubious Citizens
David Gutman

The Kizilbash-Alevis in Ottoman Anatolia: Sufism, Politics and Community
Ayfer Karakaya-Stump

Çemberlitaş Hamamı in Istanbul: The Biographical Memoir of a Turkish Bath
Nina Macaraig

The Kurdish Nobility in the Ottoman Empire: Loyalty, Autonomy and Privilege
Nilay Özok-Gündoğan

Nineteenth-Century Local Governance in Ottoman Bulgaria: Politics in Provincial Councils
M. Safa Saraçoğlu

Prisons in the Late Ottoman Empire: Microcosms of Modernity
Kent F. Schull

Ruler Visibility and Popular Belonging in the Ottoman Empire, 1808–1908
Darin N. Stephanov

The North Caucasus Borderland: Between Muscovy and the Ottoman Empire, 1555–1605
Murat Yasar

Children and Childhood in the Ottoman Empire: From the 15th to the 20th Century
Edited by Gülay Yilmaz and Fruma Zachs

euppublishing.com/series/esoe

THE NORTH CAUCASUS BORDERLAND

BETWEEN MUSCOVY AND THE OTTOMAN EMPIRE, 1555–1605

Murat Yaşar

EDINBURGH
University Press

Edinburgh University Press is one of the leading university presses in the UK. We publish academic books and journals in our selected subject areas across the humanities and social sciences, combining cutting-edge scholarship with high editorial and production values to produce academic works of lasting importance. For more information visit our website: edinburghuniversitypress.com

Edinburgh University Press Ltd
The Tun – Holyrood Road
12 (2f) Jackson's Entry
Edinburgh EH8 8PJ

First published in hardback by Edinburgh University Press 2022

Typeset in Jaghbuni by
Cheshire Typesetting Ltd, Cuddington, Cheshire,

A CIP record for this book is available from the British Library

ISBN 978 1 4744 9869 2 (hardback)
ISBN 978 1 4744 9870 8 (paperback)
ISBN 978 1 4744 9871 5 (webready PDF)
ISBN 978 1 4744 9872 2 (epub)

Contents

List of Illustrations vii
Acknowledgements viii
A Note on Transliteration and Spelling of Terms and Names x

Introduction: Sources, Methodology and Terminology 1
Sources 4
Terminology 9
Structure of the Book 12

1. The Land and Peoples of the North Caucasus in the Sixteenth Century: An Overview 19
1.1 The Land 19
1.2 The Peoples 23
1.3 The North Caucasus: An Overview of the First Half of the Sixteenth Century 36

2. Tracing the Milky Way: The North Caucasus and the Two Empires 49
2.1 The North Caucasus within Ottoman Northern Policy 49
2.2 The North Caucasus within Muscovite Steppe Frontier Policy 55
2.3 The Road to Astrakhan: Towards a Mature Ottoman Policy in the North 63
2.4 Muscovite 'Ghost Fortresses' and Muscovite Ways of Defining Loyalties in the North Caucasus 69

3. Bargaining for the Milky Way: The Astrakhan Campaign and the North Caucasus Borderland 86
3.1 The Astrakhan Ordeal: Preparation, Campaign and its Aftermath 86
3.2 The Muscovite Responses to the Campaign 98

4. The Milky Way Fades: Post-Astrakhan Ottoman and Muscovite Strategies in the North Caucasus 115
4.1 Out of the Ashes, the Tsar's Prestige Born Again: Revival of Muscovite Power in Kabarda 115
4.2 Killing Two Birds with One Stone: The Ottoman–Safavid War of 1578–90 and the North Caucasus 118
4.3 Muscovite Attempts to Contain Ottoman Activities in the North Caucasus 138

5. The Milky Way Vanishes: The Denouement of the Ottoman–Muscovite Rivalry in the North Caucasus, 1605 155
5.1 Pacification and Muscovite Domination of Kabarda 155
5.2 The Final Act of the Imperial Rivalry in the North Caucasus: The Muscovite Offensives in Daghestan 162

6. Searching for the Milky Way: A Tale of Five Narts 177
6.1 Kansavuk and Sibok of the Janey Circassians 178
6.2 Solokh of Kabarda 181
6.3 Urus of the Greater Nogays 189
6.4 Alexander II of the Kingdom of Kakheti 194

Conclusion: Imperial Entanglements and Borderlandisation of the North Caucasus 202

Appendix I: Selected Ottoman Documents from *Mühimme* Registers 218
Appendix II: Selected Muscovite Documents from *Posol'skii Prikaz* Records 232
Appendix III: Glossary of Terms 244
Appendix IV: Chronology 247
Bibliography 250
Index 266

Illustrations

Figures

1.1 Map of the Black Sea and Circassia by Piri Reis, 1525 20
2.1 Baptism of Temriuk's son, Saltankul, in Moscow, 1558 70
2.2 Ivan IV sends aid to his father-in-law, Temriuk, 1563 72
3.1 Ivan IV sends Prince Vyshnevetskyi to attack the Crimean Khanate, 1553 87
3.2 Ivan IV sends soldiers and material to build a fortress in Kabarda, 1567 94
4.1 Osman Pasha and Ottoman troops in Derbend, 1578 131
4.2 Ottoman troops attack the Kaytaks in Daghestan 132
6.1 Prince Vyshnevetskyi and Prince Sibok in Ivan IV's service, 1560 180
6.2 King Alexander with Lala Mustafa Pasha, 1578 195

Maps

1.1 The North Caucasus before the Ottoman–Safavid War of 1578–90 38
5.1 The North Caucasus, 1583–1603 and the Ottoman supply route 161

Acknowledgements

I am indebted to many colleagues, friends and family in the course of my research and writing this book. Among them, I am forever thankful to Victor Ostapchuk, who encouraged me to consider specialising in the early modern history of the North Caucasus and allowed me to use his personal microfilm library for my research. I benefited greatly from his mentorship and friendship. Many thanks to Virginia Aksan, Maria Subtelny, Brian Boeck and Alison Smith for their comments on the original dissertation. Virginia Aksan also helped me with the initial process of figuring out how to turn it into a manuscript. I also owe much to İsenbike Togan, who showed me the way when I was a clueless undergraduate student and instilled in me a love for languages and an interest in Russian history and borderlands.

I am grateful for numerous travel grants, awards and fellowships from several institutions. The Department of Near and Middle Eastern Studies at the University of Toronto provided fellowships and several grants that funded my archival visits in Turkey. The History Department at the State University of New York at Oswego was generous with conference and research grants for this endeavour. I also thank the helpful and kind staff members of the Ottoman Archives, Istanbul University Library and Süleymaniye Library in Istanbul as well as Robarts Library and Thomas Fisher Rare Book Library in Toronto.

My thanks also go to my amazing friends and colleagues in Canada, Turkey and the United States who assisted my research agenda and book project. I thank Maryna Kravets for reading parts of this work and her comments. Natalie Rothman, Mehmet Kuru, Lale Javanshir, Gülay Yılmaz, Joo-Yup Lee, Kayla Kavanagh and Metin Bezikoğlu in Toronto, and Geraldine Forbes, Frank Byrne, Jennie Han, Christopher Mack, Mary McCune and Richard Weyhing in Oswego provided intellectual and emotional support. My colleagues Courtney Doucette and Candis Haak read and commented on several chapters of the manuscript, for which I am thankful.

I owe special thanks to Kent Schull, editor of the series, and a great colleague who has supported this book project since we first talked about my research in 2015. He read my proposal and manuscript several times. His comments and insights have benefited this book greatly. I also thank Nicola Ramsey, publisher in Islamic history for Edinburgh University Press, for her patience and support in the publication process. Many thanks to the anonymous reviewers for their comments, suggestions and sensible criticism that helped me improve the final version of this work.

I have a great debt of gratitude to my families, both in Turkey and in Canada, who have always supported me. For many years, my partner Candis Haak and I have shared a love for history, cats, museums and libraries. My greatest thanks go to her for years of support and encouragement. Lastly, I dedicate this book to my father, who bought me my first history book when I was a primary school student and taught me the meaning of history.

A Note on Transliteration and Spelling of Terms and Names

The Ottoman Empire and the Tsardom of Muscovy ruled over peoples speaking a plethora of languages, which is reflected in their archival material as well as names and terms referenced throughout this book. For convenience, I have rendered Ottoman terms and names based on modern Turkish orthography. In the case of Russian terms and names, I have employed a modified form of the Library of Congress transliteration system. However, I have opted to use Anglicised versions of both Ottoman and Russian terms when available. Thus, the reader will see 'pasha', not '*paşa*'. The North Caucasus names and terms have been rendered as they appeared in the Ottoman or Russian documents or in their modern standardised versions. Lastly, frequently used non-English terms appear in italics only in their first usage. They appear in normal script thereafter in an attempt to make the text more accessible to the reader.

For the sake of simplicity, I have opted to use place names as they were in the polity, state or empire to which they belonged during the early modern era. As such, I use Kefe, instead of Caffa or Kaffa. The exception to this rule is that I have preferred commonly known standard English equivalents of place names for the convenience of the reader. For example, the capital of Muscovy is Moscow in this book, not Moskva.

Introduction: Sources, Methodology and Terminology

Прощай, немытая Россия,
Страна рабов, страна господ,
И вы, мундиры голубые,
И ты, им преданный народ.
Быть может, за стеной Кавказа
Сокроюсь от твоих пашей,
От их всевидящего глаза,
От их всеслышащих ушей.
Mikhail Lermontov (1840)*

An ancient Circassian Nart saga, Tlepsh and Lady Tree, inspired the titles of the chapters herein. Nart sagas are legends of the North Caucasus peoples. The Narts are virtuous heroes and familiar figures in the folklore of the diverse North Caucasus societies regardless of their ethnic or linguistic origins. The saga of Tlepsh and Lady Tree tells the story of the Milky Way, the guiding light of the Narts. Accordingly, worrying about the future and survival of his Narts, Tlepsh, the god of fire and forge, went on a quest to find an answer to ensure their prosperity and endurance. During his travels, he came across Lady Tree, a goddess

* Mikhail Lermontov, *Sobranie sochinenii v chetyrekh tomakh* (Moscow: Izdatel'stvo Akademii nauk SSSR, 1961), 1:524. Lermontov articulates the perception of the North Caucasus by the surrounding empires as an impregnable area of refuge. The translation by Anatoly Liberman in Mikhail Lermontov, *Major Poetical Works* (Minneapolis: University of Minnesota Press, 1983), 556 is as follows:

Farewell, unwashed Russia,
land of slaves, land of lords,
and you, blue uniforms,
and you, people, obedient to them.
Perhaps beyond the ridge of Caucasus
I will hide from your pashas,
from their all-seeing eye,
from their all-hearing ears.

who was 'a tree yet not a tree, a person yet not a person'.[1] Intrigued by Tlepsh, Lady Tree invited him in and made love to him. After staying with her for a while, Tlepsh decided to continue his quest. Despite Lady Tree's protests, Tlepsh left her for the sake of his Narts. The quest was unfruitful, and yet upon Tlepsh's return, Lady Tree presented him with a baby born out of their union. Their baby was the Milky Way.[2] On the advice of Lady Tree, Tlepsh took their child, the Milky Way, to the Narts and told them to follow him in the sky so they would never get lost. One day, however, the Milky Way wandered off to play and vanished. Tlepsh rushed to Lady Tree, who told him that the child was not with her. 'A time may come when he returns on his own ... If you all return alive from raids, then you will be happy. If you do not return, then it will be your calamity and you will have perished because of this,' she warned.[3] And perish the Narts did. Not only did they lose their mountains, valleys and rivers to the imperial powers encroaching on the North Caucasus, but they were also driven away from their homeland. This book is a history of the process in which the North Caucasus peoples lost their 'milky way'.

Many people have been fascinated for the first time with the North Caucasus – the variety and beauty of its landscapes as well as its unique social and political structures – upon reading famous Russian classics of prose or poetry by Leo Tolstoy, Mikhail Lermontov or Alexander Pushkin. The region, as told by these writers, has inspired scholars, writers, artists and filmmakers for generations. This was also the case for the present author. The North Caucasus and its idiosyncratic peoples fascinated me for the first time when I was a high school student reading a novel whose protagonist had the same name as me, Tolstoy's *Hadji Murat*. I was even more enthralled upon reading the North Caucasus sections of the seventeenth-century Ottoman traveller Evliya Çelebi's multi-volume account in which he describes giant Circassian vampire witches fighting in the sky, animists worshipping trees, or people keeping bees in groins of their dead relatives. Yet, when I looked for scholarly works on the North Caucasus and its peoples to understand the history that enabled such an exciting fictional world, I was surprised to find a dearth of such books in the history section of bookstores and libraries.

Two decades later, the scholarship on the region has not advanced much. The history of the North Caucasus and its peoples, especially in the early modern period, has still not received adequate academic attention either within the historiographies of the Ottoman and Russian Empires or as a separate area of research. However, scholarly interest in the North Caucasus and the demand for academic work have continued to increase. The war in Chechnya following the break-up of the Soviet Union and the ongoing conflicts in the North Caucasus have been influential. Besides, the plight of the native North Caucasus populations, subjected to a genocide in the hands of the Russian Empire in the nineteenth century, was once more remembered by the world during the 2014 Winter Olympics, which took place in that region, in Sochi. Some scholars claim that Sochi was the site of the first modern genocide in Europe.[4] The Circassian genocide caused mass and forced migrations of many native North Caucasus peoples from their homeland into the Ottoman Empire, whose descendants today amount to millions of people living in large diasporas. Many diaspora organisations formed by the people of North Caucasus origin have been actively seeking recognition of the genocide and repatriation, which has so far been denied by the Russian Federation. Some of these repatriation claims have become more serious and feasible, particularly from war-torn countries such as Syria. Moreover, existing histories of the region and its peoples have been written from rather nationalist or ideological perspectives by Russian or Turkish historians. They are not helpful for understanding from a more objective viewpoint what happened in the North Caucasus that turned it into a borderland between the two empires in the sixteenth century, shaping the future engagements between these two powers in broader Eurasia and ending in the forced migration of the North Caucasus peoples from their homeland in the nineteenth century.

This book aims to address the aforementioned shortcomings of the current scholarship by analysing the hitherto poorly understood first encounter between the Ottoman Empire and the Tsardom of Muscovy in the North Caucasus, from the Muscovites' annexation of the nearby Khanate of Astrakhan in 1556 to their expulsion from the region by the Ottomans and their allies in 1605. It also details a process of borderlandisation in the North Caucasus between the two rival imperial powers, which encroached on the region with their territory- and subject-making strategies in the second half of the sixteenth century. Considering that imperial powers applied such strategies in their purest forms in borderlands, the North Caucasus borderland provides us with a concrete sample to examine the Ottoman and Muscovite policies in the early modern period. This book is not, however, solely a study of an imperial rivalry in a contested borderland. The Ottoman and Muscovite involvement brought about immense and irreversible changes to the internal dynamics and strategies of the polities within the North Caucasus, shaping the region, its political structures and the lives of its peoples in the following centuries, and this is examined in the chapters below.

Sources

The present book relies on the relevant primary sources from the Turkish and Russian archives as well as the sixteenth- and seventeenth-century chronicles. Two major collections of archival sources utilised for our purposes are the Ottoman *mühimme defterleri* (registers of important affairs, hereafter MD) and the Muscovite compilations of *posol'skie knigi* (ambassadorial books). These sources contain invaluable information regarding the subject- and territory-making strategies of the Ottoman Empire and Muscovy and the relations of these imperial powers with the local polities of the North Caucasus borderland, with their vassals in their broader shared frontier zones, and with each other.

The MD collection contains copies of the imperial orders issued by the Ottoman Imperial Council and the sultan concerning domestic and international affairs in their political, social and military dimensions. There are 263 volumes of MD registers, which together form the *mühimme defterleri* fond at the Turkish Presidency State Archives' Department of Ottoman Archives (Cumhurbaşkanlığı Devlet Arşivleri, Osmanlı Arşivi). The available MD collections cover approximately 350 years between 1544 and 1905.[5] Compared to the later centuries, the sixteenth-century MD collections are more comprehensive in terms of the range of issues with which they deal.[6] Ottoman historian Suraiya Faroqhi argues that the sixteenth- and seventeenth-century MDs encompass the majority of the affairs handled by the Ottoman Porte and its agents.[7] Covering over three centuries and containing invaluable information on various aspects of the functioning of the Ottoman Empire, the MD collections are unquestionably one of the most prized series in the Ottoman archives for historians working on the early modern Ottomans.

The grand vizier, viziers at the Porte, the *kadıasker* (chief judge) of Anatolia and Rumelia, the *defterdar* (treasurer) and the *nişancı* (chief of chancellery) attended the meetings at the Imperial Council to discuss and make decisions on a variety of issues regarding the administration and everyday affairs of the Ottoman Empire. Every decision made at the council needed the sultan's approval before it could be written as an imperial order (*hükm*) and sent out to its addressees. The records in the MDs could be copies of the imperial orders dispatched to the Ottoman officials, vassals or foreign rulers. As Uriel Heyd claims, this does not necessarily diminish the authenticity of these records. The great majority of the entries in these registers were dispatched, as some entries have marginal notes indicating that they were not sent out.[8] It is also true, however, that the final texts of the orders could be different in their wording and orthography. We know that in case of significant differences between the text in a register and its final form, the same order was entered again into the MD, or corrections were made alongside the entry.[9] These differences were not related to the content but only to the language and wording.[10] In most cases, there was no significant difference between the texts in MD entries and the final orders. We have examples of orders recorded in the MD collections after the final copy was made or after they were dispatched.[11] Cancellation of a registered order was also possible, but only with the written approval of the sultan.[12]

The final forms of the orders sent to the provinces or foreign rulers can sometimes be found in local or foreign archives, as evidenced in this book. However, there are examples of orders sent to the provinces or foreign rulers discovered in local or foreign archives but not extant in the Ottoman MD collections.[13] Some of the MD volumes were perhaps lost, as we understand from the lack of registers for certain years. A possible cause for these losses might be that the grand viziers took then-current registers with them during campaigns or other Ottoman officials sometimes left a part of these registers in different locales where they served.[14] So far, the Department of Ottoman Archives has published nine MD volumes.[15] These publications contain full transcriptions, modern Turkish summaries and an index for each *defter*. Halil Sahillioğlu published a volume from the Archives of Topkapı, which covers the years of 1544 and 1545.[16] In addition to these, Mehmet Ali Ünal and Hikmet Ülker edited and published two more volumes.[17]

The unpublished Muscovite sources used in this book are mostly the documents contained in *posol'skie knigi* (ambassadorial books) from the Russian State Archives of the Ancient Acts (Rossiiskii gosudarstvennyi arkhiv drevnikh aktov, henceforth RGADA). This archive is home to documents dating from the earliest periods of Eastern Slavic history. It contains approximately 1,600 fonds covering a period from the eleventh century to the nineteenth.[18] *Posol'skie knigi* were compiled by the Posol'skii Prikaz (Ambassadorial Office), which was the Muscovite government's office for foreign affairs. Its jurisdiction included sending and receiving embassies as well as establishing and maintaining commercial relations with foreign governments.[19]

Ambassadorial reports (*stateinye spiski*, literally, 'article lists'), which are a part of the *posol'skie knigi*, are valuable sources for historians, as the Muscovite envoys prepared these reports in rather exact and often vivid detail. These reports contain documents such as speeches delivered to foreign rulers and interactions and discussions between the envoys and those rulers or other high-ranking officers.[20] They also include information on Muscovite envoys' travel routes from their departure point to their destination and back to Moscow. The envoys purposely noted chiefs, rulers and other important personalities they came across and negotiated with during their travels as well. These reports were written in a daybook form and provided the Muscovite government with a day-to-day record of an embassy.[21] Therefore, the ambassadorial books and specifically the ambassadorial reports are significant sources not only for understanding Muscovite foreign policy and its functioning but also for gathering factual information on the political and social structure of the countries where the envoys conducted their embassies and of the polities and peoples encountered on the envoys' routes.

The Ambassadorial Office produced the most valuable documents regarding Muscovy's relations with the Ottoman Porte, the Crimean Khanate and the North Caucasus rulers.[22] These documents are classified by country or region, including the Crimean Khanate (*Krymskie dela*, 'Crimean Dossiers') and the Ottoman Empire (*Turetskie dela*, 'Turkish Dossiers'). Documents are preserved in chronological order within the framework of the aforementioned geographical classification. The Turkish and Crimean dossiers contain reports of Muscovite envoys to the Porte and the Crimean Khanate, as well as documentation on envoys and letters from the Ottoman sultan and the Crimean khan. There are three books preserved under the title *Turetskie dela* (fond no. 89) for the second half of the sixteenth century. Moreover, twenty-one books are catalogued under *Krymskie dela* (fond no. 123) for the same period.[23] Two books of the fond no. 89 (*Turetskie dela*) are especially crucial for information on Muscovite and Ottoman designs and negotiations on the status and affairs of the North Caucasus. *Turetskie dela* book no. 2 contains documentation of Ivan Novosiltsev's embassy to the Porte in 1570 and his ambassadorial report providing detailed information on his negotiations in the Ottoman Empire. It also has the documentation for the embassies of Andrei Kuzminskii in 1571 and Boris Blagovo in 1584. Book no. 3 contains the documents of Grigorii Nashchokin's embassy in 1592–3 and his ambassadorial report. The relevant books from the fond for Crimean affairs (fond no. 123) for the second half of the sixteenth century are numbers 13, 14, 15 and 16, which contain the documentation of A. F. Nagov and negotiations between Devlet Girey and Ivan IV partly related to North Caucasus affairs.

Sergei L. Belokurov compiled and published an extensive collection of archival documents on the relations of the principalities and rulers in the Caucasus with the Tsardom of Muscovy as early as 1889 in his monumental *Snosheniia Rossii s Kavkazom: Materialy izvlechennye iz Moskovskago glavnago arkhiva Ministerstva inostrannykh diel, 1578–1613 gg.* It encompasses archival documents related to the North Caucasus rulers and reports of Muscovite envoys on missions to the Georgian Kingdoms passing through Kabarda.[24] Additionally, *Kabardino-russkie otnosheniia v 16–18 vv* was published as an official contribution to the celebrations of 'the four hundredth anniversary of the voluntary adherence of Kabarda to Russia' in 1957 in the Soviet Union. It came out in two volumes, which present sixteenth- and seventeenth-century documents about the relations of the Kabardinian rulers and numerous other North Caucasus chieftains with Muscovy/the Russian Empire.[25] These two publications contain the essential Muscovite documents on the early modern history of the North Caucasus, including archival material from the *Kabardinskie dela* ('Kabardinian Dossiers').

The different natures of the Ottoman and Muscovite primary sources are worth some elaboration. Robert Croskey states that the basic unit of an ambassadorial book is the embassy itself, including the instructions to the envoys and their reports,[26] whereas the *mühimme* entries, which are copies of imperial orders, constitute the basic unit of a *mühimme* register. The Ottoman imperial order was a direct response by the sultan to a petition by an individual or community or a letter describing an event or situation by an Ottoman magistracy or vassal. The Muscovite documents, however, were prepared by the Ambassadorial Office for the envoys based on general principles, known realities of the region, and also some assumptions which might turn out to be pertinent to the embassy. The Ambassadorial Office provided its envoys with multiple alternative answers, questions, lines of action depending on what might transpire during their embassy. As these documents were prepared in advance, what was expected in Muscovy before an envoy's departure and what transpired during the embassy could be different. The nature of an Ottoman imperial order was not the same at all. What the sultan ordered was the final word on the issue unless it was an order asking for a report or further information on specific events. In the Muscovite case, most of the time, we know what happened during the negotiations with foreign rulers or local chiefs as Muscovite envoys submitted them in a written format following their return to Moscow. However, sometimes, we do not know what sorts of actions the Muscovite government took after envoys submitted their reports. Thankfully, for the North Caucasus affairs, we have a fairly complete picture of the Muscovite responses and actions in the sixteenth-century Muscovite archival records.

The Ambassadorial Office had also a particular code of conduct and way of translation, which was sometimes at odds with what was understood by local chiefs or foreign rulers at the negotiations, especially with the local rulers in borderlands or frontier zones. For example, when Temriuk of Kabarda swore allegiance to the Muscovite tsar, the Ambassadorial Office recorded it as though the whole of Kabarda was now a part of the Muscovite realm, which was far from the truth on the ground. In comparison, although they had a strong sway over the Western Circassian tribes, the Ottomans in their internal documents did not claim that the whole area or all the tribes in that region were an integral part of the Ottoman realm. The internal Ottoman documents, for example, show that the Porte enquired time and again with the governors of Azak and Kefe about the tribes and chiefs that were either loyal or rebellious in the North Caucasus.

However, when issues of sovereignty were discussed with Muscovite envoys or in letters to foreign rulers, the Ottomans never hesitated to claim that the sultan and the Crimean khan were the legitimate rulers of the North Caucasus or the Pontic–Caspian steppes. Therefore, due to the nature of the *mühimme* documents in this connection – especially the internal correspondence between the Porte and its governors – researchers can obtain more precise information about the smaller polities or chiefs in the North Caucasus. Although the Muscovite diplomatic parlance, even in internal correspondence, claims these smaller polities or local chiefs as subjects of the tsar, the Ottoman documents distinguish which ones were loyal and which ones were 'still' rebellious or independent. This stems from the fact that while the Porte was already an established imperial power with an imperial ideology that was respected by its rivals and neighbours, the Tsardom of Muscovy was just beginning its imperial career and needed to enforce its imperial claims and legitimacy, both internationally and domestically.

In terms of details regarding the peoples, rulers and polities of the North Caucasus, the Muscovite documents have an abundance of factual information about the names of chieftains, settlements, borders and travel routes. In contrast, the Ottoman orders related to the same issues or areas lack such factual information. To illustrate, one can extract from Ottoman documents that Aslanbek of Kabarda was a chief in the North Caucasus serving the Ottoman sultan.[27] However, the Muscovite documents provide us with further details such as the names of his relatives, his network, his settlements, and the power and limits of his position among other chiefs in Kabarda in the 1580s.[28]

The number of scholars working on the North Caucasus in the early modern period and producing works in Western languages, using both Ottoman and Muscovite primary sources, remains low compared to those interested in broader Ottoman or Russian histories or those interested in the post-Soviet history and status of the North Caucasus. Exceptions to this are Chantal Lemercier-Quelquejay, Marie Bennigsen Broxup, Alexandre Bennigsen, Michael Khodarkovsky and C. Max Kortepeter.[29] However, Russian and Turkish historians writing on the North Caucasus present and interpret its history from a nationalist viewpoint, utilising only Russian or Turkish archival materials, as if North Caucasus rulers and peoples were unreservedly ready to submit to the Muscovite tsar or Ottoman sultan. This approach of Russian and Turkish historians, relying solely on their own archival sources and ignoring perspectives of the local peoples and other imperial powers, has so far been an obstacle to understanding the history of the region objectively. While Soviet and Russian historians have tirelessly attempted to establish an ideological motivation for applauding and justifying Russia's annexation of the region, Turkish historians have presented the history of the North Caucasus as a history of Russian aggression against the local peoples who strove to be under Crimean/Ottoman/Turkish rule because they were Muslims.[30] Lastly, another shortcoming of the scholarship on the North Caucasus is what we can call 'source bias'. Most western scholars working on the North Caucasus can read and consult Russian sources, but not necessarily Ottoman/Turkish ones. These historians using solely Russian sources examine the North Caucasus history through Russian lenses, by which they may see an aggressive and slave-harvesting Ottoman Empire and Crimean Khanate preying on the North Caucasus peoples until Muscovy emerges as their saviour.[31] By utilising both Ottoman and Muscovite primary sources and examining the North Caucasus borderland from multiple perspectives, this book aims to address the aforementioned issues and limitations related to the nature of archival materials.

Terminology

As Owen Lattimore states in his seminal essay on frontier history, 'the linear frontier as it is conventionally indicated on a map always proves, when studied on the ground, to be a zone rather than a line'.[32] Scholars following in Lattimore's footsteps have further conceptualised the idea of the zone in the last decades; the term 'frontier' is being replaced by a more comprehensive term, 'borderland', which embraces other actors and agents in addition to states surrounding a frontier zone.[33] Among multifarious overlapping and similar terms such as 'border region', 'frontier' or 'middle ground', I prefer to use the term 'borderland' in the following chapters for examining the North Caucasus and its polities between the Ottoman Empire and Tsardom of Muscovy. The term 'borderland' denotes a peripheral region and a zone of fluidity straddling two or more imperial systems and inhabited by independent or autonomous groups of people with their own cultural, social and political structures caught between imperial powers vying for hegemony over their lands. Being on the edges of empires or states, a borderland is an interpenetrable territory, incorporated, or in the process of incorporation, into an imperial system or state through cooptation or force.[34] Admittedly, the term 'frontier' has comparable connotations and is often used interchangeably. However, a frontier implies the prominence of state-sponsored military interactions, whereas a borderland denotes that of other autonomous or independent actors besides states and their military operations. Two or more empires or states could contest a borderland where they engage with its local rulers as well as with each other, relying on sophisticated strategies not solely based on military prowess. While a frontier evokes the idea of eventual annexation or military occupation by a state or empire, a borderland can be dominated through clients and vassals without being fully integrated into an imperial system for a relatively long time.[35]

In that regard, a borderland is a permeable region of interaction and transition with nebulously defined limits. Its refractory peoples and polities can quickly shift their allegiances and political alignments not only among themselves but also with the surrounding imperial powers or other forms of states. Throughout this book, similar to what Michiel Baud and Willem Van Schendel or A. I. Asiwaju propose in their respective works, I consider borderlands as a cross-imperial and cross-cultural phenomenon, instead of looking at them merely as border regions of an empire.[36] As stated earlier, the term 'borderland' encompasses a myriad of players besides imperial centres or their administrative units in a complex relationship of subject- and territory-making processes. Among these players, we can undoubtedly count peoples and polities inhabiting a borderland.[37] This is important, considering that empires or states vying for control over a borderland make it possible for the borderland peoples to play one power against the other for negotiating autonomy, independence or other privileges. Inhabitants of borderlands form a common identity and establish a functionally recognised community around their joint interests. These people, Lattimore points out, become a 'we' group, as opposed to 'they' who are perceived as rivals, even including people from their own nationalities or authorities.[38] Borderland peoples are connected by a multitude of networks, 'as well as a frontier ethos that transcend[s] geography and environment'.[39] In the early modern period, empires or states trying to establish hegemony over a borderland had to understand the local political and social dynamics and relationships and figure out creative and flexible strategies to convince the local rulers to accept their definition of sovereignty.[40] Considering that empires and states could not always rely on their military capabilities in borderlands, negotiation and cooptation were often the preferred methods in larger and difficult-to-control areas such as the North Caucasus.[41]

The North Caucasus functioned as a perennial borderland for centuries between numerous empires expanding in Eurasia, thanks to its idiosyncratic socio-political organisations, diverse peoples and political structures, and arduous geographical features. The North Caucasus was an 'ancient interacting frontier', not a 'sudden' one created by colonising European powers.[42] A borderland between the empires surrounding it, the North Caucasus in the second half of the sixteenth century had a plethora of geographical, political and linguistic frontiers and ill-defined borders within itself. The North Caucasus borderland remained an area in which, until its violent annexation by the Russian Empire in the nineteenth century, the nearby empires and states preferred the method of 'occupation without annexation'.[43] In the sixteenth century, it emerged as a dynamic borderland where both the Ottomans and Muscovites promoted their rule and imperial ideology while incorporating the local ruling elite into their imperial systems and, in the process, fostering antagonism towards the rival power.[44] Both the Ottomans and Muscovites used religion and local power struggles and differences as the ideological background of this antagonism in the sixteenth-century North Caucasus. The status of a borderland with the surrounding imperial systems trying to incorporate it is, however, not static, which was the case with the North Caucasus in the second half of the sixteenth century. Both the Ottoman Empire and the Tsardom of Muscovy desired to establish suzerainty over the region and turn it into an area controlled from the nearby centrally governed provinces – Kefe for the Ottomans and Astrakhan for the Muscovites.

As is typical in borderlands, the imperial rivalry over the North Caucasus allowed the peoples inhabiting the region to have broad autonomy, which reached the level of independence for some local rulers. Besides playing one empire against the other, the North Caucasus peoples also benefited from the geographical features of the region, which allowed them to evade imperial control, whether in taxation, occupation or annexation. However, certain parts of the North Caucasus, due to their proximity to imperial centres or accessibility for regular armies, were susceptible to imperial exploitation and were incorporated into an imperial system in the sixteenth century. The imperial rivalry slowly but surely changed the socio-political and economic patterns of the relationship among the peoples of the North Caucasus borderland, gradually depriving them of their independence, their autonomy and, finally, their lands. However, as Sabri Ateş in his book on Ottoman–Iranian borderlands nicely puts it, 'the borderland peoples were not merely swallowed up by the imperial cultures that encroached on them. Instead, they actively participated in, or fought against, the creation of imperial frontiers.'[45] Empires surrounding a borderland and their subject- and territory-making strategies do indeed affect the political, social, cultural and economic life of the borderland peoples. However, this relationship is reciprocal. A contested borderland can affect the imperial or state centres. This was the case in terms of the North Caucasus borderland and the imperial centres of Istanbul and Moscow. The Ottoman Porte changed its administrative structure and units in its northern territories and in the Caucasus due to the imperial rivalry over the North Caucasus. The elevation of Kefe from a province (*sancak*) to a governor-generalship (*beylerbeyilik*) in 1568 is an excellent example of how a borderland can affect the centre. Similarly, the evolution of the relationship of the Muscovite tsars with the Ottoman sultans and their diplomatic efforts was one result of the rivalry over the North Caucasus borderland.

Structure of the Book

This book examines the sixteenth-century history of the North Caucasus and its process of borderlandisation between the Ottomans and Muscovites in six chapters, besides an introduction and a conclusion. The first chapter, entitled 'The Land and Peoples of the North Caucasus in the Sixteenth Century: An Overview', is a survey of the North Caucasus in the sixteenth century with a focus on its landscape, peoples and political units, and the religious culture in the region. It introduces the main actors, states, polities, cultures, economic relations, rulers and various socio-political formations in the North Caucasus, providing the reader with the necessary background information to tackle the complex yet distinctive social hierarchies of the North Caucasus societies. This chapter also examines religious life among the peoples of the North Caucasus and some of the peculiarities unique to this region, where animism, Islam and Christianity were practised and, among some groups, existed in a syncretic way.

The second chapter, 'Tracing the Milky Way: The North Caucasus and the Two Empires', sets the stage for the direct Muscovite and Ottoman involvement in the North Caucasus by examining the frontier policies of the two imperial powers. The chapter analyses the reasons for Muscovite expansion into the region, treating the North Caucasus as a part of the broader Muscovite steppe policy, which eventually put an end to the 'bane of existence' of the Slavic states, that is, invasions and raids by various Eurasian nomadic confederations, and brought about the Russian Empire. I argue that the Muscovite ambitions and strategies in the North Caucasus altered the policies of the Ottoman Empire and forced the latter to assume a more active role in the region that the Porte initially considered a part of its lax northern policy. This chapter includes new perspectives on Ottoman relations with several influential North Caucasus peoples who lived in the areas adjacent to the Ottoman possessions to the north of the Black Sea, as well as new documentary evidence of the activities and allegiances of the famous Ukrainian Cossack leader Dmytro Vyshnevetskyi.

The third chapter, 'Bargaining for the Milky Way: The Astrakhan Campaign and the North Caucasus Borderland', focuses on the Ottoman Empire's military campaign in 1569 to take the city of Astrakhan from the Tsardom of Muscovy and, in the process, establish its sphere of influence in the North Caucasus and increase its control over the Crimean Khanate. The objective was to turn the region into an Ottoman-controlled territory after capturing a major city like Astrakhan in the lower Volga and making it an Ottoman province ruled from the centre. This chapter offers fresh insight into this infamous campaign, considered the reason for Ottoman reluctance to expand further north. I claim that despite its failure, the campaign galvanised the Ottomans in the North Caucasus and transformed the region into a discernible borderland between the two imperial powers. This chapter also explores the questions of the impact of the imperial centre on the borderland as well as vice versa in the context of Ottoman and Muscovite strategies and their transformations in the North Caucasus borderland.

The fourth chapter, 'The Milky Way Fades: Post-Astrakhan Ottoman and Muscovite Strategies in the North Caucasus', explores the imperial rivalry in the region in the aftermath of the Astrakhan campaign, with particular attention on the Ottomans' large-scale military undertaking against the Safavid Empire from 1578 to 1590. I argue that in this long war, the Ottoman Porte used the North Caucasus as a supply route and aimed to solidify its presence in the region. This chapter shows the nuances and flexibility of Muscovite policy and their mastery of using vassals in their steppe frontier zones, which allowed them to retain their sphere of influence in certain parts of the North Caucasus. It also analyses the Ottoman policy in Daghestan and the career of the famous Ottoman commander Osman Pasha and his strategies in the North Caucasus during the Ottoman–Safavid War.

The fifth chapter, 'The Milky Way Vanishes: The Denouement of the Ottoman–Muscovite Rivalry in the North Caucasus, 1605', examines the end of the first round of the imperial rivalry that affected the entire northern frontier zone of the Ottoman Empire and played out in a variety of versions throughout this zone. In this chapter, I explain how the Ottoman Porte harnessed the energies of its vassal states and masterfully organised them to oust the Muscovites from the region, even when the Porte was facing the renewed vigour of the Safavid Empire in the South Caucasus. The first encounter between the Ottoman Empire and the Tsardom of Muscovy in 1555–1605 transformed the North Caucasus into a borderland and ended up in a Muscovite defeat, but it was the harbinger of future engagements in the region and beyond in broader Eurasia.

The sixth chapter, 'Searching for the Milky Way: A Tale of Five Narts', details the strategies and policies of five local rulers caught between the two rival imperial powers. An analysis of the strategies of local rulers based on the juxtaposition of Ottoman and Muscovite sources provides us with a framework to understand the internal mechanisms of their political structures, as well as the functioning of these mechanisms within their own polities and with the expanding imperial powers in the region. The local chiefs examined in this chapter are Kansavuk and Sibok of the Janeys, Solokh of the Kabardinians, Urus of the Greater Nogays and Alexander II of Kakheti. Besides these individual local rulers, I explore the rivalry between the Kaytuk(ov)s and the Idar(ov)s of Kabarda, which led to the numerous invasions of the Kabardinian territories by different powers in the second half of the sixteenth century. This chapter explains the paths of accommodation and resistance that the peoples of the North Caucasus took as the imperial rivalry over their territories intensified.

The end matter of the book contains a conclusion and beneficial appendices. In the conclusion, I synthesise the main arguments and conclusions from each chapter, highlighting the importance of the North Caucasus in the long-lasting and impactful rivalry between the Ottoman Empire and Russia over a large part of the Eurasian landmass. The appendices include six Ottoman and Muscovite documents with transcriptions and translations into English, a chronological list of sixteenth-century events covering Muscovy, the Ottoman Empire and the North Caucasus, and a glossary of terms and personalities.

Notes

1. John Colarusso, ed., *Nart Sagas from the Caucasus: Myths and Legends from the Circassians, Abazas, Abkhaz, and Ubykhs* (Princeton, NJ: Princeton University Press, 2002), 100.
2. Ibid., 103.

3. Ibid., 101.
4. Walter Richmond, *The Circassian Genocide* (New Brunswick, NJ, and London: Rutgers University Press, 2013), 2.
5. *Başbakanlık Osmanlı Arşivi rehberi*, ed. Hacı Osman Yıldırım, Nazım Yılmaz and Yusuf İhsan Genç (Istanbul: Başbakanlık Devlet Arşivleri Genel Müdürlüğü Osmanlı Arşivi Daire Başkanlığı, 2000).
6. Chantal Lemercier-Quelquejay, 'Une source inédite pour l'histoire de la Russie au XVIe siècle: Les registres des 'Mühimme Defterleri' des Archives du Baş-Vekâlet', *Cahiers du monde russe et soviétique* 8 (1967): 335–43.
7. Suraiya Faroqhi, 'Mühimme defterleri', in *Encyclopaedia of Islam*, 2nd ed. (hereafter *EI2*), ed. P. Bearman et al. (Leiden: Brill, 1998–2009), 7:471.
8. Uriel Heyd, *Ottoman Documents on Palestine, 1552–1615: A Study of the Firman According to the Mühimme Defteri* (Oxford: Clarendon Press, 1960), 23–24.
9. Ibid., 25.
10. Ibid., 25.
11. Ibid., 27–8.
12. *Başbakanlık Osmanlı Arşivi rehberi*, 61.
13. For example, N. A. Smirnov lists 37 letters from Ottoman sultans to Muscovite tsars between 1497 and 1667 found in the Russian archives. Most of these letters are not extant in the available *mühimme* volumes. See his *Rossiia i Turtsiia v XVI–XVII vv*. (Moscow: Izdatel'stvo Moskovskogo gosudarstvennogo universiteta, 1946), 42.
14. Faroqhi, 'Mühimme defterleri', 7:470; Heyd, *Ottoman Documents on Palestine*, 4–5.
15. *3 numaralı mühimme defteri, 966–968/1558–1560*, ed. Nezihi Aykut et al. (Ankara: Türkiye Cumhuriyeti Başbakanlık, Devlet Arşivleri Genel Müdürlüğü, 1993); *5 numaralı mühimme defteri, 973/1565*, ed. Hacı Osman Yıldırım et al. (Ankara: Türkiye Cumhuriyeti Başbakanlık, Devlet Arşivleri Genel Müdürlüğü, 1994); *6 numaralı mühimme defteri, 972/1564–1565*, ed. Hacı Osman Yıldırım et al. (Ankara: Türkiye Cumhuriyeti Başbakanlık, Devlet Arşivleri Genel Müdürlüğü, 1995); *7 numaralı mühimme defteri, 975–976/1567–1569*, ed. Hacı Osman Yıldırım et al. (Ankara: Türkiye Cumhuriyeti Başbakanlık, Devlet Arşivleri Genel Müdürlüğü, 1997); *12 numaralı mühimme defteri, 978–979/1570–1572*, ed. Hacı Osman Yıldırım et al. (Ankara: Başbakanlık, Devlet Arşivleri Genel Müdürlüğü, 1996); *82 numaralı mühimme defteri, 1026–1027/1617–1618*, ed. Hacı Osman Yıldırım et al. (Ankara: Başbakanlık, Devlet Arşivleri Genel Müdürlüğü, 2000); *83 numaralı mühimme defteri, 1036–1037/1626–1628*, ed. Hacı Osman Yıldırım et al. (Ankara: Başbakanlık, Devlet Arşivleri Genel Müdürlüğü, 2001); *85 numaralı mühimme defteri, 1040–1041/1630–1631*, ed. Hacı Osman Yıldırım et al. (Ankara: Başbakanlık, Devlet Arşivleri Genel Müdürlüğü, 2002); *91 numaralı mühimme defteri, 1056/1646–1647*, ed. Murat Cebecioğlu et al. (Istanbul: Başbakanlık, Devlet Arşivleri Genel Müdürlüğü, 2015).

16. *Topkapı Sarayı Arşivi H.951–952 tarihli ve E-12321 numaralı mühimme defteri*, ed. Halil Sahillioğlu (Istanbul: IRCICA, 2002).
17. *Mühimme defteri 44*, ed. Mehmet A. Ünal (İzmir: Akademi Kitabevi, 1995); *Sultanın emir defteri, 51 numaralı mühimme defteri*, ed. Hikmet Ülker (Istanbul: Tarih ve Tabiat Vakfı Yayınları, 2003).
18. Patricia Kennedy Grimsted, *Archives and Manuscript Repositories in the USSR: Moscow and Leningrad* (Princeton, NJ: Princeton University Press, 1972), 153–4; Olga E. Glagoleva, *Working with Russian Archival Documents* (Toronto: Centre for Russian and East European Studies, 1998), 101.
19. N. M. Rogozhin, *Posol'skii prikaz: Kolybel' rossiiskoi diplomatii* (Moscow: Mezhdunarodnye otnosheniia, 2003). For a comprehensive list of *posol'skie knigi* preserved at the RGADA, see ibid., 333–52.
20. Robert M. Croskey, *Muscovite Diplomatic Practice in the Reign of Ivan III* (New York: Garland, 1987), 18.
21. Smirnov, *Rossiia i Turtsiia, 31–3; Charles Halperin, 'Russia between East and West: Diplomatic Records during the Reign of Ivan IV', in Saluting Aron Gurevich: Essays in History, Literature and Other Related Subjects*, ed. Yelena Mazour-Matusevič and Alexandra S. Korros (Leiden: Brill, 2010), 82–3.
22. Smirnov, *Rossiia i Turtsiia*, 29.
23. N. M. Rogozhin, *Posol'skie knigi Rossii kontsa XV–nachala XVII vv.* (Moscow: Institut rossiiskoi istorii, 1994), 181.
24. *Snosheniia Rossii s Kavkazom: Materialy izvlechennye iz Moskovskago glavnago arkhiva Ministerstva inostrannykh diel, 1578–1613 gg.*, ed. S. L. Belokurov (Moscow: Universitetskaia tipografiia, 1889).
25. *Kabardino-russkie otnosheniia v 16–18 vv.*, ed. T. Kh. Kumykov and E. N. Kusheva, 2 vols (Moscow: Izdatel'stvo Akademii nauk SSSR, 1957).
26. Croskey, *Muscovite Diplomatic Practice*, 18.
27. MD 25, no. 2052; MD 44, nos 182, 190; MD 51, no. 10.
28. RGADA, F. 123, *Krymskie dela*, kniga 13, fol. 275b; *Snosheniia Rossii s Kavkazom*, 112, 131.
29. Marie Bennigsen Broxup, ed., *The North Caucasus Barrier: The Russian Advance towards the Muslim World* (London: Hurst, 1992); Chantal Lemercier-Quelquejay, 'La structure sociale, politique et religieuse du Caucase du nord au XVIe siècle', *Cahiers du monde russe et soviétique* 25 (1984): 125–48; Alexandre Bennigsen, 'L'expédition turque contre Astrakhan en 1569, d'après les Registres des "Affaires importantes" des Archives ottomanes', *Cahiers du monde russe et soviétique* 8 (1967), 427–46; Michael Khodarkovsky, *Russia's Steppe Frontier: The Making of a Colonial Empire, 1500–1800* (Bloomington: Indiana University Press, 2002); Michael Khodarkovsky, 'Of Christianity, Enlightenment, and Colonialism: Russia in the North Caucasus, 1550–1800', *Journal of Modern History* 71 (1999): 394–430; Michael Khodarkovsky, *Bitter Choices: Loyalty and Betrayal in the Russian Conquest of the North Caucasus* (Ithaca, NY:

Cornell University Press, 2011); C. Max Kortepeter, *Ottoman Imperialism during the Reformation: Europe and the Caucasus* (New York: New York University Press, 1972). There are also several English-language works that examine the broader Caucasus region, covering several centuries: James Forsyth, *The Caucasus: A History* (Cambridge: Cambridge University Press, 2013); Thomas de Waal, *The Caucasus: An Introduction* (New York: Oxford University Press, 2010); Charles King, The *Ghost of Freedom: A History of the Caucasus* (New York: Oxford University Press, 2008).

30. Among numerous Soviet-era scholars and works, N. A. Smirnov and E. N. Kusheva produced several seminal monographs on the history of the North Caucasus and its role in Ottoman–Russian relations. N. A. Smirnov, *Politika Rossii na Kavkaze v XVI–XIX vekakh* (Moscow: Izdatel'stvo sotsial'no-ekonomicheskoi literatury, 1958); N. A. Smirnov, *Kabardinskii vopros v russko-turetskikh otnosheniiakh XVI–XVIII vv.* (Nal'chik: Kabardinskoe gosudarstvennoe izdatel'stvo, 1948); E. N. Kusheva, *Narody Severnogo Kavkaza i ikh sviazi s Rossiei: vtoraia polovina XVI–30-e gody XVII veka* (Moscow: Izdatel'stvo Akademii nauk SSSR, 1958). While both scholars extensively used Muscovite primary sources, Kusheva also consulted several early modern Ottoman chronicles in her discussions of Ottoman ambitions over the region. A useful survey on the history of the North Caucasus published in the Soviet era is B. B. Piotrovskii and A. L. Narochnitskii, eds, *Istoriia narodov Severnogo Kavkaza s drevneishikh vremen do kontsa XVIII v.* (Moscow: Nauka, 1988). Significant Turkish-language monographs with chapters on the early modern history of the region include Fahrettin Kırzıoğlu, *Osmanlılar'ın Kafkas elleri'ni fethi (1451–1590)* (Ankara: Sevinç Matbaası, 1976); Cemal Gökçe, *Kafkasya ve Osmanlı İmparatorluğu'nun Kafkasya siyaseti* (Istanbul: Has Kutulmuş Matbaası, 1979); M. Sadık Bilge, *Osmanlı Devleti ve Kafkasya* (Istanbul: Eren, 2005); Yahya Kanbolat, *1864'e kadar Kuzey Kafkasya kabilelerinde din ve toplumsal düzen* (Ankara: Bayır Yayınları, 1989).
31. Walter Richmond, *The Northwest Caucasus: Past, Present, Future* (Abingdon: Routledge, 2008); Firuz Kazemzadeh, 'Russian Penetration of the Caucasus', in *Russian Imperialism from Ivan the Great to the Revolution*, ed. Taras Hunczak (New Brunswick, NJ: Rutgers University Press, 1974), 239–63.
32. Owen Lattimore, 'The Frontier in History', in *Studies in Frontier History: Collected Papers, 1928–1958* (London: Oxford University Press, 1962), 469–70.
33. Mark Elliott, 'Frontier Stories: Periphery as Center in Qing History', *Frontiers of History in China* 9 (2014): 340; Sabri Ateş, *The Ottoman–Iranian Borderlands: Making a Boundary, 1843–1914* (New York: Cambridge University Press, 2013), 8.
34. Alfred Rieber, *The Struggle for the Eurasian Borderlands: From the Rise of Early Modern Empires to the End of the First World War* (Cambridge:

Cambridge University Press, 2014), 15; Elliott, 'Frontier Stories', 339; Omer Bartov and Eric D. Weitz, 'Introduction: Coexistence and Violence in the German, Habsburg, Russian, and Ottoman Borderlands', in *Shatterzone of Empires: Coexistence and Violence in the German, Habsburg, Russian, and Ottoman Borderlands*, ed. Omer Bartov and Eric D. Weitz (Bloomington: Indiana University Press, 2013), 1.

35. Daniel Power and Naomi Standen, 'Introduction', in *Frontiers in Question: Eurasian Borderlands, 700–1700*, ed. Daniel Power and Naomi Standen (New York: St Martin's Press, 1999), 5.
36. Michiel Baud and Willem Van Schendel, 'Toward a Comparative History of Borderlands', *Journal of World History* 8 (1997): 216; A. I. Asiwaju, 'Borderlands in Africa: A Comparative Research Perspective with Particular Reference to Western Europe', *Journal of Borderlands Studies* 8/2 (1993): 1–12.
37. Ateş, *The Ottoman–Iranian Borderlands*, 8; James Anderson and Liam O'Dowd, 'Borders, Border Regions and Territoriality: Contradictory Meanings, Changing Significance', *Regional Studies* 33 (1999): 595.
38. Lattimore, 'The Frontier in History', 470.
39. Ateş, *The Ottoman–Iranian Borderlands*, 4.
40. Power and Standen, 'Introduction', 15, 22.
41. Ibid., 22.
42. Ibid., 1; Lattimore, 'The Frontier in History', 25.
43. Rudi Matthee, 'The Safavid–Ottoman Frontier: Iraq-i Arab as Seen by the Safavids', *Journal of Turkish Studies* 9 (2003): 170.
44. Lattimore, 'The Frontier in History', 477; Power and Standen, 'Introduction', 22.
45. Ateş, *The Ottoman–Iranian Borderlands*, 7.

1

The Land and Peoples of the North Caucasus in the Sixteenth Century: An Overview

Today the notion of the North Caucasus evokes highlands, untamed tribal societies, bandits, warfare and fierce freedom-loving people, thanks to various infamous Russian literary classics and their representation in Western media. The sixteenth-century North Caucasus, however, was much more complex and diverse than such stereotypical representations portray. It was an idiosyncratic region compared to the lands surrounding it in terms of its geographical features, social and political structures, and the diversity among its peoples. The sixteenth century marked the beginning of a new phase in the history of the North Caucasus, its border-landisation between the Ottoman Empire and the Tsardom of Muscovy. In this process, the landscape and geography of the North Caucasus played a significant role for both the imperial powers and the peoples of the region.

1.1 The Land

Geographically, the North Caucasus is bounded by the Black and Azov seas to the west, the Caspian Sea to the east, the southern slope of the Greater Caucasus Mountains to the south, and the Kuma-Manych Depression and the Kuban River to the north. The northern slopes and westernmost part of the Greater Caucasus Mountains, including its southern slopes at the western end, are also considered a part of the North Caucasus region. The North Caucasus terrain comprises various types of landscapes – coastlines along the Black and Caspian seas, fertile plains, steppes, valleys, high and low mountains, and foothills.[1]

With a width of 50 to 200 kilometres, the Greater Caucasus mountain range not only divides the Caucasus into its northern and southern parts but also constitutes the traditional border between Europe and Asia. Stretching over 1,200 kilometres from southeast to northwest, it has been a formidable barrier throughout history. The Greater Caucasus Mountains are divided into three sections – western, central and eastern. The western section stretches from the Taman Peninsula as far as the source of the

Kuban River with an average height of 2,500–3,000 metres. The mountain range in the west, lying parallel with the shore, leaves a very narrow coastal strip with rugged terrain. The central section is the widest and highest of the Greater Caucasus Mountains, going as far as the Daryal Pass, which stands at 2,382 metres. This section includes Mount Elbrus, the highest mountain in Europe with a height of 5,629 metres, and Mount Kazbek at 4,877 metres. Daghestan constitutes the eastern section of the main mountain range. It covers the area from the Daryal Pass as far as the Absheron Peninsula. The northern slopes of the main range of the Greater Caucasian Mountains merge with the North Caucasian Steppe, which is a part of the Great Eurasian Steppe and the Pontic–Caspian steppe system. As for its rivers, the Terek, the Kuban and the Kuma make up the three major river systems in the North Caucasus. The Kuban originates in the western section of the Greater Caucasian Mountains and follows a north-westerly direction, falling into the Sea of Azov. The Kuma and Terek rivers originate in the central section and fall into the Caspian Sea. Many smaller rivers feed the three major systems of the North Caucasus. The major rivers and most of the tributaries rely on the seasons to the extent that in the winter, most tributaries and smaller rivers freeze over, and in the spring, the melting snow and rains make the rivers more manoeuvrable for navigation.

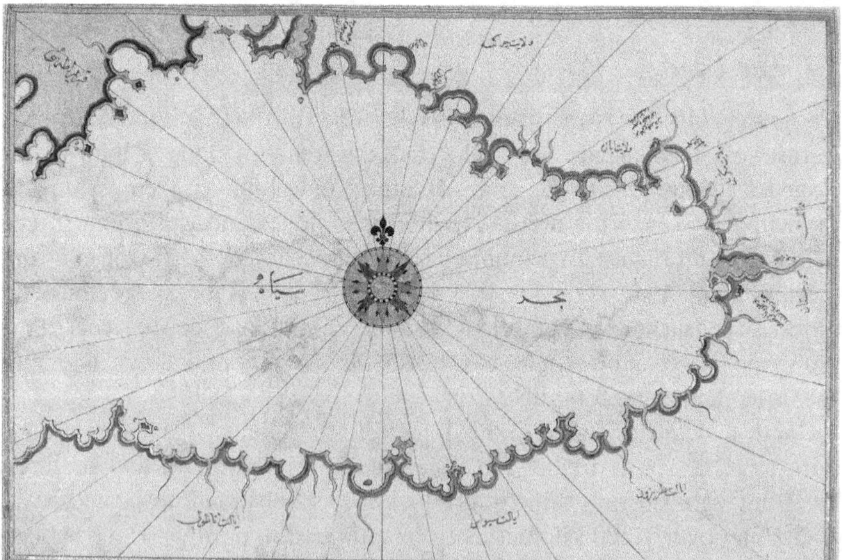

Figure 1.1 Map of the Black Sea and Circassia by Piri Reis, 1525.
Source: David Rumsey Historical Map Collection.

The western part of the North Caucasus is traditionally known as the Kuban region in scholarly literature. Several Western Circassian tribes and polities inhabited the sixteenth-century Kuban region, including the Taman Peninsula. The northeast part, including the Kuma-Manych Depression, was the Nogay Steppe, named after the Nogay nomads who inhabited the region in the sixteenth century. The area along the shores of the Caspian Sea in the east was Daghestan, where in the same century, several local political entities composed of various ethnic groups such as Kumyks, Laks and Avars existed. The central part of the Caucasus was Kabarda, inhabited by the Kabardinians, who belonged to the broader Circassian people.

As the Greater Caucasus Mountains formed a barrier between the North and South Caucasus, mountain passes were of strategic importance both for the local peoples and for the imperial powers trying to control the region in the medieval and early modern times. In this period, three principal mountain passes connected the North and the South Caucasus. The most famous and perhaps the most convenient one for troops and transport was the Derbend Pass in the easternmost section, where the Greater Caucasus Mountains fall to the Caspian Sea. The width of this strip of the shore is between 2 and 30 kilometres. The Derbend Pass had the renowned name of *Bab al-Abwab* (Gate of the Gates) among Islamic empires and the peoples of Daghestan, a name originally given by the Arab armies in the eighth century. In the sixteenth century, the Derbend Pass was the most critical pass thanks to the trade routes that connected the Safavid Empire with the Tsardom of Muscovy, reaching as far as the Baltic region. In the same period, another strategic passageway was the Daryal Pass in the central section of the Greater Caucasus Mountains, starting from Kabarda and following the Terek Valley to the Georgian kingdoms. The Daryal Pass was the primary connection as well as a raid route between Kabarda in the North Caucasus and the Georgian kingdoms in the South Caucasus, conveniently reaching the Araghi Valley in the south. The last possible passage was in the western part along the eastern shoreline of the Black Sea. However, it was narrow and its terrain extremely rugged, and in the sixteenth century, this passageway was easily controlled from the sea by the Ottoman naval forces. Therefore, the Ottomans strictly controlled the Black Sea route, while local Daghestani rulers and occasionally the Safavids were in charge of the Derbend Pass. When Muscovy appeared as yet another player in the region, the only passage they were able to use to connect with the South Caucasus, especially the Georgian kingdoms, in the second half of the sixteenth century, was the Daryal Pass, which was then dominated by the

Kabardinian rulers in its northern part and by the Georgian kings in its southern part.[2]

Besides the evident geographical north–south variation in the broader Caucasus region, there was also an east–west political variation based on the Ottoman and Safavid spheres of influence in the sixteenth and seventeenth centuries. The western part was traditionally claimed by the Ottoman sultan and the eastern part, including Shirvan and some Daghestani principalities, by the Safavid shah. Before the Muscovite presence in the North Caucasus, however, Safavid claims over Daghestan or Ottoman control beyond the Taman Peninsula was limited and nominal. The same east–west variation existed especially in the South Caucasus among the Georgian kingdoms, in Armenia and among the Turkic khanates in Azerbaijan, which found themselves in either the Ottoman or the Safavid sphere of influence.[3]

The geographical conditions manifestly affected the social and political preferences of the North Caucasus peoples. Landscapes such as high mountains, deep valleys, steppes and foothills, which were hard to dominate or unite, forced the peoples of the North Caucasus to adopt smaller and fragmented polities or tribal communities as their social and political structures. Within this framework, they developed remarkably local identities peculiar to the North Caucasus, especially compared to their neighbours in the south and north. And this unusual topography has made the North Caucasus since ancient times an area of refuge for those escaping authorities, enemies or oppression. For example, in the sixteenth century, some Nogays who were not content with the policies of their ruler split from the main horde and migrated to the North Caucasus, where they were able to avoid punitive raids or getting captured by their former ruler. Similarly, Slavic-speaking people, either fugitives or adventurers, came to the region to form Cossack hosts. It was not only groups of people who found refuge in the early modern era in the North Caucasus, but also individuals who were disgraced or starting a fight for a position of power. These chapters provide several examples of such Crimean and Ottoman princes who ended up in the North Caucasus vying for the throne.

It was, however, these very same geographical features that posed the most arduous challenges for the surrounding imperial powers aiming to encroach upon the North Caucasus. Thus, establishing palpable sovereignty over the region and its peoples required much materiel, manpower and resources from any power in the sixteenth century. Partially for this reason, imperial powers initially preferred to find trustworthy vassals in the region and assert their sovereignty over certain parts of the North Caucasus through them. The vassals and allies they could find in the region varied significantly in terms of their location and capabilities. In the mid-sixteenth century, there were several stable and relatively strong polities in the North Caucasus, specifically in Kabarda and Daghestan. The Kabardinians and Daghestanis developed stratified social and political organisations compared to their neighbours in the west or those living in the highly mountainous parts of the North Caucasus. Regardless of their social and political hierarchies, however, the authority held by the local rulers in Kabarda and Daghestan was still limited, and none of the chiefs proved strong enough to exercise rule over the others.[4] From the imperial viewpoint, whether it was Muscovy or the Ottoman Porte, the North Caucasus societies and polities were borderland peoples with primitive means of political and social organisation. As of the sixteenth century, while employing their territory- and subject-making strategies to integrate the region into their imperial systems, both imperial centres viewed the North Caucasus through lenses that exoticised it and its peoples.[5] These two empires competing over the region further divided the already separate peoples and polities of the North Caucasus in the second half of the sixteenth century.

1.2 The Peoples

The North Caucasus is globally known for its ethnic, linguistic and religious diversity. Nearly fifty languages with no cognates to the major linguistic families are a testament to the impact of geography and the role of the North Caucasus as a refuge. The situation in the sixteenth century was no different. Historians can trace the origins of specific ethnic or linguistic groups in the North Caucasus, such as the Nogays, Kalmyks or Slavs. However, the theories regarding the origins of its most ancient inhabitants, such as the Circassians, are not conclusive. One of the major ethnic groups in the region until their forced expulsion by the Russian Empire in the nineteenth century was the Circassians, also known as the Adyghe. The name 'Circassian', originating from Turkic *çerkas*, encompasses the Kabardinians and Western Circassians, who speak languages that are related, but excludes the Daghestanis and certain smaller groups of people living in and around Kabarda and the Kuban region such as the Vainaks or the Turkic-speaking Karachai-Balkars.

The ethnonym 'Adyghe', with which the Circassians refer to themselves, is sometimes used in the scholarly literature to denote the Western Circassians.[6] In the sixteenth century, however, the Ottoman and Muscovite officials and historians referred to both the Kabardinians and the Western Circassians using the term 'Circassian'. Apart from the

Circassians, other peoples and polities targeted by the subject-making strategies of the imperial powers in the sixteenth-century North Caucasus were the Daghestanis, including the Kumyks, Laks, Avars and Kaytaks, as well as the Nogays and Cossacks, who were relative newcomers to the region. Understandably, each society listed here had its own social and political hierarchies and established patterns of relationships. However, the geography of the North Caucasus engendered isolated and very local forms of social and political structures as well as identities, to the extent that even among the peoples who shared the same language and history, such as the Circassians, it was possible to see different forms of social and political hierarchies and relations. To illustrate, while the Kabardinians were known for their stratified society and relatively sophisticated polities, their cousins in the Kuban region, such as Hatukhays or Shapshugs, had no social hierarchy and comprised free peasants with equal rights.

There were, however, certain social and political traditions respected and upheld by most of the North Caucasus societies and occasionally by their neighbours. A significant and perhaps universal aspect of the North Caucasus social life was the *adat*.[7] It was the customary law, which was the main conduit for the peoples of the region. Predating Islamic, Christian or other religious influences, the *adat* dictated the social norms in the North Caucasus for individuals and groups, enabling the diverse inhabitants to interact with each other within the framework of this widely accepted set of rules. It regulated practically every aspect of social life, from conflict resolution to hospitality and from inheritance to marital unions. Despite the omnipresent linguistic and ethnic, as well as the early modern religious, diversity in the North Caucasus, its peoples adhered to their customary law, which provided the legal and societal order until the Russian Empire colonised the region.[8] Even among the more traditional Islamic societies such as the Daghestanis, the *adat* in the sixteenth century was more prevalent than religious codes (sharia) for regulating social relations. For some anthropologists, the tension between various religious codes and the *adat* and the triumph of the latter is explained by the flexibility of the *adat* compared to religious law.[9] In the sixteenth century, imperial powers vying to create new vassals and allies in the North Caucasus understood and respected the *adat* in their dealings with the local peoples.[10]

Another important tradition common among the North Caucasus peoples and some of their neighbours was *atalyk* (*atalık*). The *atalyk* institution involved entrusting the children of princely or noble families, usually at two or three years old, to a less noble family until the age of fifteen or sixteen. *Atalyk* children lived with their host families and received training in horse riding, wrestling, swordsmanship and other highly regarded skills. They constituted a strong bond between their biological royal or noble families and their host families. Thus, this institution contributed to creating a sense of alliance, allegiance or partnership. Interestingly, this tradition was not only respected but also practised by the Crimean khans and nobles, who regularly sent young Crimean Tatar elites to their Circassian or other North Caucasus vassals. By doing so, the Crimean Tatars cemented the loyalty of the desired local rulers in the North Caucasus. Even the Golden Horde rulers before the Crimean khans were known to have sent their children to the North Caucasus.[11] While the Ottoman sultans and nobility did not partake, they saw no reason to interfere in this relationship between the North Caucasus peoples and the Crimean Tatars, even though some of those Crimean elites sent to the North Caucasus through the *atalyk* system were Girey princes eligible for the Crimean throne. As is known, the Porte always preferred to control and sometimes retain viable candidates for the Crimean throne in Istanbul or other parts of the Ottoman Empire as a way of manipulating Crimean politics.[12]

The North Caucasus peoples prided themselves on their hospitality and protection of guests travelling through their lands. In most parts of the region, the guest stayed in an adjacent building on the land of the host (*konak*), who was responsible for the guest's protection and well-being. The tradition of hospitality was common among the peoples of the North Caucasus and could be extreme to the extent that it was not unusual for a host to give his or her own life for the protection of their guest.[13] The host was responsible for guests until they reached the next *konak*. Meanwhile, the host was obliged to seat the guest in the most revered seat, facing the entrance, and provide feasts in the guest's honour. Most free peoples of the North Caucasus, regardless of their wealth or social status, observed and respected this tradition.[14]

Lastly, raiding and kidnapping were universal in the North Caucasus in the sixteenth century. These two activities, being both martial and economic, were considered by the North Caucasus peoples as an acceptable norm of behaviour.[15] The foreign travellers who visited the region in the early modern era or even in the nineteenth century observed the prevalence of the custom of raiding and kidnapping. While sons of wealthy families could be kidnapped for ransom, sons and daughters of poor families could fall victim to being sold as slaves or servants to the neighbouring imperial centres. In the sixteenth century, the Crimean Tatars or Ottoman merchants facilitated the slave trade in the north of the Black Sea.[16] Slaves were one of the major commodities for export coming from the North Caucasus.[17] There was a continuous and robust demand in the Ottoman markets for slaves from the North Caucasus, considered by the Ottoman elites as highly valuable.[18] While the social and political organisations of the North Caucasus peoples differed depending on their geographical location and tribal, linguistic and religious traditions, these four institutions and customs were common to almost all of them. They were also understood and respected by their imperial neighbours in the sixteenth century, including the Ottomans, the Crimeans and the Muscovites.

1.2.1 The Kabardinians

Kabarda was in the Terek river basin in the central section of the Greater Caucasus Mountains and covered the area from the Beshtau region to Daghestan. It comprised two distinct parts, Greater Kabarda in the west around the Kuma River and Lesser Kabarda in the east along the Terek River. The Kabardinian territories occupied a strategically important part of the North Caucasus where the trade routes, especially the Central Asia–Astrakhan–Crimea route, intersected. The Kabardinians could also control northern parts of the Daryal Pass. Lastly, they were in the middle of the north–south and east–west connections in the North Caucasus. This geographically advantageous position of Kabarda and related strategic calculations were the main reasons for Muscovy's initial objective of obtaining the allegiance of the Kabardinian chiefs more than other North Caucasus rulers despite the fact that Western Circassians such as the Besleneys and Janeys submitted to the Muscovite tsar as early as 1552, five years before the Kabardinians.

Kabardinian society was highly stratified and sophisticated. It was also flexible, allowing vast freedom to each prince and his nobles, which created practical problems for the imperial powers to understand and manipulate, but at the same time prevented the local rulers from unifying against external powers. A large number of princely clans ruled over the Kabardinians. The heads of these princely clans had the title of *pshi*, whose power stemmed from the number of *burg*s they possessed.[19] *Burg*s were fortified strongholds made of stones where pshis could take refuge and defend their lands. The Ottomans used the term *bey*, which once meant 'ruler', then 'prince', and in the sixteenth century was mainly used to denote a governor, or mirza (originally from Persian *emir-zade* 'prince'), to refer to a pshi. The Muscovites used *kniaz*, meaning 'prince', and a variant of 'mirza', *murza*. The Kabardinian princely families traced their ancestry to the semi-legendary Inal Teghen, who united the Circassians under one state in the late fifteenth century. Thus, they shared a common lineage and considered themselves as related to each other.[20] Mirza (*mirze*, *murza*) was the title for pshis' children with women of the same rank, while children born from women of lower status had the title of *tuma*. This obviously created confusion for the Ottomans and Muscovites, who at times used the term 'mirza' to refer to a pshi, while at other times to refer to a pshi's son. However, in the Ottoman diplomatic parlance of the sixteenth century, there is a rather clear preference to refer to a pshi with *bey*. But most of the time, the Muscovites used *kniaz* for a pshi. In fact, both imperial centres paid little attention to the real status of any Kabardinian political elite with whom they were corresponding.

The Kabardinian princely families were extended families. The oldest member was the head of the family. The inheritance was not linear (vertical), i.e., from father to son, but rather lateral (horizontal), i.e., from brother to brother. Their estates were the rural settlements known as *kabak*s. A pshi could own numerous *kabak*s and *burg*s, which again determined his overall status among the Kabardinian princely families.[21] There was an ancient tradition among the Kabardinians of choosing a *pshihua*/*pshim yapsh* (grand prince/prince of the princes) from among the pshis. An assembly of gentry composed of all the princes and nobility of Kabarda, known as *zeuche*, elected the pshihua.[22] Despite the supposed loftiness of this title, in reality, the pshihua held no practical power or authority over other pshis.

Beneath the pshis were the *work*, sometimes transcribed as *werk* or *uork*, which constituted the nobility of Kabarda. The Muscovite officials used the Turkic term *uzden* (or *özden*) to refer to the Kabardinian *work*s. *Work*s were divided into two groups – *tlakotlesh* (nobler) and *dezhenugo* (less noble) in Kabardinian. The Muscovites occasionally agreed to take members of the *work* as hostages instead of the sons of the Kabardinian chiefs, which was a concomitant of submission to the tsar. Thus, these nobles were evidently valuable to the pshis. They had a certain degree of autonomy and had the privilege of changing their patron or even entering into an alliance with different external powers.[23] The pshis had to consult with their *work*s before making important decisions.[24] As for the lower classes, there were two categories of peasants. The first was the *tlfekotl*, land-owning peasants. They constituted the most populous class of the Kabardinian society. The second was the *og* or *loganapit*, peasants upon whom forced labour was imposed on behalf of the nobles. Slaves, called *azat*s, constituted the lowest-ranking group in Kabardinian society.[25]

In the sixteenth century, there were no proper cities in Kabarda, as was the case in Beshtau or the Kuban region, but there was urban development in forts.[26] The Kabardinian economy relied on farming, animal husbandry and apiculture besides commerce. They traded with their neighbours and with the merchants who visited or travelled through the North Caucasus. Of all the economic activities, perhaps animal husbandry, specifically cattle, was the most significant, as the Kabardinians' lands were not very fertile. The number of animals one owned determined the prosperity of a Kabardinian person.[27] Besides the famed Circassian horses, which were in high demand in Eurasia, major Kabardinian commodities that found their way to the international markets in the sixteenth and seventeenth centuries were the apiculture products such as honey and beeswax.[28] Hunting, fishing and craftsmanship were other economic activities. The Kabardinians mostly bartered, despite the presence of money that came through commerce and from the imperial powers interested in creating vassals in Kabarda.[29]

Until the late 1590s, most of the Kabardinian population were animists.[30] Some groups in Kabarda practised Christianity with an influence of animism. Christianity in the North Caucasus had been introduced to the local population by the Byzantine Empire in the sixth century. After that, especially between the thirteenth and fifteenth centuries, the Genoese, having established colonies on the northern shores of the Black Sea, attempted to convert Circassians to Catholicism by sending missionaries and building churches.[31] And the Georgian Christians, living across the Caucasus Mountains, also influenced the Kabardinian elites and population.[32] However, starting in the second half of the sixteenth century, Kabardinian chiefs or nobility gradually accepted either Islam or Orthodox Christianity, following their political alliances with the Ottomans or Muscovites respectively, although their religious beliefs did not necessarily define their political alliances with foreign powers. As the Muscovite records show, Kabardinian chiefs or nobles who travelled to Moscow in 1557 converted to Orthodoxy, but those who remained in Kabarda were not pressured to convert. Similarly, we see in the Ottoman documentation that Kabardinian chiefs who travelled to Istanbul converted to Islam. This pattern held throughout the second half of the sixteenth into the seventeenth centuries. It was possible in Kabarda for Christians, Muslims and animists from the same family to serve different patrons, be it the Muscovite tsar, Crimean khan or Ottoman sultan. The family of Prince Temriuk, who submitted to the Muscovite tsar in 1557, illustrates this point well. We cannot claim with certainty that Temriuk himself was Muslim or Christian or animist, but his son Saltankul and his daughter Kuchenei were baptised into Orthodoxy. However, Temriuk's other sons, especially Mamstriuk, who stayed in Kabarda, were Muslims. The family remained loyal to the Muscovite tsar rather than other imperial powers in the region, regardless of their religious affiliations, throughout the sixteenth century.[33]

1.2.2 The Western Circassians and Abkhaz-Abazas

To the west of Kabarda were the Western Circassians with more flexible social and political organisation compared to their neighbours to the east. The Western Circassians consisted of several related tribes who inhabited the Taman Peninsula as well as the middle and lower basins of the Kuban River. The strongest and most influential groups of the Western Circassians in the sixteenth century were the Janeys, Kemirgoys and Besleneys. The first two lived in the Kuban region, while the Besleneys inhabited the Beshtau region. Perhaps due to their proximity and often intermingled history, the Besleneys were sometimes considered part of the Kabardinian people rather than the Western Circassians. There is no clear-cut classification of the Circassian tribes. The Besleneys, supposedly originating from 200 families, had split from the Kabardinians and left Kabarda under their prince, Kanoke, during the reign of Idar, son of the aforementioned Inal, in the first years of the sixteenth century.[34] In accordance with the Ottoman and Muscovite documentation, the Besleneys are examined as part of the Western Circassians in this book. Both Muscovites and Ottomans treated them separately from the Kabardinians and dealt with the Besleneys as part of the Western Circassians.

The social organisation of the Western Circassians was similar to that of the Kabardinians. However, their feudal hierarchy was less rigid in comparison with their cousins in the east. Politically, by being closer to the Crimean Khanate and Ottoman strongholds in the north of the Black Sea, they were undoubtedly less independent. Just like the Kabardinians, the Western Circassian rulers were called pshis. Their pshis traced their lineage back to the same Circassian ruler, Inal, and claimed their princely legitimacy through him.[35] The Western Circassians had the tradition of choosing a grand prince as well. There is an example of a Kemirgoy grand prince recognised among the Western Circassians who was a son of Prince Inal. However, by the sixteenth century, this tradition was no longer continued. The noble class of the Western Circassians was known as *uzden* or *özden*. Beneath the noble class was the *tekhoqotle*, peasants with no obligation of forced labour, and the *pshitle*, peasants upon whom forced labour was imposed. The last stratum, similar to the Kabardinians, were slaves, called *unatle*.[36]

The Western Circassian tribes mentioned in the Ottoman and Muscovite documents most often are the Janeys in the Taman Peninsula, the Besleneys in Beshtau and the Kemirgoys in the Kuban region. Besides these, there were the Abadzehs, the Shapshugs and the Hatukhays in the mountainous areas of the southern Kuban region. The last three tribal groups mentioned had no feudal hierarchy, and their societies comprised free peasants with equal rights organised into *cema'at*s ('communities', originating from Arabic).

There are two linguistically and ethnically related groups of people in the western part of the North Caucasus who sometime before the sixth century split from the Circassians. These were the Abkhazis-Abazas and the Ubykhs, whose histories were intertwined with their Western Circassian neighbours.[37] The social structure of the Abkhazi-Abazas, who were linguistically related to the Western Circassians and inhabited the area south of the Greater Caucasus Mountain chain between the Kuban and Kabarda rivers, was the same except that their chiefs did not even have the authority of the chiefs of the other Circassian peoples, and they used different names for their social classes. Their feudal ladder comprised the *akha* or *ah* (lords, chiefs), *aamistadi/aamista/tawad* (nobles), *anyay-outskia/tefekashou* (land-owning peasants), *ahipshi* (serfs) and *unavi* (slaves).[38] While their names were occasionally referred to in the Ottoman sources of the sixteenth century due to their proximity to the Ottoman lands, the Muscovites were not interested in or capable of drawing them to their side.

Like the Kabardinians, the main economic activities of the Western Circassians were animal husbandry, farming and apiculture. The lands in the Taman Peninsula and the Kuban region were, however, more fertile, which allowed them to farm more extensively compared to the Kabardinians. Millet and barley were the most common agricultural products. Similar to their neighbours, the Western Circassians were engaged in hunting and fishing, as well as craftsmanship performed locally at people's houses.[39] Slaves were the desired commodity in the adjacent markets and were one of the major exports coming from these Circassian lands. In terms of trade, the Western Circassians mainly exchanged goods with the Crimean Tatars and Ottoman merchants in the cities of the Taman Peninsula and the Black Sea shores.[40]

The majority of the Western Circassians in the sixteenth century were animists. However, there was a populous Christian community that practised a heterodox version of Christianity. As we can gather from Ottoman and Muscovite sources, in the second half of the sixteenth century, most of the Janey chiefs were Muslim, but Besleney and Kemirgoy chiefs were Christians. Similar to the Kabardinian rulers, Western Circassian chiefs sometimes converted in accordance with their political arrangements.

Those who went to Moscow to submit to the tsar in 1552 and 1555 were, for example, baptised. Available Ottoman sources prove that in the 1590s, the Besleneys and Kemirgoys were increasingly converting to Islam. As it was the case in Kabarda, conversion to Islam among the Western Circassians in the sixteenth century was superficial, and a Christian chief could serve the sultan, or a Muslim chief could serve the tsar. To illustrate, a Muslim Janey ruler, Tsurak, was a loyal ally of the Zaporozhian Cossack leader Dmytro Vyshnevetskyi against the Ottomans in the early 1560s. Even in the seventeenth century when most of the Circassians had already converted to Islam, their religious beliefs had elements stemming from their ancestral animist traditions, and many Circassians, even in the Taman Peninsula under the direct influence of the Crimean Tatars and Ottomans, were still animists but had some connection or familiarity with Islam.[41]

1.2.3 The Daghestanis

Daghestan means 'the land of mountains' in Turkish. This region constitutes the eastern section of the Greater Caucasian Mountains. As its name implicates, Daghestan is a very mountainous area; thus, it was hard to control in the sixteenth century. It was a microcosm of the North Caucasus, as its peoples were ethnically, linguistically and religiously heterogeneous.[42] In the sixteenth century, Daghestan was predominantly inhabited by Kumyks, Laks, Avars, Kaytaks and various other smaller groups. The strongest polity in the region was the Shamkhalate of Daghestan, with its complex feudal system. It was traditionally called the Shamkhalate of Tarku, named after its political centre, the town of Tarku. The Kumyks, who were pastoralists and spoke a Kipchak dialect of Turkic, constituted the most populous ethnic group of this polity. Besides the Kumyks, the shamkhalate had a Lak population. The family of the *shamkhal*s was originally of Lak origin, coming from the village (*aul*) of Gazi-Kumuk, which had been the centre of the shamkhalate until the sixteenth century. Known as Gazi-Kumuks (Kazi-Kumukh in the Muscovite documents), the Laks spoke an Eastern Ibero-Caucasian language. As in the rest of the North Caucasus, the social life of the shamkhalate was regulated by the *adat*, customary law.[43]

At the zenith of the political pyramid was their ruler, the shamkhal. He belonged to a princely clan, which included the princes called khans and extended relatives who possessed the titles of mirza and *beg*.[44] The shamkhalate was divided into *yurt*s, each of which was governed by the members of its princely clan. The heir apparent of the shamkhalate was called *krym-shamkhal* and governed lands assigned to him from the village of Buinak.[45] Beneath the princely clan was the *chanka*, which comprised the children of the princely clan members with women of lesser classes. The third stratum, called *uzden*, consisted of free noble agricultural lords, who were considered vassals of the shamkhal. The shamkhal granted the best lands to his favoured *uzden*s, known as *sala uzden*s. Next to the *uzden*s were the land-owning peasants, who constituted the bulk of the shamkhalate's population. They organised themselves into *cema'at*s, which helped them to preserve their tribal and domestic relations, known as *tukhum*. The peasants with forced labour obligations were the *cagar* or *rayat*, from Arabic *ra'iyah*, meaning 'subject' or 'flock'. At the bottom of the social ladder, as usual, were the slaves, called *yasir*s or *kul*s, a Turkic term for slave.[46]

Another important Daghestani polity was the Kaytak Principality. This principality was ruled by a chief called an *usmi*, originating from Arabic *ism* and sometimes transcribed as *ustmii* in the Muscovite sources; hence, the principality was sometimes known as the usmiate. Its territories covered the area between the Kura River in the south and the shamkhalate to the north. Their political centre was the fortress of Quraysh, named after their claims of ancestry from the tribe of the Prophet Muhammad. The population of the principality was heterogeneous, though it mostly consisted of the Kaytaks, who spoke an Ibero-Caucasian language. The *usmi* was the strongest ruler in the mountainous areas and could muster an army of thousands of people.[47] Due to the proximity of the principality to Derbend, the Kaytaks controlled the Tarku–Derbend road and had a wealthier polity compared to the others of Daghestan, except for the shamkhalate. The *usmi* was chosen from among the elders of the dynastic family.[48]

The Khanate of the Avars, along the Koysu Andi, Koysu Avar and Kara Koysu branches of the Sulak River, was another influential political unit in the region. Its centre was the town of Hunzah. The Avar ruler was known as the *nutsal*. The Daghestani Avars spoke an Eastern Ibero-Caucasian language, known as *maaroul mats* (mountain language), and called themselves *maaroulal* (mountaineers). The Avars of Daghestan were Ibero-Caucasian and had no connections to the nomadic Avars who famously established an empire centred on Pannonia and from the mid-sixth century threatened Europe for about a century and a half. Some claim that the name Avar, which in Turkic means 'free' or 'vagabond', was given to them by the Turkic Kumyks due to their mountainous lifestyle. The Avars were less feudal, and their social organisation was laxer and more flexible.[49] Lastly, the principality of Tabarasan was a small but important polity located around the fortress of Derbend. Its ruler had the title *ma'sum* (sometimes known as *tabarasan shah*); in the 1570s, their *ma'sum* was Gazi Salih.[50] The population of this principality comprised Tabarasans and Lezgins, both of whom spoke Ibero-Caucasian languages.[51] Compared with other Daghestani polities, Tabarasan was a minor principality, which could muster only a few hundred mounted warriors.[52]

The Daghestani peoples in the sixteenth century were mainly engaged in sheep- and cattle-based animal husbandry, farming and manufacturing. Animal husbandry was common in the mountainous areas and the flatlands in the northern part of Daghestan and on its coastal strips, while farming was restricted to arable lands. Some manufacturing, such as silk production, took place in towns.[53] The religious composition of the Daghestani population was more homogeneous than the other parts of the North Caucasus. Islamisation of the Daghestani peoples began in the first half of the eighth century when the Caliphate invaded the Caucasus and took several centuries before most of the Daghestanis converted to Islam.[54] Among the Muslim population in Daghestan, Sunni Muslims of the Shafi'i school of law formed the majority.[55] Sunni Islam emerged in the medieval and early modern ages as the main bond that connected the numerous ethnic and linguistic populations in Daghestan. There were some Shi'ite Muslims and even a small Jewish population, who claimed that their ancestors were brought to Daghestan by the conquering Assyrians and Babylonians.[56] Unlike the other peoples of the North Caucasus, religion was a significant constituent of identity for the Daghestanis, whose elites even claimed to have Arab ancestry, as their royal titles such as shamkhal or *usmi* and legends about their origins indicate. Islam in Daghestan was an established religion. Daghestani rulers did not change their religious affiliation, as they changed their political orientation in the sixteenth and seventeenth centuries.

1.2.4 The Cossacks

Cossacks inhabited the North Caucasus from the second half of the sixteenth century. The first mention of Cossack villages in the North Caucasus occurred in 1563. These were probably the Greben Cossacks living near the mountain range on the left bank of the Sunzha River.[57] The origins of the Greben Cossacks are murky. One tale claims they were originally Ryazan Cossacks, who fled from the oppression of Muscovite Grand Prince Ivan III (r. 1462–1505) and eventually reached the Terek where they founded their settlement.[58] Another tale states they were descendants of Novgorod pirates of the fourteenth century (the so-called *ushkuiniks*).[59]

They most likely arrived in the foothills along the Sunzha in the sixteenth century and were mostly composed of outlawed fugitives. These Cossacks were known as *Grebentsy* because of the ranges of hills around their settlements; *greben'* means 'ridge' or 'crest'.[60] They remained a Christian community and accepted only Christians or converts into their ranks, playing essential roles in sixteenth-century North Caucasus politics.[61]

At around the same time, another group of Cossacks, who came from the lower Volga and Don rivers in the middle of the sixteenth century, settled and colonised the region along the Terek River. Thus, these Cossacks became known as the Terek Cossacks.[62] Compared to the Greben Cossacks, the Terek Cossacks were more inclusive and are even known to have accepted non-Christians into their ranks. Both the Greben and Terek Cossacks of the North Caucasus were eventually collectively known as the Terek Cossacks. In the sixteenth century, the Cossacks inhabiting these frontiers and steppes organised themselves into similar socio-military formations. Every Cossack host elected its own officials.[63] Although the Cossacks usually acted independently, the Ottomans, the Crimean Tatars and the North Caucasus peoples considered them as being natural allies or proxies of the Tsardom of Muscovy. Both Greben and Terek Cossack hosts continuously replenished their ranks with the influx of peoples from the surrounding lands. Besides their role as the proxy forces of Muscovy, the Cossacks in the North Caucasus were engaged in economic activities such as trade, raiding, animal husbandry, fishing, hunting and farming.[64]

Apart from these Cossack hosts that settled in the North Caucasus and despite living outside of the region, two other Cossack hosts played significant roles in North Caucasus affairs in the sixteenth century. These were the Zaporozhian and Don Cossacks. The Zaporozhian Cossacks, primarily ethnic Ukrainians who had migrated from their original lands in southeastern Poland-Lithuania, operated from their *sich*, a fortified settlement and administrative centre, located just below the Dnieper rapids. Under Hetman Dmytro Vyshnevetskyi, they were heavily involved in the North Caucasus in the years 1556–61, targeting Ottoman/Crimean possessions.[65] In the sixteenth century, the Don Cossacks were clients of Muscovy and living along the middle and lower sections of the Don River. They were active in the North Caucasus as allies of Muscovy, especially during the Ottoman campaign of 1578–90.[66]

1.2.5 The Nogays

Another consequential migrant group of people in the North Caucasus was the Nogays. The Nogays were Turkic-speaking pastoral nomads with a rigid social hierarchy similar to other Turkic peoples in Eurasia. In the sixteenth century, they were the most nomadic people in the North Caucasus. Throughout the fifteenth and sixteenth centuries, they were an effective military power along the Volga. By the 1550s, the Nogays occupied the vast area stretching from the Yaik River to the lower Volga. Since the Nogay rulers did not have a Chinggisid lineage, they had the title of mere *beg* (*biy*, *bey*), not khan. Sons of a *beg* were given *yurt*s (appanages) and were known as mirzas (*murza*). The heir apparent of the Nogay Horde had the title of *nureddin*, and in line with the Turko-Mongolian traditions, he was customarily assigned to the western borders of the horde. The second in line to the succession in the Nogay Horde was the *kekovat* (*keykuvat*), and he was assigned to the eastern borders of the horde.[67] Akin to the other post-Golden Horde political entities, the power of the Nogay ruler was limited. The Nogay mirzas and nobility enjoyed broad autonomy, and the former even conducted their own external affairs with the surrounding powers.

The Nogays split into two groups in 1557 when Kazy (Ghazi) Mirza and his followers separated themselves from the Nogays of İsmail Beg, who was a staunch ally of Muscovy. This alliance ultimately enabled the Muscovite annexation and retention of Kazan and Astrakhan. Kazy Mirza and his Nogays migrated to the Kuban region close to the Ottoman province of Azak and came to be known as the Lesser Nogay Horde (*Kiçi Ulus*).[68] They were allowed to inhabit this region as a vassal of the Crimean Khanate by the Ottoman Porte. The Greater Nogay Horde (*Ulug Nogay*) remained in the lower Volga region as a client of Muscovy for the rest of the sixteenth century, except for the periods when their leadership approached the Porte and joined Ottoman campaigns in the Caucasus.[69]

The Nogays were pastoral nomads. The major components of their economy were animal husbandry, raiding and trading. Perhaps thanks to the massive swathe of land they controlled in the sixteenth century along the lower Volga River, the Nogays considered the steppes and nomadic lifestyle the source of their political and military power.[70] However, as V. V. Trepavlov argues, at least one city, their capital Saraichuk, existed as an urban centre.[71] Similar to other nomadic peoples of Eurasia, the Nogays traded with their settled neighbours and collected taxes and duties from merchants in transit over or visiting their lands. Hunting and fishing were other significant economic activities for the Nogays, who were not engaged in animal husbandry, in addition to small-scale craftsmanship and farming.[72] Lastly, both the Greater and the Lesser Nogays were homogeneously Sunni Muslims.[73] Although the Greater Nogays were allies of the Muscovite tsar, they did not change their religious beliefs, nor did the Muscovites encourage the Nogay rulers to convert.

The North Caucasus has been famous for the vast variety of languages and peoples, a situation which prevailed in the sixteenth century. Besides the larger and more influential groups of people introduced above, there were other North Caucasus peoples with whom the imperial powers interacted or established contacts. In the sixteenth century, however, these were rather smaller groups, such as Chechens, Ossetians, Balkars and Karachais. Their impact in the region and on imperial policies and strategies remained limited due to the locations of their settlements and the nature of their political and social organisations, which were free societies with vague political boundaries and certainly limited political influence.

1.3 The North Caucasus: An Overview of the First Half of the Sixteenth Century

Three major imperial powers surrounded the North Caucasus in the sixteenth century: the Ottoman Empire, the Tsardom of Muscovy and the Safavid Empire. In the second half of the century, the region became a proper borderland between the Ottomans and Muscovites. This, however, was not the first time the North Caucasus had served as a borderland between imperial powers. In the thirteenth and fourteenth centuries, the area was a part of the borderland between the Ilkhanid Empire and the Golden Horde. Armies of the Ilkhanids and the Golden Horde fought near the Terek River in 1262, which ended in an Ilkhanid defeat and placed the North Caucasus under the rule of the Golden Horde.[74] It was again in the North Caucasus by the Terek River that the troops of the Timurid Empire annihilated a Golden Horde army led by Tokhtamysh in 1395.[75] Times of trouble notwithstanding, it was the Golden Horde that dominated the steppes to the north of the Black and Caspian seas from the thirteenth to the fifteenth century. Following a pattern common in empires of the steppes, in the first half of the fifteenth century, the Golden Horde eventually broke up into several states, each ruled by a different Chinggisid dynasty. These new states were the Great Horde, the Crimean Khanate, the Khanate of Kazan and the Khanate of Sibir. The Khanate of Astrakhan was the last post-Golden Horde state to come into existence following the fall of the Great Horde to the Crimean Tatars in 1502.[76] The Nogays were also a part of the former Golden Horde realm and continued their unaltered nomadic ways in the Volga basin as a formidable military power until the seventeenth century. These political powers laid claim to the heritage of the Golden Horde. Besides these, perhaps an illegitimate yet not surprising and equally able contender forged in steppe politics was the Principality of Muscovy, which had been assigned to handle taxation and other affairs of the Golden Horde khans in the Rus' territories before the collapse of the Golden Horde.[77]

While these states were struggling for primacy and power to the north of the Black Sea for Eastern Europe, a new power replaced the Byzantine Empire and made Constantinople its capital in 1453. With the conquest of Constantinople, the Ottoman Empire not only inherited certain Byzantine imperial traditions of administration but also adopted Byzantine strategies for controlling the Black Sea. Just as the Byzantine emperors had to be attentive to the developments in the Pontic–Caspian steppes for the protection of their imperial domains, the Ottoman sultans found themselves as natural players in the affairs of the Eurasian steppes in the fifteenth century.[78]

After his conquest of Constantinople, Sultan Mehmed II (r. 1444–6, 1451–81) annexed the Empire of Trebizond in 1461 and sent a fleet to conquer the northern shores of the Black Sea in 1475. The fleet, under the command of Gedik Ahmed Pasha, conquered Caffa (Ottoman, Kefe) and Tana (Ottoman, Azak) and reduced the Crimean Khanate to vassalage.[79] Four years later in 1479, another Ottoman fleet, under the command of Cezeri Kasım Pasha, captured Anapa, Koba and Taman, subduing the 'Circassians of the shore'.[80] The reign of Selim I (1512–20), who had been the governor of Trabzon and presumably knew adequately about the Black Sea region and the Crimea, saw more Ottoman activity in the North Caucasus.[81] In 1519, the Ottomans constructed two forts, Temrük and Kızıltaş, at the mouth of the Kuban River and a third, Cane (Janey), in the south of the Taman Peninsula to strengthen their control over the Circassians living in the vicinity.[82] With these conquests and construction of new forts, Black Sea shipping and shores were under an effective Ottoman monopoly by the late fifteenth and early sixteenth century.

While the Ottomans were furthering their conquests in the Black Sea area, the Safavid dynasty, which would be influential in the affairs of the North Caucasus, emerged in Tabriz, Azerbaijan in 1501. It became the flag bearer of Shi'a Islam and thus emerged as a natural rival to the Sunni Ottoman Empire. The Safavids united Iran and Azerbaijan and ruled these lands until their demise in 1736.[83] Despite territorial losses, the Safavid Empire survived its rivalry with the Ottomans, only to be overthrown within Iran proper and replaced by Nadir Shah.[84] As far as the Caucasus region was concerned in the sixteenth and seventeenth centuries, the Safavids were mostly active in southern polities of Daghestan and the eastern parts of the Georgian and Armenian lands.

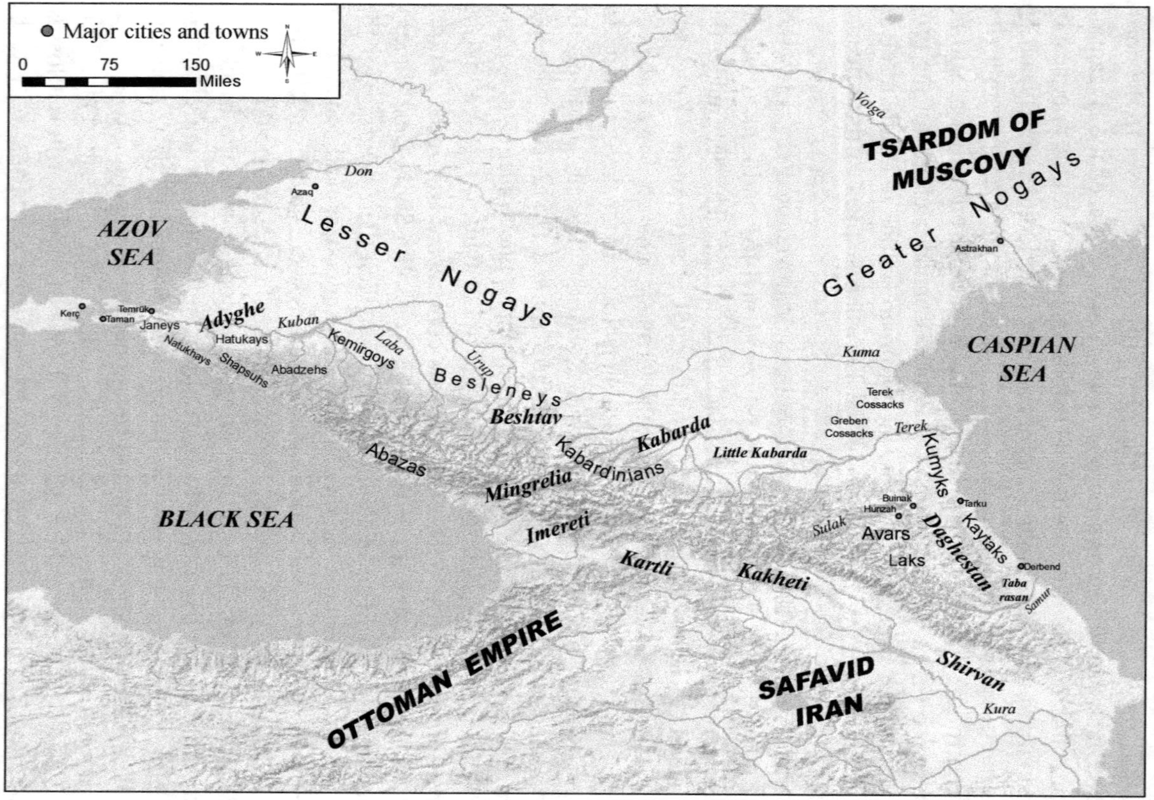

Map 1.1 The North Caucasus before the Ottoman–Safavid War of 1578–90.

In the sixteenth century, the main areas of conflict between the Ottomans and Safavids were in the South Caucasus. The warfare between these empires that started in 1514 ended in 1555 with the first official treaty, the Treaty of Amasya, signed during the reigns of Süleyman I of the Ottomans and Tahmasp I of the Safavids.[85] According to this document, the Safavids recognised the Ottoman annexation of Iraq and sovereignty over eastern Anatolia. The western Georgian kingdoms (Imereti, Goria, Mingrelia) and western Armenia were left under the suzerainty of the Ottoman sultan while the eastern Georgian kingdoms (Kartli and Kakheti) and eastern Armenia remained under the Safavid shah.[86] The initial warfare between the Ottomans and Safavids and the following peace treaty essentially divided the South Caucasus into western and eastern sections dominated by Ottomans and Safavids, respectively. This peace treaty would remain in effect until 1578 when the Ottoman Porte started a long campaign in the east, which lasted for twelve years and this time involved the North Caucasus.

The Crimean Khanate, as a contender for the Golden Horde territories, claimed suzerainty over the North Caucasus lands as far as the Caspian Sea. The Ottoman Porte recognised and respected the Crimean claims. It was at the beginning of the sixteenth century that the Porte found itself more and more embroiled in the affairs of the North Caucasus. Although Ottoman–Crimean control was sufficient over some of the Western Circassian lands, Kabarda and Daghestan were only under a nominal claim and never entirely under the control of the Ottomans until the second half of the sixteenth century. From the Crimean Tatar perspective, raiding the North Caucasus was always a welcome option as an economic activity, and as nominal overlords, the Crimean khans received tribute in the form of slaves from the Circassians and sent some to the Porte.[87] In the first half of the sixteenth century, especially during the reign of Sahib Girey I (1532–51), the Crimean army raided the North Caucasus four times on a large scale, in 1539, 1542, 1544 and 1551.[88] There were many smaller raids besides these campaigns.[89] The campaigns in 1539 and 1542 were carried out to subdue the Janey Circassians, and during them the Crimean Tatars enslaved thousands of Circassians and destroyed their troops. In 1544, they raided Kabarda, enslaving thousands of Kabardinians and tearing down churches in that region. In his last campaign in the North Caucasus, Khan Sahib Girey I attacked the Janeys and the Kabardinians in 1551, which resulted in thousands more Circassians enslaved and their lands devastated.[90] Sahib Girey I was one of the most ambitious Crimean khans. He was also interested in Nogay affairs and strived to control and eventually subordinate them to the khanate. But the Nogays desired to contain the growing power of the Crimean khans in the steppes by allying themselves in the 1530s with the khanates of Astrakhan and Kazan and later with Muscovy. In 1546, a Nogay army attacked Crimea but was checked by the Crimean Tatars. In the ensuing battle, the Nogay troops were violently decimated, which further deteriorated the already strained relationship between the Crimean Tatars and the Nogays. Therefore, by the mid-sixteenth century, the eastern campaigns of the Crimean Tatars brought about discontent with the Crimean claims in the North Caucasus and resistance from the Nogays. In this period, local North Caucasus polities and the Nogays were ready to enter into negotiations with any power that could oppose and protect them from the Crimean Khanate.

The history of Eurasia took an interesting turn in 1552 when Muscovy captured and annexed the Khanate of Kazan. This event marked the beginning of the transition of power in the Eurasian steppes from Turkic states to Muscovy. The year 1552 also marked the beginning of Muscovy's imperial career, as it was the first time it had conquered a non-Russian sovereign state and a centre of its former Tatar overlords.[91] Following the annexation of Kazan other remnants of the former Golden Horde, except the Crimean Khanate, came to be first controlled and then annexed by Muscovy in a relatively short period. The only power that could compete with Muscovy for the lands of the Golden Horde in the sixteenth century was the Crimean Khanate.

Muscovy and the Crimean Khanate were not, however, always rivals. The reign of Mengli Girey, which began in 1468, saw the first attempts to establish an alliance with Muscovy against the Great Horde of Seyyid Ahmed, which was a threat both to Muscovy and to the Crimean Khanate. The Great Horde supported Mengli Girey's elder brother, Nurdevlet, in his bid for the khanate's throne. In 1478, this struggle ended when Mengli Girey took the Crimean throne with Ottoman help as an Ottoman vassal. This event also signalled the end of Great Horde's ambitions in the north of the Black Sea.[92] Subsequently, Mengli Girey continued a policy of friendship and alliance with Muscovy against the alliance of the Great Horde and Poland-Lithuania.[93] It was also Mengli Girey who initiated diplomatic relations between Muscovy and the Ottoman Empire.[94] The Ottoman Porte supported its new vassal in his struggle against the Great Horde. Eventually, the Crimean–Muscovite alliance delivered the final blow to the Great Horde in 1502 when the Crimean army captured the city of Saray. However, once the threat from the Great Horde was eradicated, the rivalry between the Crimean and Muscovite allies surfaced. In 1507, Mengli Girey approached Poland-Lithuania to form an alliance against Muscovy, and in the 1520s, the Crimean Tatars raided southern Muscovy.

Despite the rivalry and enmity between Muscovy and the Crimean Khanate, the former continued to provide the latter with an annual tribute or gifts until the reign of Peter I in the eighteenth century, mostly to prevent Tatar raids on its southern frontier.[95]

The Crimean Khanate and Muscovy were militarily the most robust and most plausible competitors for the Golden Horde lands in the sixteenth century. The Khanate of Kazan was fragmented by internal strife and reduced to a near-vassal status already during the reign of Muscovite Grand Prince Ivan III. The Khanate of Astrakhan was a latecomer and in no position to enter into a power struggle with the Crimean Tatars or Muscovy. The Crimean–Muscovite competition over the lands of the Golden Horde that started after 1502 lasted for almost a century. In 1521, Crimean Khan Mehmed Girey I (r. 1515–23) succeeded in installing his son, Sahib Girey, on the throne of Kazan. Thus, the Girey dynasty in 1521 united the khanates of Kazan and Crimea. Sahib Girey, who left Kazan for Istanbul in 1524 hoping to become a khan in the Crimea, was later replaced by Sefa Girey, who ruled the Khanate of Kazan until 1532 when Can Ali, a pro-Muscovite khan, deposed him. However, Sefa Girey would gain power in Kazan twice more until his final dethronement by the pro-Muscovite faction in 1549.[96]

The same year when Sefa Girey was dethroned, Khan Sahib Girey I of Crimea (r. 1532–51) captured Astrakhan, supported by Ottoman soldiers and weapons.[97] Khan Yağmurcu of Astrakhan left the city and took refuge with the Nogays. The Porte, however, was not pleased with Sahib Girey's ambitions over the Khanate of Astrakhan. The Ottoman sultan ordered him to return Astrakhan to Khan Yağmurcu and withdraw his forces. Interestingly, Sultan Süleyman I (r. 1520–66) willingly hampered the Crimean Tatar struggle for the Golden Horde lands against Muscovy by dethroning Sahib Girey in 1551 due to the complaints of some Ottoman officials about Sahib Girey's ambitious policies in the north and the danger he could pose to the Porte in the future.[98] However, it proved to be ill advised for the Ottomans to impinge on Crimean politics as Muscovite Tsar Ivan IV (r. 1547–75) reached his long-awaited prize and annexed Kazan in 1552 – one year after the dethronement of Sahib Girey – and Astrakhan in 1556. Most of the Nogay rulers had become clients of Muscovy before 1552, mostly due to the successful Muscovite policy of cooptation and the Nogays' resentment of Crimean khans who desired to control them. The pro-Muscovite Nogays and their services rendered for the Muscovite tsar – or, sometimes, their neutrality in the conflicts between Muscovy and the post-Golden Horde khanates – to a great extent facilitated the Muscovite annexation of Kazan and Astrakhan.

In 1555, pro-Muscovite İsmail Beg became the ruler of the Nogay Horde, igniting more conflicts among the princes and eventually splitting the Nogays into two hordes. Thus, by 1556 Muscovy added to its realm the heartland of the former Golden Horde—the Volga basin as far as the Caspian Sea in the south.

With the Muscovite annexations of Kazan and Astrakhan and control over the Greater Nogays, the Ottomans were to face a power to be reckoned with in their northern frontiers. Muscovy gained considerable gravity and became closer to being an equal rival to the other powers in the north. The balance of power between Muscovy, Poland-Lithuania and the Crimean Khanate tipped in favour of Muscovy. However, Muscovite ambitions did not end there. The transition of Muscovy from a principality and a second-rate power into a tsardom with imperial ambitions over Eurasia, as well as its success over the former Golden Horde territories in the 1550s, prompted the North Caucasus polities, burdened by the policies of Khan Sahib Girey and frustrated with Ottoman attempts at establishing direct rule, which included its taxation system, to approach to the Muscovite tsar. Muscovy, seeming by then an option for the North Caucasus chiefs for an alliance, geographically was far from the region. It did not appear capable of posing an immediate threat to the independence of the North Caucasus rulers; instead, it could offer an opportunity to counteract the Crimean dominance over the region. For these reasons and more, the North Caucasus rulers sent their envoys to the tsar as early as 1552 and began a process whereby their lands would turn into a borderland between the two major imperial powers of the sixteenth century in Eurasia.

Notes

1. For geographical descriptions of the North Caucasus, see James Forsyth, *The Caucasus: A History* (Cambridge: Cambridge University Press, 2013), 11–13; Thomas de Waal, *The Caucasus: An Introduction* (New York: Oxford University Press, 2010), 6–9; W. E. D. Allen and Paul Muratoff, *Caucasian Battlefields: A History of the Wars on the Turco-Caucasian Border, 1828–1921* (Cambridge: Cambridge University Press, 1953), 1–12; Charles King, The *Ghost of Freedom: A History of the Caucasus* (New York: Oxford University Press, 2008), 3–12; Semen Bronevskii, *Noveishiia geograficheskiia i istoricheskiia izvestiia o Kavkaze*, vol. 1 (Moscow: S. Selivanovskii, 1823); E. N. Kusheva, *Narody Severnogo Kavkaza i ikh sviazi s Rossiei: vtoraia polovina XVI–30-e gody XVII veka* (Moscow: Izdatel'stvo Akademii nauk SSSR, 1958), 39–154; Amjad Jaimoukha, *The Circassians: A Handbook* (New York: Palgrave, 2001), 65–8; Kadircan Kaflı, *Şimali Kafkasya* (Istanbul:

Vakit, 1942), 5–9; Douglas W. Freshfield, *The Exploration of the Caucasus* (London: Edward Arnold, 1896), 1:1–59.

2. *Russian Embassies to the Georgian Kings (1589–1605)*, ed. W. D. Allen, texts trans. Anthony Mango (London: Hakluyt Society, 1970), 1:10–11.
3. King, *The Ghost of Freedom*, 12–13.
4. *Tarih-i Osman Paşa*, ed. Yunus Zeyrek (Ankara: Kültür Bakanlığı Yayınları, 2001), 44–5; Michael Khodarkovsky, *Russia's Steppe Frontier: The Making of a Colonial Empire, 1500–1800* (Bloomington: Indiana University Press, 2002), 15–16, 26.
5. Stefanos Yerasimos, 'Türklerin Kafkasları: egzotizmle jeopolitik arasında-II', *Toplumsal Tarih* 37 (1997): 7–13; Murat Yaşar, 'Evliya Çelebi in the Circassian Lands: Vampires, Tree Worshippers, and Pseudo-Muslims', *Acta Orientalia Academiae Scientiarum Hungaricae* 67 (2014): 75–96; Michael Khodarkovsky, '"Ignoble Savages and Unfaithful Subjects": Constructing Non-Christian Identities in Early Modern Russia', in *Russia's Orient: Imperial Borderlands and Peoples, 1700–1917*, ed. Daniel R. Brower and Edward J. Lazzerini (Bloomington: Indiana University Press, 2001), 9–27; Michael Khodarkovsky, 'Of Christianity, Enlightenment, and Colonialism: Russia in the North Caucasus, 1550–1800', *Journal of Modern History* 71 (1999): 394–430.
6. Chantal Lemercier-Quelquejay, 'Cooptation of the Elites of Kabarda and Daghestan in the Sixteenth Century', in *The North Caucasus Barrier: The Russian Advance towards the Muslim World*, ed. Marie Bennigsen Broxup (London: Hurst, 1992), 27; Walter Richmond, *The Northwest Caucasus: Past, Present, Future* (Abingdon: Routledge, 2008), 8.
7. John Colarusso, *A Grammar of the Kabardian Language* (Calgary, AB: University of Calgary Press: 1992), 5.
8. For an examination of the *adat* among the North Caucasus peoples, see Fedor I. Leontovich, *Adaty Kavkazkikh gorstsev: Materialy po obychnomu pravu Severnogo i Vostochnogo Kavkaza* (Odessa: P. A. Zelenyi, 1883); and Aleksandr Ladyzhenskii, *Adaty gortsev Severnogo Kavkaza* (Rostov on Don: SKNTs VSh, 2003).
9. Ladyzhenskii, *Adaty gortsev Severnogo Kavkaza*, 45.
10. MD 40, no. 278; Fahrettin Kırzıoğlu, *Osmanlılar'ın Kafkas elleri'ni fethi (1451–1590)* (Ankara: Sevinç Matbaası, 1976), 439.
11. Ali Barut, 'Kırım Hanlığı ile kuzey-batı Kafkasya ilişkilerinde Atalık müessesesinin yeri', *Emel* 219 (1997): 21–4; S. Kh. Khotko, 'Matrimonial'nye soiuzy i sistema priemnogo rodstva kak instrumenty vneshnei politiki cherkesskikh kniazhestv (XIII–XVII vv.)', *Nauchnaia mysl' Kavkaza* 2 (2016): 76–86; Ufuk Tavkul, 'Kırım-Kafkas ilişkilerinde "Atalık" kurumunun kökeni üzerine değerlendirmeler', *Karadeniz Araştırmaları* 51 (2016): 223–32.
12. This tradition began during the reign of Selim I and princes in Istanbul received a daily allowance of 1,000 *akçe*. Özalp Gökbilgin, *1532–1577*

yillari arasinda Kırım Hanlığı'nın siyasi durumu (Ankara: Sevinç Matbbası, 1973), 30.

13. Colarusso, *A Grammar of the Kabardian Language*, 7.
14. Jaimoukha, *The Circassians*, 188–9.
15. Richmond, *The Northwest Caucasus*, 25–6; King, *The Ghost of Freedom*, 4–5, 12.
16. Richmond, *The Northwest Caucasus*, 26; Colarusso, *A Grammar of the Kabardian Language*, 7.
17. R. A. Panesh, 'Sotsial'no-ekonomicheskoe i politicheskoe razvitie zapadnoadygskogo sotsiuma v poslednei chetverti XV–pervoi polovine XVI vv.', *Vestnik Adygeiskogo gosudarstvennogo universiteta* 135 (2014): 68–77.
18. The sixteenth-century Ottoman statesman Gelibolu Mustafa Ali states that Circassian and Abaza slaves can be trained well and are all brave and that Circassians are of good race. *Gelibolulu Mustafa Ali ve meva'idü'n-nefais fi-kava'idi'l-mecalis*, ed. Mehmet Şeker (Ankara: Türk Tarih Kurumu Basımevi, 1997), 117–19; Alan Fisher, 'Chattel Slavery in the Ottoman Empire', *Slavery and Abolition* 1 (1980): 25–45, esp. 44–5; Mária Ivanics, 'Enslavement, Slave Labour and the Treatment of Captives in the Crimean Khanate', in *Ransom Slavery along the Ottoman Borders*, ed. Géza Dávid and Pál Fodor (Leiden: Brill, 2007), 193–221.
19. For the social structure and titles of the nobility of Kabarda in detail, see Jaimoukha, *The Circassians*, 156–60.
20. *Snosheniia Rossii s Kavkazom: Materialy izvlechennye iz Moskovskago glavnago arkhiva Ministerstva inostrannykh diel, 1578–1613 gg.*, ed. S. L. Belokurov (Moscow: Universitetskaia tipografiia, 1889), 2–3.
21. Jaimoukha, *The Circassians*, 156–60.
22. Ibid., 62.
23. Lemercier-Quelquejay, 'Cooptation of the Elites of Kabarda', 26.
24. *Snosheniia Rossii s Kavkazom*, 143–6.
25. Ibid., 157–8.
26. Colarusso, *A Grammar of the Kabardian Language*, 4.
27. Panesh, 'Sotsial'no-ekonomicheskoe i politicheskoe razvitie zapadnoadygskogo sotsiuma', 68–77.
28. Richmond, *The Northwest Caucasus*, 25.
29. Yaşar, 'Evliya Çelebi in the Circassian Lands'.
30. Lemercier-Quelquejay, 'Cooptation of the Elites of Kabarda', 26.
31. Jaimoukha, *The Circassians*, 49, 148–9.
32. Ibid., 149.
33. Lemercier-Quelquejay, 'Cooptation of the Elites of Kabarda', 27.
34. Jaimoukha, *The Circassians*, 51–5.
35. Ibid., 54.
36. Ibid., 162.
37. Jaimoukha, *The Circassians*, 16; R. Abaza, 'The Abazinians', *Caucasian Review* 8 (1959): 34–40; T. Tatlok, 'The Ubykhs', *Caucasian Review* 7

(1958): 100–9; Şerafettin Terim, *Kafkas tarihinde Abazalar ve Çerkeslik mefhumu* (Istanbul: Murat Matbaacılık, 1976).
38. Lemercier-Quelquejay, 'Cooptation of the Elites of Kabarda', 27.
39. Panesh, 'Sotsial'no-ekonomicheskoe i politicheskoe razvitie zapadnoadygskogo sotsiuma', 68–77.
40. Yaşar, 'Evliya Çelebi in the Circassian Lands'.
41. Ibid., 75–96.
42. B. G. Aliev and M. S. K. Umakhanov, *Dagestan v XV–XVI vv.: Voprosy istoricheskoi geografii* (Makhachkala: Institut istorii, arkheologii i etnografii dagestanskogo nauchnogo tsentra RAN, 2004), 49–95.
43. W. Barthold and A. Bennigsen, 'Dāghistān', *EI2*, 2:86–7.
44. Ibid.; M. Sadık Bilge, *Osmanlı Devleti ve Kafkasya* (Istanbul: Eren, 2005), 24; Anna Zelkina, *In Quest for God and Freedom: The Sufi Response to the Russian Advance in the North Caucasus* (New York: New York University Press, 2000), 14–21.
45. Barthold and Bennigsen, 'Dāghistān', 2:87; Lemercier-Quelquejay, 'Cooptation of the Elites of Kabarda', 32. Lemercier-Quelquejay states that the title *krym-shamkhal* could be *yarim-shamkhal*, 'half-shamkhal' in Turkish.
46. D. M. Ataev et al., *Istoriia Dagestana* (Moscow: Glavnaia redaktsiia *vostochnoi literatury*, 1967), 1:239–40.
47. Kusheva, *Narody Severnogo Kavkaza*, 48.
48. Barthold and Bennigsen, 'Dāghistān', 2:87.
49. H. Carrère d'Encausse and A. Bennigsen, 'Avars', *EI2*, 1:755–6.
50. Gelibolulu Mustafa 'Âli, *Nusret-nâme*, ed. Mustafa Eravcı (Ankara: Türk Tarih Kurumu, 2014), 167.
51. Bilge, *Osmanlı Devleti ve Kafkasya,* 20–22.
52. Kusheva, *Narody Severnogo Kavkaza,* 47.
53. M. G. Gadzhiev, O. M. Davudov and A. P. Shikhsaidov, *Istoriia Dagestana s drevneishikh vremen do kontsa XV v.* (Makhachkala: DNTs RAN, 1996), 309–14; Kusheva, *Narody Severnogo Kavkaza*, 39.
54. Michael Kemper, *Herrschaft, Recht und Islam in Daghestan: von den Khanaten und Gemeindebünden zum Ǧihad-Staat* (Wiesbaden: Reichert, 2005), 65–72; Zelkina, *In Quest for God and Freedom*, 26–30.
55. Zelkina, *In Quest for God and Freedom*, 26–28.
56. They are called Dag-Chufut (Mountain Jews) in Daghestan. Barthold and Bennigsen, 'Dāghistān', 2:86–7.
57. Thomas Barrett, *At the Edge of Empire: The Terek Cossacks and the North Caucasus Frontier, 1700–1860* (Boulder, CO: Westview Press, 1999), 13.
58. J. F. Baddeley, *The Russian Conquest of the Caucasus* (London: Longmans, Green, 1908), 7.
59. Barrett, *At the Edge of Empire*, 13; A. A. Kudriavtsev, 'Spetsifika formirovaniia i istoricheskaiia rol' grebenskogo i terskogo kazachestva na rannem etape razvitiia', *Gumanitarnye i iuridicheskiie issledovaniia* 4 (2015): 82–4;

V. A. Potto, *Dva veka terskogo kazachestva (1577–1801)* (Vladikavkaz: Tipografii Terskago oblastnogo pravleniia, 1912), 1:24–35.

60. Barrett, *At the Edge of Empire*, 7.
61. *Russian Embassies to the Georgian Kings*, 19.
62. Potto, *Dva veka terskogo kazachestva*, 13–23.
63. Ibid., 13; I. *Popko, Terskie kazaki s starodavnikh vremen* (St Petersburg: Tipografiia Departamenta udielov, 1880), 35–7.
64. Kudriavtsev, 'Spetsifika formirovaniia i istoricheskaiia rol' grebenskogo i terskogo kazachestva', 86.
65. Mykhailo Hrushevsky, *History of Ukraine-Rus'*, vol. 7, *The Cossack Age to 1625*, trans. Bohdan Struminski and ed. Serhii Plokhy and Frank E. Sysyn (Edmonton, AB: Canadian Institute of Ukrainian Studies Press, 1999), 88–98. Also see Liubomyr Vynar, *Kniaz Dmytro Vyshnevets'kyi* (Munich: Ukrainian Free Academy of Arts and Sciences, 1964).
66. Brian Boeck, *Imperial Boundaries: Cossack Communities and Empire-Building in the Age of Peter the Great* (New York: Cambridge University Press, 2009), esp. 14–17, 27–30.
67. V. V. Trepavlov, *Istoriia Nogaiskoi Ordy* (Kazan: Kazanskaia nedvizhimost', 2016), 532–44.
68. Ibid., 86, 171.
69. For Muscovite–Nogay relations in this period, see *Posol'skie knigi po sviaziam Rossii s Nogaiskoi Ordoi (1551–1561 gg.)*, ed. D. A. Mustafalina and V. V. Trepavlov (Moscow: Institut rossiiskoi istorii RAN, 2003); Trepavlov, *Istoriia Nogaiskoi Ordy*, 580–625; B. B. Kochekaev, *Nogaisko-russkie otnosheniia v XV–XVIII vv.* (Alma-Ata: Nauka kazakhskoi SSR, 1988).
70. Trepavlov, *Istoriia Nogaiskoi Ordy*, 497–8.
71. Ibid., 566.
72. Ibid., 504, 507, 511.
73. Ibid., 547–61.
74. George Lane, *Early Mongol Rule in Thirteenth-Century Iran: A Persian Renaissance* (London: RoutledgeCurzon, 2003), 76.
75. Bertold Spuler, *Die Goldene Horde: Die Mongolen in Rußland, 1223–1502* (Leipzig: Otto Harrassowitz, 1943), 133–4; A. Yu. Yakubovskii, *Altın Ordu ve çöküşü*, trans. Hasan Eren (Ankara: Türk Tarih Kurumu, 1992), 180–2.
76. I. V. Zaitsev, *Astrakhanskoe khanstvo* (Moscow: Vostochnaia literatura, 2004), 32–58.
77. For the relations between the Golden Horde and the Principality of Muscovy, see George Vernadsky, *The Mongols and Russia* (New Haven, CT: Yale University Press, 1953); Leo de Hartog, *Russia and the Mongol Yoke: The History of the Russian Principalities and the Golden Horde, 1221–1502* (London: British Academic Press, 1996); Charles J. Halperin, *Russia and the Golden Horde: The Mongol Impact on Medieval Russian History* (London: I. B. Tauris, 1987).

78. Halil İnalcık, 'The Question of the Closing of the Black Sea under the Ottomans', *Archeion Pontou* 35 (1979): 74–110; Nagu Pienaru, 'The Black Sea and the Ottomans: The Pontic Policy of Beyazid the Thunderbolt', in *Ottoman Borderlands: Issues, Personalities, and Political Changes*, ed. Kemal H. Karpat and Robert W. Zens (Madison: University of Wisconsin Press, 2003), 33–59.
79. Halil İnalcık, 'Yeni vesikalara göre Kırım hanlığının Osmanlı tabiliğine girmesi ve ahidname meselesi', *Belleten* 8 (1944): 185–229; Kefeli İbrahim bin Ali, *Tevarih-i Tatarhan ve Dağıstan ve Moskov ve Deşt-i Kıpçak ülkelerinindir*, ed. Cafer Seyit Kırımer (Pazardzhik, 1933), 23.
80. Abdülgaffar ibn Hasan Kırımi, *Umdetü't-tevarih* (Istanbul: Matbaa-i Amire, 1924), 103; Ahmed Cevded Paşa, *Tezakir*, ed. Cavid Baysun (Ankara: Türk Tarih Kurumu, 1953), 97.
81. Ahmet Uğur, 'Yavuz Sultan Selim ile Kırım Hanı Mengli Giray ve oğlu Muhammed Giray arasında geçen iki konuşma', *Ankara Üniversitesi İlahiyat Fakültesi dergisi* 21 (1963), 357–61.
82. Akdes Nimet Kurat, *Türkiye ve İdil boyu* (Ankara: Türk Tarih Kurumu, 1966), 54; Bilge, *Osmanlı Devleti ve Kafkasya*, 45.
83. Roger Savory's *Iran under the Safavids* (Cambridge: Cambridge University Press, 1980) is one of the most comprehensive books on the Safavid dynasty of Iran. For a recent study on the Safavids, see Colin P. Mitchell, ed., *New Perspectives on Safavid Iran: Empire and Society* (Abingdon: Routledge, 2011). For a general history and the place of the dynasty in the history of Iran, see Peter Jackson and Laurence Lockhart, eds, *The Cambridge History of Iran,* vol. 6, *The Timurid and Safavid Periods*. (Cambridge: University Press, 1986). Also see Sibylla Schuster-Walser, *Das safawidische Persien im Spiegel europäischer Reiseberichte (1502–1722): Untersuchungen zur Wirtschafts- und Handelspolitik* (Baden-Baden: B. Grimm, 1970); Metin Kunt, 'Ottomans and Safavids: States, Statecraft, and Societies, 1500–1800', in *A Companion to the History of the Middle East*, ed. Youssef M. Choueiri (Malden, MA: Blackwell, 2005), 191–207; Colin P. Mitchell, *The Practice of Politics in Safavid Iran: Power, Religion and Rhetoric* (New York: Palgrave Macmillan, 2009); Andrew J. Newman, *Safavid Iran: Rebirth of a Persian Empire* (London: I. B. Tauris, 2006).
84. Ernest S. Tucker, *Nadir Shah's Quest for Legitimacy in Post-Safavid Iran* (Gainesville: University Press of Florida, 2006), 35–8.
85. Kırzıoğlu, *Osmanlılar'ın Kafkas elleri'ni fethi*, 243.
86. Ibid., 245–9.
87. Remmal Hoca, *Tarih-i Sahib Giray Han*: *Histoire de Sahib Giray, khan de Crimée de 1532 à 1551* (with French translation by M. Le Roux), ed. Özalp Gökbilgin (Ankara: Atatürk Üniversitesi Yayınları, 1973), 39, 76.
88. Victor Ostapchuk, 'Crimean Tatar Long-Range Campaigns: The View from Remmal Khoja's *History of Sahib Gerey Khan*', in *Warfare in Eastern Europe, 1500–1800*, ed. Brian L. Davies (Leiden: Brill, 2012), 153–5,

158–64; Gökbilgin, *1532–1577 yılları arasında Kırım Hanlığı'nın siyasi durumu*, 18–22, 26–9.

89. Remmal Hoca, *Tarih-i Sahib Giray Han*, 39; K. F. Dzamikhov, *Adygi v politike Rossii na Kavkaze, 1550-e–nachalo 1770-kh gg.* (Nal'chik: El'-Fa, 2001), 260.
90. Remmal Hoca, *Tarih-i Sahib Giray Han*, 39, 76.
91. Geoffrey Hosking, *Russia: People and Empire, 1552–1917* (Cambridge, MA: Harvard University Press, 1997), 3–4.
92. İnalcık, *'Yeni vesikalara göre'*, 228–9.
93. Janet Martin, 'Muscovite Relations with the Khanates of Kazan' and Crimea (1460s to 1521)', *Canadian-American Slavic Studies* 17 (1983), 442–3.
94. Halil İnalcık, 'The Origin of the Ottoman–Russian Rivalry and the Don-Volga Canal (1569)', *Annales de l'Université d'Ankara* 1 (1947): 47–55; Croskey, *Muscovite Diplomatic Practice*, 129.
95. Alan Fisher, *The Crimean Tatars* (Stanford, CA: Hoover Institution Press, 1978), 40; Halil İnalcık, 'Power Relations between Russia, the Crimea and the Ottoman Empire as Reflected in Titulature', in *Turco-Tatar Past, Soviet Present: Studies Presented to Alexandre Bennigsen*, ed. Ch. Lemercier-Quelquejay, G. Veinstein and E. Wimbush (Paris: École des hautes études en sciences sociales, 1986), 175–215.
96. Akdes Nimet Kurat, *IV–XVIII. yüzyıllarda Karadeniz kuzeyindeki Türk kavimleri ve devletleri* (Ankara: Murat Kitabevi Yayınları, 1992), 173–4.
97. Remmal Hoca, *Tarih-i Sahib Girey Han*, 115–32.
98. Ibid., 132.

2

Tracing the Milky Way: The North Caucasus and the Two Empires

A major turning point in the history of the early modern North Caucasus that marks the beginning of its borderlandisation was the annexation of Astrakhan on the northern shores of the Caspian Sea in 1556 by the Tsardom of Muscovy. Muscovy subsequently and successfully expanded its sphere of influence further south into the region. Muscovy's ambitions and overtures in the North Caucasus, specifically in Kabarda, eventually forced the Ottoman Empire to redefine its priorities and strategies in its northern frontier zones. Hence, it was in the North Caucasus that these two empires, with their subject- and territory-making strategies, confronted each other for the first time in a long list of encounters which would shape the history of Eastern Europe in the following centuries.

2.1 The North Caucasus within Ottoman Northern Policy

The North Caucasus was a part of the Ottoman Empire's northern frontier, which stretched from Poland-Lithuania in Eastern Europe to the lower Volga River in the north of the Caspian Sea. The Ottoman Porte implemented in the North Caucasus a version of its northern policy, the essential objective of which was to secure and control the Black Sea as a *mare nostrum*. Ensuring the flow of wealth from the Black Sea shores to the Ottoman capital and its hinterland was a critical aspect of this policy. Because of this mostly effective strategy, the Ottomans for a long time were able to centrally control and prevent increases in prices of foodstuffs and other goods thanks to the resource-rich Black Sea littoral, while securing the core provinces of their empire from threats coming from the north.[1] While its control of the Black Sea was never static and complete, the Ottoman Empire was undoubtedly the most potent political power in and around the Black Sea throughout the sixteenth century.[2]

With their expansionist energies spent on their western and eastern frontiers, the Ottomans preferred to operate in the north, especially in the Pontic-Caspian steppes, through their vassal, the Crimean Khanate. In the sixteenth century, the khanate provided the Ottomans with a reliable proxy power and an army capable of raiding or checking the power of the northern states such as the Tsardom of Muscovy and Poland-Lithuania. Similarly, the Crimean khans played significant roles in the North Caucasus as self-proclaimed overlords of the region and its peoples, which was accepted and, to an extent, respected by the Ottoman Porte. Except for certain Western Circassian tribes living in the lands adjacent to the centrally governed Ottoman territories, the North Caucasus in its entirety was under the sway of the Crimean Khanate. Moreover, as the Crimean khans were vassals of the Ottoman sultan, the Porte also considered the North Caucasus as being under Ottoman sovereignty. In the sixteenth century, the Crimean Tatars used the North Caucasus as a source of tributes and slaves, which resulted in frequent Crimean raids in the region, especially during the reign of Khan Sahib Girey.[3]

The Crimean Khanate was also essential in checking the power of the northern states, which was another major element of Ottoman northern policy. The Ottomans considered the Tsardom of Muscovy and Poland-Lithuania as second-rate powers with which their vassal, the Crimean Khanate, could deal and strove to maintain a balance of power between Muscovy, Poland-Lithuania and the Crimean Khanate.[4] In this way, while they used their vassal to render the Muscovites and Polish-Lithuanians incapable of expanding southward to the Black Sea, they ensured these powers kept the Crimean Tatars occupied so that the expansionist ambitions of the khans as the Chinggisid heirs to the legacy of the Golden Horde were in return checked by these northern states. During this time, the Ottoman Porte also preferred to negotiate with the Muscovite rulers through the Crimean khans, who considered Muscovy as a tribute-paying vassal state.

The pre-Muscovite Ottoman policy in the North Caucasus sought to ensure several specific outcomes for the Porte. First, following their broader northern policy, the main objective of the Ottomans was to establish an imperial order around the Black Sea littoral of the North Caucasus by coopting and subduing the Western Circassian rulers and their tribes in the Taman Peninsula controlling the shores and the mouth of the Kuban River. In line with the traditional Ottoman diplomatic practices of the sixteenth century, the sultan granted banners, diplomas of investiture and often salaries to some of the strong local rulers or the rulers of larger tribes in the North Caucasus. At this stage, the Ottomans did not necessarily aspire to annex the territories of these local rulers but instead wanted to keep them under control as proper vassals and gradually integrate them into the Ottoman imperial system.

Second, the provinces of Kefe and Azak functioned as the headquarters of information gathering for Ottoman priorities in the North Caucasus. Through Kefe and Azak the Ottomans applied what they called a strategy of *istimalet*, that is, appeasement or accommodation, to draw the local rulers to their side by rewarding them with annuities and imperial titles. The Ottomans expected loyalty and service from these local rulers, especially when they were on the Porte's payroll. They tasked the local rulers, who submitted to the sultan, with the protection of Ottoman possessions from raids of 'unruly' tribes or with other duties such as manning the nearby Ottoman forts or fortresses. The extant Ottoman documents confirm that some of these chiefs and their soldiers were stationed in Azak and were actively responsible for helping with the defence of Ottoman possessions to the north of the Black Sea.[5] Lastly, the Porte employed the Crimean Khanate as the 'stick' for punishing local peoples if the policy of *istimalet* did not yield the desired results.[6]

Therefore, the Ottoman Porte preferred to apply a manipulative yet lax policy whose main objective was to maintain its exclusive control over the Black Sea and ensure the security of its centrally administered provinces in the region. While establishing order and creating loyal vassals or administrative districts along the Black Sea shores, the Ottomans trusted the Crimean khans to handle the affairs of the broader North Caucasus and the steppes to the north. The Ottomans' initial policy in the North Caucasus derived from their long-term understanding of their northern frontier. The Crimean Khanate controlled the region militarily with broad powers to punish the local populations, while the Porte applied a 'carrot and stick' policy in the strategically important areas of the North Caucasus. Local rulers deemed obedient and loyal were adorned with imperial titles and granted salaries from the revenues of Kefe or Azak. If a local ruler failed to fulfil his promises or was no longer loyal, the Ottoman Porte sent the Crimean khan to punish him. The Crimean Tatars often welcomed such punitive opportunities, as it allowed them to exact tributes and slaves from the region.[7]

While the Crimean khans possessed an extensive authority amounting to independence in their dealings with the North Caucasus polities, the Western Circassians in the Taman Peninsula were an exception to this. The Ottoman governors, the *sancakbeyi*s of Kefe and Azak, encouraged the submission of these local rulers to the Porte due to their proximity to Ottoman possessions and in line with the Ottoman notion of centrally governing the Black Sea coasts. After capturing Taman in 1479 and constructing the Temrük, Kızıltaş and Cane fortresses in 1516, the Ottomans were able to effectively control some of the Circassian tribes living near these fortresses, in the most strategic areas of the Taman Peninsula.

Most of these local rulers were from the Janeys, the most influential group in the western part of the North Caucasus. The Ottoman Porte provided the Janey chiefs with standards of investiture, which typically included a golden banner, a drum and robes of honour (*hil'at*), as well as the title of *sancakbeyi*, which came with an annual salary.[8] And some of these Circassian chiefs in the region received annuities with no titles. Such sorts of annuities were usually paid from the revenues of Kefe.[9] The number of local rulers who were allocated salaries from Kefe was rather high in the second half of the sixteenth century. In 1564, the governor of Kefe wrote to the Porte that numerous Circassian chiefs were travelling to his province, seeking permission to visit Istanbul to submit to the sultan, from whom they would request salaries. The sultan responded that the governor should no longer allow Circassian chiefs to travel to Istanbul without obtaining prior permission from the Porte.[10] To illustrate, in 1578, salaries paid from Kefe to the Circassian rulers, including some Kabardinian chiefs, amounted to 1,206,274 *akçe*; the figure rose to 1,918,480 *akçe* in 1579.[11]

Interestingly, Circassian chiefs could even receive salaries from the revenues of remote parts of the Ottoman Empire. One of the Janey chiefs, for example, was granted a timar (land revenue) from Aleppo.[12] As we understand from the available Ottoman documents, the Circassian rulers receiving salaries from the Porte were mostly loyal to the sultan. However, it was not unusual for some to switch sides. For example, in 1565, the same Janey chief with a timar revenue out of Aleppo rebelled against the Porte and joined the Zaporozhian Cossacks of Dmytro Vyshnevetskyi, whose activities against the Ottomans and Crimean Tatars are examined below.[13]

Being close to Ottoman possessions, the Janeys were even registered for taxes and in 1539 were required to pay *cizye* as non-Muslims by order of Halil Bey, the governor of Kefe.[14] Theoretically, their registration for taxation made the Janeys Ottoman subjects. In 1565, when some Janeys were attacked and enslaved in the Taman region, the Porte ordered the governor of Kefe to prevent such attacks on 'Ottoman subjects' and not to allow slave traders to buy or sell these enslaved Circassians. The Porte dispatched this order upon the request of Janey Chief Mustafa, who had sent a man to Istanbul with a petition stating, '[May] slave traders be warned that people of his (Mustafa's) *sancak* who are sold as slaves must not be purchased. Following this warning, his people are to be freed regardless of who owns them.'[15] The governor was to find those enslaved people and free them by any means necessary. The Porte also instructed him 'to imprison those who enslaved these people', as they were now Ottoman subjects.[16]

In another instance, the Porte ordered the Crimean khan and the governor of Kefe that without causing disturbance and disorder in the region of Taman, they were to capture and punish certain Circassian chiefs who oppressed their own Circassian subjects by illegally seizing their herds.[17] These documents prove that the Ottomans attempted to establish a degree of direct authority and the rule of law, especially among the Circassians living in the Taman Peninsula, as they inhabited an outlet to the Black Sea whose control was imperative to the Ottoman Empire. A seventeenth-century chronicle by Hezarfen Hüseyin shows that the Ottomans reached their objectives regarding the Circassians of the Taman Peninsula. Hezarfen Hüseyin writes that the Janeys were Muslims and had judges appointed by the Porte, which was a proof of central authority.[18] Thus, with the Janeys, we see both the establishment of the Ottoman rule of law and Islamisation of a native North Caucasus tribe, a successful result for the Porte.

However, being registered as Ottoman subjects with an obligation to pay taxes caused disturbances among the Circassian population in the Kuban–Taman region. Local chiefs and *sipahis*[19] often appealed to the governor of Kefe, complaining about these taxes: 'The provincial secretary registered us as subjects and demanded payments of *'öşr* and *resm-i çift*. But, we have no means of paying such taxes.'[20] When their complaints fell on deaf ears, Circassian tribes tended to flee from their lands into the northwestern regions of the Caucasus Mountains where they could avoid the Ottoman tax machine, given that neither the Ottomans nor the Crimean Tatars controlled such mountainous areas effectively. In response, the Porte sent orders to Kefe and the Crimea Khanate in 1570 and 1571 instructing them to prevent such migrations from the Taman Peninsula and return the fleeing Circassians: 'It is ordered that if the aforementioned people [Circassians] want to leave the island [Taman Peninsula], you should return them to their lands, if possible, in peace and by applying *istimalet* [reconciliation or accommodation]. If they do not comply or rebel, punish them.'[21] The discontent of the Western Circassian chiefs and tribes with Ottoman taxation is evident in the Ottoman documents in which they repeatedly appealed to the Porte or the governor of Kefe. Therefore, despite frequent tribal revolts or sometimes attacks on Ottoman possessions, most rulers in the North Caucasus, going all the way east but not including the realm of the Daghestani shamkhals, were under the punitive and robust hand of the Crimean khan or, depending on their proximity to Ottoman possessions and peaceful subordination, under the control of the Ottoman governors. The former group included the Kabardinians, and the latter the Janeys, Besleneys and Kemirgoys.

The situation further east of the Beshtau Mountains was politically more complicated but of less concern to the Ottomans. The Porte considered Kabarda nominally to be under the sovereignty of the sultan through his Crimean vassal. However, before the Muscovite interest and activities in Kabarda, the Ottomans had no intention of establishing any form of real control over it. It means that the areas further east, including Daghestan and its Muslim rulers, did not interest the Ottoman officials, as attested by the lack of references to them in the official Ottoman sources. This Ottoman policy over the North Caucasus remained the same until the appearance of Muscovy in the region as a rival power in the second half of the sixteenth century. It was only after the rise of Muscovite power and their ambition to establish a sphere of influence in the North Caucasus that the Ottomans felt the need to modify their strategies in the region.

Beyond the North Caucasus and for the post-Golden Horde steppe powers, the Ottomans preferred to use the conceit of being far distant, despite these steppe polities approaching the Ottoman Porte for support against their foes several times in the sixteenth century. Sultan Süleyman I (r. 1520–66) stated this in his letter dated 1551 to İsmail Beg of the Nogays. Just before the imminent capture of Kazan by Muscovy, he wrote, 'We are all Muslims, and we should unite against Moscow … and you should help Kazan and Azov [*sic*], which are too far away for me to aid; then I shall make you a khan in Azov.'[22] İsmail was the staunchest ally of Muscovy among the Nogay elites. In his pro-Muscovite policies, he was opposed by his brother, Yusuf Mirza, but in 1555 emerged victorious in this power struggle. Süleyman also wrote to Yusuf Mirza and, in 1548, recognised him as the *emirü'l-umera*, the supreme commander of the Nogays as an Ottoman vassal.[23] The Porte had to thread a very delicate policy with the post-Golden Horde steppe powers, as this relationship was intertwined with the politics of the Crimean Khanate, a contender for the heritage of the Golden Horde in Eurasia. Süleyman I and certain Ottoman officials during and after his reign were perceptibly aware of the delicate situation to the north of the Black Sea. Among these officials, Sokullu Mehmed Pasha, who became the grand vizier in 1565 and *de facto* ruled the empire after Süleyman's death in the following year, was the most stalwart supporter of an active Ottoman policy in the north.

Süleyman's knowledge of the northern affairs was sufficient to understand the possible danger that Muscovy could pose for Crimea and the Ottoman possessions in the north of the Black Sea. Khan Sahib Girey, who was pursuing a fierce anti-Muscovite policy in the former Golden Horde territories, was a close friend of Süleyman.[24] He had even installed himself as the khan of Kazan (r. 1521–4) before he became the khan of the Crimean Khanate in 1532. Sahib Girey met Süleyman on several occasions during the Ottoman campaigns in Central Europe, and, according to Remmal Hoca's chronicle, they had long conversations together.[25] Thus, although Süleyman I probably comprehended the intricacies of the northern affairs and Muscovite ambitions over the former Golden Horde territories, he did not have the opportunity to devise policies to neutralise Muscovy. We understand from his letter to the Nogays that the Porte had more pressing priorities than the developments in the north and decided not to interfere in the affairs of the Pontic–Caspian steppes actively. Instead, the Ottomans tried to prevent the fall of the khanates of Kazan and Astrakhan by forming an alliance of Muslim polities to check Muscovy or at least by trying to reverse the pro-Muscovite orientation of the Nogays.

Historians sometimes raise the question of why the Ottoman Porte failed to help its vassal the Crimean Khanate to take over the lands and heritage of the Golden Horde when it was evident that the Tsardom of Muscovy would conquer the khanates of Kazan and Astrakhan in the mid-sixteenth century. In line with its northern policy, the Ottoman Empire actively limited the power of the Crimean Khanate. Worse than the Muscovite capture of Kazan and Astrakhan for the Ottomans was their annexation by the Crimean khan, as it meant that the former Golden Horde territories would be united once more under a Chinggisid ruler. Such a neighbour to the north – vassal or not – would have been problematic for the non-Chinggisid Ottoman dynasty and state. The Crimean Khanate as a potent Chinggisid and Muslim power controlling Kazan, Astrakhan and possibly the Nogays would likely be a direct rival and a severe threat to the Ottoman Empire, not only in the north of the Black Sea but also in greater Eurasia. However, the Ottomans had no intention of accepting the Muscovite annexation of Kazan and Astrakhan, either. As W. E. D. Allen points out, Süleyman I agreed to sign a peace treaty with the Safavid Empire in the east on 1 June 1555, right after the effective occupation of the Khanate of Astrakhan by Muscovy, and this could be an indication of his intentions for organising a campaign in the north.[26]

2.2 *The North Caucasus within Muscovite Steppe Frontier Policy*

The history of Muscovy and later the Russian Empire is also a history of an ever-expanding southern frontier. In their early contacts with the North Caucasus rulers and peoples following their consequential conquests of

Kazan and Astrakhan, the Tsardom of Muscovy and its officials preferred to apply their strictly formulated and well-tested steppe frontier policy in the North Caucasus. The instruments of the Muscovite steppe frontier policy seemed to bear fruit in the first decades of their active involvement in the region. These were the same strategies that had previously enabled them to annex Kazan and Astrakhan, and control the Nogay Horde on their eastern and southern frontiers.[27] In 1556, Ivan IV's court was divided between boyars and officials promoting a westward expansion into Livonia versus those arguing for the continuation of the Muscovite push into the Golden Horde territories, which included Crimea and the North Caucasus.[28] Ivan sided with the first group and dedicated the most of Muscovy's military resources to the Livonian War, which began in 1558. Although the tsar prioritised an expansion in the west, the Muscovites could not solely dedicate all of their resources to the Livonian War due to the developments that followed their conquests of the Tatar Khanates and the constant threat of Crimean raids. The wheels of the Muscovite steppe frontier policy continued to turn and do what they did best in Muscovy's southern frontier zones: manipulate and establish suzerainty over the local peoples, build fortresses, and eventually integrate new lands into the Muscovite imperial system. Hence, when their success against Kazan and Astrakhan brought them to the North Caucasus, the Muscovite officials ostensibly assumed that the peoples of the region did not differ much from the nomadic or semi-nomadic groups they had encountered on their southern frontier, namely those who already were or would eventually be 'tamed'. However, the political and social hierarchies of the North Caucasus peoples were quite different from those of the Turkic nomadic societies in the south and east frontier zones of Muscovy.[29]

At first, to the local rulers in the North Caucasus, the Tsardom of Muscovy was evidently a potential ally that could help them with their political ambitions in a region where conflicts between the local rulers, foreign invasions and slave raids were a way of life. For the Western Circassians, the Muscovites were a possible power that could help relieve the nearby Crimean pressure over them. As understood from the Muscovite chronicles, the Kabardinians also saw in Muscovy an opportunity to protect themselves from the Crimean Tatars and the shamkhal of Daghestan.[30] But the Muslim Daghestani rulers were also among the local rulers soliciting an alliance with Muscovy, for they wanted military assistance against the Safavid Empire and for their domestic rivalries and power struggles within Daghestan.[31]

In its arsenal for engaging and controlling its nomadic and semi-nomadic neighbours, Muscovy had some effective weapons. One of them was systematic cooptation, an essential element of Muscovite policy on its southern frontier. The Muscovite cooptation strategy aimed to incorporate native elites into the Muscovite imperial system. Its principles were formulated on the basis of the long-lasting and largely successful Muscovite practice of dealing with the nobility of the post-Golden Horde polities. A ruler, social group or entire tribe could be granted economic and political advantages over the others and thus be expected to act in the interest of Muscovy.[32] Cooptation might include religious conversion, cultural assimilation, and even marital ties with the Muscovite tsar depending on the status of the elites or peoples targeted.[33]

The Muscovite cooptation strategy went hand in hand with another Muscovite method – delegating power to one of the local rulers and subduing other chiefs in the area through him. This was related to the Muscovite practice of designating a Chinggisid prince when the Muscovites coopted Turko-Mongolian polities. Chantal Lemercier-Quelquejay argues this policy brought about what she calls 'Chinggisid syndrome' in Muscovite foreign relations. The Muscovite officials designated one chief as the supreme ruler, regardless of the social and political structures of the peoples they encountered.[34] Michael Khodarkovsky describes this Muscovite method as finding 'a khan or a search for central authority'.[35] In its relations with the post-Golden Horde polities on its eastern and southern frontiers, Muscovy implemented the same strategy of creating a supreme ruler by using Chinggisid nobility to secure the loyalty of the steppe peoples. This strategy yielded very favourable results when applied to the Turco-Mongolian societies, which were hierarchical and rarely questioned the decisions of their Chinggisid rulers. Thus, it was a productive method with Tatar nobilities of Kazan and Astrakhan, and with the Nogays.[36]

Compared to this, it was rather tricky for the Ottoman Porte to play the 'Chinggisid card' since Crimean khans were Ottoman vassals. The Crimean dynasty was Chinggisid and claimed the heritage of the Golden Horde. Therefore, the Crimean khans recognised no other Turkic steppe ruler equal to themselves and demanded their submission or destruction, which left little room to manoeuvre for the Ottomans to cement a separate alliance with the Nogays or other steppe powers without intervention or recognition by the Crimean khans. The Crimean khans expected that the Ottoman sultans would allow them the independence to deal with steppe peoples and former Golden Horde territories, and the Ottomans mostly respected this, at least until they modified their strategies in the North Caucasus.

There were several other tools used by the Muscovite officials within the framework of their steppe frontier policy in the sixteenth century.

These were obtaining a pledge of allegiance (*shert'*), taking of hostages (*amanat*), and providing gifts and annuities (*pominki* and *zhalovaniia*).[37] The Muscovite officials negotiating treaties or alliances with local rulers in their southern frontier zones always acted within the limits of instructions given to them regarding the prescribed rituals of the *shert'*, receiving hostages, and distributing presents and annuities among local rulers. Every procedure was arranged ahead of time by the centre – even sentences that envoys or officials would utter or the manner in which they would act was written down by officials in Moscow.[38]

From the Muscovite perspective, *shert'*, a word of Arabic origin that the Muscovite chancellery borrowed from the Tatars, denoted a kind of pledge that a local ruler was required to take to document his loyalty to the Muscovite tsar.[39] Originally a Chinggisid practice called *möchälgä*, these sorts of binding pledges in a document were widely used in post-Chinggisid states in Eurasia.[40] Non-Chinggisid states such as the Safavid Empire[41] or the Tsardom of Muscovy established in lands once ruled by the Chinggisid dynasties also adopted the practice. The *shert'* remained a part of Muscovite diplomatic practice well into the eighteenth century.[42] Signing of the *shert'* went hand in hand with monetary allowances and gifts given to local rulers by the tsar as well as hostage taking. On the one hand, Muscovite officials were insistent upon the oath of alliance and considered it as proof of submission by local rulers. It was a pivotal element of the whole clientage system of Muscovy. On the other hand, many local rulers in the southern and eastern frontier zones of Muscovy, especially in the North Caucasus, regarded the *shert'* instead as a military league between them and one of the potential allies.[43]

Amanat was another essential strategy in the complex relationship between Muscovy and its clients. Sons or close relatives of local rulers allying with or submitting to the tsar or, sometimes, their nobility were taken hostage as surety by the Muscovites. This common practice in Eurasia became a cornerstone of Muscovite diplomacy in the North Caucasus.[44] For the Muscovite officials, the *shert'* coupled with *amanat* reflected Muscovy's own image of sovereignty over the local rulers whom they wanted to coopt. Just as was the case with the *shert'*, the Muscovites were rigid in their demands for hostages in their negotiations for a new alliance or submission with a local ruler. Muscovy applied the same rigidity in its dealings with the North Caucasus chieftains, among whom hostage taking was also common.[45]

The tsar of the centralised and 'civilised' 'Third Rome' was benevolent and generous to local rulers for their submission and loyalty to him. At the same time, local rulers were content to receive protection against their enemies as well as money and gifts in exchange for their military 'alliance'. Gift and payments (*pominki* and *zhalovaniia*) were indeed intended to keep these local rulers loyal. However, as mentioned above, with or without the tsar's 'royal bounty', many local rulers in the North Caucasus did not imagine their relationship with the tsar as submission to Muscovy.[46] The Muscovites also used presents and annuities to prevent steppe powers such as the Crimean Tatars or the Nogays from raiding Muscovite territories and subjects. Moreover, by providing its clients and neighbours with presents and annuities, Muscovy was making them more and more economically dependent.

Besides these, the Muscovite conquests in the sixteenth century show us a specific pattern in terms of subduing the local population, including assimilation policies. Newly conquered areas could be subject to the expulsion of some local elements such as tribes or groups that Muscovy considered enemies and found dangerous for its further expansion and eventual annexation of the area. While the people expelled from their native lands were, most of the time, relocated within the boundaries of the Tsardom of Muscovy, a Slavic population and elites were settled in their stead. To illustrate, it took only a few years to transform Kazan and its hinterland from a Muslim Tatar city into a proper Muscovite one, in which Muscovite nobles and Slavic people constituted the majority of the inhabitants. Similarly, the Muscovites deported the Tatar population of Astrakhan to the surrounding areas and settled Slavic-speaking people in the new city and fortress of Astrakhan, in which the majority of the population consisted of Russians.[47] Therefore, expulsion and, later in the following centuries, deportation were sometimes used as a component of Muscovy's policy in its steppe frontier zones.

At times the Muscovites applied this policy to people coopted peacefully. The Nogays, controlling an area that covered most of the lower Volga and Yaik rivers as well as the steppes around these rivers, provide a good example. [48] As we understand from the Muscovite sources, the Nogays almost always complained that they were losing their rivers and lands to the Muscovite settlers and could not use the pastures they had previously freely enjoyed. Slowly but gradually, those lands that belonged to the Nogays, who were clients of Muscovy, were transformed into centrally administered Muscovite territories or districts wherein fortresses were built, soldiers stationed and Slavic peasants settled. By contrast, the Ottomans strove to retain the local populations in their own lands in the northern borderlands, as exemplified above with the Janey Circassians. As one may remember, the Ottoman Porte sent orders to the governors of Azak and Kefe and to the Crimean khan regarding Circassians that attempted to flee their lands due to being subjected to Ottoman taxation.[49] As far as the Porte was concerned, keeping the local populace and registering them for taxation was preferable to deporting and replacing them with Muslim or Turkish people in its territory north of the Black Sea.[50]

Attempting to achieve their objectives in the North Caucasus, the Muscovites realised that their steppe frontier strategies needed to be adjusted, as this time they would be operating in an area close to the Ottoman territories and traditionally regarded as belonging to the Ottoman Porte through their vassal the Crimean Khanate. Therefore, there was an imminent threat of military reaction from the Ottoman Empire. A direct military intervention in the North Caucasus by the Muscovites would guarantee a similar response from the Porte and the Crimean Khanate. This reality and Muscovite officials' understanding of their political and military limits brought about a significant component of Muscovite policy in the North Caucasus: the avoidance of direct military conflict with the Ottoman Empire. The Muscovites, especially in the first phases of their activities in the region, were careful not to provoke the Ottoman Porte. They had from the beginning no desire to become embroiled in direct conflict with the Ottomans in which a combined Ottoman–Crimean power might put an end to Muscovy's expansionist ambitions and even reverse its latest territorial annexations along the Volga River. However, Muscovite officials in the sixteenth century noticeably differentiated between the Ottoman Empire and its vassals in applying this policy, as Muscovy did not hesitate to confront the Crimean Khanate and other Ottoman vassals in the Pontic–Caspian steppes or the North Caucasus.[51]

Understanding the strategic value of the region for the defence of their newly acquired possessions in the north of the Caspian Sea and their future expansion, the Muscovites sought ways to contain possible Ottoman and Crimean reactions to their political and territorial objectives, which now included lands claimed by the Ottoman sultan. As a common imperial practice in Eurasian history, using centrifugal frontier forces was one option available to the Muscovites in this endeavour. The Muscovites employed the Cossacks in the first phase of their involvement in the North Caucasus, for the Muscovite tsar could easily disown their attacks on the Ottoman–Crimean possessions.

In the steppe frontier zone, the Cossacks were the equivalent of the Crimean Tatars both for the Tsardom of Muscovy and for Poland-Lithuania. By using them effectively, the Muscovites incorporated the frontier zones and colonised the southern steppes from the sixteenth to the eighteenth centuries, regardless of their sometimes uneasy relations with various Cossack hosts. Similar to the relationship between the Ottomans and the

Crimean Tatars, there was a special understanding of rights and responsibilities between the Cossack hosts and Muscovy. No person accepted into a Cossack host was subject to Muscovite jurisdiction. Even if they were a fugitive or criminal, as soon as they became a member, Muscovite officials had no authority over the person. The Muscovites comprehended that services rendered by the Cossacks on the steppe frontier were much more important than following and apprehending fugitives, who initially constituted the bulk of the Cossack hosts.[52] The Cossacks inhabiting the southern steppes and borderlands of Muscovy and lands in the North Caucasus were also settlers. Organised as military societies, they were able to defend themselves and even attack local peoples and polities in their vicinity.[53] In fact, the Cossacks proved to be the cheapest and most effective way of colonising the steppes for Muscovy.[54]

Upon settling on the Pontic–Caspian steppes, in Ukraine or in the North Caucasus, the Cossacks enabled an influx of Slavic settlers by providing them with much-needed security against attacks by nomadic and semi-nomadic steppe polities or other external enemies of Muscovy.[55] For example, the Greben and Terek Cossacks became an integral part of the North Caucasus, where they established their hosts, while creating a symbiotic relationship with the Muscovite officials in the lower Volga region.[56] Their social structure, organised into military fraternities and their idea of *vol'nost'* (freedom), conformed to the ideals of the North Caucasus societies and polities. Compared to the Crimean Tatars, who considered the North Caucasus as a source of slaves and tribute and themselves as the masters of the region, the Cossacks were more successful in interacting with the local populations. The Cossacks intermarried and had neighbourly relations with the local North Caucasus societies, promoting Muscovite interests within their locality in a way that Muscovy could not possibly do with its own military, political or economic means. Therefore, the most significant contribution of the Cossacks to Muscovy's ambitions was their military prowess and mobility, which Muscovy itself could not muster in the southern frontier zones, and their ability to colonise. Being outlawed people from Muscovy, Poland-Lithuania and other states, the Cossacks opted to settle in borderlands and uninhabited frontier zones. Precisely for the same reason, it was difficult to control them, as they did not always obey the Muscovite tsar and could prioritise their own interests if the situation required it.

As the proxy forces of the two imperial powers bordering the Pontic–Caspian steppes, the Cossacks and the Crimean Tatars adhered to a particular code of conduct for warfare and raiding. Conflicts between the Crimean Tatars and Cossacks coexisted with periods of peace and amicable relations. Thus, the objective of warfare in the steppes through the Crimean Tatar or Cossack prism was to 'procure resources' rather than annihilate the adversary. The prominent Ukrainian historian Mykhailo Hrushevsky refers to this phenomenon from the Cossack perspective as a 'border sport'.[57] From the perspective of the imperial powers trying to puppet-master them, the aim was to disturb the other state's order and subjects settled in or near the borderlands or frontier zones.[58]

Another critical aspect of relying on clients and vassals in the frontier zones was the notion of 'plausible deniability'. Conflicts and warfare between the clients in the borderlands did not necessarily exacerbate the relationship between the imperial powers.[59] Thus, the imperial powers could have cordial relations with one another while their clients in the steppes carried out raiding and plundering, which were often protested against but not seen as a reason for a full-scale campaign. Just as the Ottomans punished the Cossacks when they had the chance, the Muscovites had the perfect right to stop the Crimean Tatars' raiding activities, if they could.[60]

It was in this context and setting that the expansion of the Ottoman Empire and Tsardom of Muscovy brought them to a region wherein their subject- and territory-making strategies clashed in the second half of the sixteenth century for the first time. The relationship and diplomacy of the Ottoman Porte with the local North Caucasus peoples examined above remained the same until the Tsardom of Muscovy emerged as an imperial contender in the region. Muscovy found itself as a player in the North Caucasus affairs as early as 1552 following its annexation of Kazan when Tsar Ivan IV received Circassian envoys from the region of Beshtau. In November of that year, the Circassian princes Maashuk, Ezbozluk and Tanashuk arrived in Moscow, requesting the tsar's protection against the Crimean khan.[61] These local rulers knew that the Muscovites and Crimean Tatars were at odds over the conquest of Kazan by Ivan IV, and thus enemies. That is why these North Caucasus chieftains considered Muscovy a potential ally against the Crimean Tatars in 1552. The Crimean and Ottoman pressures over the Western Circassians and frequent slave raids by the Crimean Tatars were possible other reasons for the Circassian appeals to the rising power of Muscovy.

In August 1555, another group of Circassian princes, this time from the Kuban-Taman region of the North Caucasus, travelled to Moscow requesting Muscovite protection against the Crimean Tatars and the Ottomans.[62] This embassy was important, as Prince Sibok, his brother Atsymguk and his son Kudadik were from the Janey tribe of the Western Circassians. As one may recall, the Ottoman Porte considered them as the sultan's subjects.

One other prince who travelled to Moscow with the same party was Prince Tutaryk from Beshtau. Tutaryk's father was Ezbozluk, who had submitted to the tsar in 1552. Such appeals were welcome developments for the Muscovite tsar because they provided Muscovy with an opportunity to claim these areas as under the tsar's sovereignty, which is stated in the Muscovite chronicles: '[A]nd they, with their wives and children, remain as servants of the Tsar and Great Kniaz for centuries.'[63] Tsar Ivan IV granted them salaries and promised protection against the Crimean khan, but specifically not against the Ottomans, as 'he was in peace with the sultan'. This last part is a good illustration of the Muscovite strategy of avoiding direct military conflict with the Ottoman Porte. Kudadik was baptised, taking the name Alexander, remained in Moscow and joined the tsar's service. Tutaryk was also baptised and given the name Ivan.[64]

In 1557, perhaps the most pleasing diplomatic news about the North Caucasus came from several Kabardinian rulers. Temriuk and Tazriut, significant rulers in Kabarda, sent their envoys to newly conquered Astrakhan to ask for Muscovite assistance against their Kabardinian rivals and foreign enemies, especially the Daghestani shamkhal.[65] This petition ideally suited the objectives the Muscovite officials had in the North Caucasus, as Kabarda was a strategic location controlling a passage to the South Caucasus, the Georgian kingdoms and the Safavid Empire.[66] A possible Muscovite control over Kabarda would be a natural defence line for Astrakhan and a springboard for southward expansion. The Muscovite tsar gladly accepted their submission and promised them military assistance against their enemies. The Kabardinian princes did not list the Ottomans as one of their enemies, which is an indication of the limits of the pre-Muscovite Ottoman ambitions in the North Caucasus. The Porte was not interested in this faraway land. However, the developments that followed the Kabardinian request for an alliance in 1557 caused the Ottoman Porte to alter its previously lax strategies in the North Caucasus and in their broader northern frontier zones.

2.3 The Road to Astrakhan: Towards a Mature Ottoman Policy in the North

The Ottoman Porte was undoubtedly cognisant of the ideological and strategic consequences in Eurasia of the annexation of Kazan and Astrakhan by the Tsardom of Muscovy in 1552 and 1556 respectively. However, to limit the power and prestige of the Crimean Khanate, the preferred scenario devised by the officials at the Porte was to take over Astrakhan rather than allowing it to fall under the rule of the khanate. Even though the Crimean Khan Sahib Girey had captured Astrakhan with the help of Ottoman soldiers already in 1549, seven years earlier than Ivan IV of Muscovy, he was instructed by the Ottoman sultan to reinstall Yağmurcu Khan of Astrakhan and withdraw his forces.[67] His appeals to the Porte to help Kazan and Astrakhan by sending Ottoman troops along with the Crimean army fell on deaf ears. The Porte eventually deposed Sahib Girey, for the sultan considered him to be too ambitious.[68] A sixteenth-century Crimean chronicler, Remmal Hoca, blames several high-ranking Ottoman officials at the Porte and their intrigues for the dethronement of Sahib Girey by the sultan. Accordingly, certain viziers spread rumours and swayed the sultan's opinion by lying that, conceited about his Chinggisid ancestry, Sahib Girey repeatedly ignored the orders from the Ottoman sultan and looked down on Ottoman governors and viziers.[69] By taking Astrakhan, the Ottomans would keep their Crimean vassal under tighter control, obtain a strategic upper hand against the Safavids, neutralise the newly emerging Muscovite threat from Kabarda, and control the flow of commercial revenues from the region, which was quite handsome, as stressed in the letters sent to the sultan by Central Asian rulers and local Tatars.[70]

Regardless of the Porte's apprehensions about the ambitions of the Crimean khans, the annexation of Kazan and Astrakhan, both Sunni Muslim territories, by a non-Muslim state was a severe blow to the Ottoman imperial ideology and the historical perception of everlasting imperial conquests to expand *darü'l-islam*, the abode of Islam.[71] The Ottoman sultans considered the protection and steady expansion of *darü'l-islam* territories as their duty. Therefore, the Ottoman sultan, as the self-proclaimed leader of the Sunni Muslim world, needed to listen to the appeals coming from Central Asian khanates about the closure by the Muscovites of the pilgrimage route from their lands to Mecca that passed through Astrakhan and from the local Tatars and Nogays about the duty of the sultan to rescue them from the 'infidel' Muscovites 'who destroyed their mosques and enslaved Muslims'.[72]

The Ottoman Porte planned a campaign to take Astrakhan at least three times in the second half of the sixteenth century. The earliest recorded occasion was during the reign of Süleyman I. In 1563, he sent an order to the Crimean khan, instructing him to muster his army for a campaign in the spring of 1564 to conquer Astrakhan.[73] However, due to the military engagements of the Porte and the political situation in Central Europe, as well as the response of Crimean Khan Devlet Girey (r. 1551–77) regarding the impracticality of retaining the city following its conquest, this project was shelved. The second was in 1569, when the Ottomans carried out a campaign. The third and the last one was planned in 1587. However, the Porte once again abandoned the plan due to the ongoing war with the Safavid Empire and the tense situation on the western frontiers of the Ottoman Empire.

There is a common thread that wove its way through the discussions and plans for the conquest of Astrakhan at the Ottoman Porte. In all three instances, there was a military threat created or supported by the Muscovite forces stationed in Astrakhan. In 1563, it was the activities of the Zaporozhian Cossack leader Dmytro Vyshnevetskyi in alliance with some Circassian chiefs. Vyshnevetskyi and his allies received Muscovite support from Astrakhan and Kabarda, as the Ottoman and Muscovite documents related to their activities indicate. In 1569, it was the Muscovite fortress and military activities in Kabarda, operating out of Astrakhan, besides other strategic calculations about the rising power of Muscovy and encircling the Safavid Empire. The 1569 plan was the only one that materialised, although its result was a failure. In 1587, it was the Cossacks hindering the Ottoman efforts to establish a more defined presence and sovereignty in the North Caucasus. The Cossacks blocked or harassed the Ottoman supply and transportation route in the region during the Ottoman–Safavid War of 1578–90, again supported by the Muscovites in Astrakhan. That a Crimean prince, Murad Girey, took refuge in Astrakhan and was reportedly recruiting men to take over the Crimean Khanate in the 1580s was indeed another major reason for the Porte to consider capturing Astrakhan in 1587.

Among the irritants that triggered a more active Ottoman involvement in the north in the 1560s, and an actual military campaign in 1569, was the sudden and very effective cooperation of some prominent North Caucasus local rulers with Muscovy, starting in 1552, and more alarmingly their raids in alliance with the Zaporozhian Cossacks under Vyshnevetskyi in the Ottoman/Crimean territories. Vyshnevetskyi, dissatisfied with his overlord Sigismund II (king of Poland and grand duke of Lithuania, r. 1548–72) and his policy of Catholicisation in traditionally Orthodox Ukraine, entered into the service of Ivan IV in 1556.[74] The Cossack/Circassian attacks under his command on the Ottoman/Crimean possessions around the north of the Black Sea from the mid-1550s to the early 1560s were of great concern to the Porte. By supplying him money, weapons and men, the tsar and his officials took excellent advantage of Vyshnevetskyi, who targeted some strategic Ottoman and Crimean territories in the region such as the fortresses of Islam Kerman, Taman, Temrük and Azak, all vital for the Ottoman control of the Black Sea.[75]

Another shocking reality for the Ottoman Porte was that many Circassian rulers joined Vyshnevetskyi in the years 1556–62. Among those Circassian rulers was Kansavuk of the Janeys, who, in 1539, received the title of *sancakbeyi* and a salary from the Porte.[76] Another Janey chief, receiving a timar from the revenue of Aleppo, also allied with Vyshnevetskyi, though he ended up losing his life in 1560 in a battle with the Ottomans, according to the Ottoman sources.[77] Sibok of the Janeys, Atsymguk and Kanuko of Kabarda were also first among those who sided with the Cossack/Muscovite front in the region and fought against the Ottomans and Crimean Tatars.[78] As one may remember, Sibok was one of the sons of Kansavuk.[79] Moreover, in a letter to the Crimean khan, the sultan stated that Circassian chiefs Polad Sultan and Cantemir were likely to travel to Muscovy and submit to the tsar, eventually harming the Ottoman lands or Muslim subjects in the Taman region. The sultan instructed the khan to protect the Ottoman possessions and assist in the repairs of the fortress of Özi.[80] The abundance of such Ottoman documents dealing with the Cossack/Circassian attacks demonstrates that the Ottomans came to understand how ineffective their policies were for controlling the Circassian tribes in the Kuban–Taman region.

Four possible reasons explain why so many Circassian chiefs readily abandoned the Porte and approached Muscovy. First, both the Western Circassians and the Kabardinians had been raided time and again by the Crimean Tatars in the first half of the sixteenth century and were forced to pay substantial annual tributes to the khan.[81] Especially in the 1540s, Khan Sahib Girey I raided the Janeys and Kabardinians often and inflicted serious harm on their lands.[82] In addition to these campaigns, it was customary for the Crimean khans to exact slaves as tribute from the Circassians. Second, although Ottoman direct rule was flexible, it brought about taxation and other intrusive administrative practices, which led the Circassians to flee or migrate to the mountainous regions to avoid taxes and central authority. Third, the Muscovite–Cossack alliance offered the Circassians economic benefits in terms of more stipends from the tsar and booty from the raids. Lastly, Muscovite lands were far from the Kuban–Taman region of the North Caucasus compared to the Crimean Khanate and Ottoman provinces. The Circassian chiefs possibly hoped that Muscovy's presence and involvement would be less intrusive and mostly directed at the Crimean Khanate. As soon as a new power emerged with a policy of systematic cooptation rather than direct exploitation in the form of Tatar slave raids or Ottoman taxation, the Janey, Besleney and Kabardinian Circassians were ready to negotiate their alliances.

Vyshnevetskyi's activities and success showed the Ottomans that usually restful or at least benign Circassian tribes could turn into a significant security problem for the Porte if they could unite and rally around a leader. There indeed had been revolts by the Western Circassians and Kabardinians before the 1550s, and sometimes they harmed Ottoman subjects and shipping in the Black Sea, but they hardly damaged Ottoman possessions on this scale before the Muscovite involvement, which brought with it the Cossack element. Besides the scale and success of the attacks, Vyshnevetskyi, his Circassian allies and the Muscovite soldiers directly attacked the Crimean Khanate, which was unprecedented.

It was undoubtedly the alliance with Dmytro Vyshnevetskyi and the support of the Muscovites that encouraged the Circassian tribes to raid Ottoman/Crimean possessions. With the help of the Circassians, Vyshnevetskyi captured the fortresses of Taman and Temrük in 1557. The fall of Taman and Temrük was a cause for true alarm at the Porte and in Bahçesaray, the capital of the Crimean Khanate. Vyshnevetskyi even threatened Azak, a very strategic fortress for the security of Kefe and the Black Sea. The Ottomans recaptured Taman and Temrük in the following year. In 1559, the Janey and Kabardinian Circassians resumed the attacks on Azak and Taman, but the governor of Kefe defeated them. Meanwhile, Kansavuk, who was fighting with Vyshnevetskyi, lost his life in a battle. His head was sent to Istanbul, a symbolic act that indicates his importance to the Ottoman Porte at that time.[83]

While engaging the Crimean Tatars and the Ottomans through the Cossacks and Circassians in the western section of the North Caucasus and the Pontic–Caspian steppes, the Muscovites concentrated their diplomatic and military overtures on Kabarda, which until the end of the Vyshnevetskyi affair would be out of the reach of Crimean punitive power, as we understand from the *Nikonian Chronicle*. The chronicle reads, 'Prince Dmitrei [Dmytro] said that he was a slave of the tsar and grand prince … and he went to fight against the Crimean *ulus* and took Islam-Kermen [Islam-Kerman] … From another side, Beshtau Circassians took two towns, Temriuk (Temrük) and Taman.'[84]

When the Ottoman Porte and the Crimean Khan protested, Ivan IV denied any involvement with the Cossacks of Vyshnevetskyi as he and his successors would deny their patronage of the Don, Terek and Zaporozhian Cossacks in the following decades and centuries. However, as the *Nikonian Chronicle* indicates, Vyshnevetskyi was in the pay and service of the Muscovite tsar and was supported by Muscovite troops. These raids proved to be an effective tool for keeping the Ottomans and Crimean Tatars in defence of their own lands while the Muscovite officials were solidifying relationships and creating vassals in the Kabardinian part of the North Caucasus. Ivan IV certainly appreciated Vyshnevetskyi's services and success and in 1560 appointed him as a *voevoda*, or governor, in the North Caucasus.[85]

Although the Muscovites officially repudiated any connection with the activities of Vyshnevetskyi, the Porte certainly knew about the direct Muscovite support for the Cossack–Circassian alliance and attacks.[86] Ali Reis, sent to Azak for its defence, reported to the Porte in August 1559 that 'Muscovy sent one of its own commanders named Anyan with four thousand infidels to assist Dimitrash (Dmytro Vyshnevetskyi) and to attack us'.[87] We know that two Muscovite commanders fought with Vyshnevetskyi against the Ottomans and Crimeans, Ignatii Veshniakov and Danilo Adashev.[88] This particular Ottoman report might be referring to the raid of Adashev via the Dnieper River, which was quite destructive.[89] Besides, the Porte confirmed in a letter sent to the Crimean khan that Vyshnevetskyi was 'loyal to the Muscovite tsar'.[90] The Ottomans also received news that Vyshnevetskyi gathered 70,000 musketeers in Astrakhan ready to attack Ottoman territories, especially Kefe and Azak, in the spring of 1560. Though the figure of 70,000 musketeers is certainly an exaggeration, this report is important for showing that Vyshnevetskyi was receiving support from Astrakhan and the level of anxiety that his attacks caused in the north of the Black Sea.[91] Similarly, the khan informed the Porte after a Crimean spy returned from Muscovy with the information that the Cossacks were preparing to assault the nearby Ottoman and Crimean lands.[92] The Porte, in response, organised its governors in the region to stop the Cossack/Circassian assaults. In May 1560, Istanbul sent a series of letters to the provinces of İskenderiyye, Çirmen, Vidin, Vulçitrin, Selanik, İnebahtı, Alacahisar and Akkerman ordering the governors in these provinces to muster their timariots and volunteers (*dirliksüz*) and send them to Silistre.[93] An imperial order also went out to the *voivode*s of Wallachia and Moldavia, asking them to go to Silistre with their troops.[94] Subsequently, the governor of Silistre, Sinan Pasha, was instructed that provincial cavalry as well as the Wallachian and Moldavian troops would gather in Silistre under his command. The Porte ordered him to assemble these forces to defend Azak and other Ottoman lands from the attacks of Vyshnevetskyi and his 'cursed' Cossacks.[95] The Crimean khan and the governor of Kefe also received letters, instructing them to communicate with Sinan Pasha of Silistre regarding their defence strategies.[96]

2.4 *Muscovite 'Ghost Fortresses' and Muscovite Ways of Defining Loyalties in the North Caucasus*

Due to the eventually successful military operations of the Ottomans and Crimean Tatars as well as Vyshnevetskyi's decision in 1562 to return to the service of Sigismund II, the Muscovite influence through their proxies in the Kuban-Taman region came to an end. Although the Circassian chiefs who fought with Vyshnevetskyi were the first ones in the North Caucasus to submit to the tsar, Ivan IV did not try to revive his sphere of influence there.[97] However, from the Muscovite perspective, the defeat of Vyshnevetskyi's forces and the loss of influence in the Western Circassian lands were not significant in terms of their long-term objectives. By that time, the Muscovites had succeeded in realising one of their main goals: creating a sphere of influence in Kabarda through which they could control the Daryal Pass to the South Caucasus, approach the Georgian kingdoms and Safavid Empire, and possibly expand their influence into the Daghestani lands.

Temriuk, a prominent Kabardinian ruler, submitted to the tsar in 1557. Between 1557 and 1563, while the Ottomans and Crimean Tatars were dealing with Cossack and Circassian attacks, the Muscovites gradually elevated Temriuk to the position of the most prominent ruler in Kabarda by providing him with continuous and generous military and financial support. Temriuk used this opportunity well and defeated his domestic rivals.[98] The Muscovite officials considered Temriuk 'the prince of Kabarda', and through his allegiance, they thought that the entire Kabardinian territory was now a part of the tsar's realm.[99] The substantial assistance Temriuk and his family received from the Muscovite tsar through Astrakhan made them loyal vassals of the Muscovite tsar for generations. None of Temriuk's sons ever tried to approach the Ottoman Porte or Crimean Khanate in their struggles for power in Kabarda or against their non-Circassian foes. One of them, Saltankul, came to Moscow in 1558 to enter the service of the tsar. He was baptised as Mikhail and became an influential politician and military leader in Muscovy.[100] Mikhail Temriukovich Cherkasskii, brother-in-law of the tsar, rose quickly in the Muscovite hierarchy and ended up serving as one of the top commanders in the infamous *oprichnina* of Ivan IV.

Another reason for the allegiance on the part of the Temriuk family was that the Muscovite tsar also used marriage to cement more robust ties with his Kabardinian vassal. When Ivan IV's first wife, Anastasia Romanovna, died, the tsar decided to marry Temriuk's daughter Kuchenei. On 15 June 1561, Kuchenei arrived in Moscow from Kabarda. The tsar then ordered

Figure 2.1 Baptism of Temriuk's son, Saltankul, in Moscow, 1558.

Source: *Litsevoi letopisnyi svod XVI veka*, vol. 23, https://runivers.ru/upload/iblock/06d/LLS23.pdf.

that Kuchenei be brought to the palace, where 'he saw her and loved her'.[101] On 6 July she was baptised as Maria, and on 21 August Tsar Ivan IV married her.[102] Ivan IV's decision to strengthen the loyalty of Temriuk through marriage, which happened only four years after the latter's submission to Muscovy, proves that establishing sovereignty over Kabarda was a significant objective of the Tsardom of Muscovy in the North Caucasus. In fact, a quick look at Temriuk's marital connections shows an impressive diplomatic network for a local ruler in the North Caucasus and perhaps is a testament to the strategic importance of Kabarda. Another daughter of Temriuk, Altynchach, was married to Prince Bekbulat of Astrakhan, who following the annexation of the Astrakhan Khanate ended up in Moscow in the service of Ivan IV.[103] Besides this, Malkhurub, also a daughter of Temriuk, was the wife of Tinahmet Beg of the Greater Nogays, a major ally of Muscovy in the lower Volga region.[104]

While the Muscovite officials considered the submission of Temriuk and marriage of his daughter to Ivan IV as the proof of Kabarda's acceptance of the tsar's sovereignty, from the Kabardinian perspective, Temriuk was one of the chiefs, and his power was still limited in the Kabardinian political structure. Temriuk was indeed the pshihua of Kabarda; however, this title did not grant him real political power or authority over other chieftains. As the previous chapter explains, it was rather an honorary title with a symbolic authority. What is certain is that Temriuk's submission to Muscovy and the support he received from the tsar made him more enemies in Kabarda, among whom Psheapshoko and Aslanbek of the Kaytuk family were the most prominent. Understandably, these rival chiefs did not want Temriuk to gain too much power that would threaten their independence within Kabarda. Temriuk's rivals, in their bid to balance his power, sought military backing from the Crimean Khanate. As may be remembered, following the triumph of İsmail as the leader of the Nogays in 1555, the horde split into two. The smaller group of Nogays who migrated to the Kuban region in the North Caucasus in 1557–8 came to be known as the Lesser Nogays. Their leader, Kazy, officially pledged allegiance to the Crimean khan in 1560.[105] During their migration through the North Caucasus and in his struggle against the Greater Nogays, Kazy of the Lesser Nogays received the protection of Psheapshoko and Aslanbek and took refuge in their lands, which were inaccessible for the Greater Nogay troops.[106] Therefore, in the early 1560s, there were two opposing coalitions in Kabarda. Temriuk in alliance with the Muscovites and Greater Nogays stood against Psheapshoko and Aslanbek backed by the Crimean Tatars, the Lesser Nogays, and indirectly the Ottomans.[107] Despite Temriuk's early successes, the opposition to him in Kabarda led

Figure 2.2 Ivan IV sends aid to his father-in-law, Temriuk, 1563.

Source: *Litsevoi letopisnyi svod XVI veka*, vol. 23, https://runivers.ru/upload/iblock/06d/LLS23.pdf.

by Psheapshoko and Aslanbek of the Kaytuks steadily gained strength and became powerful enough to force Temriuk to flee his lands with his sons to Astrakhan in 1563.[108]

Faced with this danger, namely losing his valuable client and father-in-law in Kabarda, Ivan IV acted quickly and decisively. Temriuk received military support from Astrakhan consisting of 500 musketeers (*strel'tsy*) and 500 Cossacks, which was a large number in sixteenth-century Kabarda. Only with this Muscovite assistance, a thousand men under the command of Prince Ivan Dashkov, was Temriuk able to drive his enemies out of his lands.[109] By 1566, Temriuk recovered from his earlier defeat, though his rivals remained powerful. There is no record of actual Crimean or Ottoman aid to Temriuk's rivals in Kabarda. However, there are records of the Lesser Nogays militarily collaborating with Psheapshoko to attack the nearby Muscovite or Greater Nogay possessions.[110] The Crimean khan was undoubtedly aware of the rising power of Temriuk and his ambition to unite not only Kabarda but also the Western Circassians in the North Caucasus with the help of the Muscovites.[111] Regardless, the Ottomans and Crimean Tatars were in no position to interfere in the affairs of Kabarda as they were dealing with their own defence problems that had become apparent during the Cossack/Circassian attacks on their possessions from 1556 to 1562. As stated above, the Muscovites benefited from this reality immensely in terms of establishing their vassal Temriuk as one of the strongest rulers in Kabarda.

In 1566, Temriuk petitioned the tsar for a fortress to be erected in his lands in Kabarda so he could protect himself from the rival Kabardinian chiefs and from the Daghestani shamkhal, who occasionally raided his territories.[112] Temriuk's request for a fortress is mentioned in the Muscovite sources. Unfortunately, there is no possibility of confirming it from the primary sources of the Ottomans or Crimean Tatars. However, there is no reason to doubt that the proposal came from Temriuk if only for personal interests, considering that his rivals in Kabarda were still powerful. From the Muscovite perspective, a fortress in Kabarda conformed to the basic tenets of their steppe frontier policy. An ever-expanding line of fortresses was the backbone of the Muscovite territory-making strategy on their southern frontier.[113] Initially, fortresses were built in the frontier zones to protect the Muscovite subjects from nomadic raids. They provided Muscovy with much-needed security and a military footing for further expansion.[114] Muscovite settlers engaged in agriculture and established villages behind those lines of defence. As new villages and towns sprang up around the fortresses, these defence lines showed a trend to move further south.[115] The Muscovites associated a fortress on their southern frontier with creating a sphere of influence beyond this area and gradually expanding when an opportunity presented itself. Although, in theory, the Muscovites constructed these fortresses to protect their clients upon their request, that they housed Muscovite *strel'tsy* and Cossacks made them an effective method of direct control and dominance over local rulers and their peoples.

It is generally accepted that the first Muscovite fortress was completed in February 1567. However, as early as 1563, Prince Sibok of the Janeys, who first fled to Lithuania from Muscovite service and then opted to serve the Crimean khan, reported to the khan that the Muscovites intended to erect a fortress in Kabarda.[116] In the same year, a certain Kulgun Mirza said to the khan that a *voevoda* with a thousand *strel'tsy* came to Temriuk from the tsar and constructed him a 'town' (fortress). Kulgun Mirza might be referring to Ivan Dashkov's troops that helped Temriuk recover his lands in Kabarda in 1563. Based on these primary sources, N. A. Smirnov claims that the fortress Sibok and Kulgun Mirza mentioned in 1563 was the first Muscovite fortress in Kabarda.[117] That is before Temriuk officially requested a fortress to be built for his protection in 1566. Yet, we cannot say with certainty that a fortress was actually constructed in 1563.

We understand, however, from Devlet Girey's letter to Ivan IV dated September 1567 – months after the construction of the Terek Fortress – that the Muscovites had a fort in the lands of the Circassians and another in the lands of the shamkhal.[118] The fortress built in 1567 was definitely in Kabarda. Therefore, rather than a fully fledged fortress, the one built in 1563 might have been a blockhouse-type structure in Daghestan, which could facilitate Muscovite military assistance for Temriuk from Astrakhan in 1563 when Temriuk was trying to oust the anti-Muscovite party in Kabarda. As such, there were possibly two Muscovite fortified structures in the North Caucasus by 1567, a blockhouse or redoubt in Daghestan and a fortress in Kabarda. What is certain is that the Muscovites certainly welcomed the opportunity to build a fortress in Kabarda. However, they did not impose this forcefully without a request from their vassal Temriuk. As we understand from the chain of events, Temriuk felt the need for consistent Muscovite presence and military support against his enemies in Kabarda, as the very nature of the Kabardinian and, in general, North Caucasus societies was such that a single dominant ruler could not easily exert power over other chieftains.

Another critical point is that, as seen on two occasions, the extant primary sources mention Muscovite fortresses in various locations in the North Caucasus at different times, as if they could appear and disappear out of thin air. For this reason, these fortresses, forts and perhaps blockhouses are like ghosts. Numerous sources talk about their existence yet at different times and in different places, with an ability to quickly disappear into nothingness when rival imperial powers challenged Muscovy.

The *Nikonian Chronicle* records in no uncertain terms 1566 that 'they petitioned the Sovereign Tsar and Great Kniaz on behalf of his father[-in-law] Temriuk-Kniaz that the Sovereign order the building of a fortress at the mouth of the Sunzha River on the Terek for the for protection of Temriuk from his enemies'.[119] This also means that despite their defeat in 1563 by Temriuk, his rivals, especially the Kaytuk family led by Aslanbek and Psheapshoko, were still active and powerful. The Muscovite tsar immediately granted his vassal's request and, in February 1567, sent necessary equipment and labourers to Kabarda to build a fortress there. In his letter to the Polish king, the Crimean khan confirmed that the grand prince of Muscovy had 'sent many people to his father-in-law to build a fortress on the Terek'.[120]

Constructing this fortress triggered an Ottoman–Crimean reaction in the North Caucasus against the Muscovite designs. The annexation of Astrakhan was a shock to the Porte, and its recovery was on the agenda of the Ottomans. However, it was not a priority until Muscovy made its true intentions clear by erecting a fortress on the Terek River and thus made a move to control this strategic part of the North Caucasus that the Ottomans considered under their sovereignty.[121] For this reason and in line with the traditional Ottoman strategies in the north, the Crimean Tatars raided the Kabardinian lands to punish those who sided with Muscovy.[122] Yet, this raid as well as the pressure from the Crimean khan and the Ottoman sultan did not engender the desired results – the fortress and the Muscovite influence in Kabarda remained intact, at least for the time being.

The fortress and the Muscovite troops stationed in it were apparent signs of Muscovite dominance in Kabarda, and this is also a good example of direct Muscovite military involvement in, even beyond, its southern frontier zones. By relying on his own military prowess rather than solely employing his clients, the Muscovite tsar gained prestige and influence among the rulers of Kabarda. Thanks to the Muscovite military and financial support, Temriuk's authority in 1567 spread further east into the Daghestani lands as well.[123] With his troops reinforced by the Muscovite *strel'tsy* and Cossacks, Temriuk captured some lands around Tarku, close to the capital of the shamkhalate. This Muscovite/Kabardinian aggression in Daghestan was one issue discussed in the correspondence between the Crimean khan and the Muscovite tsar. The khan warned the tsar not to interfere in the lands of the shamkhal, which was under the khan's suzerainty.[124] There was also an attempt to pacify Kabarda and expel the Muscovites in 1567 by Crimean Khan Devlet Girey. However, the Crimean attack at this time failed to oust the Muscovite forces from Kabarda or to convince Temriuk to change his alliance.[125]

Although they preferred to use their military to support their vassals, the Muscovites still avoided direct military conflict with the Ottomans at all costs. They used a clever multi-layered strategy in which they coopted Temriuk and made most of the Kabardinian chiefs their clients in the heart of the North Caucasus by establishing family ties with Temriuk and providing him with direct military aid. Then, they encouraged their Kabardinian clients to penetrate the lands of the shamkhal rather than doing it on their own with the Muscovite troops. By using the Kabardinians and Cossacks, the Muscovites were also in a position to deny their involvement in Daghestani affairs if necessary to allay possible threats from the Ottomans or Crimean Tatars.

Prior to the Ottoman Porte's decision to organise a campaign to take Astrakhan in 1569, the most influential Muscovite position in the North Caucasus was, therefore, in Kabarda around the Terek River. Given the many Circassian chiefs choosing an alliance with Muscovy or its clients in what they considered their backyard, as well as the construction of a Muscovite fortress in the North Caucasus, the Ottoman officials at the Porte realised that it was time to take action. The annexation of Astrakhan aside, the Muscovite presence and activities in Kabarda, and especially in the Western Circassian lands, were seen by the Ottomans as an unjustified occupation of Ottoman-Crimean possessions. From the perspective of the Crimean khan and the Porte, the North Caucasus was under the suzerainty of the Crimean Khanate. The westernmost part of it was, the actual situation on the ground notwithstanding, considered by the Ottomans as under their direct control, as stated in the Crimean khan's letters to the tsar in which the khan referred to these Circassian lands as *cherkasov turskogo* (Circassians of the Turk) and *turskogo sanchaki* (Turkish *sancaks*).[126]

Therefore, the extant documentation from the Ottoman and Russian archives proves that the Muscovite fortress in the North Caucasus was the last straw for the Ottoman Porte. While it was able to tolerate or at least bide its time over the Muscovite annexation of Kazan and Astrakhan, a fortress in the North Caucasus was not acceptable. As early as 1568, less than a year after the construction of the fortress in the North Caucasus, the Ottoman Porte began its campaign preparations to make Astrakhan a part of the Ottoman Empire and expel the Muscovites from the lower Volga and the North Caucasus.

Notes

1. Halil İnalcık, 'The Question of the Closing of the Black Sea', *Archeion Pontou* 35 (1979): 74–110; Victor Ostapchuk, 'Cossack Ukraine In and Out of Ottoman Orbit, 1648–1681', in Gábor Kármán and Lovro Kunčević, eds, *The European Tributary States of the Ottoman Empire in the Sixteenth and Seventeenth Centuries* (Leiden and Boston: Brill, 2013), 123–54; Victor Ostapchuk, 'The Human Landscape of the Ottoman Black Sea in the Face of the Cossack Naval Raids', *Oriente Moderno* 81 (2001): 23–95; John P. LeDonne. *The Grand Strategy of the Russian Empire, 1650–1831* (New York: Oxford University Press, 2004), 25. C. Max Kortepeter provides a comprehensive list of resources procured from the Black Sea shores by the Ottomans for their capital and its hinterland in his *Ottoman Imperialism during the Reformation: Europe and the Caucasus* (New York: New York University Press, 1972), 247.
2. Dariusz Kołodziejczyk, 'Inner Lake or Frontier: The Ottoman Black Sea in the Sixteenth and Seventeenth Centuries', in *Enjeux politiques, économiques et militaires en mer Noire, XIVe–XXIe siècles: études à la mémoire de Mihail Guboglu*, ed. Faruk Bilici, Ionel Cândea and Anca Popescu (Braïla: Musée de Braïla, 2007), 125–39.
3. For a detailed examination of the Crimean Khanate's role in the north, specifically in the North Caucasus, see Murat Yaşar and Chong Jin Oh, 'The Ottoman Empire and the Crimean Khanate in the North Caucasus: A Case Study of Ottoman–Crimean Relations in the Mid-Sixteenth Century', *Turkish Historical Review* 9 (2018): 86–103; Murat Yaşar, 'The North Caucasus between the Ottoman Empire and the Tsardom of Muscovy: The Beginnings, 1552–1570', *Iran and the Caucasus* 20 (2016): 107–11. For the Ottoman vassalage system, see Viorel Panaite, *The Ottoman Law of War and Peace: The Ottoman Empire and Tribute Payers* (Boulder, CO: East European Monographs, 2000); Viorel Panaite, 'The Voivodes of the Danubian Principalities as Haracgüzarlar of the Ottoman Sultans', in *Ottoman Borderlands: Issues, Personalities, and Political Changes*, ed. Kemal H. Karpat and Robert W. Zens (Madison: University of Wisconsin Press, 2003), 59–79.
4. Halil İnalcık, 'Power Relations between Russia, the Crimea and the Ottoman Empire as Reflected in Titulature', in *Turco-Tatar Past, Soviet Present: Studies Presented to Alexandre Bennigsen*, ed. Ch. Lemercier-Quelquejay, G. Veinstein and E. Wimbush (Paris: École des hautes études en sciences sociales, 1986), 175–215; Halil İnalcık, 'Struggle for East-European Empire, 1400–1700', *Turkish Yearbook of International Relations* 21 (1982): 1–16; Yücel Öztürk, *Osmanlı hakimiyetinde Kefe, 1475–1600* (Ankara: Kültür Bakanlığı Yayınları, 2000), 57–8.
5. MD 71, no. 162; MD 73, no. 285; MD 74, no. 137.
6. Yaşar, 'The North Caucasus', 107–8.

7. Ibid., 110–11.
8. Remmal Hoca, *Tarih-i Sahib Giray Han: Histoire de Sahib Giray, khan de Crimée de 1532 à 1551* (with French translation by M. Le Roux), ed. Özalp Gökbilgin (Ankara: Atatürk Üniversitesi Yayınları, 1973), 39.
9. Order to the governor of Kefe (November 1565), MD 5, no. 495; Order to the governor of Kefe (August 1564), MD 6, no. 37.
10. MD 6, no. 37.
11. M. Sadık Bilge, *Osmanlı Devleti ve Kafkasya* (Istanbul: Eren, 2005), 87.
12. Order to the governor of Kefe (April 1560), MD 3, no. 961.
13. Ibid.; Order to the governor of Kefe (November 1565), MD 5, no. 495.
14. Bilge, *Osmanlı Devleti ve Kafkasya*, 47.
15. MD 6, no. 623.
16. Ibid.
17. Order to the governor of Kefe (February 1566), MD 5, no. 994; Fahrettin Kırzıoğlu, *Osmanlılar'ın Kafkas elleri'ni fethi (1451–1590)* (Ankara: Sevinç Matbaası, 1976), 76.
18. Hezarfen Hüseyin Efendi, *Telhisü'l-beyan fi kavanin-i al-i Osman*, ed. Dr Sevim İlgürel (Ankara: Türk Tarih Kurumu, 1998), 87.
19. There was no timar system in the Circassian lands. Important chiefs of certain polities or tribal confederations received the title of *sancakbeyi* and a salary. However, sons of these chiefs, chiefs of lower status or *uzdens* might have also been given titles that were at the level of *bölükbaşı* or *alaybeyi*. The so-called *sipahis* in these texts may refer to the Circassian chiefs or princes of lower status or *uzdens*. See Bilge, *Osmanlı Devleti ve Kafkasya*, 87.
20. Order to the governor-general of Kefe (1571), MD 14, no. 1543. The text in this document is as follows: '*...adada olan ümera-i Çerakise ve sipahiler vilayet katibi bizi ra'iyyet kaydeyleyüb bedel-i 'öşr ve resm-i çift taleb idüb bunun emsali tekalife kadrimiz yokdur deyü re'ayayı ıdlal eyleyüb ta'un bahanesiyle adadan çıkub gitmek üzere oldukların...*'
21. Order to the governor-general of Kefe and governor of Azak (May 1571), MD 12, nos 534, 535; MD 14, nos 1543, 1544. The text in these documents is as follows: '*...anun gibi ta'ife-i mezbureden adadan çıkub gitmek isterlerse mümkün olduğu üzere tesliyet ve istimalet ile yerlü yerlerüne iskan itdürüb memnu' olmayub isyan iderlerse haklarından gelinmek emrüm oldugundan...*'
22. *Prodolzhenie drevnei rossiiskoi vivliofiki* (St Petersburg: Imperatorskaia akademiia nauk, 1793; reprint, The Hague: Mouton, 1970), 8:265–7; Michael Khodarkovsky, *Russia's Steppe Frontier: The Making of a Colonial Empire, 1500–1800* (Bloomington: Indiana University Press, 2002), 35; N. A. Smirnov, *Politika Rossii na Kavkaze v XVI–XIX vekakh* (Moscow: Izdatel'stvo sotsial'no-ekonomicheskoi literatury, 1958), 24. Indeed, Azov (Ottoman: Azak) in the text should be read 'Astrakhan'.

23. A. Zeki Velidi Togan, *Bugünkü Türkili Türkistan ve yakın tarihi* (Istanbul: Güven Basımevi, 1947), 34–5; Akdes Nimet Kurat, *Türkiye ve İdil boyu* (Ankara: Türk Tarih Kurumu, 1966), 59.
24. Remmal Hoca, *Tarih-i Sahib Giray Han*, 29–31; Alan Fisher, *The Crimean Tatars* (Stanford, CA: Hoover Institution Press, 1978), 42–3.
25. Remmal Hoca, *Tarih-i Sahib Giray Han*, 29–31.
26. W. E. D. Allen, *Problems of Turkish Power in the Sixteenth Century* (London: Central Asian Research Centre, 1963), 23.
27. Yaşar, 'The North Caucasus', 111.
28. S. F. Platonov, *Ivan the Terrible*, ed. and trans. Joseph L. Wieczynski (Gulf Breeze, FL: Academic International Press, 1986), 83–4; Charles J. Halperin, *Ivan the Terrible: Free to Reward and Free to Punish* (Pittsburgh: University of Pittsburgh Press, 2019), 154–6. For an overview of the Livonian War, see Robert I. Frost, *The Northern Wars: War, State and Society in Northeastern Europe, 1558–1721* (Abingdon and New York: Routledge, 2014).
29. Yaşar, 'The North Caucasus', 111.
30. *Kabardino-russkie otnosheniia v 16–18 vv.*, ed. T. Kh. Kumykov and E. N. Kusheva (Moscow: Izdatel'stvo Akademii nauk SSSR, 1957), vol. 1, doc. 1, 5.
31. Smirnov, *Politika Rossii na Kavkaze*, 28; Yaşar, 'The North Caucasus', 111–12.
32. Chantal Lemercier-Quelquejay, 'Cooptation of the Elites of Kabarda and Daghestan in the Sixteenth Century', in *The North Caucasus Barrier: The Russian Advance towards the Muslim World*, ed. Marie Bennigsen Broxup (London: Hurst, 1992), 18.
33. Yaşar, 'The North Caucasus', 113–14.
34. Lemercier-Quelquejay, 'Cooptation of the Elites of Kabarda', 20.
35. Khodarkovsky, *Russia's Steppe Frontier*, 30.
36. Lemercier-Quelquejay, 'Cooptation of the Elites of Kabarda', 20.
37. Khodarkovsky, *Russia's Steppe Frontier*, 51–68.
38. Examples of such instructions given to the Muscovite envoys can be seen in *Snosheniia Rossii s Kavkazom: Materialy izvlechennye iz Moskovskago glavnago arkhiva Ministerstva inostrannykh diel, 1578–1613 gg.*, ed. S. L. Belokurov (Moscow: Universitetskaia tipografiia, 1889) and in *Puteshestviia russkikh poslov XVI–XVII vv.: stateinye spiski* (Moscow: Izdatel'stvo Akademii nauk, 1954).
39. Khodarkovsky, *Russia's Steppe Frontier*, 51.
40. Maria Subtelny, 'The Binding Pledge (*möchälgä*): A Chinggisid Practice and Its Survival in Safavid Iran', in *New Perspectives on Safavid Iran: Empire and Society*, ed. Colin P. Mitchell (Abingdon: Routledge, 2011), 9–30.
41. Ibid., 9.
42. F. P. Sergeev, *Formirovanie russkogo diplomaticheskogo iazyka* (Lviv: Vyshcha shkola, 1978), 25.

43. Khodarkovsky, *Russia's Steppe Frontier*, 51–6, 69–75.
44. For an excellent analysis of the practice of *amanat*, see Sean Pollock, '"Thus We Shall Have Their Loyalty and They Our Favor": Diplomatic Hostage-Taking (*amanatstvo*) and Russian Empire in Caucasia', in *Dubitando: Studies in History and Culture in Honor of Donald Ostrowski*, ed. Brian J. Boeck, Russell E. Martin and Daniel Rowland (Bloomington, IN: Slavica, 2012), 139–63.
45. Ibid., 140. For example, in a 1576 letter to the Porte, the Ottoman governor of Azak writes that the Nogays, the Cossacks and the Circassians around the city of Azak were at peace with each other, as they all delivered hostages from among the sons of their chieftains and nobles: MD 28, no. 142; Kırzıoğlu, *Osmanlılar'ın Kafkas elleri'ni fethi*, 75.
46. Michael Khodarkovsky, 'Colonial Frontiers in Eighteenth Century Russia: From the North Caucasus to Central Asia', Marsha Siefert, ed., *Extending the Borders of Russian History* (New York: Central European University Press, 2003), 140; Khodarkovsky, *Russia's Steppe Frontier*, 69–75.
47. Halperin, *Ivan the Terrible*, 146–7; M. K. Liubavskii, *Obzor istorii russkoi kolonizatsii s drevneishikh vremen do XX veka* (Moscow: Izdatel'stvo Moskovskogo Universiteta, 1996), 246–7; Janet Martin, 'The Novokshcheny of Novgorod: Assimilation in the 16th Century', *Central Asian Survey* 9/2 (1990): 13–38; Aytek Namitok, 'The "Voluntary" Adherence of Kabarda (Eastern Circassia) to Russia', *Caucasian Review* 2 (1956): 17–28; Platonov, *Ivan the Terrible*, 71.
48. V. V. Trepavlov, *Istoriia Nogaiskoi Ordy* (Kazan: Kazanskaia nedvizhimost', 2016), 216–23.
49. MD 12, nos 534, 535; MD 14, nos 1543, 1544.
50. In the fifteenth and sixteenth centuries, Ottoman strategies of deportation and settlement of groups of people were different in the Balkans and other core territories of the empire. In these parts, deportation and forced settlements were instruments used by the Porte in controlling non-Turkish or non-Muslim populations as well as in settling centrifugal nomadic and semi-nomadic tribes of Anatolia. See Ömer Lütfi Barkan, 'Osmanlı İmparatorluğunda bir iskan ve kolonizasyon metodu olarak sürgünler', *İstanbul Üniversitesi İktisat Fakültesi Mecmuası* 11 (1949–50): 524–69; 13 (1951–2): 56–78; 15 (1953–4): 209–37. Additionally, the Ottomans often resettled rebellious populations that took refuge in mountainous or forested areas to escape the reach of central authority. Hüseyin Arslan, *16. yy Osmanlı toplumunda yönetim, nüfus, iskan, göç ve sürgün* (Istanbul: Kaknüs, 2001), 353–6; Sam White, *The Climate of Rebellion in the Early Modern Ottoman Empire* (New York: Cambridge University Press, 2011), 44–9.
51. This Muscovite policy lasted on its southern frontier until 1678 when Tsar Feodor III (Romanov, r. 1676–82) confronted the Ottoman armies in Ukraine during the siege of Chyhyryn. The tsar at that time made this decision, as Muscovy faced the danger of losing Ukraine and the Zaporozhian

Cossacks to a united hetmanate under Ottoman sovereignty, which had the potential of becoming another Crimean Khanate for Muscovy, only closer to its heartlands. Prior to this, the Muscovite tsars and officials fervently avoided any conflict with the Ottoman Empire. Even in 1637 when the Don and Zaporozhian Cossacks wrested Azak from the Ottomans and offered it to Tsar Mikhail I (Romanov, r. 1613–45), the tsar refused to take the city or provide aid for the Cossacks to keep it.

52. Brian J. Boeck, 'Containment vs. Colonization: Muscovite Approaches to Settling the Steppe', in *Peopling The Russian Periphery: Borderland Colonization in Eurasian History*, ed. Nicholas B. Breyfogle, Abby Schrader and Willard Sunderland (Abingdon: Routledge, 2007), 43; Thomas Barrett, *At the Edge of Empire: The Terek Cossacks and the North Caucasus Frontier, 1700–1860* (Boulder, CO: Westview Press, 1999), 19.
53. Barrett, *At the Edge of Empire*, 3–25.
54. Boeck, 'Containment vs. Colonization', 43; Willard Sunderland, *Taming the Wild Field: Colonization and Empire on the Russian Steppe* (Ithaca: Cornell University Press, 2004), 23–4.
55. Brian Boeck, *Imperial Boundaries: Cossack Communities and Empire-Building in the Age of Peter the Great* (New York: Cambridge University Press, 2009), 13–27; Matthew P. Romaniello, 'Grant, Settle, Negotiate: Military Servitors in the Middle Volga Region', in *Peopling the Russian Periphery: Borderland Colonization in Eurasian History*, ed. Nicholas B. Breyfogle, Abby Schrader and Willard Sunderland (Abingdon: Routledge, 2007), 61–77.
56. S. A. Kozlov, *Kavkaz v sud'bakh kazachestva* (St Petersburg: Kol'na, 1996), 8–15.
57. Boeck, *Imperial Boundaries*, 46; Mykhailo Hrushevsky, *History of Ukraine-Rus'*, vol. 7, *The Cossack Age to 1625*, trans. Bohdan Struminski and ed. Serhii Polokhy and Frank E. Sysyn (Edmonton, AB: Canadian Institute of Ukrainian Studies Press, 1999), 62–4.
58. Boeck, *Imperial Boundaries*, 46.
59. Ibid., 22–6.
60. Kortepeter, *Ottoman Imperialism*, 27. Russian/Soviet historians, not distinguishing between Crimean Tatar aggression and Ottoman defensiveness, often ignored the idea of plausible deniability and the role of vassals in the Pontic–Caspian steppes and borderlands. Examples of such works are Smirnov, *Politika Rossii na Kavkaze*; N. A. Smirnov, *Rossiia i Turtsiia v XVI–XVII vv*. (Moscow: Izdatel'stvo Moskovskogo gosudarstvennogo universiteta, 1946); and A. A. Novosel'skii, *Bor'ba moskovskogo gosudarstva s tatarami v pervoi polovine XVII veka* (Moscow: Izdatel'stvo Akademii nauk SSSR, 1948). Unlike these historians, the Muscovite officials were acutely aware of the difference and devised their strategies accordingly. Yaşar, 'The North Caucasus', 120.
61. *Kabardino-russkie otnosheniia*, vol. 1, doc. 1, 3.

62. Ibid., doc. 1, 4.
63. Ibid., doc. 1, 4.
64. Ibid., doc. 1, 4.
65. Ibid., doc. 1, 5.
66. Yaşar, 'The North Caucasus', 112–13.
67. Akdes Nimet Kurat, *IV–XVIII. yüzyıllarda Karadeniz kuzeyindeki Türk kavimleri ve devletleri* (Ankara: Murat Kitabevi Yayınları, 1992), 277–8.
68. Remmal Hoca, *Tarih-i Sahib Giray Han*, 115–32.
69. Ibid., 115–32.
70. Suret-i Name-i Harezm Han (December 1568), MD 7, no. 2723; Kurat, *Türkiye ve İdil boyu*, 79; Akdes Nimet Kurat, 'The Turkish Expedition to Astrakhan' in 1569 and the Problem of the Don–Volga Canal', *Slavonic and East European Review* 40 (1961): 14; Halil İnalcık, 'The Origin of the Ottoman–Russian Rivalry and the Don–Volga Canal (1569)', *Annales de l'Université d'Ankara* 1 (1947), 69. For the Turkish version of this last work, see Halil İnalcık, 'Osmanlı-Rus rekabetinin menşei ve Don-Volga kanalı teşebbüsü (1569)', *Belleten* 12 (1948): 349–402.
71. Yaşar, 'The North Caucasus'. 115.
72. Suret-i Name-i Harezm Han and order to the Crimean Khan (December 1568), MD 7, nos 2722, 2723.
73. İnalcık, 'The Origin of the Ottoman–Russian Rivalry', 65–6. In February 1564, the Muscovite envoy to Crimea, A. F. Nagoi, wrote to Moscow that in September 1563 the Ottoman sultan had sent a letter to the Crimean khan ordering him to muster his armies for a campaign to take Astrakhan. According to the envoy's report, the khan convinced the sultan that he was on friendly terms with the Muscovite tsar and a campaign to take Astrakhan would be futile. V. V. Ishin and I. V. Toropitsyn, eds, *Astrakhanskii krai v istorii Rossii XVI–XXI vv.* (Astrakhan: Astrakhanskii universitet, 2007).
74. Dmytro Ivanovych Vyshnevetskyi was born into the famous family of the Vyshnevetskyis in 1527. He was a magnate in the service of King Sigismund II in southern Volhynia before he started his career as a borderland warrior against the Tatars. He is considered to have built the Khortytsia fortress in the early 1550s, first of a series of Cossack *sich* forts. In these years, he also visited the Porte to negotiate with the Ottomans a possible alliance, which produced no results. Mykhailo Hurushevsky states that Vyshnevetskyi's plan was to keep the Crimean Tatars in check with Polish-Lithuanian support while maintaining good relations with the Ottoman Porte. In 1556, he decided to serve the Muscovite Tsar Ivan IV. In the first years of the 1560s, he left Muscovite service and approached Lithuania once more. Then, he militarily intervened in Moldavian affairs but in one of the battles in 1563 was taken prisoner and sent to Istanbul, where he was executed upon the orders of the Ottoman sultan. Hrushevsky, *History of Ukraine-Rus*, 88–98. Also see Liubomyr Vynar, *Kniaz Dmytro Vyshnevets'kyi* (Munich: Ukrainian Free Academy of Arts and Sciences, 1964); Remmal Hoca,

Tarih-i Sahib Giray Han, 76–90; order to the governor of Kefe (April 1560), MD 3, no. 961; *Kabardino-russkie otnosheniia*, vol. 1, doc. 1, 3.

75. *Kabardino-russkie otnosheniia*, vol. 1, doc. 1, 3.
76. Remmal Hoca, *Tarih-i Sahib Giray Han*, 76–90; Order to the governor of Kefe (April 1560), MD 3, no. 961.
77. MD 3, no. 961. The Janey chief with 200 soldiers joined Vyshnevetskyi's Cossacks. Together they were about to attack the fortress of Azak. Ottoman soldiers from Kefe managed to rout the Circassians, using the river route, before the Cossacks could come to their aid.
78. *Kabardino-russkie otnosheniia*, vol. 1, doc. 1, 3.
79. E. N. Kusheva, *Narody Severnogo Kavkaza i ikh sviazi s Rossiei: vtoraia polovina XVI–30-e gody XVII veka* (Moscow: Izdatel'stvo Akademii nauk SSSR, 1958), 205.
80. Order to the Crimean Khan (November 1559), MD 3, no. 527.
81. Remmal Hoca, *Tarih-i Sahib Giray Han*, 76–90; Yaşar and Oh, 'The Ottoman Empire and the Crimean Khanate', 96–7.
82. Remmal Hoca, *Tarih-i Sahib Giray Han*, 76–90.
83. MD 3, no. 961.
84. *Polnoe sobranie russkikh lietopisei* [henceforth PSRL], vol. 13, *Lietopisnii sbornik, imenuemyi Patriarshei ili Nikonovskoi lietopis* (St Petersburg, 1904; reprint, Moscow: Nauka, 1965), 275–7. (*'A prikazal Kniaz' Dmitrei chto on kholop tsaria i velikogo kniazia ... a poshel voevati Krymskykh ulusov i pod Islam-Kirmen' ... a s druguiu storonu Cherkasy Pyatigorskie vziali dva goroda, Temriuk da Toman'*.')
85. PSRL, 13:324; *Kabardino-russkie otnosheniia*, 1:8.
86. Order to the governor of Kefe (June 1560), MD 3, nos 1265, 1266. The Muscovites sent an envoy to the Crimean khan informing him of Vyshnevetskyi's forthcoming attacks in 1560 by saying, 'Dimitrash is on his way to attack the Ottoman lands. You should know that it is not our doing.' The governor of Kefe reported this to the Porte in a letter.
87. MD 3, nos 266, 278. Ali Reis and the Ottoman fleet under his command remained in the Sea of Azov until the Cossack threat was over. In September 1559, the governor of Kefe was ordered to provide them with foodstuffs and protect the ships.
88. Brian L. Davies, *Warfare, State and Society on the Black Sea Steppe, 1500–1700* (Abingdon: Routledge, 2007), 56; B. N. Floria, 'Proekt antituretskoi koalitsii serediny XVI v.', in *Rossiia, Pol'sha i Prichernomor'e v XV–XVIII vv.*, ed. B. A. Rybakov (Moscow: Nauka, 1979), 71–86.
89. Floria, 'Proekt antituretskoi koalitsii', 74.
90. Order to the Crimean Khan (May 1560), MD 3, no. 1048.
91. Ibid.
92. Order to the Crimean Khan (April 1560), MD 3, no. 954.
93. MD 3, no. 1054.
94. MD 3, no. 1050.

95. MD 3, no. 1047. In May 1560, the governor was also instructed to include the Tatar troops of Silistre in this force and that an Ottoman fleet was being sent to the region through the Black Sea.
96. Orders to the Crimean Khan and governor of Kefe (May 1560), MD 3, nos 1048, 1049.
97. *Kabardino-russkie otnosheniia*, vol. 1, doc. 1, 3.
98. PSRL, 13:371.
99. *Kabardino-russkie otnosheniia*, vol. 1, doc.4, 7–13.
100. *Kabardino-russkie otnosheniia*, vol. 1, doc. 4, 7; Paul Bushkovitch, 'Princes Cherkasskii or Circassian Murzas: The Kabardians in the Russian Boyar Elite, 1560–1700', *Cahiers du monde russe* 45 (2004): 14–15.
101. PSRL, 13:333. ('*Togo zhe lieta iiunia v 15 den', v nadeliu, priekhala k Moskve iz Pyatigorskikh cherkas Kabardinskogo kniazhe Temriukova Aidarovicha doch' kniazhna Kuchenei ... Togo zhe mesiatsa Tsar' i Velikii Kniaz' Ivan Vasil'evich vsea Rusii kniazhne cherkaskoi velel byti na svoem dvore, smotrel ee i poliubil.*')
102. Ibid., 333. ('*Togo zhe lieta avgusta v 21 den', na pamiat' sviatago apostola Faddeia, v chetverg, Tsar' i Velikii Kniaz' Ivan Vasil'evich vsea Rusii zhenilsia vtorym brakom, a vzial za sebia Kabartinskogo iz Cherkas Temriuka-kniazia Aidarovicha doch', narechennuiu vo sviatom kreshchenii tsarevnu Mariiu...*') The tsar's marriage with Kuchenei was also recorded by Antonio Possevino, who was Pope Gregory XIII's envoy to Ivan IV and spent the years 1581–2 in Moscow. In his report, Possevino writes, 'Contiguity and the common possession of the Greek rite have enabled the Prince of Muscovy to draw very close to the Circassians; he married to the daughter of one of their chief men, although she later died.' Antonio Possevino, *The Moscovia of Antonio Possevino SJ*, trans. Hugh F. Graham (Pittsburgh: University of Pittsburgh, 1977), 2. Interestingly, the tsar's marriage to Kuchenei must have made Possevino think that the Circassians (Kabardinians) were Orthodox Christians. In fact, we know certainly that neither Temriuk nor his family were Orthodox Christians.
103. Bushkovitch, 'Princes Cherkasskii or Circassian Murzas', 14.
104. Kusheva, *Narody Severnogo Kavkaza*, 217, 236.
105. Trepavlov, *Istoriia Nogaiskoi Ordy*, 392.
106. Ibid., 394; S. Kh. Khotko, 'Protivostoianie voenno-politicheskikh koalitsii v Cherkesii: Na osnove soobshchenii Elizara Rzhevskogo (1578 g.)', *Klio* 7 (2019): 79.
107. Trepavlov, *Istoriia Nogaiskoi Ordy*, 394–5; *Snosheniia Rossii s Kavkazom*, lxi; Khotko, 'Protivostoianie voenno-politicheskikh koalitsii', 79. Kazy of the Lesser Nogays married a daughter of Psheapshoko to cement their alliance. Kusheva, *Narody Severnogo Kavkaza*, 236.
108. PSRL, 13:370–1; *Kabardino-russkie otnosheniia*, vol. 1, doc. 4, 10–12.
109. PSRL, 13:370–1; *Snosheniia Rossii s Kavkazom*, lxi; *Kabardino-russkie otnosheniia*, vol. 1, doc. 4, 13.

110. Trepavlov, *Istoria Nogaiskoi Ordy*, 395.
111. *Snosheniia Rossii s Kavkazom*, lviii.
112. PSRL, 13:405; *Kabardino-russkie otnosheniia*, vol. 1, doc. 4, 13; Yaşar, 'The North Caucasus', 114.
113. V. V. Kargalov, *Na granitsakh stoiat' krepko! Velikaia Rus' i Dikoe pole – protivostoianie XII–XVIII* (Moscow: Russkaia panorama, 1998), 301–20.
114. Davies, *Warfare, State and Society*, 40.
115. Ibid., 40; Kargalov, *Na granitsakh stoiat' krepko!*, 301–20.
116. Kusheva, *Narody Severnogo Kavkaza*, 217.
117. Smirnov, *Rossiia i Turtsiia*, 91.
118. RGADA, F. 123, *Krymskie dela*, kniga 13, fols 71b–75a; *Kabardino-russkie otnosheniia*, vol. 1, doc. 6, 13.
119. PSRL, 13:405 ('...*biti chelom gosudariu tsariu i velikomu kniaziu ot ottsa svoego Temriuka-kniazia Aidarovicha, chtoby gosudar' pozhaloval dlia berezhenia ot nedrugov ego velel gorod na Terke ust'Siuiunchi reki postaviti*').
120. *Kabardino-russkie otnosheniia*, vol. 1, doc. 7, 15–16.
121. Yaşar, 'The North Caucasus', 115.
122. *Kabardino-russkie otnosheniia*, vol. 1, doc. 7, 15–16.
123. Ibid., docs 6 & 7, 14–16; RGADA, F. 123, *Krymskie dela*, kniga 13, fols 71b–75a.
124. RGADA, F. 123, *Krymskie dela*, kniga 13, fols 71b–75a; *Kabardino-russkie otnosheniia*, vol. 1, doc. 6, 14.
125. *Kabardino-russkie otnosheniia*, vol. 1, doc. 7, 15–16.
126. Kusheva, *Narody Severnogo Kavkaza*, 222.

3

Bargaining for the Milky Way: The Astrakhan Campaign and the North Caucasus Borderland

The Tsardom of Muscovy witnessed the early success of its steppe frontier strategies in the North Caucasus in 1567 when Ivan IV constructed the Sunzha fortress on the Terek River and stationed a thousand soldiers in it upon the request of his loyal client and father-in-law Temriuk of Kabarda.[1] While the Muscovites were creating vassals and strengthening their loyalty to the tsar through marriage, conversion of elites, and construction of a fortress in Kabarda, the Ottomans and Crimean Tatars had to repel the incursions and attacks in the Kuban–Taman region of the Muscovite clients led by Dmytro Vyshnevetskyi. This was a brilliant strategy on the part of Muscovy and kept the Ottomans and Crimean Tatars out of Kabarda at this crucial time. Muscovy could also deny its association with Vyshnevetskyi or his Circassian allies when the Ottomans or Crimean Tatars protested. Once the threat of Vyshnevetskyi was eliminated, and understanding the objectives of Muscovy in the North Caucasus, the Ottoman Porte resolved to take a more active stance in the region. Preparing a campaign to conquer Astrakhan was a harbinger of a series of new strategies that the Ottomans were to employ in the North Caucasus in the following decades.

3.1 The Astrakhan Ordeal: Preparation, Campaign and its Aftermath

In line with the Ottoman methods of conquest, snatching Astrakhan from the Muscovites, who were engineering their operations in the North Caucasus from there, was naturally the first order of business for the Porte. After conquering and subduing an area, establishing direct rule and imposing the Ottoman rule of law was the desired outcome of the Ottoman methods of conquest. First, the Ottomans sought to create a degree of suzerainty over the area or state they targeted. If this was successful or following their conquest, they gradually eliminated the native ruling elite in those lands and established direct rule by reorganising land ownership under their infamous timar system.[2] The local rulers and other elites, however, were not entirely deprived of their previous rights; on the contrary, they could be included in the timar system and therefore accommodated within the Ottoman administration, whose aim was the assimilation of such elites and nobility.[3] Small garrisons were immediately stationed in several fortresses in the conquered areas while remaining fortresses were demolished to prevent their new subjects from using them to form centres of resistance against Ottoman rule and to lessen the cost of maintenance. To secure the loyalty of their new subjects, the Ottomans might also grant the native population tax exemptions for a specific period of time.[4] Besides these, containing centrifugal forces within the Ottoman borderland system was a significant part of this strategy, as seen often in the western and eastern frontier zones and borderlands of the empire. The Ottomans preferred to surround their unruly vassals or more tribal and less centralised groups of people by creating centrally administered provinces around them. These

Figure 3.1 Ivan IV sends Prince Vyshnevetskyi to attack the Crimean Khanate, 1553.
Source: *Litsevoi letopisnyi svod XVI veka*, vol. 23, https://runivers.ru/upload/iblock/06d/LLS23.pdf.

provinces had governors appointed from the Porte as well as janissaries and other standing troops for their protection and for intervention in the affairs of nearby vassal states.[5]

Therefore, the conquest of Astrakhan by the Ottomans would conform to the Ottoman methods of conquest. If the Ottomans took Astrakhan from the Tsardom of Muscovy and turned it into an Ottoman province, they would have a good chance of subduing those loosely allied, disobedient or even hostile North Caucasus rulers and polities by encircling them in both the east and the west. As Khan Devlet Girey justly feared, it would also increase the Ottoman Porte's control over the Crimean Khanate. Another dimension of a successful move into the Astrakhan area would be threatening the Safavid Empire from the Caspian Sea. This would have given the Ottomans, who by then demonstrated the capability to build and use sea power effectively, a substantial strategic advantage over their arch-enemy in the east. An Ottoman fleet sailing from Astrakhan in the Caspian Sea would be disastrous for the Safavids, who did not possess a navy comparable to that of the Ottomans. When the Ottoman statesmen discussed the plans to conquer Astrakhan at the Imperial Council, those who supported the campaign emphasised its value for encircling the Safavid Empire to convince the opposition.

According to the Ottoman chroniclers, the idea of a campaign to capture Astrakhan came from Kasım Bey, who 'was a *mutasarrıf* [a provincial administrator] in Kefe for many years'. Despite some viziers' arguments about the futility of such a campaign, Grand Vizier Sokullu Mehmed Pasha sided with Kasım Bey and convinced the sultan to approve Kasım's proposal.[6] The objections to the campaign came mostly from the viziers and other officials who were opposed to the power that Sokullu Mehmed Pasha held at the Ottoman court, rather than the campaign itself. The Ottoman chronicler İbrahim Peçevi adds that Sokullu Mehmed Pasha always contemplated potential strategies to conquer Iran and that 'some wise people' advised him to dig a canal between the Don and Volga rivers,[7] which became one of the major undertakings of the Astrakhan campaign in 1569.

The khanates of Central Asia and the Muslim peoples of the Pontic–Caspian steppes, whose access to the pilgrimage route to Mecca was now controlled and blocked by the Muscovites, as well as local Tatars around the newly conquered Astrakhan and Kazan, who now lived under the rule of the Muscovite tsar, petitioned the Ottoman sultan. In their correspondence, they stressed the notion of Muslim solidarity and the Ottoman sultan as the protector of the Sunni Muslims to encourage the Ottomans for a campaign in the north to take Astrakhan.[8] Indeed, the proponents of the campaign, such as Sokullu Mehmed Pasha, used these arguments at the Ottoman court to secure the approval of Sultan Selim II (r. 1566–74). A northern campaign was unusual for the Ottomans, considering that their campaigns focused on their western and eastern frontiers. Being the leading supporter of this project, however, Sokullu Mehmed Pasha was convinced of the benefits of capturing Astrakhan, which would engender an Ottoman control of the Caspian Sea.[9]

Lastly, Astrakhan had a geostrategic position, as it was necessary for securing the control of two key military and commercial roads – Crimea–Astrakhan–Central Asia from west to east and Astrakhan–Derbend–Tabriz from north to south.[10] Related to this, Astrakhan was also on the trade routes that connected China and Central Asia with Anatolia and the Levant and which passed through the North Caucasus. Built at the mouth of the Volga River, Astrakhan could act as a control point for shipping in the Caspian Sea, as Kefe and Azak did for the Black and Azov seas respectively.

In the end, the Ottoman Imperial Council accepted the proposal for a campaign to conquer Astrakhan, and Sultan Selim II approved it. In accordance with the sixteenth-century Ottoman campaign planning methods, preparations for the Astrakhan campaign began a year in advance. In February 1568, Governor Cafer Bey of Kefe received an imperial order from the Porte asking him to consult with the Crimean khan about the campaign for Astrakhan and to submit a report on the timing of and essential preparations for such an undertaking.[11] The Porte also sent a letter to Crimean Khan Devlet Girey with more or less the same message, but including a few questions on the history of Astrakhan. The khan was instructed to write back with detailed suggestions on campaign preparation.[12] The earliest Ottoman documents related to the preparation for the Astrakhan campaign show that the officials at the Ottoman Porte sought the most up-to-date information about the city, its history and its geography. However, the letters sent to the Crimean Khan and governor of Kefe indicate that the level of knowledge in Istanbul about Kazan and Astrakhan and the North Caucasus beyond the Black Sea littoral was somewhat limited. Considering that the previous sultan, Süleyman I, communicated with Nogay rulers such as İsmail and Yusuf regarding the affairs of Kazan and Astrakhan and even planned a campaign in the north, familiarity of the Ottoman Porte with recent events and the situation in and around Astrakhan in 1568 was surprisingly inadequate. However, as seen in the relevant documents, the Porte tried to remedy the situation by asking for detailed reports from its vassals and governors to facilitate the preparations for the campaign.

To achieve a successful campaign in the north, Sokullu Mehmed Pasha arranged for Kefe to be upgraded to the status of a governor-generalship (*beylerbeyilik*) as the centre for the preparations.[13] In 1568, Kasım Pasha, originally a Circassian with a broad knowledge of the North Caucasus and possibly the architect of the campaign, was appointed as the governor-general (*beylerbeyi*) of Kefe where he swiftly started the preparations. One of the key objectives of the proposed campaign was to dig a canal connecting the Don and Volga rivers, as this would be the fastest and most efficient way to transport Ottoman soldiers and materiel needed for the siege of Astrakhan. Kasım Pasha sent men to the area where the distance between Don and Volga rivers was the shortest to investigate the feasibility of the proposed canal between these two rivers. He then submitted his findings to the Porte in a report. Unfortunately, we do not know the details of this report because it is not extant. However, according to the Ottoman chronicles of the sixteenth century, it was claimed in this report that a canal connecting the Don and Volga rivers was feasible and the campaign to capture Astrakhan would succeed with a small army supported by the Crimean Tatar and Nogay cavalry and the Circassians of the North Caucasus.[14] This was a long-distance campaign that needed careful planning; it required the Porte to obtain men and materiel from the areas surrounding the Black Sea and then send them to Astrakhan via Kefe and Azak using a flotilla that would sail between the Don and Volga rivers. The distance that the troops and materiel needed to travel was over 1,000 kilometres, and the terrain, unlike the traditional areas of campaigning for the Ottomans, was not familiar to the Ottoman soldiers and commanders.

The Porte also sent a series of orders in early 1568 to the provinces regarding the recruitment of soldiers and procurement of weapons and food for the campaign.[15] The ammunition, cannons, guns and bullets collected in this process were shipped to Azak from Kefe, and the castellan of Azak was instructed to ensure their safety until the commencement of the campaign.[16] Engineers and craftsmen were sent to Kefe in April 1568 to build new ships suitable for river transportation.[17] A document dated June 1568 indicates that constructing these ships was almost complete by then.[18] In July, the Porte appointed a certain Hızır Reis as the captain of the fleet that would sail to Astrakhan via the Don–Volga canal.[19] The procurement of supplies and their transportation were critical due to the distance to be travelled to reach Astrakhan. In 1568, the sultan ordered the governor and judge of Çorum, a province in Anatolia, to prepare foodstuffs for the army.[20] A similar order went to the judges of Kefe, Maykop, Soğucak, Kerç and Taman, administrative units in the north of the Black Sea, for the procurement of over 141 tonnes of *peksimet* (hard tack).[21] Kasım Pasha of Kefe received the food supplies shipped from the provinces and promptly stocked them in the stores in the fortress of Azak.[22] In May 1568, the Ottoman Porte purchased 800 draft horses from Moldavia and 300 from Wallachia to be sent to Kefe. The money owed for these horses was deducted from the tribute exacted from Moldavia.[23]

The central government sent more orders to muster soldiers from different parts of the empire. The timariots from the provinces of Köstendil, Silistre, Niğbolu, Canik, Amasya and Çorum were to gather for the campaign under the command of Kasım Pasha of Kefe. The timariots were the provincial cavalry forces, which, in the sixteenth century, constituted the bulk of the Ottoman armies. As usual, the sultan warned them that those who failed to report would face severe punishment.[24] Kasım Pasha received another imperial order in December 1568, informing him of the expected date of arrival of these troops and the procedures to be followed once they arrived.[25] Additionally, some Roma people from the Balkans who were registered as infantry soldiers joined the Ottoman army as one of the auxiliary troops.[26] Historian Halil İnalcık calculates that the timariot soldiers from the provinces totalled around 10,000 to 11,000.[27] The Porte commanded the castellan of Kefe to provide as many men as Kasım Pasha demanded from the resident soldiers (*hisar erleri*) of the fortress.[28] We know that Kasım Pasha added a thousand of these soldiers to his army.[29] Therefore, the main Ottoman army that set off for Astrakhan was about 13,000–15,000 strong. Besides these, workers (*cerahor*s) from the Kefe and Taman regions reported for duty to dig the proposed canal between the Don and Volga rivers.[30] As we understand from the available Ottoman documents, and contrary to what the contemporary Muscovite or European sources claim, this was a small-scale campaign, mostly because the Porte predicted that the conquest of Astrakhan would be relatively easy to achieve. The Ottomans were skilled in siege warfare, and their enemy was not that powerful. The Porte also expected substantial support from the local Tatars and Nogays in this military endeavour.

Russian and Western scholarly works, which are mostly based on Russian sources, traditionally exaggerate the importance of the Astrakhan campaign. They portray it as a typical grand imperial campaign similar to other sixteenth-century Ottoman military operations in Europe.[31] However, it was not a full-scale imperial campaign, as the planners at the Porte assumed that a small Ottoman army supported by the Crimean khan, local Circassian rulers and Nogay chieftains could capture Astrakhan. Compared to their major operations on their western and eastern frontiers, where they could easily field an army of 100,000 led by a grand vizier or the sultan himself, for Astrakhan, the Ottomans prepared a rather small army of 13,000–15,000 troops under the command of a mere governor-general. The Ottoman primary sources show us that the Porte completed the preparations for this campaign in a short time and that the expended effort was quite limited. Considering that the main rivals of the Ottoman Empire were the Habsburgs in the west and the Safavids in the east, Poland-Lithuania and Muscovy were regarded as second-rate, tribute-paying states, be it directly to the Ottoman Porte or to the Porte's vassal, the Crimean Khanate. Therefore, the campaign preparations reflected this very Ottoman perception of their northern neighbours.

In contrast to their western and eastern frontiers, the planned area of operation for the Astrakhan campaign was not familiar to the planners at the Porte. One feature that the Ottoman officials knew, however, was that the steppes, mountains and other unique terrains of the North Caucasus were hard for regular armies to traverse. For example, Prince Beyazıd, son of Süleyman I and a contender to the throne, sought his way to the North Caucasus in 1559 to avoid capture by his father's forces.[32] Similarly, various Crimean princes throughout the sixteenth century took refuge in the North Caucasus to escape the wrath of the Crimean khans or Ottoman sultans. In addition to the difficulty of transporting armies through the North Caucasus, not all of the peoples and polities in the region were allies or vassals of the Ottoman sultan or the Crimean khan. Based on the extant documentation, the Ottomans seemed to understand that alliances with the local rulers were extremely fluid. Regardless, the Ottoman Porte was keen on inviting the North Caucasus local rulers to join its campaign, at least to provide information and intelligence about the terrain, route and possible attacks by the Muscovites or their Cossacks.

Certain Nogay chieftains, including several from the Greater Nogay Horde, which was in alliance with or under the control of Muscovy, some local chiefs in the North Caucasus, and some Tatar nobles from Astrakhan and Kazan had appealed to the Ottoman sultan for a campaign and promised support.[33] Perhaps for this reason, the Ottomans calculated that their army would receive substantial help in terms of men and materiel from these rulers. There are several imperial orders addressed to the Circassian chiefs about the Astrakhan campaign dispatched in October 1568. The sultan instructed Janey Chief Ahmed to gather his men equipped with weapons and join the approaching Ottoman army under the command of Kasım Pasha.[34] More orders with the same message were also forwarded to six other Janey and Besleney Circassian rulers in the Kuban–Taman and Beshtau regions. One of them was a certain Mustafa Bey, who, three years later, would receive permission from the Ottoman Porte to resettle in the Taman Peninsula.[35]

Moreover, there was an imperial order for the ruler of Terek (*Terek hakimi*) sent in October 1568, asking him to join the Ottoman army along with other Circassian chiefs for this campaign. Under his name in this Ottoman document, a note reads, 'Order sent to him was written with some *ri'ayet* [esteem, observance].'[36] This marginal note implies that he was the most important ruler among the recipients of these orders. The name *Terek* in this document evidently refers to the Terek River, and therefore, *Terek hakimi* was one of the prominent chiefs of the Lesser Kabarda region, along this river.

As of 1557, Temriuk and his allies, who were clients of the Muscovite tsar, dominated Kabarda. However, due to the fragmented politics and internal rivalries within Kabarda, other Kabardinian rulers were still strong and sought more support at least several times from the Crimean khan and the Ottoman Porte to check the rising power of Temriuk. We know that these rulers repeatedly warned the Crimean khan that if the tsar built a fortress in Kabarda, not only Terek but also the Tiumen and Shevkal rivers in Daghestan would be lost to the Muscovites.[37] Although there are no other orders in the Ottoman registers besides the documents mentioned above in connection with the Astrakhan campaign explicitly addressing the Kabardinian rulers by name, we can assume that the Crimean chancellery might have sent such orders as the Crimean khans considered Kabarda and beyond to be under their sovereignty. With an understanding of how the Porte prepared for the Astrakhan campaign and conducted its business with the rulers of the North Caucasus, we can now look at what the expectations were and what actually took place during and after the campaign, which was the first direct military involvement of the Ottoman Empire against the Tsardom of Muscovy.

After the Porte sent the final imperial orders to the Ottoman governors, the Crimean khan and local rulers of the North Caucasus, an Ottoman fleet carrying 3,000 janissaries arrived in Azak in April 1569. In May 1569, another Ottoman fleet carrying the timariot cavalry, janissaries and workers left for Azak. Despite the letter from the sultan instructing that the Crimean khan was to send his army under the command of his representative (*kethüda*) and that the khan himself was to stay in Crimea to protect the peninsula, Khan Devlet Girey joined the campaign with an army of 30,000 to 50,000 Crimean troops.[38] This supports the argument that some officials at the Porte were aware of the priorities of the Crimean khan and his reluctance to see Astrakhan turned into an Ottoman province. By instructing the khan to stay in the Crimean Khanate, the Porte tried to solve this problem as well as address the issue of sending a governor-general as the commander of its army to be accompanied by the Crimean

Figure 3.2 Ivan IV sends soldiers and material to build a fortress in Kabarda, 1567.
Source: *Litsevoi letopisnyi svod XVI veka*, vol. 23, https://runivers.ru/upload/iblock/06d/LLS23.pdf.

khan, whose position was higher in the Ottoman military hierarchy. The Porte must have thought that the participation of the Crimean khan in the campaign was likely to cause problems of hierarchy within the Ottoman–Crimean army, which could have negative consequences regarding the command of the campaign. However, when the khan joined the campaign himself in command of the Crimean army, the Porte did not protest or stop him, perhaps to avoid more complications in the north by antagonising its principal vassal.

In the summer of 1569, the Ottoman army of 13,000–15,000 and the Crimean Tatar cavalry of 30,000–50,000 set out to take Astrakhan. In line with the campaign plans, Kasım Pasha first attempted to dig the proposed canal to connect the Don and Volga rivers. The distance between the two rivers at their closest point was 101 kilometres. However, after working on it for a while, he came to understand that it was impossible to dig the proposed canal before the campaign season was over and instead resolved to take the army by land to lay siege to Astrakhan.[39] To reach the city before the winter, Kasım Pasha decided to leave the heavy cannons and some other vital supplies behind. In making this decision, he was encouraged by Nogay and Tatar leaders from Astrakhan, who promised to aid the Ottoman army by providing supplies and troops once the army had besieged the city.[40] During this very vulnerable march to Astrakhan through the steppes and lowlands of the North Caucasus, there were no Muscovite attempts to stop the Ottoman–Crimean army.[41] The bulk of the Muscovite armies were then engaged in a war in Eastern Europe against Poland-Lithuania. As one may remember, the Muscovites also intentionally avoided any direct military confrontation with the Ottoman Empire in the sixteenth century.

As for the expected support from local North Caucasus rulers, Ottoman chronicles and other primary sources indicate that such help in terms of men or supplies never materialised, even from the Western Circassians, under tighter control of the Ottoman Empire and the Crimean Khanate. However, the Daghestani shamkhal approached the Porte in 1569 by sending a letter with an envoy to Kasım Pasha. In his letter, the shamkhal swore loyalty to the sultan and promised, '[The shamkhal] will be a friend to the friends of the sultan and enemy to the enemies of the sultan.'[42] The submission of the shamkhal in 1569 – even if it was more of a gesture at this point – was significant because the Daghestani shamkhals would become key players in the new Ottoman policy that would take shape in the North Caucasus following the failure of the Astrakhan campaign.

The Ottoman–Crimean army reached Astrakhan in September 1569, which was already late in the campaign season.[43] There were skirmishes between the Muscovite and Ottoman forces, but the Ottomans could not lay a full siege of Astrakhan due to the lack of heavy weapons. Kasım Pasha, following the Ottoman plans, wanted to repair the old fortress of Astrakhan and winter there with his army to begin the siege in earnest the following year. However, there was unrest among the Ottoman troops caused by rumours circulating in the camp that the Muscovite tsar had sent an army of relief, and the Safavids would also send support from the south to attack them. The Ottoman soldiers also complained about the harshness of the winters in Astrakhan and the declining food rations.[44] The unfeasibility of properly besieging and taking the city without heavy weapons and the restiveness of the army made retreat seemingly the sole option for Kasım Pasha. He began the preparations for a retreat on 26 September.[45] Meanwhile, the Porte dispatched an order with a certain Ahmed Çavuş, who arrived in the Ottoman camp while the Ottoman army was on its way to Kefe through the North Caucasus. In this order, the grand vizier instructed Kasım Pasha to build a fortress on the site of old Astrakhan and winter there with his army until next spring so they could capture Astrakhan with more soldiers and weapons sent by the Porte.[46] However, Kasım Pasha was in no position to obey this order from the Porte, as the army was already retreating, and forcing the already aggravated and almost mutinous soldiers to stay was simply impossible.

The retreat of the Ottoman army was exacerbated by significant losses of men and materiel. Upon the advice of Devlet Girey, the Ottoman army withdrew through a different route – across the North Caucasus passing through Kabarda and Beshtau to Taman and Kefe. Due to the harsher conditions of the North Caucasus terrain, the Ottoman casualties were high. More than half of the soldiers in the retreating Ottoman army lost their lives, and the majority of the survivors lost their belongings. To add insult to injury, some Kabardinians attacked and looted the Ottoman soldiers whenever an opportunity presented itself.[47] The failure of the campaign and the undisciplined retreat of the army possibly encouraged certain Kabardinian chiefs to prey on the Ottoman troops. In contrast, on the way to Astrakhan, the Ottoman army did not have to fend off any attacks from the local peoples or rulers of the North Caucasus.[48]

Contemporary Ottoman chroniclers and some modern scholars agree that Crimean Khan Devlet Girey sabotaged the campaign by spreading rumours that negatively affected the morale of the army.[49] Devlet Girey's valid foresight that an Ottoman province in Astrakhan would reduce his freedom as an Ottoman vassal, especially in his dealings with Poland-Lithuania, Muscovy and the polities of the North Caucasus, can indeed explain his attitude. Thus, he did not hesitate to discourage the

Ottoman commanders and the army when they had the choice of staying in Astrakhan for the next campaign season. Interestingly, however, the Muscovite sources mention both Devlet Girey and Kasım Pasha as the key people responsible for convincing the Ottoman sultan to wage the Astrakhan campaign. Perhaps, both Muscovites and Ottomans found in those two, at least in Devlet Girey, a scapegoat for the materialisation and the failure of the campaign, respectively. Even more interesting is that according to the report of the Muscovite envoy to the Ottoman Porte in 1570, when he met Kasım Pasha in Kefe on his way to Istanbul, the pasha himself blamed Devlet Girey for convincing the Ottoman sultan to start a war against Muscovy.[50]

Thus, the campaign in 1569 was an utter failure for the Ottomans. Following the campaign, the power of Sokullu Mehmed Pasha weakened, and his rivals at the Imperial Court convinced the sultan to direct the Ottoman military resources towards the conquest of Cyprus rather than engaging in more 'futile' wars in the north against Muscovy. Although Sokullu Mehmed Pasha's reputation at the Porte was tarnished and the Ottoman Empire was now waging war against Venice for Cyprus, he still had the ear of Sultan Selim II. More important, Sokullu Mehmed Pasha and some other Ottoman officials did not abandon the developments in the north following the disastrous result of the Astrakhan campaign. They were now perhaps even more concerned about the possibility of expansion of the Muscovite sphere of influence in the North Caucasus. The post-Astrakhan changes in the Ottoman strategies in their northern frontier zones and in their diplomatic relations with the Tsardom of Muscovy are indeed signs of this new understanding at the Porte.

The increasing number of orders after the Astrakhan campaign in the Ottoman *mühimme* registers about the Circassian and Daghestani rulers, which will be examined in the following sections and chapters, proves that the Ottoman Porte altered its strategies in an attempt to establish a defined presence in the North Caucasus. The most notable modification in its policy over the region was that the Porte implemented a better form of diplomacy by corresponding with the local rulers of the North Caucasus directly rather than through the Crimean khan. This does not mean, however, that the Crimean Khanate was no longer a key player in the North Caucasus affairs. The Ottomans understood that the khanate was still indispensable for the control of the region, mainly because it was an unswerving foe of Muscovy in the Pontic–Caspian steppes, where the Ottoman armies were not effective. This is also why, although the Ottoman officials openly blamed Khan Devlet Girey for the failure of the Astrakhan campaign, they did not dare to remove him, as it would likely create more problems on the northern frontier and in the North Caucasus than it would solve. The military power of the Porte in the north, specifically in Kefe, was substantially reduced, and the governor-general of Kefe, Kasım Pasha, fell out of grace for his role in the Astrakhan campaign. Had the Porte removed Devlet Girey, who had the support of the Crimean aristocracy and people, and had there been resistance in the Crimea, it would not have had enough troops and resources to fight a rebellious khan in the north of the Black Sea.

3.2 The Muscovite Responses to the Campaign

Due to its policy of avoiding conflict with the Ottoman Empire in the North Caucasus and the delicate situation in Eastern Europe against Poland-Lithuania, the Tsardom of Muscovy could not risk a war with the Porte over Astrakhan or even to protest against the Ottoman aggression. The failure of the Astrakhan campaign notwithstanding, the Muscovites considered active political involvement and military actions of the Ottomans in their southern steppe frontier zone a grave threat to their interests. They were probably apprehensive that the Ottomans could eventually take Astrakhan and manipulate the Nogays, who had been by the mid-sixteenth century coopted by Muscovy. Considering that Tsar Ivan IV conquered Kazan and Astrakhan in 1552 and 1556 respectively, by the 1560s, their hold over these territories was still tentative. From the Muscovite perspective, if the Porte was not appeased and considered Muscovy a threat, not only Astrakhan but also Kazan could be in the crosshairs of the Ottoman–Crimean war machine. The possibility of such outcomes encouraged the tsar not to provoke the Porte and instead offer an amicable alternative to the Ottoman sultan.[51]

Therefore, a peaceful diplomatic resolution to the Ottoman aggression was the best option for the Muscovites in 1569. In January of the following year, the tsar sent his envoy to the Porte, officially to congratulate Selim II on his ascension to the Ottoman throne, which had taken place in 1566. However, this was clearly a pretext; the real reason for the embassy was to appease the Ottoman Porte and secure some sort of peace with the sultan. The Muscovite officials also instructed their envoy to assess the intentions of the Ottomans towards Astrakhan and the North Caucasus as well as to negotiate possible scenarios to keep the Ottomans out of the Muscovite steppe frontier zone and the North Caucasus, in which the Muscovites were prepared to compete with the Crimean Khanate but not with the Ottoman Empire. Ivan IV's representative to Sultan Selim II was Ivan Novosiltsev, who served the tsar as an envoy on multiple occasions, including an embassy to Temriuk of Kabarda in June 1565.[52] Ivan IV's or his ambassadorial office's choice to send Novosiltsev could be related to his carrying out an embassy in the North Caucasus. The negotiations at the Ottoman Porte would also be about this region.

Despite his claims to the contrary, Novosiltsev was not received warmly by the sultan in Istanbul, as we understand from his report submitted upon his return to Moscow in September 1570.[53] In accordance with the sixteenth-century Muscovite diplomatic practices, Novosiltsev's report contained prescribed speeches delivered to the Ottoman sultan and Ottoman officials, the routes taken from Moscow to Istanbul and back, and descriptions of influential people he interacted with during his embassy, as well as minute details of his conversations and reception at the Ottoman Porte.[54] Although diplomatic relations between the Tsardom of Muscovy and the Ottoman Empire began in 1497, Novosiltsev's report is the earliest extant ambassadorial report on the Ottomans in the Posol'skii Prikaz records available to historians.[55] Previously, Muscovite envoys were instructed to visit the Crimean khan before travelling to the Ottoman capital, thus acknowledging the khan's authority and role as an intermediary between the sultan and the tsar. In 1570, the tsar ordered Novosiltsev to go to the Porte directly without visiting the khan in Bahçesaray, which was a new practice and perhaps Ivan IV's way of refusing to recognise the khan's authority or position as an intermediary.

The ambassadorial report lists the issues that Novosiltsev sought to enquire into during his embassy. These included Selim II's thoughts on the Astrakhan campaign, in-depth information on the campaign including the size of the army, Ottoman losses and the routes taken, the relationship between the sultan and the Crimean khan, whether the sultan was upset with the khan or not, Ottoman officials close to the sultan, and Ottoman relations with Poland-Lithuania and the Safavid Empire.[56] Novosiltsev provides in his report a short history of the recent events in the Ottoman Empire with a focus on the Astrakhan campaign. He claims, perhaps drawing on what he heard from various officials at the Porte, that Sultan Süleyman I was opposed to the plans for an Ottoman conquest of Astrakhan, saying it was never a 'Turkish [Ottoman] city'.[57] He further writes that Crimean Khan Devlet Girey and Kasım Pasha were the culprits who convinced the new sultan, Selim II, in 1568 to organise a campaign to take Astrakhan. Novosiltsev gives the size of the Ottoman army as 80,000, which includes the Crimean Tatar forces.[58] This number seems to be a little higher than the one calculated from the extant Ottoman sources, which is 43,000–65,000. The majority of this army in 1569 was the Crimean Tatar troops, which numbered anywhere between 30,000 and 50,000 soldiers.

According to Novosiltsev, a certain Mehmed Çelebi assisted him at the Porte to gather information as demanded by the tsar and Muscovite officials. There are a few Mehmed Çelebis mentioned in the report. This particularly helpful Mehmed Çelebi must be the Ottoman merchant who had visited Moscow for commercial purposes in previous years. Novosiltsev claims that Mehmed Çelebi delivered him a copy of the map of Astrakhan sent by Kasım Pasha to Sokullu Mehmed Pasha in a letter while he was conducting his embassy. He also writes that when the grand vizier read the letter, he was angry that despite the failure of the campaign in 1569, Kasım Pasha was still insistent on pursuing the idea of conquering Astrakhan. Novosiltsev then concludes that Selim II was not planning a new campaign for Astrakhan.[59] In fact, he emphasises several times in his report that the sultan was no longer interested in organising another campaign in the north, which was undoubtedly good news for the Muscovite tsar. Perhaps surprisingly, Ivan Novosiltsev points out the willingness of numerous Ottoman statesmen, from local administrators such as the governor of Azak to the viziers of the Imperial Council, to promote peaceful relations between the sultan and the tsar.

In the course of the Muscovite envoy's stay at the Porte, Grand Vizier Sokullu Mehmed Pasha questioned him on a few occasions regarding the ambitions and objectives of Muscovy in the lower Volga and North Caucasus, specifically about the Muscovite fortress in Kabarda, Muscovy's relations with the Crimean Khanate, and their blockage of the pilgrimage route from Central Asia to Mecca at Astrakhan. He first enquired about the route Novosiltsev took to come to the Ottoman capital. The grand vizier asked why the envoy preferred not to take the shorter route from Astrakhan through the Northern Caucasus to Azak, which, he claimed, would have taken only seventeen days. By doing so, he was trying to ascertain whether the Muscovites had settled in Astrakhan and were regularly using the North Caucasus route.[60] The envoy simply replied by saying he took the route his sovereign ordered him to take. When asked about the Muscovite blockage of the Central Asian Muslims' pilgrimage route, Novosiltsev denied it. He assured the Ottoman grand vizier that the tsar allowed all travellers to pass through, detaining no one, and added that Muslims lived in peace in the Tsardom of Muscovy. The envoy then blamed those who wanted to create enmity between the two rulers for such accusations.[61] Regardless of his denial, these accusations were right, and the grand vizier was aware of it.

Among the several issues deliberated, the Muscovite fortress in Kabarda was one of the most frequently asked about during the embassy. Stressing the Ottoman claims over the North Caucasus, Sokullu Mehmed

Pasha queried the envoy, 'Why did your sovereign order a city to be built in the lands of our sovereign?' In response, Novosiltsev justified the Muscovite fortress with the marriage of Ivan IV to Temriuk's daughter and as a case of voluntary submission of the Kabardinian chief to the Muscovite tsar. Temriuk requested this fortress for protection from his enemies, which included some Circassian princes under his rule and the Daghestani rulers. Novosiltsev further claimed that the lands along the Terek River all the way to the Caspian Sea belonged to Temriuk, to which Sokullu Mehmed Pasha responded, 'All of the lands of the Circassians, Kumyks and shamkhals belong to our sovereign, and are of our religion.'[62] As Novosiltsev's report shows, the Muscovite fortress in Kabarda was the primary point of contention between him and the Ottoman officials with whom he negotiated. Compared to this issue, the status of Astrakhan and Kazan was hardly a topic of discussion.[63]

During his reception by the sultan on June 10, Novosiltsev delivered Ivan IV's gifts and a letter in which the tsar assured Sultan Selim II of Muscovy's proper treatment of Muslims and his desire to be at peace with the sultan.[64] After the reception at the Topkapı Palace, Selim II neither invited Novosiltsev for a feast nor provided him with food. But Novosiltsev tried to portray the reception positively by claiming that the soldiers around the sultan were not armed, which was the sultan's way of honouring him and, in his person, the tsar.[65] In accordance with the Ottoman palace traditions and diplomatic regulations during the reign of Selim II, this was highly unlikely. Thus, the Muscovite envoy in 1570 was not received warmly at the Porte and indeed not shown the diplomatic niceties afforded to the representatives of other states.

Novosiltsev received permission to return to Moscow in July 1570 after his second reception with the sultan, during which he was told that the sultan was to send a letter with him to the tsar.[66] This letter with a golden stamp was delivered to Novosiltsev in Istanbul in early August 1570. Because of the failure of the campaign in 1569, the loss in a fire of the munitions stockpiled in Azak for a possible future campaign to capture Astrakhan,[67] and the war in Cyprus, the Ottomans knew that another campaign against Muscovy in the near future was impossible. Therefore, Selim II wrote to Ivan IV that there could be peace between the two of them if the tsar agreed to certain conditions – opening and security of the route through Astrakhan for Muslim pilgrims from Central Asia, demolition of the fortress in Kabarda, which, according to the sultan, belonged to the Ottoman Empire since the conquest of Kefe by Mehmed II (r. 1451–81), and return of the Crimean khan's envoy detained in Moscow for the last four years.[68] What is noteworthy about the discussion of the

North Caucasus during Novosiltsev's embassy or in the sultan's letter, as N. A. Smirnov argues, is that neither the Ottomans nor the Muscovites mentioned or acknowledged any Crimean claims to Kabarda or the North Caucasus in general.[69] This shows the ongoing change in Ottoman perception of the North Caucasus borderland and their role in it.

The Ottoman sultan did not even ask for or pay lip service to the issue of Astrakhan or Kazan in his letter but specifically demanded the Muscovite fortress in Kabarda to be demolished, which indicates the priorities of the Ottomans in their newly reformulated strategies in the North Caucasus and on their broader northern frontier. For the Porte, withdrawal of the Muscovites from Kabarda and the North Caucasus, which was considered as being under the sovereignty of the sultan and directly affected the status of their possessions in the north of the Black Sea, was more critical than 'saving' or annexing the former Muslim khanates of Kazan and Astrakhan. This particular demand shows that among the priorities of the Porte, the destruction of the Muscovite fortress in Kabarda was the highest one. The Ottomans certainly understood the value of fortresses in establishing sovereignty over a polity or people in a borderland or a frontier zone, and in the 1560s, a Muscovite fortress was standing in an area that the Crimean khan and the sultan considered as being under their rule. Therefore, the Ottomans categorically rejected the argument of the Muscovite envoy in 1570 that the Muscovite fortress in Kabarda was a legitimate possession of the tsar thanks to the tsar's marriage to Temriuk's daughter and Temriuk's submission to Muscovy, and unwaveringly demanded its demolition at once. To perhaps encourage the tsar to accept these conditions, Selim II's letter included claims that the Porte had two years' worth of campaign materiel stocked in all of its frontier provinces and that the Ottomans were familiar with all the routes and directions in the north. The sultan further stated that he had instructed the Crimean khan not to raid Muscovy despite the khan's insistence, 'only because your [Ivan IV's] devotion and amity to us [Selim II] is well known'.[70]

Selim II's letter to Ivan IV and its Muscovite translation are excellent examples of how early modern states embedded their imperial and ideological claims in their diplomatic correspondence. Among those, claims of dynastic legitimacy and of patrimony over contested lands were common. This practice was not trivial. In fact, it affected and shaped relationships between empires and states in Eurasia. An integral part of diplomatic correspondence in the sixteenth century was translators and translations. Any translation from one language and cultural realm to another is intertwined with interpretation of meaning and the question of faithfulness to the original. As products of their own cultural and linguistic milieu, translators construct meaning by selecting vocabulary and terminology and if necessary by omitting foreign concepts and terms in their translations. In constructing meaning, translators and chancelleries navigate the issues of power, resistance and dominance.[71] Early modern chancelleries of empires such as the Ottomans and Muscovites were no exception to this phenomenon.

Securing an international acceptance of their legitimacy was especially important to the Muscovite Tsardom, as its imperial claims were the most recent among its neighbours such as the Ottoman Empire, the Crimean Khanate or Poland-Lithuania. Muscovite imperial ideology and claims of equality of their ruler to the contemporary emperors of Eurasia intensified during the reign of Ivan IV, who, for the first time in Muscovy's history, was crowned as tsar in January 1547.[72] Ivan IV's conquest of Kazan in 1552, a sovereign non-Russian state, added further legitimacy to his claims. The Ambassadorial Office worked meticulously to embed this ideology in their diplomatic relations.[73] Muscovite envoys to foreign states were provided with instructions about how to defend their ruler's new titles and imperial ideology. To illustrate, during an embassy to Poland-Lithuania, the Muscovite envoy was told to refer to Ivan IV's predecessors who were also tsars and that it was Ivan IV who conquered Kazan, if the Polish officials questioned him about Ivan's usage of the title 'tsar'.[74] Similarly, during his embassy to the Ottoman Porte, Ivan Novosiltsev worded his answers painstakingly to portray the relationship between the sultan and the tsar as brotherhood between two equal rulers in his conversations with the Ottoman officials and in his report prepared after his return to Moscow. Evidently, this new imperial title of the Muscovite ruler and its complex ideological connotations were also for domestic consumption within Muscovy. The Ambassadorial Office did not hesitate to alter diplomatic correspondence or other documents in translation in accordance with the accepted ideological framework of their imperial claims. For example, when the Orthodox Patriarch of Constantinople, Joasaph II, confirmed Ivan IV's title but refused to recognise the Muscovite Metropolitan Makarii's authority to crown the tsar, the Ambassadorial Office simply changed the meaning of the patriarch's letter in translation.[75] Likewise, Antonio Possevino, visiting Muscovy as a diplomat in 1581–2, reported that envoys of countries at war with the tsar should bring their own interpreters and not trust the Muscovites.[76]

A comparison of the Ottoman version of Selim II's letter with its Muscovite translation reveals how the Muscovite chancellery used translation as means of upholding their self-image and imperial ideology, equating the two rulers and getting rid of Ottoman claims of superiority.[77] As the reader can see in the appendices, the Muscovite version is much shorter. For the sake of simplifying convoluted Ottoman sentences, the translation omits several large sections from the original version. The Ottoman chancellery produced such letters based on a formula with pre-determined praises of the Porte and the addressee as well as prayers for any official whose name was mentioned. Omitting these perfunctory parts may be practical, but is certainly not faithful in translation. However, the Muscovite distortion of the Ottoman version was not limited to such practical omissions. The Muscovite translation also ignores passages that convey the ideological and imperial claims of the Porte in relation to the Muscovite tsar. In the Ottoman version, there is an entire section that portrays the Ottoman Porte as a refuge for loyal kings who submit to the sultan and in exchange are rewarded for their loyalty and amity. With such phraseology, the Ottoman text clearly expresses the notion that the Ottoman sultan was above all other rulers and certainly not equal to the Muscovite tsar, a claim that was typical for sixteenth-century Ottoman diplomatic correspondence. In this section, Selim II invites Tsar Ivan IV to submit to the Porte as a vassal:

> Now, from the old times, those loyal kings who submit with a mature sincerity to our benevolent court … are adjoined to those who attain the state of peace … if you are to be at the front line of being ready to support and be unwavering in your amity with your earnest desire and clear affectionate devotion to our threshold of the highest felicity and to our noble religion and state … you too will be honoured with our constantly increasing magnificent blessings and our royal grace.

The Muscovite Ambassadorial Office, where letters from foreign rulers were translated, simply omitted the aforementioned part. As such, the translation fails to convey the Ottoman sultan's perspective and voice; it rather renders him as addressing an equal in the person of the tsar. The translation adjusted the language and tone of the Ottoman original in accordance with the self-image and ideological concerns of the tsardom.

Interestingly, the Muscovite translator not only disregarded the parts that did not align with the tsarist imperial and ideological claims but also added sentences not found in the original letter. For example, while the Ottoman version remarks on the Astrakhan campaign of 1569 without mentioning the Muscovite conquest of the city in 1556, the translation reads, 'From your majesty's side, you [Ivan IV] sent your army to the khans [*sic*] of Astrakhan, and owing to your … good fortune, God entrusted Astrakhan to your majesty.' This addition to the translation reflects how the Muscovites legitimised their presence in Astrakhan and simply does not exist in the Ottoman version. A similar addition in the translation is the part that reads, '[P]rior to that [Muscovite conquest], from time immemorial Astrakhan had been our majesty's [the sultan's], of the same faith … and for the sake of our majesty and crown we sent to Astrakhan our army.' The Ottoman version does not claim that Astrakhan, having the same religion, belonged to the Ottoman Porte before its conquest by the Muscovites. The official argument for the campaign in the original letter was about the Ottoman conquest of Kefe and the Muscovite blockage of the pilgrimage route from Central Asia at Astrakhan. The Muscovite translation also omits the part that explains the sultan's claims to the North Caucasus. The Ottoman version argues that since the conquest of Kefe by Mehmed II, the Crimeans and the Circassians had been subjects of the Porte. As Novosiltsev's report indicates, the Ottoman officials countered the envoy's arguments about the legitimacy of the Muscovite fortress in Kabarda by claiming the entire region to be under Ottoman sovereignty because of their conquest of Kefe.

There are also several critical translation errors in the Muscovite version. For example, the translation refers to Mehmed II as if he was with the Ottoman army during the Astrakhan campaign, whereas the Ottoman text mentions him in the context of his conquest of Kefe. Besides this, the Ottoman version states that although the Crimean khan wished to raid Muscovite lands, the Porte refused to grant him permission, so he did not do so. The Ottoman sentence reads, 'And [the khan's request for permission to raid] has been refused and stopped many times, only because your devotion and amity to us is well known.' This part in the translation reads, 'And it was without our permission that he [the Crimean khan] came to your country with an army.' Lastly, the *hijri* date on the Muscovite translation is 979 AH, which corresponds to 1571. However, we know that Ivan Novosiltsev carried out his mission between January 1570 and September 1570. According to his ambassadorial report, he received Selim II's letter on 30 July 1570. The aforementioned ideological omissions and additions aside, the translation of Selim II's letter into Russian seems rudimentary and problematic, certainly not faithful to the original. This is noteworthy, considering that the Ambassadorial Office had officials and translators who were competent in Turkic languages thanks to its long-established diplomatic relations with powers such as the Crimean Khanate or the Nogay Horde.

Although the Porte did not possess substantial military materiel stockpiled in its northern provinces for another campaign and was militarily engaged in Cyprus, the Ottoman officials were not turning a blind eye to the North Caucasus affairs and the rising Muscovite threat in the north. The sultan encouraged the Crimean khan to raid not only the North Caucasus but also Muscovy, contrary to what he claimed in his aforementioned letter to the tsar. While Novosiltsev was still in Istanbul, the Porte unleashed the Crimean Tatars in the North Caucasus. The Crimean forces raided Kabarda in June and July 1570, inflicting severe damage to the pro-Muscovite rulers in several battles. In one of these battles, Temriuk himself was heavily wounded while two of his sons were captured and taken to Crimea by Prince Adil Girey, who commanded the Crimean army.[78] Compared to the previous punitive raid in 1567, when Muscovy's clients in Kabarda suffered but survived, the 1570 campaign was most effective as a punishment both for the Muscovite orientation of some Kabardinian rulers and for their attacks on the Ottoman soldiers returning from Astrakhan in 1569.

Muscovite records indicate that the campaign took place upon the request of Aslanbek (Arslan Bey in the Ottoman sources) and Psheapshoko from the Kaytuk family, who were the major rivals of Temriuk in Kabarda.[79] Aslanbek's relationship with the Ottomans and Crimeans dated to the early 1560s when he and his Kabardinian allies tried to check the rising power of Temriuk supported by Muscovy in 1562–3.[80] A certain Gazi Mirza, according to the Ottoman sources (Kazy Murza in Muscovite sources, possibly Psheapshoko's son), guided the Crimean Tatars in 1570.[81] In the end, this Crimean campaign was better organised and instrumental in curtailing the power of Muscovy in Kabarda. Devlet Girey's apprehensions about a possible Ottoman take-over of Astrakhan, a city that was a vital part of the Golden Horde's heritage, could be the reason for the surprising and effective success of the 1570 Crimean raid in Kabarda. Devlet Girey might have thought that if the Crimean Tatars expelled the Muscovites from Kabarda, the Ottomans would shelve their plans to annex Astrakhan and allow a return to the *status quo ante*, leaving northern affairs once again to the Crimean khans.

In the same year or 1571, Muscovy's key client in Kabarda and Ivan IV's father-in-law, Temriuk, died of his wounds. His two sons were now in the Crimean Khanate as prisoners. In response, the tsar opted to use diplomacy and sent a letter in December 1570 to the Crimean khan, inquiring about the well-being of Temriuk's sons and requesting their release from captivity in exchange for a ransom payment. A month later, the tsar sent another letter with salaries for Temriuk's sons.[82] Therefore, by 1571, the Crimean Tatar army had inflicted a severe blow to the Muscovite sphere of influence and prestige in Kabarda, but they could not eliminate it. The Muscovites preserved their connection to Kabarda and Temriuk's family through one of his sons, Mamstriuk, who had led an embassy to Moscow on behalf of his father in June–September 1565.[83]

Although the pro-Muscovite party lived on with some members of Temriuk's family, the Idars, they lost their power in Kabarda and started biding their time. After his death, Temriuk was replaced by his brother, Kanbulat, as the pshihua. The Muscovites seemed to have no say in Kanbulat's election, as he was elected solely by the Kabardinian princes. Due to the Crimean forces at their doorstep and with the demise of Temriuk, initially Kanbulat had no option but to respect the old Kabardinian–Crimean pattern of relations rather than solely submitting to Muscovy.[84] Thus, this pattern of relationship, with a more active Ottoman involvement, dominated the Kabardinian part of the North Caucasus following the Crimean campaign of 1570 and the death of Temriuk. The Muscovite presence in Kabarda in the form of *strel'tsy* and Cossacks ended by 1571, and the Crimean/Ottoman-backed Kabardinian chiefs controlled the area for almost a decade thereafter.

The possibility of another campaign for Astrakhan by the Porte as insinuated by the sultan in his letter dated 1570, the successful Crimean raid in Kabarda, and Ivan IV's military engagements in the Livonian War convinced the latter to fulfil the demands of the Ottoman Porte. In response to the letter of Selim II, Ivan IV sent another embassy in April 1571, led by Andrei Kuzminskii, to the Ottoman Porte, which was received by the sultan in May. The Muscovite tsar, in his letter to Selim II, wrote, '[O]ut of our love and friendship for our brother [the Ottoman sultan], we ordered the fortress on the Terek to be demolished, and the people stationed there to be sent to Astrakhan.' The tsar assured the sultan that his people would not obstruct the pilgrimage route through Astrakhan, and Muslim pilgrims could travel through the city with no hindrance.[85] Although the tsar promised to order the demolition of the fortress in Kabarda, it is not clear whether it was actually razed, because time and again throughout the second half of the sixteenth century, at the most opportune moments, fortresses seemed to pop up in the same location. According to his ambassadorial report, Kuzminskii said to the Ottoman officials that the tsar ordered the demolition of the fortress, but his word had not yet reached Kabarda.[86] Therefore, when the envoy was in Istanbul, the fortress was still standing on the Terek River. What is fairly certain is that the Muscovite troops stationed in the fortress withdrew to Astrakhan and that Muscovy maintained a steady relationship with the princely family of Temriuk.[87]

Thus, in 1571, Ivan IV accepted the conditions for peace proposed by the sultan, according to his letter delivered by Kuzminskii. This was fortunate for the Ottomans, as in the same year, they were fighting the Venetians for the island of Cyprus. Meanwhile, following his victory in the North Caucasus, Crimean Khan Devlet Girey organised a major campaign into Muscovy in 1571, reaching and burning the suburbs of Moscow and forcing the tsar to flee the capital in May of the same year when Kuzminskii was still in the Ottoman Empire. After this dramatic event reminiscent of the glorious days of the Golden Horde, Devlet Giray became known as '*Taht Algan*' ('The Taker of the Capital').[88] This Crimean Tatar campaign was indeed impressive, but its success was exaggerated by the Crimean khan on purpose so that it would prove to the Ottoman Porte that the Tsardom of Muscovy was not an imminent threat and the khanate was still able to contain it and even 'take' its capital. Perhaps most important, the khan wanted to show the Ottoman sultan that another Ottoman campaign in the north against the Muscovites would not be needed.

Khan Devlet Girey immediately sent a letter to Selim II to announce his victory over the Muscovites and his demand for Kazan and Astrakhan after eighteen days of raiding and plundering the capital province.[89] We know that Ivan IV agreed to give Astrakhan but not Kazan. However, this was a stalling strategy, and the tsar was simply trying to gain time to regroup.[90] In the aftermath of the Crimean campaign, the tsar sent an envoy to Crimea for further negotiations. A testament to the significance of Kabarda for the Muscovites, even after the destruction of the 1571 Crimean raid, was that Ivan IV requested the release of Temriuk's sons from Crimean captivity as a part of the negotiations.[91] Devlet Girey refused, arguing that the tsar had just executed their brother, Mikhail Temriukovich Cherkasskii. This son of Temriuk's, who entered the service of the tsar in 1558, was indeed executed upon the orders of Ivan IV, for reasons that might be related to his role in the *oprichnina* or alleged claims of treasonous relationships with the Crimean khan.[92]

The successful campaigns against Kabarda in 1570 and Muscovy in 1571 by the Crimean Tatars encouraged the Ottoman officials to demand from Ivan IV far more than they had during the embassy of Novosiltsev. Therefore, in his response letter to the Muscovite tsar dated October 1571, Selim II wrote that he was pleased with the news about the demolition of the fortress in 'the province of Kabarda' and the withdrawal of the Muscovite troops to Astrakhan. Stating that 'loyalty and vassalage of the tsar to the Porte' was known, Selim II asked for Astrakhan to be given to the Ottoman Empire and Kazan to the Crimean Khanate besides the official submission of the tsar to the sultan as the conditions for peace between Muscovy and the Ottoman Empire.[93]

The campaign for Astrakhan in 1569 was for the Ottomans the first experience of active involvement in the North Caucasus and on their northern frontier against Muscovy. It turned out, however, to be a complete military fiasco. Although by the time they started the campaign, the Ottomans had acquired adequate knowledge of the North Caucasus and its intricacies, they failed to realise that their aim of digging a canal to connect the Don and Volga rivers was far from attainable and that their authority over local North Caucasus rulers was rather liminal. The Ottomans accurately comprehended that neither the Porte nor the Crimean Khanate had the true allegiance of the majority of the North Caucasus rulers outside of the Taman Peninsula. In the events that followed, the Ottomans recognised that for any military undertaking in this borderland or the northern frontier zones, the local rulers of the North Caucasus were to be directly communicated with and encouraged to draw closer the Porte. The Ottoman Porte also realised that the Crimean khans had their own prerogatives and interests in the region, which did not always overlap with those of the Ottoman Empire. Most important, however, contrary to what the histories of the Ottoman and Russian empires suggest, for the Ottomans, the Astrakhan campaign became instrumental in changing their perception of the North Caucasus as a part of their northern policy and modifying their strategies in the region, which had broad implications for their northern frontier zones.

Notes

1. *Kabardino-russkie otnosheniia v 16–18 vv.*, ed. T. Kh. Kumykov and E. N. Kusheva (Moscow: Izdatel'stvo Akademii nauk SSSR, 1957), vol. 1, doc. 4, 13; PSRL, 13:405.
2. Halil İnalcık, 'Ottoman Methods of Conquest', *Studia Islamica* 2 (1954): 103–7; Metin Kunt, '17. yüzyılda Osmanlı kuzey politikası üzerine bir yorum', *Boğazici Üniversitesi dergisi* 4–5 (1976–7): 111–15; Gábor Ágoston, 'A Flexible Empire: Authority and Its Limits on the Ottoman Frontiers', in *Ottoman Borderlands: Issues, Personalities, and Political Changes*, ed. Kemal H. Karpat and Robert W. Zens (Madison: University of Wisconsin Press, 2003), 18.
3. İnalcık, 'Ottoman Methods of Conquest', 103.
4. Ibid., 107.
5. Kunt, '17. yüzyılda Osmanlı kuzey politikası üzerine bir yorum', 111–15; Kahraman Şakul, 'Siege Warfare in Verse and Prose: the Ottoman Conquest of Kamianets-Podilsky (Kamaniçe), 1672', in *The World of the Siege: Representations of Early Modern Positional Warfare*, ed. Anke Fischer-Kattner and Jamel Ostwald (Leiden: Brill, 2019), 211.

6. *Gelibolulu Mustafa Ali ve Künhü'l-ahbar'ında II. Selim, III. Murat ve III. Mehmet devirleri*, ed. Faris Çerçi (Kayseri: Erciyes Üniversitesi Yayınları, 2000), 2:6–7; *Puteshestviia russkikh poslov XVI–XVII vv.: Stateinye spiski* (Moscow: Izdatel'stvo Akademii nauk, 1954), 82–3.
7. İbrahim Peçevi, *Peçevi tarihi*, ed. Fahri Derin and Vahit Çabuk (Istanbul: Enderun, 1980), 1:468.
8. *Gelibolulu Mustafa Ali ve Künhü'l-ahbar'ında*, 2:6–8; Peçevi, *Peçevi tarihi*, 1:468–9.
9. *Gelibolulu Mustafa Ali ve Künhü'l-ahbar'ında*, 2:6–7.
10. Chantal Lemercier-Quelquejay, 'Cooptation of the Elites of Kabarda and Daghestan in the Sixteenth Century', in *The North Caucasus Barrier: The Russian Advance towards the Muslim World*, ed. Marie Bennigsen Broxup (London: Hurst, 1992), 22; Halil İnalcık, 'The Origin of the Ottoman–Russian Rivalry and the Don–Volga Canal (1569)', *Annales de l'Université d'Ankara* 1 (1947), 69.
11. MD 7, no. 838, Order to the governor of Kefe (February 1568).
12. MD 7, no. 2722.
13. *Gelibolulu Mustafa Ali ve Künhü'l-ahbar'ında*, 2:7; Peçevi, *Peçevi tarihi*, 1:468–9.
14. *Gelibolulu Mustafa Ali ve Künhü'l-ahbar'ında*, 2:6–8; Peçevi, *Peçevi tarihi*, 1:468–70; Murat Yaşar, 'The North Caucasus between the Ottoman Empire and the Tsardom of Muscovy: The Beginnings, 1552–1570', *Iran and the Caucasus* 20 (2016): 116.
15. See especially MD 7, nos. 1554, 1738, 2076, 2252, 2745. Some of these documents are summarised by Alexandre Bennigsen and Halil İnalcık. See Bennigsen, 'L'expédition turque contre Astrakhan en 1569, d'après les Registres des "Affaires importantes" des Archives ottomanes', *Cahiers du monde russe et soviétique* 8 (1967), 427–46; İnalcık, 'The Origin of the Ottoman-Russian Rivalry', 101–6.
16. Order to the *dizdar* and *azablar agası* of Azak (June 1568), MD 7, no. 1554. They were also instructed to register every item they received in a *defter*.
17. MD 7, no. 2722.
18. MD 7, no. 1749.
19. Order to the governor-general of Kefe (July 1568), MD 7, no. 1738.
20. MD 7, no. 2076.
21. MD 7, no. 2252. Akdes Nimet Kurat claims that this amount could certainly be procured by the time of the campaign. See Kurat, *Türkiye ve İdil boyu* (Ankara: Türk Tarih Kurumu, 1966), 22.
22. Order to the governor-general of Kefe (November 1568), MD 7, no. 2599; İnalcık, 'The Origin of the Ottoman–Russian Rivalry', 79.
23. MD 7, no. 2230.
24. MD 7, nos 2692, 2693.
25. Order to the governor-general of Kefe (December 1568), MD 7, no. 2691.
26. MD 7, no. 2644.

27. İnalcık, 'The Origin of the Ottoman–Russian Rivalry', 78.
28. MD 7, no. 2275.
29. İnalcık, 'The Origin of the Ottoman–Russian Rivalry', 79; Ahmed Refik, 'Bahr-i Hazar – Karadeniz kanalı ve Ejderhan seferi', *Tarih-i Osmani Encümeni mecmuası* 43 (1917): 8.
30. Peçevi, *Peçevi tarihi*, 1:469; İnalcık, 'The Origin of the Ottoman–Russian Rivalry', 78.
31. See, for example, Walter Richmond, *The Northwest Caucasus: Past, Present, Future* (Abingdon: Routledge, 2008) and Firuz Kazemzadeh, 'Russian Penetration of the Caucasus', in *Russian Imperialism from Ivan the Great to the Revolution*, ed. Taras Hunczak (New Brunswick, NJ: Rutgers University Press, 1974), 239–63, or a contemporaneous European source such as Antonio Possevino, *The Moscovia of Antonio Possevino SJ*, trans. Hugh F. Graham (Pittsburgh: University of Pittsburgh, 1977), 29–30.
32. Order to the governor-general of Diyarbakır (June 1559), MD 3, no. 32. This document clearly indicates, 'Most probably he [Prince Beyazıd] plans to reach the Circassian lands through Georgia.' Related to the same issue, the report of the Muscovite envoy to the Porte, Ivan Novosiltsev, in 1570 states, 'Beyazıd intended to take refuge in the land of Rus' with the sovereign tsar and grand prince…' RGADA, F. 89, *Turetskie dela*, kniga 2, fol. 96a–97b; *Puteshestviia russkikh poslov*, 81. The Muscovite document claims that Beyazıd wanted to make his way to Muscovy. However, the Ottoman sources note that he wanted to reach the Circassian lands in the North Caucasus. However, it can be argued that 'the land of Rus'' in the Muscovite envoy's report might refer to the Circassian lands, which were claimed by the tsar following the submission of Temriuk.
33. MD 7, no. 2723.
34. MD 7, no. 2246.
35. MD 14, no. 1621.
36. MD 7, no. 2246.
37. S. M. Solov'ev, *Istoriia Rossii s drevneishikh vremen* (Moscow: Izdatel'stvo sotsial'no-ekonomicheskoi literatury, 1959–66), 3:604.
38. Order to the Crimean Khan (October 1568), MD 7, no. 2757; Yaşar, 'The North Caucasus', 116.
39. *Gelibolulu Mustafa Ali ve Künhü'l-ahbar'ında*, 2:7–9; Peçevi, *Peçevi tarihi*, 1:469–70. İnalcık agrees with the Ottoman chronicles and says that one-third of the canal was completed in three months. İnalcık, 'The Origin of the Ottoman–Russian Rivalry', 79–80. However, Kurat argues that the main objective of the campaign was to capture Astrakhan. He claims that it took the Ottoman only two weeks to understand that digging a canal between the Don and Volga rivers was not feasible. Kurat, *Türkiye ve İdil boyu*, 18. Also see his 'The Turkish Expedition to Astrakhan' in 1569 and the Problem of the Don–Volga Canal', *Slavonic and East European Review* 40 (1961)': 17.

40. Report of Kasım Pasha to the Porte on the Astrakhan Campaign (1569), published in French in Tayyib Gökbilgin, 'L'expédition ottomane contre Astrakhan en 1569', *Cahiers du monde russe et soviétique* 11 (1970): 118–23 (for a facsimile of the original document see Alexandre Bennigsen et al., *Le Khanat de Crimée dans les archives du Musée du palais de Topkapi* (Paris: Mouton, 1978), 135–8); Report of Simon Maltsev (1569), in P. A. Sadikov, 'Pokhod tatar i turok na Astrakhan' v 1569 g.', *Istoricheskie zapiski* 22 (1947): 153–64; Kurat, *Türkiye ve İdil boyu*, appendices, 6–7.
41. Yaşar, 'The North Caucasus', 116–17.
42. Report of Kasım Pasha to the Porte on the Astrakhan Campaign (1569), in Bennigsen et al., *Le Khanat de Crimée*, 136–7.
43. Bennigsen et al., *Le Khanat de Crimée*, 135–8.
44. *Gelibolulu Mustafa Ali ve Künhü'l-ahbar'ında*, 2:8–10.
45. Sadikov, 'Pokhod tatar i turok'; Kurat, *Türkiye ve İdil boyu*, appendices, 6–7.
46. Report of Kasım Pasha to the Porte on the Astrakhan Campaign (1569), in Bennigsen et al., *Le Khanat de Crimée*, 136–7. A Polish envoy, Andrzej Taranowski, also came with Ahmed and witnessed the situation around Astrakhan and within the Ottoman camp. 'Istoriia o prikhode turetskogo i tatarskogo voinstva pod Astrakhan v lieto ot Rozhdetsva Khristova 1677', trans. N. N. Murzakevich, *Zapiski Odesskago obshchestva istorii i drevnostei* 8 (1872): 479–88; N. A. Smirnov, *Rossiia i Turtsiia v XVI–XVII vv.* (Moscow: Izdatel'stvo Moskovskogo gosudarstvennogo universiteta, 1946), 93; Yaşar, 'The North Caucasus', 117.
47. Order to Şirin Ali Bey of the Crimea (October 1586), MD 62, no. 226; Report of Simon Maltsev (1569), in Sadikov, 'Pokhod tatar i turok'; Kurat, *Türkiye ve İdil boyu*, appendices, 6–7.
48. Yaşar, 'The North Caucasus', 117–18.
49. *Gelibolulu Mustafa Ali ve Künhü'l-ahbar'ında*, 2:8–10; Peçevi, *Peçevi tarihi*, 1:469–71; Kurat, *Türkiye ve İdil boyu*, 96–7; İnalcık, 'The Origin of the Ottoman–Russian Rivalry', 82–6; M. Sadık Bilge, *Osmanlı Devleti ve Kafkasya* (Istanbul: Eren, 2005), 55; Bennigsen, 'L'expédition turque contre Astrakhan', 440. According to Antonio Possevino, Pope Gregory XIII's envoy to Ivan IV, Polish King Stefan Bartory told him that the defeat of the Ottomans at Astrakhan was inflicted not by the Muscovites but by the Crimean Tatars, who led them through inhospitable terrain. Possevino, *The Moscovia*, 29–30.
50. RGADA, *Turetskie dela*, F. 89, kniga 2, fol. 98–102b; *Puteshestviia russkikh poslov*, 82–3.
51. Yaşar, 'The North Caucasus', 119–21.
52. Murat Yaşar, 'Ivan Petrovich Novosiltsev', in *Christian–Muslim Relations. A Bibliographical History*, vol. 7: *Central and Eastern Europe, Asia, Africa and South America, 1500–1600*, ed. David Thomas and John Chesworth (Leiden: Brill, 2015), 426–9; PSRL, 13:383.

53. Halil İnalcık, 'Osmanlı-Rus rekabetinin menşei ve Don-Volga kanalı teşebbüsü (1569)', *Belleten* 12 (1948): 386.
54. Yaşar, 'Ivan Petrovich Novosiltsev', 428.
55. İlyas Kamalov, *Rus elçi raporlarında Astrahan seferi* (Ankara: Türk Tarih Kurumu, 2011), 15.
56. RGADA, F. 89, *Turetskie dela*, kniga 2, fol. 96b; *Puteshestviia russkikh poslov*, 80.
57. RGADA, F. 89, *Turetskie dela*, kniga 2, fol. 97–97b; *Puteshestviia russkikh poslov*, 81.
58. RGADA, F. 89, *Turetskie dela*, kniga 2, fol. 98–102b; *Puteshestviia russkikh poslov*, 82–3.
59. *Puteshestviia russkikh poslov*, 86.
60. Smirnov, *Rossiia i Turtsiia*, 121; Yaşar, 'The North Caucasus', 122.
61. *Puteshestviia russkikh poslov*, 77.
62. RGADA, F. 89, *Turetskie dela*, kniga 2, fol. 118b–119a; *Puteshestviia russkikh poslov*, 90.
63. RGADA, F. 89, *Turetskie dela*, kniga 2, fol. 117a–127b; *Puteshestviia russkikh poslov*, 89–92.
64. Selim II's letter to Ivan IV dated 1570. This document was first published in Ahmed Feridun Bey, *Münşa'atü's-selatin* (Istanbul, 1858–9 (AH 1275)), 460–1. See also İnalcık, 'Osmanlı-Rus rekabetinin menşei', 400–1. The Muscovite copy of this letter is in RGADA, F. 89, *Turetskie dela*, kniga 2, fol. 56b–59a.
65. RGADA, F. 89, *Turetskie dela*, kniga 2, fol. 118a–118b; *Puteshestviia russkikh poslov*, 79.
66. RGADA, F. 89, *Turetskie dela*, kniga 2, fol. 126; *Puteshestviia russkikh poslov*, 92.
67. Order to the governor of Azak (February 1570), MD 8, no. 10.
68. Feridun Bey, *Münşa'atü's-selatin*, 460–1; İnalcık, 'Osmanlı-Rus rekabetinin menşei', 400–1; Yaşar, 'The North Caucasus', 122.
69. Smirnov, *Rossiia i Turtsiia*, 32.
70. Feridun Bey, *Münşa'atü's-selatin*, 460–1; İnalcık, 'Osmanlı-Rus rekabetinin menşei', 400–1.
71. E. Natalie Rothman, *Brokering Empire: Trans-Imperial Subjects between Venice and Istanbul* (Ithaca, NY: Cornell University Press, 2012), 165–211. Also see Maria Tymoczko and Edwin Gentzler, eds., *Translation and Power* (Amherst: University of Massachusetts Press, 2002).
72. Michael Khodarkovsky, *Russia's Steppe Frontier: The Making of a Colonial Empire, 1500–1800* (Bloomington: Indiana University Press, 2002), 40–1; Charles J. Halperin, *Ivan the Terrible: Free to Reward and Free to Punish* (Pittsburgh: University of Pittsburgh Press, 2019), 43–8.
73. Halperin, *Ivan the Terrible*, 44; Possevino, *The Moscovia*, 135–6.
74. Khodarkovsky, *Russia's Steppe Frontier*, 40; Possevino, *The Moscovia*, 27.
75. Halperin, *Ivan the Terrible*, 47.

76. Possevino, *The Moscovia*, 34–5.
77. See Appendices I and II for transliteration and translation of the two versions of this letter into English.
78. RGADA, F. 123, *Krymskie dela*, kniga 13, fol. 284a–285b; *Snosheniia Rossii s Kavkazom: Materialy izvlechennye iz Moskovskago glavnago arkhiva Ministerstva inostrannykh diel, 1578–1613 gg.*, ed. S. L. Belokurov (Moscow: Universitetskaia tipografiia, 1889), LXXVIII; *Kabardino-russkie otnosheniia*, vol. 1, doc. 11, 21–2.
79. RGADA, F. 123, *Krymskie dela*, kniga 13, fol. 275b, 278b, 283b; E. N. Kusheva, *Narody Severnogo Kavkaza i ikh sviazi s Rossiei: vtoraia polovina XVI–30-e gody XVII veka* (Moscow: Izdatel'stvo Akademii nauk SSSR, 1958), 253; V. V. Trepavlov, *Istoriia Nogaiskoi Ordy* (Kazan: Kazanskaia nedvizhimost', 2016), 394–5; *Snosheniia Rossii s Kavkazom*, lxi.
80. Aslanbek was one of the prominent Kabardinian chiefs who served the Ottomans in their war against the Safavids. Asafi Dal Mehmed Çelebi, *Şeca'atname*, ed. Abdülkadir Özcan (Istanbul: Çamlıca Basım, 2006), 379.
81. *Snosheniia Rossii s Kavkazom*, doc. 1, 5–6; MD 44, nos. 182, 218.
82. RGADA, F. 123, *Krymskie dela*, kniga 13, fol. 348a, 393; *Kabardino-russkie otnosheniia*, vol. 1, doc. 14, 26–7.
83. *Kabardino-russkie otnosheniia*, vol. 1, doc. 4, 12.
84. *Kabardino-russkie otnosheniia*, vol. 1, doc. 11, 21–3; *Snosheniia Rossii s Kavkazom*, doc. 2, 8–9.
85. RGADA, F. 89, *Turetskie dela*, kniga 2, fol. 149a–149b; *Kabardino-russkie otnosheniia*, vol. 1, doc. 16, 27–9.
86. RGADA, F. 89, *Turetskie dela*, kniga 2, fol. 176b; *Kabardino-russkie otnosheniia*, vol. 1, doc. 17, 29.
87. Smirnov, *Rossiia i Turtsiia*, 122.
88. MD 16, no. 26. İnalcık, 'The Origin of the Ottoman–Russian Rivalry', 90.
89. MD 16, no. 26.
90. *Kabardino-russkie otnosheniia*, 1:379. Tsar Ivan IV agreed to 'sacrifice' Astrakhan for peace and offered the khan an alliance against Poland-Lithuania.
91. *Kabardino-russkie otnosheniia*, vol. 1, doc. 20, 33–4.
92. Halperin, *Ivan the Terrible*, 69, 202–3.
93. Imperial letter to the king of Muscovy, MD 16, no. 3.

4

The Milky Way Fades: Post-Astrakhan Ottoman and Muscovite Strategies in the North Caucasus

Following the successful Crimean campaigns in Kabarda and the Tsardom of Muscovy in 1570–1, Tsar Ivan IV preferred to keep a low profile in the North Caucasus, shying away from further provoking the Ottoman Porte. At the same time, he continued to maintain a clientage relationship with the family of Temriuk, especially with his son Mamstriuk, to whom the tsar paid annuities in the 1570s. Meanwhile, Temriuk's brother, Kanbulat, replaced him in 1571 as the head of the Idars and as the pshihua of Kabarda. The new pshihua remained an ally of the Muscovite tsar but followed a fairly balanced policy with other foreign powers. The status quo lasted until 1576 when the Lesser Nogay Horde, supported by Crimean Tatars and some Ottoman volunteers from the city of Azak, attacked the lands of Kanbulat and other pro-Muscovite rulers in Kabarda.[1]

4.1 Out of the Ashes, the Tsar's Prestige Born Again: Revival of Muscovite Power in Kabarda

Although Kanbulat, with the help of his Kabardinian allies, succeeded in defeating the Nogays and even killing their leader, Kazy, in an ambush, he realised that his rivals, supported by the Ottoman–Crimean axis in Kabarda, were getting stronger and bolder. For this reason, in 1577–8, Kanbulat turned to Muscovy for assistance and travelled to Moscow with his children and the children of Mamstriuk to submit to the tsar.[2] His embassy coincided with the preparation stage of a large-scale Ottoman campaign against the Safavid Empire, during which the Porte specifically planned to assert its hegemony over the North Caucasus, in addition to acquiring territories in the South Caucasus. Soviet and Western historians who rely solely on Russian sources attribute Kanbulat's rapprochement with Muscovy in 1577–8 to his knowledge of the Ottoman designs over the North Caucasus and his determination to protect Kabardinian independence. The Muscovite tsar was a natural ally in Kanbulat's endeavour of defending Kabarda from the Ottomans and Crimean Tatars.[3] However, it is not plausible that a minor local ruler so far away from the Ottoman Porte would know about the intrinsic details of Ottoman campaign planning and their ambitions over the North Caucasus as early as 1577.

The internal dynamics of Kabardinian politics is undoubtedly a better explanation for Kanbulat's embassy, as was the case when Temriuk approached Muscovy in 1557. The Kabardinian chiefs had already experienced and, by then, known well the fact that the Tsardom of Muscovy was unwilling to confront the Ottomans in the North Caucasus, although it would provide the Kabardinians with support against the Crimean Tatars or their local rivals. The tsar's desire to be at peace with the Ottoman sultan was stated time and again in the 1550s and 1560s whenever the North Caucasus representatives visited him in Moscow, asking for his support. Therefore, there is no basis for assuming that Kanbulat went to Moscow to prevent an Ottoman military invasion or annexation of his lands. Second, we know that the Ottoman Porte designated one of the Kabardinian chiefs, a certain Mehmed, as the *sancakbeyi* (governor) of Kabarda and courted several others in the 1570s.[4] The proactive Ottoman support for the Kabardinian rulers allied with them changed the balance of power among the Kabardinian princely families. Although Kanbulat was the pshihua of Kabarda, he did not possess the practical authority that came with this title. Evidently, the Ottoman Porte did not even recognise his title when they appointed the aforementioned Mehmed as the governor of Kabarda.

Besides, following their raid in 1570, the Crimean Tatars most likely supported the Kaytuk family, led by Psheapshoko and Aslanbek. They had been the Tatars' allies in Kabarda against Temriuk, which put Kanbulat in a vulnerable situation despite his victory over a Lesser Nogay army in 1576. Considering the power relationships and domestic rivalries in Kabarda at that time, the Muscovite tsar was possibly the only ruler capable of providing military backing for Kanbulat to regain his power in the face of increased aggression from the Kaytuks and pro-Crimean/Ottoman princes. As one may remember, Temriuk's rivals sought help from the Crimean khan and the Porte in the 1560s when he was receiving substantial help from the tsar against his domestic foes. This time, rivals of the Kabardinian chiefs supported by the Ottomans and Crimeans must have thought that they could receive aid from the Muscovite tsar, who had showed interest in Kabarda since 1557 and was related by marriage to the family of Kanbulat.

Kanbulat was encouraged and assisted in his rapprochement with Muscovy by his nephew, Mamstriuk. After all, it was Tsar Ivan IV who had ransomed Mamstriuk from his captivity in Crimea after the raid of 1570 and paid him annual salaries since then. Mamstriuk remained loyal to the tsar, as stated in Ivan IV's letter delivered during the embassy of Kanbulat in 1577. According to the Muscovite sources, Kanbulat came to Moscow to petition the tsar to take him 'under his royal hand', protect him from his enemies, and construct a fortress on the estuary of the Sunzha River.[5] Tsar Ivan IV readily granted these requests. Kanbulat took the pledge of allegiance (*shert'*) and his son, Khoroshai, was baptised (Boris) and taken into the service of the tsar.[6] Kanbulat's embassy and submission to the tsar did not go unnoticed by the Ottoman Porte. The Ottoman officials recognised Kanbulat and Mamstriuk as the major pro-Muscovite princes in the North Caucasus.[7] Their staunch alliance with Muscovy definitely complicated the Ottoman designs over the region during their Safavid campaign. From the Muscovite perspective, besides taking them one step closer to their long-term goal of establishing a defined sphere of influence in the North Caucasus, the submission of several powerful Kabardinian chiefs served the tsar in two main ways in the short term. First, they could situate themselves through Kanbulat in a strategic location, controlling one of the three passageways between the North and South Caucasus just before the Ottoman–Safavid War, the preparations for which were known to the tsar. This could enable the Muscovites to check any Ottoman/Crimean attempt to expand their military operations towards Astrakhan. Second, the tsar desired to add auxiliary forces from his Kabardinian clients to the armies fighting on Muscovy's western frontier. For this reason, in his letter, Tsar Ivan IV demanded from Mamstriuk that he send 300 men to join the Muscovite army in Eastern Europe.[8]

Perhaps the most consequential aspect of Kanbulat's vassalage, however, was the reconstruction of the Muscovite fortress on the Terek River. The time was right for Muscovy because they knew that an Ottoman offensive against the Safavid Empire would intensify Crimean and Ottoman activities in the North Caucasus. A fortress in Kabarda could contain probable Ottoman efforts at expansion, in case the Ottomans wrested the South Caucasus from the Safavids. Thus, the Muscovite tsar sent Luka Novosiltsev with men and weapons to the bank of the Terek River to construct a fortress.[9] At this critical time, Muscovy built another fortress in the heart of the North Caucasus with which it could hinder the Ottoman supply route that passed through Kabarda. The strategic location of the fortress became obvious as early as its foundation date in 1578. Crimean Prince Adil Girey, who in 1570 carried out the successful campaign in Kabarda, was on his way with the Crimean troops to Shirvan in order to join the main Ottoman army when he discovered that there was now a Muscovite fortress on his route. Adil Girey had to ask permission from Novosiltsev, the commander of the Muscovite forces in Kabarda, for safe passage along this portion of the Terek River. Novosiltsev allowed Adil Girey and his army to pass without harm.[10]

Two things are important to note here. First, the Crimean army did not try nor was able to capture the fortress despite its superior numbers. Therefore, this structure was not merely a small blockhouse or a fort but a properly manned and equipped fortress. Second, the Muscovites permitted the Crimean Tatar army to pass, which shows that they continued to avoid conflict with the Ottoman Porte. Harming the Crimean Tatar forces would have certainly caused a military reaction from the Ottomans in this instance, as the Crimean army was a part of the ongoing Ottoman campaign.

However, the mere existence of a Muscovite fortress was a severe threat to the strategic and military plans of the Ottoman Porte, even though the Muscovites cooperated with the Ottomans and Crimean Tatars. In 1579, Crimean Khan Mehmed Girey II (r. 1577–84) wrote to the tsar, demanding that he demolish the Muscovite fortress on the Terek River once again.[11] Due to the Ottoman military presence in the Caucasus, the pressure from the Crimean khan and the ongoing Livonian War, Ivan IV decided to oblige.[12] This time, the pro-Muscovite party remained strong in Kabarda thanks to the continued vassalage of Kanbulat and Mamstriuk. Yet, they were not powerful enough to control the entirety of Kabarda, as they had come close to doing during Temriuk's vassalage between 1563 and 1570.

4.2 Killing Two Birds with One Stone: The Ottoman–Safavid War of 1578–90 and the North Caucasus

The failure of the Astrakhan campaign, the persistent Muscovite presence in Kabarda, and new Ottoman objectives over the Caucasus and the Caspian Sea made it clear to the Porte that its strategies in the North Caucasus ought to change. The North Caucasus borderland needed to be under Ottoman control as an integral part of the Ottoman imperial system rather than being left as a fluid region under the sway of the Crimean Khanate, pursuing a slave- and tribute-oriented strategy in the region. Therefore, the Ottoman Porte decided to kill two birds with one stone and extended its war effort against the Safavid Empire in Western Asia to the North Caucasus. The war against the Safavid Empire was a major campaign for which preparations, including the size of the army, supply lines and relations with the local rulers in the North Caucasus, were handled in a much better way compared to the Ottoman campaign for Astrakhan.

Many historians argue that the Ottomans used the North Caucasus route during the Ottoman–Safavid War due to the distance of the targeted Safavid territories in the Caucasus from major Ottoman centres in eastern Anatolia, such as Van, Diyarbakır and Erzurum. They stress that it was difficult for the Ottomans to establish order and hold the conquered territories in the South Caucasus from their eastern Anatolian strongholds.[13] In none of their previous campaigns against the Safavid Empire, however, had the Ottoman army used the route through the North Caucasus. They preferred to attack the Safavid territories from their centres in eastern Anatolia, despite claiming that the North Caucasus had been under the sovereignty of the Porte since the conquest of Kefe.[14] For example, during Süleyman I's campaigns against the Safavids in 1532–4, 1548–9 and 1553–5, the Ottoman army did not utilise the North Caucasus as a supply route.

The extant primary sources suggest that the main reason behind the Porte's preference of using the North Caucasus route was related to two significant issues – the tenacious Muscovite presence in the region and the desire to integrate the North Caucasus borderland into the Ottoman imperial system. The Ottomans were aware that the Muscovite activities in the North Caucasus were not limited to Kabarda and had influence beyond the North Caucasus. During the Astrakhan campaign, unable to confront the Ottomans directly, Tsar Ivan IV approached Shah Tahmasp I (r. 1524–76) and provided weapons to the Safavids to cement an anti-Ottoman league.[15] The Ottoman Porte, in response, reinforced its troops stationed along the Safavid border in 1569 to neutralise potential threats that might have come from them.[16] Therefore, the Ottoman officials expected a similar alliance between the Safavids and Muscovites before the war began. And they were not surprised to learn that during the Ottoman–Safavid War of 1578–90, the Muscovites were assisting the Safavids through Astrakhan and exchanging envoys to negotiate an alliance. The Ottoman sultan warned the Crimean khan in a letter dated 1579 about the Muscovite supply of weapons to the Safavids and their envoys visiting the Safavid court.[17] An alliance with the Safavid Empire against the Ottoman designs in the Caucasus was practical from the Muscovite viewpoint. A possible Ottoman hegemony over the entire Caucasus region would be disastrous since the next step for the Porte would be to capture Astrakhan and conquer the lower Volga, as they had previously attempted. Thus, the Ottomans realised that they could no longer afford to tolerate a Muscovite sphere of influence in Kabarda, nor ignore their ownership of Astrakhan at such a critical time in the Caucasus.

The architect of the 1569 Astrakhan campaign, Sokullu Mehmed Pasha, was still the grand vizier and commanded a great deal of influence at the Porte. Although the immediate objective of the 1578–90 war was to 'liberate' Shirvan and other Sunni parts of the Safavid Empire, the grand vizier was planning to build an Ottoman fleet that would sail the Caspian Sea to assist in 'conquering the surrounding lands'.[18] These lands certainly included Astrakhan and the lower Volga on the shores of the Caspian. Sokullu Mehmed Pasha sent a letter to Özdemiroğlu Osman Pasha, the commander of the Ottoman forces in the Caucasus, in July 1579 as soon as the Ottoman army secured its position in Derbend on the Caspian shore. He asked in this letter whether oak trees and iron ore needed to build ships could be found in the Caucasus. Sokullu Mehmed Pasha also queried the possibility of building ships in Tbilisi and transferring them via the Kura River and through the Caspian Sea to Derbend.[19] For these reasons, the Ottoman–Safavid War of 1578–90 was directly related to the North Caucasus and Ottoman northern policy.

As of 1569, the Ottoman Porte began to depart from its relatively lax policy in the north. A noticeable modification in Ottoman strategies in the North Caucasus was the conduct of direct diplomacy with local rulers. In contrast to its traditional method of relying on the Crimean khan as an intermediary, during the preparations and the war of 1578–90, the Ottoman Porte communicated with North Caucasus rulers directly and tried to draw them to its side with a policy of accommodation and more generous rewards. The abundance in the Ottoman archives of diplomatic records of correspondence with these local rulers evinces a major change in the Ottoman strategies, compared to the first half of the sixteenth century.

Consequently, as early as the 1570s, Ottoman control over the Kuban–Taman region reached such a level that even the Crimean khan, the self-proclaimed overlord of the North Caucasus, had to request assistance from the Porte in his dealings with the Western Circassians. For example, the khan petitioned the Porte in 1570 for an imperial letter to the Janey rulers, who refused to obey his orders regarding the rescue of some Nogays captured by the Circassians.[20] This was new in terms of the relationship patterns and diplomacy in the region. Previously, the sultan needed the Crimean khan to facilitate communication with the local rulers in the North Caucasus due to the khan's position as the sovereign of the region and his military capability of punishing them. In another instance, one of the Janey chiefs, Mustafa, visited the Porte in June 1571 to ask for permission to resettle in the Taman region. The sultan, in response, sent an order to the judges of Kefe and Taman to allow Mustafa and his brothers to settle wherever they desired.[21] What is different is that the Porte did not send a copy of this order to the Crimean khan. The affairs of the Janeys were now handled in Istanbul through the Ottoman agents in the region.

Previously, such an order would also have gone to the Crimean khan to ensure its implementation and the obedience of the Circassian vassals.

This proactive Ottoman strategy does not mean that the Crimean khan was no longer of any use in the North Caucasus. The Ottomans continued to apply their 'carrot and stick' policy, and whenever they needed to use military force, they preferred to employ the Crimean khan. To illustrate, when a Circassian chief, Bozokoğlu Mehmed, and a few other local rulers oppressed some Ottoman subjects in the Taman region in April 1574, the governor-general of Kefe was ordered to consult with the Crimean khan and take appropriate measures to capture and punish the unruly Circassian chiefs.[22] The Crimean Tatars still provided the Porte with a military arm in the region, as it was impossible or too costly for the regular Ottoman troops in Kefe or Azak to carry out such punitive tasks. The Crimean khan was happy to oblige and to exact slaves and tribute in the process. What is different, however, is that Ottoman central control over these Circassian territories increased substantially.

The same active Ottoman strategy was also evident in Kabarda, which had been the focal point of the Muscovite ambitions over the North Caucasus. Following the Crimean khan's triumphant campaign against Temriuk and his allies in 1570, the prestige and power of Muscovy in Kabarda suffered grievously. The Porte took advantage of this opportunity and courted Kabardinian chiefs to expand its sphere of influence. For this reason, a Kabardinian chief was received in Istanbul and possibly converted to Islam as he bore a generic Muslim-Ottoman name, Mehmed. On 9 May 1573, the Porte sent an order to the governor of Akkerman, informing him that 'the *sancakbeyi* [governor] of *Kabartay* [Kabarda], Mehmed, set off from the Porte to his *sancak* [province] through Akkerman and Kefe'. The governor was to ensure Mehmed Bey's safety until he reached Kefe.[23] The Ottoman Porte clearly revised its geographic considerations, which previously focused on the Kuban–Taman region, and now targeted the North Caucasus in its entirety. The granting of titles, salary and other forms of investiture was the first step in Ottoman subject- and territory-making strategies in the North Caucasus borderland, as we see in this example of a Kabardinian chief.

From the Porte's viewpoint, Kabarda was now officially an Ottoman province. The Ottomans used the title of *sancakbeyi* in their correspondence with Mehmed Bey and referred to the entirety of Kabarda as '*Kabartay sancağı*' (province of Kabarda).[24] Another famous Kabardinian chief, Aslanbek (Arslan Bey in Ottoman documents), also submitted to the Porte and received a salary from the revenue of Kefe.[25] Contemporary Ottoman chronicles and the *mühimme* registers mention his name often as a local ruler assisting the Ottoman army in Kabarda during the Ottoman–Safavid War. Therefore, despite the revival of Muscovite fortunes in Kabarda with the submission of Kanbulat to Ivan IV, the Ottomans were able to draw several important Kabardinian princes to their side in this phase of the imperial competition over the North Caucasus borderland.

Besides the Western Circassians and Kabardinians, the Ottoman Porte also approached the Daghestani rulers, whose cooperation and support for the Ottoman war effort were indispensable. Before the new Ottoman strategy of establishing a defined suzerainty, the Crimean khans and sometimes the Safavid shahs contested for a sphere of influence in Daghestan. However, neither of them territorially expanded into Daghestan, where local rulers enjoyed full independence both domestically and internationally. Following the Muscovite occupation of Astrakhan, there were several attempts at rapprochement between Muscovy and the shamkhal between 1555 and 1557, as early as the Muscovites established themselves in Astrakhan, but they did not yield viable results. When the Ottoman Porte approached them directly in the 1570s, the Daghestani rulers, including the shamkhal, showed interest in reaching an agreement with the Ottomans. Among the strategies used by the Ottomans, the Porte prioritised their religious ideology by appealing to the Sunni Muslim affiliation of the Daghestanis. The Daghestani rulers reciprocated this idea in their negotiations with the Ottoman officials. The Ottoman centres of power in the region, such as Azak and Kefe, were far from Daghestan, compared to the Muscovite position in Astrakhan. Therefore, the shamkhal and other rulers in Daghestan might have thought that an alliance with the Ottoman sultan would not hinder their independence. As one may remember, when the neighbouring Circassians petitioned the Muscovite tsar, they requested the tsar's protection against the Ottoman sultan, the Crimean khan and the Daghestani shamkhal. It was only natural that these three powers, noted as the enemies in the Muscovite–Circassian negotiations, would unite against the Muscovites and their allies in the North Caucasus.

The first direct contact between the shamkhal and the Porte in the second half of the sixteenth century took place during the Astrakhan campaign in 1569. The shamkhal sent an envoy to Kasım Pasha and affirmed his wish to be an Ottoman ally.[26] He sent another letter in 1574 through the Crimean khan, offering his submission as a vassal of the Ottoman sultan.[27] In response, the sultan accepted his submission and emphasised that the shamkhal's predecessors had also been loyal to the Porte.[28] Although there is no extant document regarding the alliance or submission of a previous shamkhal in the Ottoman archives, a similar correspondence may have taken place. Previously, the Porte entrusted the affairs of the North

Caucasus to the Crimean khan, and the Crimean officials might have handled such symbolic submissions or alliances.[29]

Another important polity with which the Ottomans wanted to establish a form of vassalage was the Nogays. Süleyman I's futile attempts to win over the Nogay hordes have already been mentioned in the previous chapter. The Muscovites appreciated the Nogay power in the Pontic–Caspian steppes and masterfully manipulated the horde in their expansion along the Volga River in the 1550s and 1560s. The Nogays were instrumental in the Muscovite annexation of Kazan and Astrakhan. In 1557, the Nogays split into two hordes – the Lesser Nogays (*Kiçi Nogay/Kazy Ulus*), who migrated to the Kuban region, and the Greater Nogays (*Ulu Nogay*), who remained on the lower Volga. While the Lesser Nogays entered the orbit of the Ottoman imperial system through the Crimean khan and the governor of Azak, the Greater Nogay rulers remained as Muscovite clients. The migration of the Lesser Nogay Horde to the North Caucasus was challenging for the local people. As newcomers to the region, they occasioned problems around Azak and in the Kuban region, harassing Ottoman subjects, including Circassians, or illegally extracting money from merchants and pilgrims.[30] In the end, the Porte and the Crimean khan managed to control them and eventually put them to use for the defence of Ottoman possessions against Cossack or Circassian raids. The Nogays were patently good mounted warriors in the steppes and the rough terrain of the North Caucasus. They provided both the Porte and the Crimean Khanate with an effective proxy force in the region. For example, when certain Circassian tribes fled from the Taman area because of Ottoman taxation, the Porte instructed the governor-general of Kefe and governor of Azak to employ the Nogays in the region to return the fleeing Circassians to back their lands.[31] In 1575, the governor of Azak, acting as the Porte's primary agent for Nogay affairs, advised Istanbul that 'there are several *palankas* [redoubts] along the Don River. Should they get repaired and given to the Nogays, it will prevent the Cossacks from descending along the river.' According to his letter, Azak was no longer dependent on Kefe for grain because the Nogays were now farming together with the local Ottoman subjects.[32] In response, the Porte ordered the governor to proceed with his already successful plans and stay on good terms with the Nogay chiefs.[33] Thus, the Lesser Nogays cooperated with the Ottoman Porte in the North Caucasus, serving Ottoman ambitions in the region.

In 1574, the Ottoman Porte received news that Urus Mirza of the Greater Nogay Horde wished to submit to the sultan. Urus Mirza was a son of İsmail Mirza, who exchanged letters with Süleyman I but eventually became a fervent supporter of the Muscovite interests in the Volga region. Like his father, Urus Mirza was a client of Muscovy and received annual payments from the tsar. Historians think that he approached the Porte in 1574 because he was dissatisfied with the amount of the annuities and concerned about Muscovite policies restricting the mobility of the Greater Nogays.[34] The Porte immediately referred this issue to the governor of Azak. The governor was to consult with the Crimean khan about Urus Mirza's submission and act accordingly.[35] Even before 1574, the Muscovites knew that Urus Mirza hoped to reduce the Greater Nogays' dependency on Muscovy by establishing a mutually beneficial relationship with the Ottoman sultan. Simon Maltsev, who in 1568 was sent to Urus Mirza as the tsar's envoy, writes in his report that during the Astrakhan campaign in 1569, Urus Mirza visited Ottoman commander Kasım Pasha and pledged his submission to the Ottoman sultan, but not to the Crimean khan, 'with whom he had a feud'.[36]

The submission of the Greater Nogay Horde would be a great boon to the objectives of the Porte in the North Caucasus. However, more important than that, and perhaps indispensable, was the Crimean khan as an Ottoman vassal. The Crimean khan's status in the Pontic–Caspian steppes was undoubtedly more valuable to the Porte than the submission of the Greater Nogays. Thanks to the Chinggisid origins of the Girey Dynasty and their military capabilities, the Crimean Khanate's role and function in the north could not be entirely replaced by the centrally appointed governors of the Porte in the region. Additionally, the Porte knew that establishing direct diplomacy without involving the Crimean khan could have caused concern among the Crimean nobility, whose loyalty was crucial for the Ottoman manipulation of Crimean politics.

During this time, the Ottomans kept a keen eye on the vexatious Muscovite activities in the North Caucasus, especially in Kabarda. The Porte was aware that the Muscovites were strengthening and repairing their fortifications along the Terek River as early as December 1575.[37] Besides their interest in the Muscovite operations engineered in Astrakhan, the Ottomans worked to establish a line of defence against the Cossacks along the Don River and other possible threats from the north, just as the Muscovites had been establishing defences in their southern frontier zones against the Tatar raids. The only difference was that, most of the time, the Ottoman plans and projects remained on paper and failed to materialise.

In the 1560s and 1570s, Cossack raids became extremely problematic for the Ottoman possessions in the north of the Black Sea. To protect the frequently targeted Ottoman towns and better control the Nogays and other tribal elements to the north of Azak, the Porte intensified its efforts to build fortifications. There were proposals to construct fortresses along the Don River, in the lands under the sovereignty of the Crimean khan. The Crimean khan and governor of Azak received several orders in 1576 and 1577 about plans for fortresses along the river.[38] As stated above, the governor of Azak proposed several redoubt-style fortifications on the banks of the Don so that the Nogays could camp in them and patrol this vital river route in both the winter and summer seasons. The governor thought that this would force the Cossacks to abandon the Don River, as the Nogays would prevent their raids on Azak or other Ottoman/Crimean settlements.[39] In 1576, the Porte instructed the Crimean khan to oversee the repairs to the Azak Fortress and the construction of redoubts, as proposed by the governor of Azak.[40] In 1577, only a year before the Ottoman–Safavid War started, the Crimean khan received word that the sultan intended to construct a fortress on the Don in 'an area that was under the khan's jurisdiction'. The khan was to send men to this particular place and submit a report on the feasibility of constructing a fortress and necessary preparations for it. The sultan also asked his opinion on what kind of material, such as stone or timber, would be better for a fortress in this location.[41] However, these plans also foundered. In the second half of the sixteenth century, Crimean khans often objected to the proposals of fortresses along the Don River or anywhere else under their jurisdiction since they were concerned about increasing Ottoman interference in their affairs.

Such was the general situation in and around the North Caucasus before the Ottoman–Safavid War broke out.[42] The Ottomans used diplomacy effectively and commenced a process of establishing a sphere of influence in the North Caucasus by creating more vassals to turn the region into an Ottoman-controlled borderland whence they would launch further military incursions towards the Caspian Sea and beyond. The palpable difference in the number of documents before and after 1569 in the Ottoman archives concerning the North Caucasus is proof of the modified and more active Ottoman strategies designed to realise the aforementioned objectives.

When the Ottoman–Safavid War began in 1578, the Porte's attempts at securing the North Caucasus region by winning over local rulers as clients accelerated. In February 1578, as soon as the Ottoman Imperial Council approved the campaign against the Safavids, the commander of the Ottoman army, Lala Mustafa Pasha, sent letters from Istanbul to the local rulers in the North and South Caucasus. Among those recipients who were asked to join the Ottoman army and serve Sultan Murad III (r. 1574–95) in the campaign were Daghestani Shamkhal Emir Mirza, Gazi Salih of Tabarasan and Tuchalav Mirza of the Avars.[43] It was only natural for the shamkhal to side with the Ottomans in 1578 because, in previous years, he had militarily supported the Sunni rulers of Shirvan against the Safavids but ended up being defeated by the Safavid armies.[44]

Besides Lala Mustafa Pasha, the Ottoman sultan also sent letters and robes of honour (*hil'at*) in May 1578 to the local rulers in Daghestan. The language used in these documents reveals that the most prominent ruler in Daghestan from the Ottoman viewpoint was the shamkhal. The phrase *cenab-ı emaret meab*, used by the Porte for important and relatively independent rulers, was added to the title of the shamkhal by the Ottoman chancellery between 1578 and 1605. Both sets of letters stated that the Ottoman army, under the command of Lala Mustafa Pasha, and the Crimean Tatar army, led by Prince Adil Girey, a brother of the Crimean khan, were marching towards the Caucasus. The Daghestani rulers were instructed to assist these armies and muster their soldiers to participate in the campaign against the Safavid Empire. The Ottoman sultan told them that they could either join the forces of Adil Girey on the North Caucasus route or merge with the main Ottoman army in the South Caucasus. The Ottoman Porte sent the same order to the *nusal* of the Avars (*Avar hakimi Nusal*), the *usmi* of the Kaytaks (*Kaytak hakimi Usmi*), the *tüki* of Tuman (Tümen, *Tuman hakimi Tüki*), the *timas* of Burgun (Balkar, *Burgun hakimi Timas*), the *ma'sum* of Tabarasan (*Tabarasan hakimi ma'sum*), and Gazi Bey of Tabarasan (*Tabarasan hakimi Gazi*).[45]

These letters from the Porte proved effective, and the Daghestani rulers offered their allegiance to the sultan. In July 1578, when Lala Mustafa Pasha camped in Çermik (in modern-day Sivas) with his army, the shamkhal's envoy, Hüseyin, arrived with a letter of submission addressed to Sultan Murad III. Moreover, the shamkhal promised 30,000 men for the campaign.[46] During the Ottoman–Safavid War, the Porte orchestrated serious efforts to turn the shamkhalate in Daghestan into a proper Ottoman vassal. Perhaps for this reason, the Ottoman historian Gelibolulu Mustafa Ali, who was with Lala Mustafa Pasha in the Caucasus, counts the lands of the shamkhal among the conquests of the Porte.[47] The correspondence between the Daghestani rulers and the Porte continued, and more letters from the sultan with similar content went out to 'the shamkhal of Tarku' and other rulers of Daghestan in the later months of 1578.[48] As stated above, the quantity of these letters and the dearth of them for the earlier Ottoman campaigns in the Caucasus indicates the newly appreciated importance of the North Caucasus for the Ottoman officials.

The Ottoman Porte dispatched orders to Circassian rulers in the North Caucasus as well. By 1578, many Circassian chiefs were clients of the Porte or the Crimean Khanate. Lala Mustafa Pasha's letter to the king of Tbilisi, Davud Khan (r. 1564–78), written in February 1578, illustrates this fact. Mustafa Pasha threatened Davud Khan that he would unleash the Tatars and Circassians upon his kingdom if the king refused to submit to the sultan.[49] Similarly, the rulers of the Georgian kingdoms of Mingrelia (Dadyan) and Goria (Guriel) responded to Mustafa Pasha's invitation letter, stating that they had already submitted to the Porte and were ready to join the pasha's army. They complained, however, about the raids of the Circassians in their lands. In his response, Mustafa Pasha promised that they no longer needed to worry about Circassian assaults, as Mingrelia and Goria were under the protection of the Ottoman sultan.[50] These examples suggest that, by 1578, the Porte had the means of controlling most of the Circassian rulers in the North Caucasus, at least in its western part.

The sultan also sent imperial orders dated May 1578, specifically to the Christian Circassian chiefs in Taman, who were receiving salaries from the Porte.[51] The letters stated that the sultan desired the conquest of Shirvan, and the Crimean Tatar army under the command of Adil Girey was participating in the Ottoman war effort. The Circassian chiefs were asked to join Adil Girey with their men and provide services for the Ottoman troops in their territories.[52] Unfortunately, this document does not mention specific names, but it shows that, in 1578, there were Christian Circassian chiefs in the region, although, as explained above, the process of Islamisation was accelerating among the Western Circassians.

Moreover, the Porte dispatched another order, also dated May 1578, to the Circassian rulers controlling the route between Kefe and Shirvan, across the entire North Caucasus. The sultan informed these chiefs that he wanted 'to conquer Shirvan and ordered the Tatar army under the command of Adil Girey to set out and assist the main Ottoman army'. 'In accordance with their submission to the Sublime Porte', the Ottomans instructed the Circassian chiefs to assist Adil Girey and his soldiers who would pass through their lands. Although the North Caucasus was still theoretically considered under Crimean sovereignty, it was now the Ottoman sultan sending orders about the movement of the Crimean army and demanding local rulers' support and obedience.[53]

Meanwhile, an approximately 100,000-strong Ottoman army setting off from the Eastern Anatolian strongholds of the empire reached the Ottoman–Safavid border in the summer of 1578. The Ottomans conquered Çıldır and Tbilisi following their victory over the Safavids on 9 August 1578. They incorporated these lands into the Ottoman administrative system as the governor-generalships of Çıldır and Tiflis. The Ottoman army then marched towards Shirvan and defeated the Safavid army once again. In September 1578, the entire South Caucasus from Eastern Anatolia to the Caspian Sea was under Ottoman control.[54] The Ottomans immediately formed a governor-generalship in Shirvan. Lala Mustafa Pasha appointed Özdemiroğlu Osman Pasha as its governor-general and commander of the Ottoman army, which would stay in the Caucasus to secure the Ottoman conquests.[55] The forming of administrative districts and obtaining allegiances from local rulers make it clear that the Ottomans intended to stay in the Caucasus.

Due to its peculiar political structures, geography and international conjuncture at the time, integrating the North Caucasus into the Ottoman system was not feasible by establishing centrally governed administrative districts; thus it necessitated the allegiance of its local rulers and turning it into an Ottoman borderland. The Porte understood this well in the 1570s. Therefore, the rewards and privileges granted by the Ottoman sultan to the North Caucasus rulers for their loyalty became substantial. For example, when the shamkhal visited the Ottoman camp in the north of Shirvan on 17 October 1578 to submit to the Porte in person, Lala Mustafa Pasha gave him the province of Şaburan in the newly formed governor-generalship of Shirvan, which was divided into thirteen provinces. Besides, the province of Ahtı in the same governor-generalship was granted to Tuchalav Burhaneddin of the Avars. The Kaytak ruler along with his son also submitted to the Ottoman sultan, as did Tabarasan ruler Gazi Salih.[56] The seventeenth-century Ottoman traveller Evliya Çelebi writes that the Ottomans allocated several important fortresses to the shamkhal and other Daghestani rulers to secure their loyalty, as they realised that without local support, they could not keep these lands.[57] To cement the submission of the shamkhal and other Daghestani rulers, Lala Mustafa Pasha arranged a marriage between Özdemiroğlu Osman Pasha, the newly appointed governor-general of Shirvan, and a niece of the shamkhal. The bride was one of the daughters of Tuchalav Burhaneddin, who was the shamkhal's brother.[58]

The Ottomans recognised that the establishment of a permanent Ottoman presence in the South and North Caucasus required the allegiance of the Daghestani rulers, especially the shamkhal – the strongest one in the region. This makes sense from the viewpoint of the Ottoman method of conquest. As one may remember, the Ottomans preferred to surround the territories they wanted to control with their provinces and vassals. If the shamkhal and other local rulers of Daghestan were to become clients of the sultan, the Porte could establish hegemony over the North Caucasus. In this way, the difficult-to-control Circassian rulers and peoples of the North Caucasus would be encircled by the vassals and provincial administrators of the Porte in the west (the Crimean Khanate), in the east (the shamkhalate) and in the south (the Ottoman province of Shirvan and the

Georgian kingdoms). Moreover, the Ottomans wanted to ensure a permanent control over Derbend. A significant passageway between the North and South Caucasus, Derbend was a heavily fortified city with a strategic position on the Caspian shore. It was a stone fortress located between the principality of Tabarasan and the usmiate of the Kaytaks. Its fortifications in the sixteenth century covered the narrow passage between the Caspian Sea and the Caucasus Mountains.[59]

In January 1579, the Porte sent another letter to the Daghestani shamkhal, asking him to help protect the Ottoman soldiers who were then in Shirvan and other parts of the Caucasus. The sultan advised him to remain loyal and expect more rewards in return.[60] He also sent a robe of honour to the shamkhal, acknowledging him for fulfilling his duties in the war effort.[61] The shamkhal surely served the Ottomans well in the Caucasus. In late November 1578, the Safavids defeated a Crimean Tatar army in Shirvan and captured their commander, Adil Girey.[62] The main Ottoman army was no longer in the Caucasus then. The remaining Ottoman troops in Şemahı, under the command of Özdemiroğlu Osman Pasha, decided to move to Derbend, where defence against the Safavid armies was more likely to succeed thanks to the strong fortifications around the city. The shamkhal was with Osman Pasha in Şemahı, and on the route, he faithfully guided the Ottoman army as far as Derbend, helping them avoid the areas where the Ottoman troops might be attacked by unruly local rulers.[63]

Aside from controlling passage along the coast, Derbend was situated at a location enabling greater control over Daghestan in the hands of a proper army. Osman Pasha used it cleverly both to fortify against the Safavids and to secure Ottoman control over the entire region. He was confident in the loyalty of the Daghestani shamkhal and Tuchalav Burhaneddin of the Avars. As it may be remembered, Osman Pasha was married to Tuchalav's daughter, and Tuchalav and the shamkhal were brothers. Based on the chronicles written by eyewitnesses such as Gelibolulu Mustafa Ali or Asafi Dal Mehmed Çelebi, the shamkhal and most other Daghestani rulers were usually loyal to the Ottoman Porte in these critical years. However, another significant ruler, the *usmi* of the Kaytaks, occasioned a complication for the Ottoman commander in Daghestan, despite his earlier submission. According to Ottoman accounts, his men stole from the Ottoman soldiers who were outside of the fortress of Derbend. The pasha, in response, ordered his soldiers to capture the thieves for punishment. In thc ensuing struggle, some Kaytaks, including a few from the retinue of the *usmi*, lost their lives. Outraged, the *usmi* ordered his men to kill every Ottoman soldier they came across.[64] Osman Pasha's reaction was equally vigorous. The Ottoman troops raided and destroyed Kaytak villages. This incident provided an opportunity for the Ottoman commander to subdue the Kaytaks and other rebellious tribes in Daghestan.[65] During this period of the war, the Porte and the commanders in the field worked in harmony. The orders sent from the Porte after this incident indicate that the *usmi* of Kaytaks fell from the sultan's grace. Although the Porte continued to send letters and gifts to the rulers in Daghestan, the *usmi* received none until April 1582, when the Porte asked him to assist Ottoman soldiers going from Kefe to Derbend. Reminding him of his submission, the sultan ordered him to let the Ottoman troops pass through his land and perform services as required by their commanders.[66] The Porte sent a similar order regarding the Ottoman soldiers to the shamkhal and several other local rulers in the region.[67]

In the 1580s, the Ottomans dispatched many orders and letters to the Daghestani rulers regarding the safety of the Ottoman North Caucasus route, through which soldiers, officials and money travelled from Kefe to Derbend.[68] This supply route was of extreme importance for the war effort and Ottoman ambitions in the region. According to the contemporary Ottoman sources, travel from Kefe to Derbend took eighty days in total. Ottoman chroniclers Gelibolulu Mustafa Ali and İbrahim Peçevi provide a detailed itinerary of Ottoman troops led by Cafer Pasha with eighty-six loads (*yük*) of treasury from Kefe to Derbend in 1582. Cafer Pasha's army, consisting of timariots from Köstendil, Silistre and Niğbolu, 3,000 janissaries, and an entire division of *silahdars* (weapon masters), took four days to travel from Kefe to Kerç. Then, they crossed the straits of Kerç with galleys and other ships in fifteen days, arriving at the fortress of Temrük in the Taman Peninsula after four more days. They rested in Temrük for four days and then set off for the Kuban River, reaching it in five days. Circassians living in the vicinity prepared rafts on the Kuban somewhere near its confluence with the Laba River. The Ottoman troops used these rafts to cross the river and paid five *akçe* per horse and fifteen *akçe* per cart to the Circassians. They followed the river for four days before arriving in the lands of the Kemirgoys and then the steppes (*heyhat sahrası*, 'the desert of regrets', in the chronicles). The Ottoman soldiers travelled through the steppes for twenty days following the Kuban and Urup rivers. It took five days to reach Beshtau from the Urup River. From Beshtau, they travelled for another five days to the Terek River. Then, the Ottoman army moved to Kabarda. Kabardinian chiefs there constructed eight portable bridges on the Terek and Sulak rivers to assist the Ottomans to cross the river.[69] It took three days to cross the two rivers and get to the lands of the shamkhal. In November 1582, and on the eightieth day of their travel, Cafer Pasha and his soldiers reached Derbend.[70]

Figure 4.1 Osman Pasha and Ottoman troops in Derbend, 1578.

Source: Asafi Dal Mehmed Çelebi, *Şeca'atname*, Istanbul University Library, TY6043.

Figure 4.2 Ottoman troops attack the Kaytaks in Daghestan.

Source: Asafi Dal Mehmed Çelebi, *Şeca'atname*, Istanbul University Library, TY6043.

However, the intensification of Ottoman activities in Daghestan, the establishment of centrally administered provinces, and the Crimean Tatar presence in the Caucasus caused distress among the Daghestani rulers. Ottoman chronicles argue that this new reality prompted the Daghestani rulers and Georgians, who were afraid of losing their independence, to send an envoy to İmam Kulı Khan of the Safavids. They knew that their military capabilities were insufficient to challenge the Ottomans and the Crimean Tatars on their own. And they were particularly concerned about the Crimean Tatar troops. The local rulers argued, 'Since nothing has been done against them [the Crimean Tatars], their number keeps increasing. If they are not put to the sword soon, they will harm us. The lands, which have been in our possession for so many years, will be lost.'[71] İmam Kulı Khan reported the alliance of these local rulers against the Crimeans and Ottomans to the Safavid shah and prepared for an offensive against the Ottomans, possibly hoping to get support from the Daghestani rulers. He did receive support, but only from some Georgian nobles. Despite their grievances and perhaps due to the fear of retribution, the Daghestani rulers decided against assisting the Safavids. The Ottomans defeated the Safavid army led by İmam Kulı in May 1583 at the infamous Battle of the Torches, during which both armies fought for three days, even at night using their torches. The Ottoman commanders ordered the execution of the captured Georgian nobles, whose heads were sent to the Georgian king, Alexander II of Kakheti, as a warning. The Daghestani rulers, who remained neutral and thus escaped the wrath of the Ottomans, had no choice but to continue serving the sultan for the time being.[72]

By 1583, the Ottomans were militarily victorious against the Safavids and consolidated their territorial gains in the Caucasus, including Shirvan and Derbend. They subdued the rebellious tribes and polities in Daghestan, thanks to the efforts of Özdemiroğlu Osman Pasha, who also employed people from the North Caucasus in his retinue. His policies in Daghestan and in other parts of the North Caucasus show that he understood the intricacies of the region well and strengthened Ottoman dominance there in a relatively short time. Following the arrival of Cafer Pasha in Daghestan and the defeat of İmam Kulı's army, the sultan ordered Özdemiroğlu Osman Pasha to travel to Istanbul via Kefe in October 1583 and to leave Cafer Pasha in Derbend.[73] The Porte also sent him 100 robes of honour for distribution among the Circassian and Daghestani rulers in the North Caucasus as a reward for their services. According to the Porte's letter dispatched in September 1583, Ferhad Kethüda, who was bringing money to Derbend, was to give twenty-one of these robes to the rulers on his route from Kefe to Derbend and the pasha would decide to whom to give the remaining seventy-nine.[74]

The Ottomans intensified their policy of subduing local chiefs and cementing their allegiance to the Porte in the western and Kabardinian parts of the North Caucasus as well. Himself being of Kabardinian origin, Özdemiroğlu Osman Pasha appreciated the strategic position of Kabarda,[75] which was vital for the Ottoman supply route in the North Caucasus and the future of Ottoman designs in the region. In fact, as soon as he established his headquarters in Derbend in November 1580, Osman Pasha proposed to the Porte that two fortresses ought to be erected in the North Caucasus – one on the Terek River and one on the Kuban, securing the supply route from Kefe to Derbend and reinforcing the Ottoman presence in Kabarda. Osman Pasha further recommended Behram Bey, who was a Circassian noble in his service, for the construction of the proposed fortresses.[76] However, this project, along with many others proposing fortress construction, was opposed by the Crimean khan and eventually abandoned.[77]

To secure the Ottoman supply route going through Kabarda, the Ottomans used diplomacy and rewards.[78] One of the most trusted Kabardinian chiefs for the Porte in these years was a local ruler whom the Ottomans called the governor of Kabarda (*Kabartay sancağı beyi*). The said governor of Kabarda was most probably Mehmed Bey, who travelled to Istanbul before the Ottoman–Safavid War and received the title of *sancakbeyi*. There are also several Ottoman documents from the same period using the designation '*Kabartay Bey*' or '*Kabartay Mirza*' without providing a specific name.[79] Beside these, some other Kabardinian chiefs were firmly on the Ottoman side. Among them, Aslanbek was a relative of Özdemiroğlu Osman Pasha through the latter's paternal side.[80] He was an influential chief in Kabarda and, at one point, became the pshihua. As one may remember, Aslanbek was an ally of the Crimeans and Ottomans from the 1560s and was one of the main rivals of Temriuk. He and his brother, Yansokh, received orders from the Porte in the 1580s about the security of the Ottoman route and providing services for the Ottoman army that passed through Kabarda.[81] We also know from contemporary Ottoman chronicles that he was one of the Kabardinian chiefs who constructed bridges on the Terek River for the Ottoman armies and guided them through Kabarda.[82] Although the Muscovites distinguished him as an important figure in Kabardinian politics, the Ottoman documents mention him as merely a regular local ruler along with several others. Clearly, the Muscovite officials corresponding with local chiefs in Kabarda had a better understanding of Kabardinian politics than the Ottoman officials at the Porte did. Özdemiroğlu Osman Pasha in the Caucasus was an exception to this.

Gazi Mirza (Kazy Murza in Muscovite sources), most likely a son of Psheapshoko, was another prominent figure on the Ottoman side. He, too, received several orders from the Porte about the safety of the supply route and constructed bridges for the Ottoman army along with Aslanbek and Kaplan.[83] Moreover, a certain Mehmed Bey of Kabarda submitted to the sultan and was invited to Istanbul on 21 January 1583.[84] He could not possibly be the same Mehmed mentioned above because the latter had already submitted and been to Istanbul in the 1570s. In September 1583, Ferhad Kethüda was traveling to Derbend from Kefe with another load of treasury. To secure his route, the Porte sent orders to the Kabardinian chiefs, Solokh, Beşir (Betsin, Başıl), Abak (Ibak in Muscovite sources), Bozok (Buzuruk in Muscovite sources), Aslanbek and Yansokh. Receiving robes of honour, they were asked to assist Ferhad Kethüda and his men. Among these chiefs, Solokh was a leading figure in Kabardinian politics. One of his daughters was married to the Crimean khan and another to the shamkhal of Daghestan. Both Muscovite and Ottoman sources confirm that he and his close ally Alkas were Muslims and sided with the Ottomans in Kabarda.[85]

As one may remember, this active Ottoman policy of subduing local rulers in Kabarda started following the Astrakhan campaign of 1569 and the Crimean raids to punish the pro-Muscovite Kabardinian chiefs in 1570. In less than a decade, the Porte managed to draw a significant number of Kabardinian chiefs to its side. The Porte's efforts intensified during the Ottoman–Safavid War, because of the Ottoman supply route in the North Caucasus. Although the Porte found support for its imperial claims among local rulers in Kabarda, establishing a defined suzerainty over Kabarda was still unattainable. There was still a robust pro-Muscovite faction kept alive by the descendants of Temriuk. These chiefs, supported by the Muscovites, were in conflict with the Kabardinian chiefs who sided with the Ottomans.

The Western Circassians, including the Janeys and Besleneys, were subject to a higher degree of Ottoman control. The Ottoman cities of Kefe and Azak housed a large number of Ottoman troops for the war in the Caucasus. Moreover, the Muscovite clients who plagued these lands for the Ottomans in the 1550s were no longer an issue. Most of the local rulers were vassals of the Ottoman Porte and received orders from the sultan during the Ottoman–Safavid War. Some Circassian chiefs in the Taman region were directly attached to Kefe, receiving salaries from its revenues and fulfilling assigned duties, such as protecting and helping with the defences of Ottoman possessions in the north. Compared with the orders dispatched to the Kabardinian and Daghestani rulers, the number of orders sent to the Western Circassian chiefs is limited. The governor-general of Kefe and the governor of Azak often communicated directly with them and arranged for the execution of services required of them.

The majority of the orders dispatched by the Porte during the war to the local rulers in the Taman and Beshtau regions were about the security of the supply route.[86] For example, in August 1581, the sultan sent orders to the local rulers in the region to ensure the safe passage of miners sent to Derbend. These miners were going to work in Shirvan, where silver mines were abundant. Among the chieftains who received the order were Mehmed who was addressed as the ruler of the Taman Peninsula (*Ada beyi*), another Mehmed who was the chief of the Janeys, as well as the chief of the Kemirgoys and the ruler of the Besleneys; the last two local rulers were Christians as we understand from their titles.[87] In September 1583, the Porte instructed the Ottoman administrators in Kefe to pay the annuities of the Circassian chiefs who were on the payroll of the city, in full and on time.[88] Payments and annuities certainly encouraged their loyalty and services, which the Porte desperately needed at this time. In the same year, Janey chiefs Ahmed and Davud, Taman chief Mehmed, Soğucak chiefs Kastok, Dutahferuk, Berduk and Kirkan, Besleney chief Mehmed, and Kemirgoy chief Kansutrak also received orders and robes of honour from the Porte regarding Fuad Kethüda's journey to Derbend with treasury.[89]

The names of the local rulers mentioned in the extant Ottoman documentation point out another process that was taking place in the North Caucasus, namely, the Islamisation of the native population. The tighter Ottoman control coupled with a noticeable lack of Crimean raids must have contributed to the process in the last two decades of the sixteenth century, especially among the Western Circassians. To illustrate, we understand from his name in the sultan's letters sent to him that the Besleney chieftain converted sometime between 1581 and 1583. As shown above, while he was addressed as a Christian ruler in 1581, two years later his name was Mehmed. Similarly, another Circassian chief, Bolayıkoğlu of the Sozomuko tribe in the Kuban area, who was a Christian, as we understand from his titles, desired to become Muslim. The Porte wrote to him that he ought to come to Istanbul to be rewarded. Undoubtedly, converting to Islam could mean potential gains for local chiefs under Ottoman rule. Their salaries and privileges could increase or they could tax their subjects under Ottoman regulations. For example, the aforementioned Bolayıkoğlu requested from the Porte the right to collect taxes (*haraç*) from his subjects, and the Porte approved it.[90] However, the process was still limited in scope. Several non-Muslim – probably Christian – Circassian chiefs, living around Soğucak, a fortress attached to Kefe on the Black Sea shore close to today's Novorossiisk, were also Ottoman clients and recipients of annuities.[91] Besides, the Kemirgoy chief at this time was not Muslim, as we understand from his name and titles. Regardless of their religious orientations, all loyal chieftains were granted salaries and some titles from the Ottoman Porte.[92] Therefore, the western part of the North Caucasus was under firm Ottoman control, and no imperial power other than the Porte could encroach on this region after 1570. The Porte erected fortresses there for its Circassian vassals who sometimes needed protection from their enemies, especially the Cossacks. One of these Circassian chiefs, Mehmed, received in October 1593 his first yearly salary of 120,000 *akçe*, a handsome amount in the sixteenth century, for defending Ottoman possessions and his subjects from the raids of the Cossacks.[93] A month later, the Porte ordered the repair of the Boğazcık Fortress for his use.[94]

It is important to note that although the Ottomans carried out an energetic policy of drawing local rulers in the North Caucasus to their side and often communicated directly with them, they still respected the Crimean Khanate's authority over the Circassian tribes and polities. The Ottoman officials were aware that they still needed the Crimean khan's collaboration in the North Caucasus and in the Pontic–Caspian steppes due to his highly effective army and experience in the affairs of these regions. For example, it was Crimean Khan Gazi Girey II who advised the Porte about the services of the aforementioned Circassian chief Mehmed. In his letter to the sultan, the khan praised Mehmed for his help in the defence of Temrük against the Cossacks.[95]

The Nogays constituted another critical piece of the North Caucasus puzzle during the Ottoman–Safavid War. The Lesser Nogays allied with the Crimean Tatars and Ottomans participated in the Crimean military operations in the Caucasus. The Porte was content as long as the Lesser Nogays obeyed the Crimean khan and the governor of Azak. However, the Ottomans were not able to exert any control over the Greater Nogays. Regardless, their ruler, Urus Beg, joined the Crimean army in 1578 to fight in the Caucasus against the Safavids. As a reward, the sultan granted him a *sancak* (a province), that is, the revenues from it. Besides, the Porte ordered the governor of Azak to give annuities to the nobility of the Greater Nogays from the custom revenues of Azak in 1579 because 'these mirzas would bring ten thousand soldiers to fight against the Safavids'.[96] It is remarkable that during the war in the Caucasus, the Ottoman Porte was using tactics similar to those of Muscovy, including sending gifts and granting annuities to multiple Greater Nogay chieftains. Urus Beg, the ruler of the Greater Nogays, was simultaneously receiving salary and gifts from the Muscovite tsar, while often complaining, according to the Muscovite sources, that the amount he received from Muscovy was meagre. This could explain why, at least for the time being, he approached the Crimean khan and Ottoman sultan in 1578, besides taking advantage of the war against the Safavids and partaking in the opportunity to gain booty and slaves. From 1578 to 1584, the Greater Nogay troops took part in many battles and economically benefited from their participation, while the Porte found in them an effective military support.

This symbiotic relationship with the Greater Nogays changed in 1584 when İslam Girey (r. 1584–8) replaced Mehmed Girey II as the new Crimean khan with the assistance of the Ottomans, which resulted in the Nogays turning against the Porte. Mehmed Girey II's sons, Saadet, Sefa and Murad, fled Crimea to fight for its throne against the Ottoman-supported İslam Girey. Murad Girey went to Moscow, which will be examined below. Saadet Girey was married to a Nogay princess, and for this reason, he took refuge with the Nogays, intending to take Crimea with an army composed of Nogays and his loyal Tatars. The alliance of the Greater Nogays with the fugitive prince caused serious concern in Istanbul. The Porte sent letters to Mirza Yahşi Saat and other Nogay chiefs in 1585 about the Crimean princes, asking them to assist Khan İslam Girey in case the princes decided to attack the Crimean capital.[97] The Porte also dispatched a similar order to the Janey chief in the Taman region because some Circassian warriors were known to have joined Saadet Girey. Despite the Porte's efforts, the Nogays collaborated with Saadet Girey and attacked the khanate, only to be defeated by the Ottoman forces at Kefe. However, thanks to the ongoing war with the Safavids, the Porte opted to use diplomacy to secure the Nogays' cooperation. The sultan sent another letter upon the advice of Khan İslam Girey to the same Mirza Yahşi Saat, along with a robe of honour. Praising him for his services, the sultan reminded him of his submission to the Crimean khan and asked him to obey the orders of İslam Girey.[98]

4.3 Muscovite Attempts to Contain Ottoman Activities in the North Caucasus

The exasperating Ottoman presence and possible near hegemony in the North Caucasus had the potential to reverse the Muscovite annexation of Astrakhan or draw the Greater Nogays to the Porte, creating severe security problems for the Tsardom of Muscovy. Yet Muscovy was still in no position to challenge the Ottoman Empire. Faced with this dilemma, Ivan IV and his officials played it safe. With the help of the Cossacks and by sending Muscovite *strel'tsy* to Kabarda only in winter, when the Ottoman troops avoided travel, the Muscovites managed to support and protect their vassals in the region from the pro-Ottoman/Crimean rulers, who, by that time, included some prominent Kabardinian chiefs. They also waged an indirect war against the Ottomans and Crimean Tatars through the Cossacks, who attacked the Ottoman supply lines that passed through Kabarda and the Terek River.

By the early 1580s, the Ottoman war effort bore fruit in the Caucasus against the Safavid Empire. The Ottomans consolidated their territorial gains in the region, including Shirvan and Derbend. They expanded their control to parts of Daghestan, subduing rebellious tribes and polities after taking Derbend. As the Porte expected, their control over Daghestan facilitated a more tangible Ottoman sphere of influence in the North Caucasus. In 1583, however, the Crimean Khanate became embroiled in a violent succession crisis, ascribed to the Ottoman plan to depose Khan Mehmed Girey II and replace him with the more obedient İslam Girey. The Ottoman sultan ordered Özdemiroğlu Osman Pasha, one of the most celebrated commanders of the Porte at the time, to assist İslam Girey in his bid for the Crimean throne. In 1583, Osman Pasha departed with his army from Derbend to Kefe via the North Caucasus route. While the pasha and his army were in Kabarda, thousands of Cossacks lying in ambush attacked them in an area that would later be known as 'The Ottoman Road' in local languages and in Muscovite sources (*Osmanovskii shliakh*).[99] The Cossacks surprised the Ottomans with musket fire near the confluence of the Sunzha and Terek rivers as the Ottoman troops were crossing the Sunzha. The battle between the Ottomans and the Cossacks continued for days, at the end of which the Cossacks fled, but only after inflicting serious harm on the Ottoman soldiers. The contemporary Ottoman sources write that they lost many men, including several high-ranking officers, and much materiel during this encounter.[100] While this was not the first instance of a Cossack attack, it was perhaps the most daring and blatant one since they targeted a famous Ottoman general. In fact, before this incident, two officers (*çavuş*) from the Porte, who were on their way to relay an order to Osman Pasha in Derbend, were captured by the same Cossacks along the Terek River. The Ottoman sultan had to send a letter to the Muscovite tsar for the safe return of these two Ottoman officials.[101] As would be the usual pattern in the sixteenth and seventeenth centuries, the Muscovite tsar renounced any connection with the activities of 'those fugitive and lawless Cossacks' operating along the Terek

River and ensured the Ottoman sultan of his desire to pursue peaceful and brotherly relations with the Porte.[102]

At the end of this saga, the Ottoman Porte succeeded in installing İslam Girey as the khan in Crimea with the help of Özdemiroğlu Osman Pasha. However, the new khan not only failed to end the Crimean succession crisis but also turned it into a very complex international quandary. As mentioned above, Mehmed Girey II's sons, Sefa, Saadet and Murad, fled the Crimean Khanate upon the accession of İslam Girey.[103] The presence of fugitive Crimean princes in the North Caucasus and one in the hands of Muscovy jeopardised the position of the new Crimean khan and the Ottoman control over the Crimean Khanate. A Crimean prince in Moscow supported by the Nogays, who once again turned against the Porte and allied with Muscovy, put the Muscovite tsar in the Ottoman sultan's cross-hairs. For the Muscovite tsar, by contrast, this offered an opportunity to pursue a sophisticated policy of establishing a broader sphere of influence in the North Caucasus, this time including Daghestan, by using Murad Girey's persona of Chinggisid and Crimean royalty.

Aside from this, the Muscovites still needed to explain the attack on Özdemiroğlu Osman Pasha's forces near the Terek River. For this reason, Tsar Feodor I (r. 1584–98) sent his envoy Boris Blagovo to the Porte in late 1584, officially to inform the sultan of the new tsar's ascension to the Muscovite throne after his father's death.[104] When the envoy arrived in Kefe, the Ottoman officials informed him that he would meet the new grand vizier, Özdemiroğlu Osman Pasha, in Kastamonu, where he was gathering troops for another campaign in the Caucasus against the Safavids. Despite Blagovo's protests, saying that he was sent to the sultan and had no business with the grand vizier, he obliged and travelled to Kastamonu in March 1585.[105] Upon his arrival, Osman Pasha questioned the envoy about the Cossack ambush in the North Caucasus, through which he had fought his way in 1583. Following the instructions given to him in Moscow, Blagovo delivered a clever answer. He said that Tsar Ivan IV built a fortress on the Terek River at the request of his father-in-law, Kabardinian Prince Temriuk, and sent a governor there to establish order, referring to the fortress built in 1567. When Sultan Selim II asked the tsar to demolish the fortress, the tsar ordered it to be razed 'out of his love and friendship with the sultan'. Blagovo claimed that lawless Cossacks then began to inhabit the lands around the Terek River, taking advantage of the lack of order caused by the demolition of the Muscovite fortress.[106] With this answer, the Muscovites were under-handedly blaming the Ottomans for the activities of the Cossacks in the North Caucasus. Osman Pasha, however, was not convinced that the

Cossacks acted independently of the tsar or the governor of Astrakhan. He responded to the envoy that due to the Cossack aggression, the sultan had considered conquering Astrakhan, tacitly threatening the Muscovites. He further claimed that conquest of the city could be quickly accomplished, but the sultan decided against it thanks to the peaceful relations between him and the tsar. The pasha further stressed that if the Terek and Don Cossacks continued their attacks on the Ottomans in the North Caucasus, the sultan was likely to order him to take Astrakhan with the help of the Crimean Tatars and Nogays.[107] Blagovo repeated that the tsar had no control over the Cossacks. He also stated that in addition to a massive number of troops stationed in Astrakhan, the city's fortifications were recently strengthened for its defence.[108]

Despite his veiled threat, Özdemiroğlu Osman Pasha's rapport with the envoy was accommodating, especially when they came to discuss the Crimean Khanate. Osman Pasha mentioned several times that the sultan ordered the Crimean khan not to raid Muscovy, as he wanted to be at peace with the tsar.[109] He might have said this to prevent a rapprochement between the tsar and the Safavid shah, which was a possibility at this time and a major topic of discussion between the envoy and the grand vizier. Osman Pasha also enquired about Muscovite relations with the Khanate of Bukhara. Blagovo responded that the tsar had diplomatic relations with the khanate. The pasha's line of enquiry about Bukhara is indicative of the Porte's consideration of the Central Asian khanates in the calculations over the Caucasus and the Caspian Sea. The Muscovite envoy then went to Istanbul and was received by the sultan in May 1585. During his stay at the Porte, he was questioned several more times about the Cossack attacks on the Ottoman officials using the North Caucasus route and Muscovy's ambitions in the region.

Meanwhile, a Chinggisid Crimean prince fighting for the throne and supported by Muscovy created mixed feelings in the North Caucasus that affected the Ottoman strategies and plans in the region. When Boris Blagovo was in Istanbul, Mesih Pasha asked him if he knew where the fugitive Crimean princes were. Blagovo, in response, said that he only learned about the princes, including one of them taking refuge in Astrakhan, when he was in Kefe en route to the Ottoman capital.[110] After concluding his embassy, Blagovo was given a letter dated May 1585 from Sultan Murad III to Tsar Feodor I, in which the sultan asked the tsar to send Crimean Prince Murad Girey to Istanbul.[111] This letter or the veiled Ottoman threats of taking Astrakhan, however, did not yield the desired results for the Porte, and Muscovite activities centred on the Crimean prince continued unabated.

Moreover, defending the North Caucasus supply route against the Cossack or combined Muscovite–Cossack attacks became a concern at the Porte. Cafer Pasha, who was in Derbend in August 1585, received an order instructing him to submit a report on the construction of a fortress on the Terek River to secure the route between Kefe and Derbend.[112] The officials at the Porte deliberated about building a fortress in Kabarda, which they calculated to be a five-day ride from Derbend. They took into account possible revenues from trade for its maintenance as well as foodstuffs that would come from the Nogays to feed the troops in their plans for this fortress. The letter also stated that the fortress would be built in the place of a previous one, possibly referring to the Muscovite fortress, as the Ottomans never built a fortress in Kabarda. Although this project failed to materialise, it was enough to alarm the Muscovites. In 1586, the governor of Astrakhan informed the tsar that the Ottomans were planning to construct several fortresses on the Terek River.[113]

In 1586, Tsar Feodor I and Murad Girey received envoys from the Daghestani shamkhal and his son. The shamkhal and his son promised to serve Murad Girey in his struggle for the Crimean throne.[114] In the same year, Murad Girey received the support of some other minor rulers in the region, as well as the Greater Nogays, and even Alexander II of Kakheti.[115] The tsar then sent Murad Girey to Astrakhan so he could organise his new-found allies against the Ottoman–Crimean axis in the Caucasus. The Muscovite officials hoped that Murad Girey's presence would help them establish their long-desired objective of creating a sphere of influence in Daghestan, which had traditionally sided with the Ottomans until 1586. In the first year following Murad Girey's arrival in Astrakhan, the Muscovite strategy woven around the Crimean prince seemed to have borne fruit. The alliance between the Muscovites, Murad Girey and the Daghestani rulers was cemented with the marriage of Murad Girey to a daughter of the shamkhal.[116]

Upon these developments and with the encouragement of the envoys to the Porte from Abdullah Khan of the Uzbeks and the Lesser Nogay Horde in 1587, the Ottoman Imperial Council resolved to organise another campaign to capture Astrakhan.[117] The sultan approved the decision and sent a letter to Urus Beg on 24 September 1587, instructing him to join the Ottoman army that would march on Astrakhan and serve the Porte as per his submission and thereby expect more rewards.[118] Piyale Pasha received an order appointing him as the commander of the Ottoman army for this campaign and asking him collaborate with Urus and the Nogays.[119] Learning some lessons from its foundered undertaking in 1569, the Porte this time sent a special letter to the strongest nobility in the Crimean Khanate, the leader of the Şirin tribe, Ali Bey. The Şirin tribe had supported the Porte since the time of Mengli Girey, the first Crimean khan installed by the Ottomans, and was very instrumental in the establishment of the Ottoman protectorate over the khanate. The sultan reminded Ali Bey that the reason for the failure in 1569 was 'because the aforementioned khan [Devlet Girey] had objections to the conquest of Astrakhan, he did not guide the army of Islam [the Ottoman–Crimean army] on the right route but instead led them through difficult roads'. The sultan ordered Ali Bey to serve him in this campaign along with Khan İslam Girey, who would also join the Ottoman army to 'serve faithfully'.[120] From the Ottoman perspective, the capture of Astrakhan could help safeguard their position and possessions in the North Caucasus while containing the Crimean Khanate and putting an end to the Muscovite ambitions in the region, especially their support of Murad Girey. However, because of the ongoing war effort against the Safavids in the South Caucasus as well as other pressing domestic and international issues, the Porte shelved the proposed campaign for Astrakhan once more.

Eventually, something other than Ottoman military prowess brought an end to the alliance spearheaded by the Muscovite tsar and Murad Girey. In 1588, Crimean Khan İslam Girey died. His successor, Khan Gazi Girey II (r. 1588–96), was accepted as a legitimate khan by the fugitive Crimean princes, and the new khan sought to reconcile with them by issuing an amnesty and appointing one of them, Sefa Girey, as the *nureddin* (second-in-line of succession to the Crimean throne).[121] Following this development, Murad Girey wrote a letter to the new Crimean khan, asking for an official pardon. Gazi Girey II relayed Murad Girey's request to the sultan and said that Murad was willing to submit to the Ottoman Porte.[122] The sultan, in response, recognised his submission and instructed the khan to convey his decision to the prince.[123] In the end, however, Murad Girey died in 1590 before he could travel back to the Crimea. While the Muscovite chroniclers and documents state that 'Tatar and Nogay sorcerers' murdered him, he was most probably poisoned by the Muscovites. The Muscovites were worried about his return to the Crimean Khanate with an intrinsic knowledge of Muscovite objectives and connections in the North Caucasus and beyond.[124]

The rumours of Ottoman fortresses in Kabarda and a new campaign to take Astrakhan combined with more effective Ottoman cooptation strategies in the North Caucasus encouraged the Muscovites to do what they had been doing best in their southern frontier zones – construction of new fortresses in strategic locations where Cossacks and *strel'tsy* could be stationed. In line with this policy, the Muscovites constructed *Terskii gorod*

(Terek Town) in 1588. To avoid the fate of other Muscovite fortresses built in the North Caucasus, this time, the tsar ordered the construction of the fortress at the mouth of the Terek River, a place which was relatively far away from the Ottoman and Crimean operations and their supply route in the North Caucasus. Meanwhile, the walls of Astrakhan were strengthened with stones.[125] Additionally, in 1589, the Muscovites erected the Tsaritsyn Fortress between the Don and Volga rivers, precisely in the same place where the Ottomans tried to dig a canal in 1569.[126] This was obviously a pre-emptive move, in case the Ottomans revived their old plans of digging a canal there. Through the construction of these fortresses, Muscovy created a new line of defence securing the city of Astrakhan. Of these, the Terek Fortress became the main centre of Muscovite operations in the North Caucasus borderland after 1590.[127] Astrakhan retained its importance as the centre for implementing strategies over the steppe frontier zone and for containing the Greater Nogays. The role of Terek for the Muscovites was similar to that of Azak for the Ottomans, while Astrakhan, as a larger city and centre, was comparable to Kefe in terms of imperial strategies in the North Caucasus.[128]

The situation in Kabarda underwent another change in 1588 – the same year as the construction of the Terek Fortress. Mamstriuk and his cousin, Kanbulat's son Kudenek, came to Moscow as envoys from Kabarda. According to the Muscovite records, Mamstriuk and Kudenek represented Kanbulat, the pshihua of Kabarda, as well as all the Kabardinian chiefs and the whole Kabardinian land, which, as pointed out several times in this book, was an exaggeration considering the political structure of Kabarda. They once again petitioned the tsar to take them 'under his royal hand' for protection against the Ottomans and the Crimean Tatars, and for the construction of another fortress on the Terek River. The tsar granted them their wishes, as usual. He also gave Mamstriuk and Kudenek their annuities. Mamstriuk received 50 rubles, sables and a fur coat, while Kudenek received 30 rubles and a fur coat.[129] When they returned, they brought an order from the tsar along with annuities for Kanbulat. The order summarised the duties of Kanbulat and other Kabardinian chiefs towards the Muscovite tsar and his representatives in Terek and Astrakhan.[130]

As the self-proclaimed representatives of the Kabardinian pshihua, all the Kabardinian chiefs and the whole Kabardinian land, Mamstriuk and Kudenek took the pledge (*shert'*) in 1588 in Moscow.[131] This *shert'* offers important clues to the extent of Muscovite influence and ambitions in Kabarda. First, by 1588 the Muscovites had grasped the social hierarchy of the Kabardinians and correctly distinguished between princes (pshis) and mirzas. For example, after the death of his father (Temriuk), Mamstriuk was a pshi, yet Kudenek was only a mirza as his father, Kanbulat, was the pshi of his clan. However, the Muscovite diplomatic language in this text indicates that the Muscovites still ignored—perhaps deliberately—the nature of Kabardinian politics. Although Kanbulat was the pshihua of Kabarda, his title predicated no practical power, and he did not possess the authority to issue orders to other Kabardinian chiefs. For this reason, he had no right to say that the whole Kabardinian land had submitted to the Muscovite tsar. Many Kabardinian rulers were still allies of the Ottoman Porte and Crimean Khanate, as this Muscovite document demonstrates. The Kabardinian chiefs who allied with the Porte and Crimea were also powerful and influential personages in Kabarda. Aslanbek, for example, would become the next pshihua after Kanbulat's death. This particular line of reasoning was not unique to the Muscovite officials; the Ottomans also considered all of Kabarda as being under their sovereignty despite the realities on the ground. As one may remember, the Ottoman Porte appointed a certain Mehmed as 'the governor of Kabarda' in 1573.[132] Therefore, both the Muscovites and the Ottomans saw their status and position in the North Caucasus through their own ideological and imperial lenses, which was a common pattern in the early modern borderlands.

Second, the *shert'* stipulates that the Kabardinians were to assist the governors of Terek and Astrakhan if the Turks or Crimean Tatars attacked 'the sovereign's patrimony of Astrakhan'. Hence, the Muscovites were expecting an Ottoman/Crimean attack on Astrakhan and Terek in these years.[133] The tsar wanted to ensure that the Muscovite troops in the region would receive military support from their vassals in their defence of Terek and Astrakhan. One of the considerations in constructing the fortress of Terek in 1588, around the time when the sultan sent out orders about a campaign for Astrakhan, was that it would be the front line of defence if an Ottoman/Crimean attack on Astrakhan materialised.

The *shert'* also lists military services required from the Kabardinian chiefs. Accordingly, the Kabardinian princes would provide troops for the tsar's armies on the western frontiers of Muscovy if needed. This was not the first time the Muscovy demanded soldiers from its clients and allies in the region. In 1578, Tsar Ivan IV ordered Mamstriuk to send men to fight in Muscovy's war against Poland-Lithuania and Sweden.[134] Muscovy also received military support from the Greater Nogays during those years.[135] Similarly, in July 1589, the Muscovite tsar instructed the governor of Astrakhan to dispatch the Circassian troops to the western front against the Swedes.[136] Letters relaying the same message were also sent to Mamstriuk and Solokh, in which the tsar demanded their services.[137] We also know that Muscovy transported and employed such auxiliary forces, including the Kabardinians, in their military operations in the Baltic Sea region against the Swedish Empire.[138] Such demands by imperial powers were common on all sides. As stated in this chapter, the Ottoman Porte sent numerous orders in 1577–8 to the North Caucasus rulers asking them to join the Ottoman war effort against the Safavid Empire.[139]

Lastly, the Muscovite sphere of influence was more tangible in Lesser Kabarda, the part of Kabarda around the Terek River. The Ottomans, Crimean Tatars and Kumyks (shamkhal) were the main enemies with whom the vassal Kabardinian chiefs were not allowed to communicate. Besides, the document makes it clear that the mountain princes (Avars) and the Tümen principality along the Tümen River in Daghestan were also refusing to cooperate with Muscovy at this time. Despite such restrictions, pro-Muscovite Kabardinian chiefs still communicated with the Ottomans, Crimean Tatars and Daghestanis. Therefore, the Muscovite influence in the North Caucasus, even in Lesser Kabarda, was constrained and shaped by internal political dynamics and institutions such as *adat*. Although he was a staunch Muscovite client, Mamstriuk, for example, allowed an Ottoman officer (*çavuş*) to stay in his village and guided him through Kabarda on his way to Derbend in 1589.[140] While this act of hospitality was a breach of his *shert'* with the Muscovites, it was also a requirement in accordance with Circassian customs. When questioned by the Muscovites, Mamstriuk explained that it was their custom to host and guide any traveller in their lands, regardless of who the guest was.[141] He needed to tread carefully between the requirements of his loyalty to the tsar and the expected norms of behaviour as a Kabardinian prince. To this end, he stalled the Cossacks who wanted to alert the governor of Terek about the Ottoman officer, but claimed in his defence that he allowed the Cossacks to travel, yet it was already too late for the alert to be of any use to the Muscovites.[142]

With Terek Town becoming a stronghold and their sphere of influence in Kabarda still operative, the Muscovites once again opted to employ their own troops to subdue the local rulers who refused to submit to the tsar. The offers of alliances against the Ottoman Empire in the east by the Safavids and in the west by the Habsburgs and the Papacy emboldened Muscovy in the last years of the Ottoman–Safavid War of 1578–90.[143] Furthermore, previous Muscovite military interventions and their successes in Kabarda encouraged the Muscovites to take bolder steps in their quest for hegemony in the North Caucasus borderland, forcing them to overextend their military capabilities. In an imperial order dated August 1588 and addressed to the governor of Terek, Andrei Khvorostinin, the tsar stated that Kanbulat, Mamstriuk, Kudenek and their brothers were on Muscovy's payroll and serving him. Explaining the conditions of the *shert'* that Mamstriuk and Kudenek signed in July 1588, the tsar's letter also listed the Kabardinian chiefs who refused to be 'under the tsar's royal hand'. Khvorostinin was instructed to send *strel'tsy* and Cossacks to subdue these chiefs. The loyal Kabardinian chiefs were to help the governor against Prince Solokh and Prince Tapshiuk, the major pro-Ottoman/Crimean figures in Kabarda.[144]

Such forceful Muscovite strategies and the Ottomans' prioritisation of their military and territorial ambitions in the South Caucasus and Daghestan in the 1580s noticeably changed the balance of power in Kabarda. In February 1589, Prince Solokh, who served the Ottoman Empire and Crimean Khanate and whom the Muscovites designated as an enemy of the tsar, was compelled to send his envoy to Murad Girey and the tsar so that he would be 'taken under the tsar's royal hand and serve him until the end of his life'.[145] Faced with the potential destruction of his lands and people in the hands of Muscovite troops supported by his Kabardinian rivals, Solokh used Murad Girey's presence in Astrakhan as an excuse to approach the tsar to prevent raids on his territory.

While its influence was on the rise, Muscovy was not yet able to control the entirety of Kabarda or alter its domestic politics at will. In July 1589, Kanbulat died at the age of ninety-seven, which brought about internal strife in Kabarda over the election of a new pshihua. Although they were the most dominant external power, at least in Lesser Kabarda, the Muscovites were unable to install their preferred candidate. However, they indirectly assisted their allies, especially Mamstriuk, Kudenek and other sons of Kanbulat, in this domestic power play among the Kabardinian chiefs for the titular position. The chiefs loyal to Muscovy wrote to the tsar, petitioning him for military aid to defeat their rivals in Kabarda by sending *strel'tsy* and Cossacks.[146] Meanwhile, the governor in Terek was making a list of Muscovy's clients and enemies in the region. Accordingly, Mamstriuk, Kudenek and his two brothers, Khotov and Ochekan, were serving the tsar faithfully but the nearby Daghestani rulers still refused to submit.[147]

Notes

1. V. V. Trepavlov, *Istoriia Nogaiskoi Ordy* (Kazan: Kazanskaia nedvizhimost', 2016), 395; S. Kh. Khotko, 'Protivostoianie voenno-politicheskikh koalitsii v Cherkesii: Na osnove soobshchenii Elizara Rzhevskogo (1578 g.)', *Klio* 7 (2019): 77–83; E. N. Kusheva, *Narody Severnogo Kavkaza i ikh sviazi s Rossiei: vtoraia polovina XVI–30-e gody XVII veka* (Moscow: Izdatel'stvo Akademii nauk SSSR, 1958), 257.

2. *Kabardino-russkie otnosheniia v 16–18 vv.*, ed. T. Kh. Kumykov and E. N. Kusheva (Moscow: Izdatel'stvo Akademii nauk SSSR, 1957), vol. 1, doc. 21, 34–5; *Snosheniia Rossii s Kavkazom: Materialy izvlechennye iz Moskovskago glavnago arkhiva Ministerstva inostrannykh diel, 1578–1613 gg.*, ed. S. L. Belokurov (Moscow: Universitetskaia tipografiia, 1889), doc. 2, 8–9.
3. N. A. Smirnov, *Rossiia i Turtsiia v XVI–XVII vv.* (Moscow: Izdatel'stvo Moskovskogo gosudarstvennogo universiteta, 1946), 122; Kusheva, *Narody Severnogo Kavkaza*, 258, 259; Walter Richmond, *The Northwest Caucasus: Past, Present, Future* (Abingdon: Routledge, 2008).
4. MD 23, no. 130.
5. *Kabardino-russkie otnosheniia*, vol. 1, doc. 21, 34–5; *Snosheniia Rossii s Kavkazom*, doc. 2, 8–9.
6. Kusheva, *Narody Severnogo Kavkaza*, 258–9; Paul Bushkovitch, 'Princes Cherkasskii or Circassian Murzas: The Kabardians in the Russian Boyar Elite, 1560–1700', *Cahiers du monde russe* 45 (2004): 15. Prince Boris Kanbulatovich became a boyar in December 1592.
7. Akif Farzaliev, *Yuzhnyi Kavkaz v kontse XVI v.: Osmano-sefevidskoe sopernichestvo* (St Petersburg: Izdatel'stvo Sankt-Peterburgskogo universiteta, 2002), 87–8; Khotko, 'Protivostoianie voenno-politicheskikh koalitsii', 81.
8. *Kabardino-russkie otnosheniia*, vol. 1, doc. 21, 34–5; *Snosheniia Rossii s Kavkazom*, doc. 2, 8–9.
9. *Kabardino-russkie otnosheniia*, vol. 1, doc. 21, 34–5, doc. 25, 46–8; *Snosheniia Rossii s Kavkazom*, doc. 2, 8–9.
10. *Kabardino-russkie otnosheniia*, vol. 1, doc. 25, 46–8; Kusheva, *Narody Severnogo Kavkaza*, 259.
11. RGADA, F. 89, *Turetskie dela*, kniga 2, fol. 254a–258a; Kusheva, *Narody Severnogo Kavkaza*, 259.
12. Kusheva, *Narody Severnogo Kavkaza*, 259–60.
13. See Halil İnalcık, 'The Origin of the Ottoman–Russian Rivalry and the Don–Volga Canal (1569)', *Annales de l'Université d'Ankara* 1 (1947): 93; Bekir Kütükoğlu, *Osmanlı-İran siyasi münasebetleri* (Istanbul: Edebiyat Fakültesi Matbaası, 1962).
14. Selim II's letter to Ivan IV dated 1570, in Ahmed Feridun Bey, *Münşa'atü's-selatin* (Istanbul, 1858–9 (AH 1275)), 552–3.
15. MD 32, no. 672; P. P. Bushev, *Istoriia posol'stv i diplomaticheskikh otnoshenii russkogo i iranskogo gosudarstv v 1586–1612 gg.* (Moscow: Nauka, 1976), 44; Rudi Matthee, 'Anti-Ottoman Concerns and Caucasian Interests: Diplomatic Relations between Iran and Russia, 1587–1639', in *Safavid Iran and Her Neighbors*, ed. Michel Mazzaoui (Salt Lake City: University of Utah Press, 2003), 108. According to the Muscovite records, the tsar sent 500 arquebuses and 4,000 muskets to the Safavids to establish an alliance with them.

16. İnalcık, 'The Origin of the Ottoman–Russian Rivalry', 80–1; S. M. Solov'ev, *Istoriia Rossii s drevneishikh vremen* (Moscow: Izdatel'stvo *sotsial'no-*economicheskoi *literatury*, 1960), 7:222.
17. MD 32, no. 672.
18. MD 37, no. 380; Safvet, 'Hazar denizinde Osmanlı sancağı', *Tarih-i Osmani Encümeni mecmuası* 3 (1912): 860–1; Fahrettin Kırzıoğlu, *Osmanlılar'ın Kafkas elleri'ni fethi (1451–1590)* (Ankara: Sevinç Matbaası, 1976), 434–6.
19. MD 37, no. 380.
20. Order to the governor of Kefe (1570), MD 9, no. 149. The Porte also enquired with the governor of Kefe whether those Circassians were in fact vassals of the sultan before an order was written.
21. MD 14, no. 1621.
22. MD 24, no. 421.
23. MD 23, no. 130.
24. MD 42, nos 382, 383.
25. MD 25, no. 2052.
26. Tayyib Gökbilgin, 'L'expédition ottomane contre Astrakhan en 1569', *Cahiers du monde russe et soviétique* 11 (1970): 118–23; Alexandre Bennigsen et al., *Le Khanat de Crimée dans les archives du Musée du palais de Topkapi* (Paris: Mouton, 1978), 135–8; P. A. Sadikov, 'Pokhod tatar i turok na Astrakhan' v 1569 g.', *Istoricheskie zapiski* 22 (1947): 153–64; Akdes Nimet Kurat, *Türkiye ve İdil boyu* (Ankara: Türk Tarih Kurumu, 1966), appendices, 6–7.
27. MD 24, no. 510.
28. Ibid.
29. Shamkhal Choban had previously submitted to the Porte in 1569 during the Astrakhan campaign. We also know that he died in 1578 and was replaced by his son Emir. Therefore, the shamkhal in Daghestan in 1569 and 1574 was the same person. *Gelibolulu Mustafa Ali ve Künhü'l-ahbar'ında II. Selim, III. Murat ve III. Mehmet devirleri*, ed. Faris Çerçi (Kayseri: Erciyes Üniversitesi Yayınları, 2000), 3:266, 306, 311–13.
30. E.g., order to the governor of Azak, MD 24, no. 421; MD 28, nos 142, 579; Trepavlov, *Istoria Nogaiskoi Ordy*, 393.
31. MD 14-2, nos 1543, 1544.
32. MD 28, no. 579; Kırzıoğlu, *Osmanlılar'ın Kafkas elleri'ni fethi*, 418–29.
33. MD 28, no. 579; Kırzıoğlu, *Osmanlılar'ın Kafkas elleri'ni fethi*, 418–29.
34. Michael Khodarkovsky, *Russia's Steppe Frontier: The Making of a Colonial Empire, 1500–1800* (Bloomington: Indiana University Press, 2002), 120; Trepavlov, *Istoria Nogaiskoi Ordy*, 320–1.
35. MD 26, no. 241.
36. Report of Simon Maltsev (1569) in Sadikov, 'Pokhod tatar i turok', and Kurat, *Türkiye ve İdil boyu*, appendices, 6–7.
37. Order to the governor of Azak, MD 28, no. 573: 'That the Muscovites began to repair fortresses [in the area] from Astrakhan through the Caspian Sea

and onto the large river known as Terek.' The Ottoman text is as follows: *'Rusun Ejderhan semtinden Bahr-i Kulzume andan Terek nam büyük su üzerine kal'a ta'mirine mübaşeret iyledigin 'ilam idüb.'*

38. MD 28, nos 142, 573, 963; Order to the Crimean Khan, MD 29, no. 332.
39. MD 28, nos 142, 573.
40. Order to the Crimean Khan, MD 28, no. 963.
41. MD 29, no. 332.
42. For a comprehensive account of the 1578–90 Ottoman–Safavid War, see Kırzıoğlu, *Osmanlılar'ın Kafkas elleri'ni fethi*; Kütükoğlu, *Osmanlı-İran siyasi münasebetleri*.
43. Gelibolulu Mustafa 'Âli, *Nusret-nâme*, ed. Mustafa Eravcı (Ankara: Türk Tarih Kurumu, 2014), 29–31.
44. MD 6, no. 1186. In 1565, Kasım Mirza of Shirvan requested Ottoman help against the Safavids' oppressive rule over the Sunni population in Shirvan. The Porte responded to him that there was peace between the Ottomans and Safavids and advised him to seek help from the shamkhal, who was his relative.
45. MD 32, no. 312; Kırzıoğlu, *Osmanlılar'ın Kafkas elleri'ni fethi*, 430–2.
46. Gelibolulu Mustafa 'Âli, *Nusret-nâme*, 65. His offer of 30,000 men, an exaggerated number, did not materialise.
47. Ibid., 62–70.
48. MD 32, 198–9, entry number illegible.
49. Gelibolulu Mustafa 'Âli, *Nusret-nâme*, 119.
50. Ibid., 122.
51. MD 32, no. 313.
52. Ibid.
53. MD 32, no. 318.
54. Gelibolulu Mustafa 'Âli, *Nusret-nâme*, 151–60.
55. Ibid., 147–8. Before its further division into three governor-generalships (Ereş, Derbend and Şemahı) in June 1583, Shirvan was initially divided into thirteen provinces: Ereş, Kabala, Aktaş, Şaburan, Zerdav, Saderu, Bakü, Salyane, Havz-ı Lahic, Karaulus, Şeki, Ahtı and Ihır. In addition to granting Şaburan to the shamkhal and Ahtı to Burhaneddin of the Avars, Serdar Mustafa Pasha gave Şeki to Irakli of Kakheti, son of King Alexander II.
56. Ibid., 163–4; Kırzıoğlu, *Osmanlılar'ın Kafkas elleri'ni fethi*, 305–6.
57. Evliya Çelebi, *Evliya Çelebi seyahatnamesi*, ed. Yücel Dağlı, Seyit Ali Kahraman and Robert Dankof (Istanbul: Yapı Kredi Yayınları, 2003), 7:298, 301.
58. *Tarih-i Osman Paşa*, ed. Yunus Zeyrek (Ankara: Kültür Bakanlığı Yayınları, 2001), 44. Mustafa Ali notes, 'After a while, his [Tuçalav's] daughter was given to Vizier Osman Pasha and it was considered suitable to have one voice and one direction with the rulers of Daghestan.' *Gelibolulu Mustafa Ali ve Künhü'l-ahbar'ında*, 2:306–7.
59. *Tarih-i Osman Paşa*, 42–3.

60. MD 32, no. 504: *''Atabe-i 'aliyyemize 'arz-ı ubudiyyet ü ihlas ve izhar-ı sadakat ü iktisas eylemişsin ... Yüz göz ak olsun ... gerekdir ki, vusul buldukda min ba'd dahi hak-i paye-i sadakatinde sabit-kadem ve rasihdem olup ol canibde alıkonulan 'asakir-i nusret-eserimizle yek-dil ü yek-cihet olup anun gibi Kızılbaş-ı bed-ma'aş tarafından üzerlerine hücum olunursa geregi gibi mu'avenet ve müzaheret olunup.*' ('You have been subservient, honest and loyal to our exalted Porte ... May you be proud ... It is commanded that when [the order] arrives you should remain firm and unwavering in your loyalty and be on the same terms with our victorious soldiers stationed in these regions and, in case of an attack by the ill-fated Kızılbaş [Safavids], you should assist and support them.')
61. MD 32, 198–9, entry number illegible.
62. Order to the Crimean Khan, MD 32, no. 457.
63. *Tarih-i Osman Paşa,* 39.
64. Ibid., 45–6.
65. Ibid., 46; Asafi Dal Mehmed Çelebi, *Şeca'atname*, ed. Abdülkadir Özcan (Istanbul: Çamlıca Basım, 2006), 187–94.
66. MD 44, no. 87.
67. Ibid.
68. Apart from these, see MD 42, no. 382; MD 44, nos 122, 182, 190; MD 51, no. 10.
69. The Ottomans paid for such services provided by the Kabardinians and other North Caucasus peoples. During his travels in the North Caucasus in the seventeenth century, Evliya Çelebi noted that the Kabardinians possessed an abundant number of Ottoman coins minted during the reign of Murad III, who was the sultan during the Ottoman–Safavid War of 1578–90. Evliya Çelebi, *Evliya Çelebi seyahatnamesi*, 7:288.
70. *Gelibolulu Mustafa Ali ve Künhü'l-ahbar'ında*, 3:401–403; İbrahim Peçevi, *Peçevi tarihi*, ed. Fahri Derin and Vahit Çabuk (Istanbul: Enderun, 1980), 2:76–8.
71. *'Bunların tedarüki görilmeye gitdükçe çogalmadın kılıçdan geçürilmeye giderek zararları bize sirayet eder bunca yıldan berü tasarrufumuzdaki mülk-i mevrusumuz elden gider...'* *Gelibolulu Mustafa Ali ve Künhü'l-ahbar'ında*, 3:403–4; cf. *'[M]ülk-i mevrusumuza ulaşmadın vaktiyle tedariklerin görmezsek bize dahi zararları sirayet itmekde iştibah yokdur'*, Peçevi, *Peçevi tarihi*, 2:78–9; C. Max Kortepeter, *Ottoman Imperialism during the Reformation: Europe and the Caucasus* (New York: New York University Press, 1972), 74.
72. *Gelibolulu Mustafa Ali ve Künhü'l-ahbar'ında*, 3:404–14; Peçevi, *Peçevi tarihi*, 2:80–5.
73. MD 44, nos. 87, 122, 182, 190.
74. MD 51, no. 23.
75. Asafi Dal Mehmed Çelebi, *Şeca'atname*, 379. Asafi Dal Mehmed Çelebi states that Osman Pasha was of Kabardinian origin on his father's side. Peçevi

records that Osman Pasha's father, Özdemir Pasha, was one of the Circassian notables (*mamluk*) of Egypt. *Peçevi tarihi*, 2:17. Also see *Gelibolulu Mustafa Ali ve Künhü'l-ahbar'ında*, 2:22, 30. Therefore, Osman Pasha was born in Egypt but was aware of his Kabardinian Circassian origins.

76. Orders to the Crimean Khan, the governor and *nazır* of Kefe, MD 43, nos. 196, 206, 247, 480.
77. Murat Yaşar and Chong Jin Oh, 'The Ottoman Empire and the Crimean Khanate in the North Caucasus: A Case Study of Ottoman–Crimean Relations in the Mid-Sixteenth Century', *Turkish Historical Review* 9 (2018): 86–103.
78. MD 42, no. 382.
79. Ibid.; order to Kabartay Bey (1582), MD 44, no. 122; order to Kabartay Mirza (1582), MD 44, no. 218.
80. Asafi Dal Mehmed Çelebi, *Şeca'atname*, 379.
81. MD 44, nos 182, 190; MD 51, no. 10.
82. Asafi Dal Mehmed Çelebi, *Şeca'atname*, 379–80.
83. MD 44, nos. 182, 218.
84. MD 48, no. 730; Kırzıoğlu, *Osmanlılar'ın Kafkas elleri'ni fethi*, 315.
85. *Snosheniia Rossii s Kavkazom*, doc. 12, 182–3; MD 44, no. 58; Kırzıoğlu, *Osmanlılar'ın Kafkas elleri'ni fethi*, 314, 441.
86. Order to the Circassian chiefs in Taman and Kuban (September 1583), MD 51, no. 11; order to the Circassian chiefs in Taman (July 1586), MD 61, no. 41.
87. MD 42, 383; Kırzıoğlu, *Osmanlılar'ın Kafkas elleri'ni fethi*, 440–1.
88. MD 51, no. 24.
89. MD 51, no. 23.
90. Ibid. *Haraç* is an Islamic tax demanded from non-Muslim subjects of the empire. The Circassian chief wanted to collect this tax from his own subjects as an Ottoman official, which means that his subjects were probably Christians, as he was prior to his conversion to Islam.
91. MD 32, no. 313.
92. MD 68, no. 96.
93. Order to the governor-general of Kefe and the judge of Taman, MD 71, no. 205.
94. Order to the Circassian Mehmed and the judge of Taman, MD 71, no. 162.
95. MD 71, no. 205.
96. MD 38, no. 98.
97. MD 58, no. 454.
98. MD 58, no. 614.
99. *Snosheniia Rossii s Kavkazom*, doc. 12, 147; *Russian Embassies to the Georgian Kings (1589–1605)*, ed. W. D. Allen, texts trans. Anthony Mango (London: Hakluyt Society, 1970), 292–3.
100. Asafi Dal Mehmed Çelebi, *Şeca'atname*, 369–79. Asafi Dal Mehmed Çelebi's brother was among the Ottoman casualties of this battle.

101. RGADA, F. 89, *Turetskie dela*, kniga 2, fol. 248b–249a; *Kabardino-russkie otnosheniia*, vol. 1, doc. 22, 35.
102. RGADA, F. 89, *Turetskie dela*, kniga 2, fol. 416a; *Kabardino-russkie otnosheniia*, vol. 1, doc. 24, 38.
103. RGADA, F. 89, *Turetskie dela*, kniga 2, fol. 291b. Murad Girey first took refuge in Astrakhan where he was quickly summoned by the tsar to Moscow.
104. *Kabardino-russkie otnosheniia*, 1:398, n. 102.
105. RGADA, F. 89, *Turetskie dela*, kniga 2, fol. 409b–411; *Kabardino-russkie otnosheniia*, vol. 1, doc. 24, 37.
106. RGADA, F. 89, *Turetskie dela*, kniga 2, fol. 277–8, 415–16; *Kabardino-russkie otnosheniia*, vol. 1, doc. 24, 35–6, 39.
107. RGADA, F. 89, *Turetskie dela*, kniga 2, fol. 416, 428b–429; *Kabardino-russkie otnosheniia*, vol. 1, doc. 24, 39, 42.
108. RGADA, F. 89, *Turetskie dela*, kniga 2, fol. 429–429b; *Kabardino-russkie otnosheniia*, vol. 1, doc. 24, 42.
109. RGADA, F. 89, *Turetskie dela*, kniga 2, fol. 416b–419; *Kabardino-russkie otnosheniia*, vol. 1, doc. 24, 39–40.
110. RGADA, F. 89, *Turetskie dela*, kniga 2, fol. 439b; *Kabardino-russkie otnosheniia*, vol. 1, doc. 24, 43.
111. MD 58, no. 203. In this letter, once again, the Ottoman sultan addressed the Muscovite tsar as a vassal of the Porte with similar phraseology used in the previous letters sent to Ivan IV.
112. MD 60, no. 271; Kırzıoğlu, *Osmanlılar'ın Kafkas elleri'ni fethi*, 317.
113. Smirnov, *Rossiia i Turtsiia*, 138.
114. Kusheva, *Narody Severnogo Kavkaza*, 263–7.
115. Chantal Lemercier-Quelquejay, 'Cooptation of the Elites of Kabarda and Daghestan in the Sixteenth Century', in *The North Caucasus Barrier: The Russian Advance towards the Muslim World*, ed. Marie Bennigsen Broxup (London: Hurst, 1992), 39; Kusheva, *Narody Severnogo Kavkaza*, 263–7.
116. *Snosheniia Rossii s Kavkazom*, doc. 12, 168, 174.
117. Mustafa Selaniki, *Tariḫ-i Selaniki*, ed. Mehmet *İpşirli* (Istanbul: Edebiyat Fakültsei Yayınları, [1864] 1999), 229–30; Kortepeter, *Ottoman Imperialism*, 100.
118. MD 62, no. 231.
119. MD 62, no. 230.
120. MD 62, no. 226 ('*Ejderhanın feth olunması müşarileyh hanın hilaf-ı mürzisi olmagla … 'asakir-i İslamı togru yoldan alub götürmeyüb sa'abü'l-mürur yollardan alub götürüb…*').
121. Kortepeter, *Ottoman Imperialism*, 101–2.
122. MD 64, no. 232.
123. Ibid.
124. *PSRL*, 14:39; Kusheva, *Narody Severnogo Kavkaza*, 268; Lemercier-Quelquejay, 'Cooptation of the Elites of Kabarda', 39.
125. Kusheva, *Narody Severnogo Kavkaza*, 270.

126. Ibid., 269; Smirnov, *Rossiia i Turtsiia*, 141.
127. Kusheva, *Narody Severnogo Kavkaza*, 284; Smirnov, *Rossiia i Turtsiia*, 138.
128. See Alan Fisher, 'Azov in the Sixteenth and Seventeenth Centuries', *Jahrbücher für Geschichte Osteuropas* 21 (1973): 161–74.
129. *Kabardino-russkie otnosheniia*, vol. 1, doc. 27, 49–50; *Snosheniia Rossii s Kavkazom*, doc. 5, 45–53.
130. *Kabardino-russkie otnosheniia*, vol. 1, doc. 29, 52–4; *Snosheniia Rossii s Kavkazom*, doc. 5, 45–53.
131. *Kabardino-russkie otnosheniia*, vol. 1, doc. 28, 50–1.
132. MD 23, no. 130.
133. MD 62, nos. 226, 230, 231.
134. *Kabardino-russkie otnosheniia*, vol. 1, doc. 21, 34–5.
135. Trepavlov, *Istoria Nogaiskoi Ordy*, 595.
136. *Kabardino-russkie otnosheniia*, vol. 1, doc. 35, 60–1.
137. Ibid., docs 36 & 37, 61–3.
138. Jukka Korpela, *Slaves from the North: Finns and Karelians in the East European Slave Trade, 900–1600* (Leiden: Brill, 2019), 157–60. Besides symbolising their loyalty to the tsar, sending men to join the Muscovite army provided an opportunity for obtaining spoils of war such as slaves for the North Caucasus troops fighting on the western frontiers of Muscovy.
139. MD 32, nos. 313, 318.
140. *Snosheniia Rossii s Kavkazom*, doc. 12, 137.
141. Ibid., doc. 12, 140.
142. Ibid., doc. 12, 140–1.
143. *Kabardino-russkie otnosheniia*, 1:46–8, 389; *Pamiatniki diplomaticheskikh snoshenii drevnei Rossii s derzhavami inostrannymi* (St Petersburg: Tipografiia II Otdielenia sobstvennoi E. I. V. Kantseliarii, 1851–71), 2:653–750.
144. *Kabardino-russkie otnosheniia*, vol. 1, doc. 29, 52–3.
145. *Snosheniia Rossii s Kavkazom*, doc. 8, 68; *Kabardino-russkie otnosheniia*, vol. 1, doc. 31, 55–6.
146. *Snosheniia Rossii s Kavkazom*, doc. 12, 84–5; *Kabardino-russkie otnosheniia*, vol. 1, doc. 33, 57–8.
147. *Kabardino-russkie otnosheniia*, 1:56–7.

5

The Milky Way Vanishes: The Denouement of the Ottoman–Muscovite Rivalry in the North Caucasus, 1605

In the last decade of the sixteenth century, the Tsardom of Muscovy achieved the establishment of a tangible sphere of influence in Kabarda despite all the odds, including the Ottoman troops and administrative units in Daghestan and the South Caucasus. Several princely families, the descendants of Temriuk and Kanbulat as well as Aslanbek and Solokh, were vying to dominate Kabarda, and both the Muscovites and Ottomans were embroiled in this power struggle. The extant Muscovite sources are quite detailed and helpful to historians for understanding the dynamics and consequences of Kabardinian domestic politics and its broader implications for the imperial rivalry in the North Caucasus. In the autumn of 1589, Tsar Feodor I's envoys travelled through Kabarda on their way to Georgian King Alexander II of Kakheti. They brought gifts from the tsar to the Kabardinian chiefs who were already Muscovite clients or whose allegiances were desired.[1] Among the latter was Aslanbek. The Muscovite officials had long recognised him as an ally of the Ottoman sultan and the Crimean khan, and the tsar ordered the governor of Terek that 'Aslanbek should be separated from the Ottomans and Crimean Tatars and be brought under the tsar's royal hand'.[2]

5.1 Pacification and Muscovite Domination of Kabarda

Following the death of Kanbulat, a staunch Muscovite client, Aslanbek became the pshihua of Kabarda. With Aslanbek's ascension to this rather honorary title, the position of the pshihua passed from the family of Temriuk, the Idars, to the Kaytuks. When the tsar's envoys arrived in Kabarda in 1589, however, they learned that Aslanbek had died, and now 'the Kabardinians wanted to make his brother Yansokh the pshihua of Kabarda'.[3] Yansokh was indeed elected the new pshihua of Kabarda in October 1589, as reported to Moscow by the governor of Terek.[4] Unlike Aslanbek, however, his brother submitted to Muscovy. This swift change in the orientation of the Kaytuk family can be explained within the context of the internal politics of Kabarda and the Ottoman focus on the South Caucasus to conclude their war with the Safavids. The Kabardinian chiefs elected Yansokh, possibly on the condition he would also collaborate with the Muscovites, as many of them did in the last two decades of the sixteenth century. More important, his main rivals, Solokh and Alkas, were in alliance with the Ottomans and Crimean Tatars.[5] At this time, numerous influential chiefs, including Kanbulat's sons and Temriuk's sons, sided with Muscovy and could receive military help from Terek, while those allied with the Porte and the Crimean Khanate lacked direct military support from those external powers due to their ongoing wars elsewhere. As such, an alignment with the Muscovites was the only way for Yansokh to secure the position of pshihua, as the events of 1589 in Kabarda detailed below prove.

Other Kabardinian chiefs known to the Muscovites as clients of the Porte or the Crimean khan were Solokh and Alkas.[6] They were both prominent rulers in Kabarda, and their cooperation with Muscovy's designs in the region was necessary. For this reason, the Muscovites planned to secure their loyalty by sending gifts and annuities, and if necessary, by forcing them with a show of military prowess. When the Muscovite envoys arrived in Kabarda in the autumn of 1589, at first Solokh and Alkas refused to meet with them despite the envoys' promise of 'royal bounty'. The Muscovite envoys, Zvenigorodskii and Antonov, learned from the Cossacks in the area that Mamstriuk and Kudenek went to Solokh to accompany him to the envoys, but Solokh 'did not welcome them because Mamstriuk and Kudenek brought the Muscovite soldiers and fortresses to Terek and Kabarda'.[7] As was often the case in the sixteenth century, some Kabardinian chiefs considered the Muscovite fortresses and troops in their lands a direct threat to their independence. Although the Ottomans planned to do so several times, neither they nor the Crimean Tatars built fortresses in Kabarda. Perhaps this encouraged certain Kabardinian chiefs to think that the Ottomans or Crimean Tatars, with no fortresses or permanent soldiers, would be a better option for an alliance that would maintain their independence.

However, the majority of the Kabardinian chiefs thought otherwise. Among those who visited the Muscovite envoys in September 1589 at their camp near the Sunzha River on their way to Kakheti and took the oath of allegiance (*shert'*) were Aslanbek's son Chopolov, Kudenek and Buzuruk Murza,[8] as well as Azlov and Shumunuk, nephews of Khotov.[9] All of these princes and mirzas 'gave their *shert'* in accordance with their Muslim faith'. Chopolov also pledged fealty in the name of his uncle Yansokh, the would-be pshihua of Kabarda.[10] Since numerous

Kabardinian chiefs were now turning to Muscovy, the pro-Ottoman/ Crimean faction was facing a larger and more robust opposition. Despite their earlier reluctance and marital connections with the Crimean khan and shamkhal, Alkas and Solokh, the most influential chiefs in the Ottoman/ Crimean camp, eventually swore the pledge of allegiance to the Muscovite tsar in the autumn of 1589.[11] During their meeting, the envoys clarified to Alkas that if he refused to submit, he would face the wrath of the tsar, 'because the sovereign's army from Terek and other Kabardinian princes loyal to the sovereign will attack him'.[12] As seen in these documents, gifts and annuities were only secondary for the local chiefs in Kabarda. Local chiefs such as Solokh and Alkas did not change their alliances because of those gifts and annuities but rather owing to the shifting balance of power in Kabarda and military threats from Muscovy and rival Kabardinian princes. In fact, such forced pledges meant little to the local rulers, who could still switch their allegiances easily and readily, if an opportunity presented itself.

To address this issue, the Muscovite officials rigorously applied their policy of hostage taking as surety (*amanat*) in their dealings with the North Caucasus rulers.[13] We know that Temriuk did not officially submit any hostages, perhaps because his daughter was married to Muscovite Tsar Ivan IV and one of his sons, Saltankul (baptised as Mikhail), was in the tsar's service in Moscow. Kanbulat and Mamstriuk did not have to deliver any hostages until 1589. In July 1589, the tsar asked Mamstriuk and Kanbulat's son Kudenek to submit hostages to the governor of Terek after they received their annuities. While Mamstriuk gave Eltiuk, his *atalyk* and one of his nobles, Kudenek delivered his son Adaruk to the Muscovites.[14] We understand from Zvenigorodskii and Antonov's conversation with the governor of Terek in 1589 that Alkas and Solokh were the only prominent Kabardinian chiefs who did not provide the governor with hostages.[15] Although the Muscovite documents suggest that all other Kabardinian chiefs submitted a hostage to the governor, thereby swearing allegiance to Muscovy, it is reasonable to assume these documents only included the politically important chiefs in Kabarda or the ones the Muscovites wanted to draw to their side.

Zvenigorodskii and Antonov's travels through Kabarda and negotiations with the Kabardinian chiefs present many examples of how rigid the Muscovites were about receiving hostages from the local rulers and how they did their best to collect them. For example, neither Alkas nor Solokh wanted to give hostages to the Muscovites despite accepting the suzerainty of the tsar and receiving gifts in return. Swearing the pledge and receiving the gifts could be reversed, but giving hostages was different.

When Alkas, through the mediation of Mamstriuk, finally visited the Muscovite envoys in 1589, he said 'he always wanted to serve the tsar'. The envoys asked him to take the pledge and give hostages as Chopolov, Mamstriuk, Kudenek and every other Kabardinian prince had.[16] Alkas told them he could not take the pledge or give hostages; instead, he could ride with the envoys to their destination, the lands of King Alexander II. The envoys refused and argued that Alkas ought not to have any problems with *amanat*, as the Circassians had the same custom of taking oaths and providing hostages among themselves. Eventually, Alkas agreed to take the pledge but still insisted on not giving any hostages. The envoys refused to consider it as submission. Then, Alkas threatened that he would not escort the envoys and remarked that the envoys' 'route went through his lands', thus implying that he could harm them during their journey. Upon this, the Muscovite envoys said that if he did not submit to the tsar, the governor of Terek and the loyal Kabardinian chiefs would send an army against him. Seeing how unyielding the envoys were with the procedures, Alkas finally agreed to take the pledge and give hostages from among his nobility.[17] A similar negotiation took place between the Muscovite envoys and Solokh, who, after a similar conversation, accepted to take the pledge and give hostages as well.[18]

Not all hostages had the same value. Muscovite officials often demanded a son from their vassals and clients. Sometimes they were satisfied with someone of noble origin from a ruler's retinue. For example, Alkas, Solokh and Mamstriuk gave their nobles as hostages, and they were accepted. However, if there was an issue of disobedience or distrust, the Muscovites required a son rather than gentry. When the Cossacks caught Alkas guiding some Kumyks travelling to Daghestan from Solokh's lands, the envoys accused him of betraying the tsar, as the shamkhal was an enemy of Muscovy and the Muscovite clients were banned from communicating with him. The Muscovites now demanded one of his sons from Alkas as a hostage.[19] Similarly, in the correspondence between Moscow and the governors of Terek and Astrakhan, taking a son of the shamkhal to secure his loyalty was an issue discussed regularly.[20]

Providing hostages and taking the oath, however, did not save Alkas and Solokh from a Muscovite attack on their lands. The rival chiefs complained about them to the Muscovite envoys, claiming that the shamkhal, Alkas, Solokh and the Nogays had allied with Crimean Prince Murad Girey, who would eventually betray the Muscovite tsar. They even contended that Murad Girey would deliver Astrakhan to the Ottoman sultan because there was Muslim unity between them.[21] In December 1589, 750 *strel'tsy* and Cossacks in alliance with Yansokh, the pshihua of Kabarda, and some other Kabardinian chiefs raided Solokh's lands. Solokh sued for peace and gave the Muscovites his son and twenty of his nobles as hostages.[22] The raid and its outcome were a true expression of power and dominance by the Muscovites. In terms of Kabardinian politics, Yansokh was probably trying to weaken Solokh, who was his main rival for the position of pshihua, rather than simply serving Muscovite interests in Kabarda. As emphasised several times in this book, the internal politics of Kabarda and power struggles among its princely families played a significant role in deciding the alignment of a particular chief with the tsar or the sultan – much more significant than historians of the Ottoman and Russian empires so far have been willing to admit. Thus, by 1590, the majority of Kabardinian princely families were clients or allies of the Muscovite tsar or were subdued by force.

The Ottomans' ongoing military engagement with the Safavids in the South Caucasus and later with the Habsburgs in Europe unquestionably encouraged Muscovy to further its ambitions in the North Caucasus. In 1590, Muscovy and the Polish-Lithuanian Commonwealth signed a peace agreement, ending the conflict on Muscovy's western frontier. Meanwhile, the Ottoman Porte ended its war against the Safavid Empire in the same year only to prepare for another long war in the west against the Habsburgs. Despite their victories, the Ottoman armies were weakened because of countless battles they fought between 1578 and 1590 in the Caucasus. Several proposals from Safavid Shah Abbas I (r. 1588–1629) in 1588 and from Habsburg Emperor Rudolf II in 1589 and 1593 to form a united front against the Ottoman Empire further encouraged Tsar Feodor I and Muscovite officials in the North Caucasus borderland.[23] The Safavid shah even offered Derbend and Baku, although he did not control them at this time, to the Muscovite tsar as a reward for Muscovy's military participation in an anti-Ottoman alliance.[24] Therefore, the conditions were just right, and these international developments paved the way for Muscovites to apply their steppe frontier strategies more aggressively in the North Caucasus.

Taking advantage of this situation in 1590, the Muscovites rebuilt their old fortress in Kabarda.[25] Compared to other Muscovite fortresses on their southern frontier zones, the fortress on the Sunzha River was a minor structure but sufficient for manipulation of the internal politics among the chiefs in the region. The Muscovites had already erected three major fortresses – Terek in 1588 and Tsaritsyn in 1589, as may be remembered, and before them Livny on Don in 1586. The intensification of Muscovite fortress building in the lower Volga region and Pontic–Caspian steppes as well as in the North Caucasus did not go unnoticed. Following an unsuccessful attack on Muscovy, Crimean Khan Gazi Girey II (r. 1588–97, 1597–1607) said to Muscovite envoy Bibikov:

> Your ruler thus wishes to do as he did with Kazan: at first he established a town [fortress] close by, then seized Kazan; but the Crimea is not Kazan, in the Crimea there are many hands and eyes; it will be necessary for your ruler to go beyond the town to the very heart of Crimea.'[26]

Notwithstanding such protests by the Crimean khan, the Muscovite activities continued unabated. Similarly, another fortress on the Yaik River was completed in 1595 to contain the Greater Nogays. Therefore, the steppe frontier defence line of Muscovy steadily extended southwards, and by the mid-1590s, it formed a streak of fortresses going through the North Caucasus: from the mouth of the Yaik River through Astrakhan to the mouth of the Terek and Sunzha rivers, and from Sunzha to Tsaritsyn between the Don and Volga and to Livny on the Don River.

Through these fortresses, Muscovy empowered its clients in Kabarda. The military value of a fortress in the early modern era is obvious. Considering that the Kabardinians could muster a limited number of soldiers, the existence of a thousand musket-bearing Muscovite *strel'tsy* and Cossacks had a substantial effect on the balance of power among the chieftains of Kabarda. Besides their military value, the Muscovite fortresses created an economic sphere of influence, which was an essential component of the fortress strategy. Fortresses enabled the Muscovites to control the nearby economic resources. These resources could be roads, fisheries, river routes, grazing lands or arable lands. The Muscovite policymakers calculated such strategic and economic issues when they built fortresses on the southern frontiers. For example, after his submission to the Muscovite tsar in 1589, Solokh requested that

> his people would be allowed to use the fisheries along the Terek River controlled by the Muscovite troops, his men would not be harmed by the Muscovite forces at the crossings, and … the tsar should help him and send him men against his enemies.[27]

Prince Alkas also made a similar request when the Muscovite envoys demanded his submission.[28]

These requests evince how the fortresses in the frontier zones affected not just the imperial rivalry over the region, but also local economies and the balance of power among local rulers. The troops stationed at the Muscovite fortress controlled the fisheries along the Terek River, which were extremely vital for the Kabardinian people living in the vicinity. The Muscovites restricted the use of these fisheries to their clients in the region

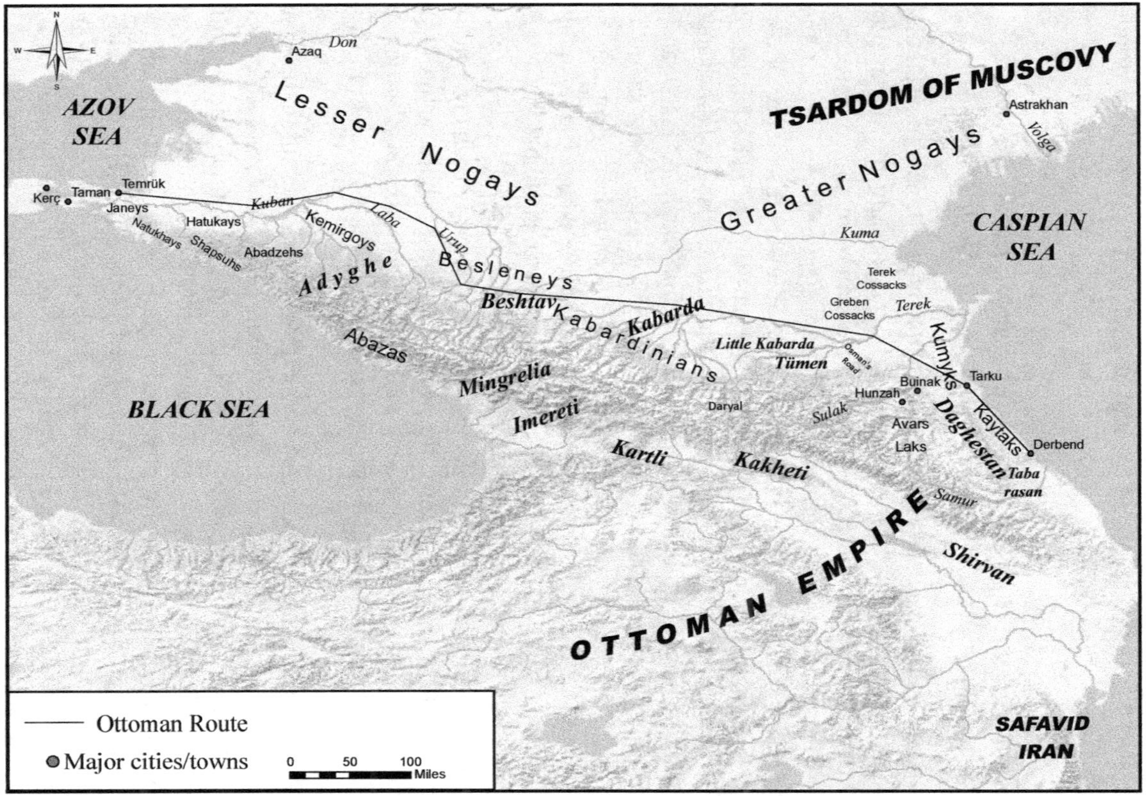

Map 5.1 The North Caucasus, 1583–1603 and the Ottoman supply route.

and effectively prevented others from using them. They also supported their allies in Kabarda against their enemies by providing them with men, including Cossacks, who were stationed in Terek or other nearby fortresses. Therefore, as stated above, the construction of a network of fortresses was the backbone of Muscovite policy in their southern frontier zones.

5.2 The Final Act of the Imperial Rivalry in the North Caucasus: The Muscovite Offensives in Daghestan

Following their success in Kabarda, the Muscovite officials focused their subject- and territory-making strategies on Daghestan, the domination of which would complete Muscovite ascendancy in the northwestern part of the Caspian Sea, providing free passage to the Safavid Empire and the Georgian kingdoms, and facilitating an in-depth defence of their lower Volga possessions from future Ottoman threats. The Muscovite officials took bolder steps in Daghestan from the 1590s to establish there the same sphere of influence as they achieved in Kabarda. Tsar Ivan IV received envoys from Daghestan as early as 1557–8. At first, the shamkhal of Daghestan requested protection from the Muscovite tsar against his Kabardinian enemies, who occasionally raided his lands. However, the negotiations between Muscovy and the Daghestani shamkhal yielded no results, as the Muscovite officials found Kabardinian rulers to be more amenable for cooptation in these early years of Muscovite interest in the North Caucasus.[29] Subsequently, the Muscovite fortress built on the Terek River in 1567 empowered Muscovy's new client in Kabarda, Temriuk, to encroach on Daghestan and control some of the shamkhal's lands, but this was short-lived.

The Ottoman–Safavid peace treaty of 1590 and the resulting Ottoman hegemony over certain parts of Daghestan and the South Caucasus were of utmost significance for every state and polity in and around the Caucasus. From the Muscovite perspective, an Ottoman military presence in Daghestan and a centrally governed administrative unit in Derbend meant a consistent threat to their then newly conquered territories along the Volga River – certainly Astrakhan and perhaps even Kazan. By the year 1590, thanks to the earlier efforts of Özdemiroğlu Osman Pasha, the Ottomans had built a navy capable of operating in the Caspian Sea.[30] While this navy was not yet a fully developed naval force similar to Ottoman units in the Mediterranean, it was decidedly the beginnings of it. A fully fledged Ottoman navy sailing in the Caspian Sea, which was an essential element in the Ottoman plans for the Caucasus in the second half of the sixteenth century, would spell grave trouble in the long term for the Safavids and Muscovites alike.

Meanwhile, the Ottoman presence in the Caucasus complicated the already precarious balance of power among the local rulers who were clients or allies of the Porte, especially in Daghestan. It was not until the Ottomans established themselves in Derbend that the shamkhal, who quite saliently sided with the Ottomans during the Ottoman–Safavid War and against the Muscovite designs, realised that a permanent and centrally governed Ottoman province bordering his polity would eventually restrict his independence. While his hands were tied when Özdemiroğlu Osman Pasha, who subdued the entirety of Daghestan, was in Derbend, as soon as the pasha left, an opportunity to challenge the Ottoman authority presented itself through the activities of Crimean Prince Murad Girey. As mentioned in the previous chapter, the shamkhal supported Murad Girey, who allied himself with the Muscovite tsar against the Ottoman sultan during the Crimean succession crisis. The relationship between the shamkhal and the Ottoman Porte became strained, but diplomatic contacts did not cease, as neither party wanted to burn its bridges. Fearing a complete Ottoman hegemony over the North Caucasus, the Muscovites paid particular attention to the shamkhal's position and sent men from Astrakhan in 1586 to learn about his orientation and the state of the Ottoman army in Derbend.[31]

Moreover, the foundation of Terek Town at the mouth of the Terek River in 1588 increased the Muscovite influence in Daghestan. The new Muscovite fortress put pressure on the shamkhal and other Daghestani rulers. In 1589, the shamkhal was clearly vacillating between the Ottoman Porte and Muscovy. According to a letter from the governor of Terek to the Ambassadorial Office, the shamkhal said to the Ottoman governor in Derbend he wished to serve neither the Ottomans nor the Muscovites.[32] The same letter also shows that the Muscovite officials at this time were trying to draw the shamkhal to their side. The tsar ordered his governor to facilitate the shamkhal's submission and take one of his sons or his *uzdens* to Terek Town as a hostage.[33]

The growing pressure and threats of war from Muscovy and the shamkhalate's continuing enmity with Georgian King Alexander II of Kakheti, who had recently allied with the tsar,[34] ultimately forced the shamkhal to choose. The end of the Murad Girey affair also helped the shamkhal in his final decision for an alliance with one of the two vying imperial powers. In 1589, he wrote a letter to the Ottoman sultan about the Muscovite ambitions in Daghestan, their new fortresses, and their anti-Ottoman alliances with Christian states in Europe and with the Safavids in the Caucasus. He pointed out that if the sultan failed to stop the Muscovite expansion and encroachment into Daghestan, the Ottoman Empire would cease to exist.[35] The shamkhal's eventual decision to side with the Ottomans and persistent petitions from Alexander II of Kakheti for a military assault on Daghestan occasioned the Muscovite tsar to issue an order in May 1591 to the governors of Astrakhan and Terek and his client Kabardinian chiefs to muster their armies for a punitive attack on the lands of the shamkhal.[36] The Kabardinian chiefs loyal to Muscovy predictably supported the tsar's efforts in Daghestan.

By 1591, the Muscovites built two more fortresses, further south from the Terek – one on the Sunzha River and another on the Sulak River in Daghestan. Keeping an eye on the Muscovite activities in the North Caucasus, Hasan Pasha of Shirvan sent a report to the Porte in 1591, informing it that the Muscovites were coopting certain tribes and rulers in Daghestan and planning an attack on Ottoman possessions in the North Caucasus. In response, the Porte advised him to watch the situation closely and cooperate with the shamkhal. The Ottomans then sent the same order to the shamkhal and other rulers in Daghestan whom they considered allies or clients.[37]

Eventually, the governor of Terek, Grigorii Zasekin, entered the shamkhal's lands in 1591 with an army of 5,000 Muscovite soldiers and 10,000 Kabardinian troops. However, this military operation was only a punitive raid. Once they raided the shamkhal's lands, the Muscovite army swiftly returned to Terek.[38] On the one hand, this raid enlivened Muscovite relations with King Alexander II of Kakheti, who had been asking the tsar to neutralise the threat posed by the Daghestani shamkhal.[39] On the other hand, it cemented the loyalty of the shamkhal and other Daghestani rulers to the Ottoman Porte. Following this campaign, the Ottoman Porte appreciated the gravity of the situation caused by the Muscovites' activities in Daghestan. The sultan ordered the Ottoman commanders in Shirvan to rally around Hasan Pasha if the pasha decided to attack the Muscovites and their allies in the North Caucasus.[40] The Porte also dispatched a letter to the shamkhal in 1592, ordering him to collaborate with Hasan Pasha in response to the increasing Muscovite aggression in the region.[41] Even more alarming for the Ottomans were the reports that the Muscovites had stationed over 10,000 musket-bearing soldiers in their fortresses along the Terek River. This rather large and certainly exaggerated number of Muscovite soldiers in the North Caucasus made the Ottomans think that the Muscovites were putting in motion a plan to unite the chiefs of Kabarda and Daghestan under the tsar's control.[42] For this reason, the Ottoman sultan ordered the Crimean khan to send an army to destroy the Muscovite fortresses in the North Caucasus. This order shows that the Porte considered the location of the Muscovite fortresses in Kabarda as a direct threat to its possessions in Daghestan, especially the centrally administered province of Derbend.[43] Additionally, the Ottoman officials at the Porte wanted to figure out the exact objectives of the Muscovite tsar in the North Caucasus borderland. They asked the Crimean khan to send spies to acquire this information and how to proceed with the preparations to capture the Muscovite fortresses.[44] The Crimean khan, however, preferred not to send military support to the Daghestani shamkhal or capture the Muscovite fortresses in the North Caucasus, but to attack the Muscovite lands directly, although this invasion of Muscovy in 1591 failed to produce the desired results.[45] Meanwhile, the Muscovites became aware that the Ottoman sultan was concerned about their activities and had instructed the khan to attack the Muscovite fortresses in the North Caucasus.[46]

The escalation of Muscovite activities in Daghestan coincided with the start of the Habsburg–Ottoman War in 1593 in Central Europe, which limited the capability of the Porte to provide support to its vassals and allies in the North Caucasus. To make matters worse, the Don Cossacks in the spring of 1593 attacked the Ottoman city of Azak, taking advantage of the Crimean Tatar army being in Central Europe for the war with the Habsburgs. Due to the absence of the main Crimean Tatar army, the Porte relied on the Western Circassians for the defence of Azak and other Ottoman possessions.[47] Meanwhile, the Muscovite tsar, following their strategy of avoiding direct military conflict with the sultan, sent an envoy, Grigorii Nashchokin, to the Porte.[48] Sinan Pasha questioned Nashchokin in Istanbul about the assaults of the Don Cossacks in the north of the Black Sea and the newly built Muscovite fortresses in the North Caucasus. The envoy answered by claiming falsely there were no new Muscovite fortresses or cities in the North Caucasus and that the Cossacks were 'lawless fugitives' who did not obey the tsar's orders.[49] Resorting to the same argument that Muscovy had used since 1567, the envoy emphasised that the fortress on the Terek was built upon the request of Ivan IV's father-in-law Temriuk, but this was not the case with the new fortresses in question. Sinan Pasha, in response, made it clear to the envoy that the Ottoman sultan considered these activities as hostile and threatened him with the possibility of an Ottoman-sponsored Crimean Tatar invasion of Muscovy.[50]

The Porte knew more than what the Muscovite envoy revealed about the new fortresses and their objectives in the North Caucasus.[51] Accordingly, Ottoman Sultan Murad III sent a letter to Tsar Feodor I in May 1593, asking him to demolish the Muscovite fortresses on the Terek and Sunzha rivers, arguing that they were built in lands belonging to the Ottoman Empire.[52] In the same year, the Ottomans and Crimean Tatars planned that Mübarek Girey, a son of the Crimean khan, would carry out a campaign to capture the Terek Fortress.[53] However, the Muscovite activities following the embassy of Nashchokin and the sultan's letter in 1593 show us that the Porte could not convince the Muscovites to give up on their ambitions over Daghestan. The Muscovite defiance was also evident in the letter sent to the sultan by the tsar in which the latter not only justified the Muscovite fortresses in the North Caucasus but also claimed that the Kabardinians and Kumyks were originally runaway people from Ryazan, hence subjects of the tsar.[54]

In fact, the Muscovites resolved to take bigger risks and target Tarku, the capital of the shamkhalate, to establish their authority over Daghestan decisively. In the summer of 1593, the Muscovite tsar ordered preparations to begin for a decisive campaign in Daghestan under the command of Kniaz Andrei Khvorostinin. The tsar informed Georgian envoys Aram and Kiril, who were in Moscow representing Alexander II, that the shamkhal would be replaced by Alexander II's ally, the *Krym-shamkhal* of Daghestan.[55] With no Ottoman and Crimean assistance to the Daghestanis, Kniaz Khvorostinin captured Tarku effortlessly in July 1593. The shamkhal himself was wounded in the battle and retreated to the mountains. Khvorostinin then began preparations for securing Tarku, as the shamkhal remained a threat. The Muscovite commander was also expecting more troops from Georgian King Alexander II, who had promised to send soldiers if the Muscovites attacked the shamkhal.

Meanwhile, the envoys of Habsburg Emperor Rudolf II (r. 1576–1612) and Safavid Shah Abbas I met in Moscow in 1593–4 to discuss an anti-Ottoman league, which must have also been known to the Porte.[56] Upon these developments, which indicated that the Muscovites were in Daghestan to stay and the international balance of power favoured them, the Ottoman Porte intervened. In 1594, Sultan Murad III sent an imperial order to the governor-general of Shirvan, Cafer Pasha. According to this letter, the Porte learned from one of its agents in the area that the Muscovites had gathered 5,000–6,000 troops in Astrakhan and were building a fortress on the Koysu River in Daghestan, where they planned to muster an army of 40,000 soldiers to conquer Daghestan and then march on Derbend. The sultan ordered the governor-general of Shirvan to send men to the area to ascertain the Muscovite strategies and prevent them from building more fortresses by any means necessary.[57] In his response to the Porte, Cafer Pasha wrote that the Muscovites had indeed invaded the shamkhalate with a 20,000-strong army and already built two fortresses in Daghestan.[58] The Ottoman sultan then sent a letter in April 1594 to the shamkhal, promising him liberation from the invading Muscovite troops by the Ottoman soldiers arriving from Shirvan. Moreover, Cafer Pasha was preparing an army supported by cannons to assist the shamkhal.[59] Based on the information gathered by Cafer Pasha in 1594, the Ottomans were concerned that the eventual goal of Muscovy after conquering Daghestan was to take Derbend.[60] The extant Muscovite sources, however, do not confirm that the Muscovites had any plans or even desire to capture Derbend. This would be contrary to their strategy of avoiding direct military confrontation with the Ottoman Empire, to which they rigorously adhered in the sixteenth century. However, it was not odd for the Ottomans to assume this could happen, as they were closely watching Muscovite activities such as constructing fortresses in Daghestan and negotiating with the Safavids and Habsburgs for an alliance against the Porte.[61] As we understand from the letter sent to Cafer Pasha, the Porte was also worried that the Muscovite fortresses and troops in Daghestan could compel the Daghestanis to submit to the tsar by force. The Ottomans were apprehensive that this outcome would encourage the Georgian kings, of whom the Porte was already suspicious, to approach the tsar. The sultan stated in his letter to Cafer Pasha that if the Muscovite fortresses could be razed, the Daghestani vassals would be liberated from their pressure, and the Georgian kings would have no choice but to accept the sultan's sovereignty for good.[62]

In the end, the Ottomans formed a coalition which included their centrally appointed administrators in Derbend and Shirvan as well as certain local rulers in Daghestan, such as the shamkhal, the *usmi* of the Kaytaks and the *ma'sum* of Tabarastan, to facilitate a complete removal of the invading Muscovite troops from Daghestan.[63] The Porte sent copies of the letters addressed to the shamkhal, *usmi* and *masum* to Cafer Pasha so he would know the arrangement between the Porte and the local rulers and strategise accordingly. The sultan also ordered the Ottoman governors in Revan, Gence, Lori and Hoşab in the Caucasus to dispatch soldiers to Cafer Pasha for this military endeavour. Cafer Pasha was instructed to collaborate with the local rulers and together 'raze the Muscovite fortresses in the lands of the shamkhal to the ground'.[64] Interestingly, despite knowing that Alexander II was in an alliance with the tsar,[65] the sultan even wrote a letter to order him to help the shamkhal against the Muscovites. In order to intimidate him, the sultan stated in his letter that the Ottoman governors of Van, Diyarbakır and Gence, all close to Kakheti, would combine their troops and set off to expel the Muscovites and Cossacks from Daghestan.[66] This was obviously a veiled threat to Alexander II.

Thanks to the Porte's diplomacy and promise of military aid, the Daghestani rulers united their forces. Including the Ottoman soldiers from the Caucasus, they gathered 15,000 troops, as detailed in the Muscovite sources.[67] Eventually, in the summer of 1594, the combined forces of the Daghestanis under the command of Adil Girey, a son of the shamkhal, supported by the provincial Ottoman soldiers and cannons from Derbend and Shirvan, took Tarku by defeating the 7,000-strong Muscovite army.[68] The Muscovites lost 3,000 men in the battle, and this defeat briefly put an end to the Muscovite activities in Daghestan. The Muscovite fortresses were destroyed, and the Muscovite soldiers were expelled. Thus, in the same year, the Ottomans and Muscovites returned to acceptance of the *status quo ante* in this part of the North Caucasus borderland. The shamkhal sent one of his sons to the Ottoman Porte perhaps to show his gratitude and to renew his submission to the sultan.[69]

This war and defeat revealed to the Muscovites a few critical matters for their future engagements in the region. First, whenever a military invasion took place, despite their mutual enmities, Daghestani rulers could unite against an invading army of a foreign power. Second, King Alexander II of Kakheti, who promised to send troops to Daghestan, could not be trusted. Third, despite the ongoing war in Central Europe, the Ottoman Porte was determined to preserve its sphere of influence over Daghestan and could raise troops to secure it. In the case of Alexander II, the Muscovites openly accused him of causing the defeat because he failed to send his soldiers.[70] Apparently, a subtle threat from the Porte was enough to prevent Alexander II from fulfilling his promise to the Muscovite tsar. Following this failure, Tsar Feodor I wrote a letter to the Porte, emphasising his desire to have peaceful relations with the sultan and guaranteeing once more that Ottoman troops and subjects could travel through the Muscovite-controlled part of Kabarda without hindrance. However, the tsar still refused to comply with the Ottoman request to demolish the Muscovite fortresses in the North Caucasus, merely reminding the sultan that the Kabardinians had been subjects of the tsar since Ivan IV. The tsar did not forget to stress that the envoys of the Safavid shah, Habsburg emperor and French king came to Moscow to establish alliances with the Tsardom of Muscovy.[71]

As a result of their failed invasion, the Muscovites also recognised that the shamkhal of Daghestan was a formidable ruler. The position of the shamkhal held a certain prestige that could unite the Daghestani rulers. In 1599, Muscovite officials calculated that if the shamkhal was to bring together the local rulers, mountaineers and allied Circassians in the North Caucasus, he could muster an army of 15,000 horsemen and many more infantry.[72] In the same year, however, a Muscovite ambassador at the Habsburg court claimed to have Daghestan under Muscovite sovereignty and that along with the Georgian kings, the Daghestani rulers would join the tsar to fight the Ottomans, which was clearly a lie.[73] Thus, at the end of the sixteenth century, the shamkhal could pose a serious threat to Muscovite ambitions not only in Daghestan but also in the entire North Caucasus, especially when Ottoman soldiers and cannons supported him. The Muscovites were also concerned because the Daghestani rulers collaborated with the Ottoman provinces in the Caucasus and one of the shamkhal's sons, Sultan Mahmud, stayed with the Ottomans in Şemahı.[74]

The Muscovite envoys who travelled to Kakheti in 1604 were told by the Georgians that should the sultan send men to support him, the shamkhal would attack the Muscovite fortresses in the North Caucasus. They learned that Kazy (Gazi) and Solokh in Kabarda were in alliance with the Ottomans and the shamkhal.[75] In fact, only a year before in 1603, envoys from Solokh and Kazy were in Moscow, and as usual, they claimed to be 'under the royal hand of the tsar'.[76] Nonetheless, despite the *shert'* given in 1589 and the envoys sent to Moscow several times since, neither Solokh nor Kazy was genuinely loyal to the Muscovite tsar, and both were waiting for an opportunity to oust the foreign troops from their lands. We know that the aforementioned Sultan Mahmud's representatives were also with the Kabardinian envoys in Moscow.[77] Besides, in 1602, Tsar Boris Godunov (r. 1598–1605) had received envoys from another son of the shamkhal, Andi. However, these missions to the Muscovite tsar by the Daghestani rulers were most probably there to dissuade the Muscovites from organising more punitive campaigns in Daghestan, as most of the Daghestani rulers still retained their contacts with or submitted to the Ottoman sultan or the Crimean khan.

While the Ottoman Porte was keeping an eye on the Muscovite activities in the North Caucasus, its arch-enemy in the east, Shah Abbas I of the Safavid Empire, was readying for a major campaign against the Ottomans in the Caucasus and Western Asia. Following the Treaty of Istanbul signed in 1590, he rebuilt the Safavid armies, which by the beginning of the seventeenth century matched their Ottoman counterparts. It was the right moment for a campaign, as the Ottomans were fighting a long war in Central Europe against the Habsburgs, and the empire was plagued by domestic uprisings in Anatolia and Rumelia. The Safavids started their offensive in 1603 to retake the territories lost to the Ottomans. The reinvigorated Safavid armies were victorious and swiftly expelled the war-weary Ottoman troops from Tebriz, Yerevan and the Georgian kingdoms, as well as Shirvan.

The success of the Safavid armies and the unnerving news about Ottoman plans to assemble a coalition comprising the shamkhal, Daghestani rulers and pro-Ottoman Kabardinian chiefs to march on the Muscovite fortresses in the first years of the seventeenth century occasioned Muscovite preparations for another campaign in Daghestan. This second attempt to establish sovereignty over Daghestan aimed to preempt the threat that could come from the combined forces of the Daghestanis and Kabardinians supported by the Ottomans. The Ottomans were fighting two major wars in 1604, one against the Habsburgs in the west and one against the Safavids in the east. Therefore, the timing for an assault on Daghestan was just right. In 1604, Tsar Boris Godunov ordered the governor of Terek, Ivan Baturlin, to invade the lands of the shamkhal once and for all with a 10,000-strong army. The Muscovite offensive began in the spring, and as early as April, Baturlin's army captured Tarku, Anderi, Koysu and Kara-Budak, the most strategic settlements in the region. The shamkhal again retreated into the mountains. Meanwhile, perhaps drawing lessons from the failure of 1594, Baturlin strengthened the walls of Tarku with stone, building a *kamennyi gorod* (stone town), and constructed several other forts in other critical locations. The fall of Tarku and construction of new Muscovite forts caused further concerns among the local rulers.[78] Fearing a total Muscovite hegemony over Daghestan and eventual loss of their independence, they once more opted to unite under the authority of the shamkhal.

By this time, the armies of Safavid Shah Abbas I were advancing into the Caucasus, defeating the Ottoman units. Despite such an imminent threat from the Safavid Empire, the Ottoman Porte supported the Daghestani forces with troops and cannons from Derbend.[79] The Ottomans, by then, were appreciative of the loyalty of the Daghestani rulers for their own ambitions in the North Caucasus. With the Ottoman support, the Daghestani forces once again united under the command the shamkhal's sons, Adil Girey and Sultan Mahmud. In fact, Sultan Mahmud was on the tsar's payroll, but he did not hesitate to lead the Daghestani armies against the Muscovites. The Daghestani forces swiftly took the Muscovite fort on the Koysu River and besieged Tarku, where Baturlin was commanding the remaining Muscovite troops, which comprised 7,000 men. Tarku was bombarded heavily by the Ottoman cannons that arrived from Şemahı.[80] Baturlin did not possess enough provisions and weapons to defend Tarku, especially in the face of the heavy artillery bombardment. He and Sultan Mahmud eventually agreed on terms in June 1605 for handing over Tarku to the Daghestanis, allowing the Muscovite soldiers to withdraw with their arms. The Daghestanis, however, failed to honour their promise and unexpectedly attacked the retreating Muscovite troops, annihilating them all, including Baturlin and other Muscovite commanders.[81]

The year 1605 marked the date of the final act of the first confrontation between the Ottoman Empire and the Tsardom of Muscovy in the North Caucasus borderland. After this defeat, the Daghestani–Ottoman forces and their Kabardinian allies captured the remaining Muscovite fortresses in Daghestan and Kabarda. The Muscovites could not take any measures to reverse their misfortune, as Tsar Boris Godunov died in April 1605, starting a succession crisis that would last until 1613. Therefore, following the defeat of the Muscovite army in Daghestan in 1605, the Ottoman Porte emerged as the victor of this first round in the imperial rivalry with their northern neighbour over the North Caucasus. The Ottomans, however, failed to take full advantage by expanding their conquest into the lower Volga and the Pontic–Caspian steppes, because the South Caucasus slipped away from their hands as a result of the successful Safavid campaign and they were still fighting a war against the Habsburgs in the west.

The Muscovite policy in the North Caucasus was effective, as over a short period of time and despite a few setbacks, they established their hegemony over Kabarda and become a power to be reckoned with in Daghestan. This achievement was indeed a result of their clever steppe frontier policy that included military intervention and economic and political incentives for local rulers for cooptation, as well as their superior diplomatic skills, out of which the expansionist policy of the Russian Empire eventually sprang.[82] Despite wars on their western frontier, power struggles among the boyars after the death of Ivan IV in 1584 and even the dynastic extinction in 1598, Muscovite policy on their southern frontier, including the North Caucasus borderland, continued almost unabated based on their long-term strategies.[83] Compared to the Ottomans' initially lax northern policy, which depended ultimately on the opinions of influential politicians at the Porte and was partially shaped by their Crimean vassals, the rigid and centrally planned Muscovite steppe policy was undoubtedly more effective in the shared steppe frontier zone in the north of the Black Sea and the North Caucasus borderland.

It was only in the late 1560s that some prominent officials in Istanbul realised the danger for the Ottoman Empire coming from the north with the expansion of the Tsardom of Muscovy into the North Caucasus. After 1569, the Ottomans implemented rather active and modified strategies of subject- and territory-making in the North Caucasus. This proactive change in Ottoman policy did not have a parallel in the sixteenth-century Muscovite strategies. The Muscovites continued to pursue the same steppe frontier policy, which had produced favourable results in their eastern and southern frontier zones earlier in the same century when applied to the Turco-Mongolian peoples and polities. The Ottoman–Safavid War of 1578–90 presented another opportunity for the Porte to build on this new foundation. Instead of attacking the Safavid Empire's possessions in the South Caucasus from their Eastern Anatolian strongholds, the Ottomans used the North Caucasus as a supply route, which brought about a palpable Ottoman presence in this borderland.

While the changes in their policy helped the Ottomans oust the Muscovites in the first phase of the imperial rivalry in the North Caucasus, even this improved Ottoman policy had specific weaknesses. The Ottoman bureaucratic machine was slow compared to the Muscovite decision-making process in taking necessary actions or precautions in the North Caucasus in a swift manner. The Ottoman system continued to rely on other players, such as the Crimean khans, who favoured policies and strategies that allowed them to have a form of independence in the Pontic–Caspian steppes and the North Caucasus borderland. In spite of several attempts, as exemplified above from the Ottoman sources, the Porte remained unable to construct much-needed fortifications in the North Caucasus due to the conflicting opinions of officials, including the Crimean khan, and ever-changing military priorities of the empire. But the Muscovites constructed fortresses with ease, as it was a part of their strategies on their southern frontiers, including in the sixteenth century the North Caucasus borderland. Thus, they built numerous forts, fortresses and redoubts in the North Caucasus in a relatively short time. The Ottomans or the Crimean Tatars often forced the Muscovites to demolish these fortifications. However, the speed with which these fortresses were built and their territorial span, ranging from Kabarda to Daghestan, provided them with the aura of ghost fortresses that might or might not have been there, to the extent that it confuses modern historians writing on the subject. It mostly likely confused the policymakers at the Ottoman Porte and in the Crimean Khanate as well in the second half of the sixteenth century.

With skilful diplomacy and sometimes by backing off, the Muscovites succeeded in maintaining their presence in the North Caucasus for a long time, although militarily, Muscovy was no match for the Ottoman Empire in an area close to some important Ottoman centres such as Kefe and later Derbend. The Muscovite officials, however, overextended their resources and overestimated their power when they made their first mistake of trying to conquer Daghestan with their own armies, which differed from their methods of controlling and coopting the Kabardinian chiefs. Because of overextending their resources and confronted by modified Ottoman strategies, Muscovy had to abandon its ambitions in the North Caucasus by the beginning of the seventeenth century and leave the region. It was only a century later, during the reign of Peter the Great (r. 1682–1725), that the Russians would return to the North Caucasus to annex Derbend and Mazandaran, this time as the Russian Empire under the famous Romanov dynasty.

Notes

1. *Snosheniia Rossii s Kavkazom: Materialy izvlechennye iz Moskovskago glavnago arkhiva Ministerstva inostrannykh diel, 1578–1613 gg.*, ed. S. L. Belokurov (Moscow: Universitetskaia tipografiia, 1889), doc. 12, 108–9. For English translation of parts of the ambassadorial report for this Muscovite embassy to the Kingdom of Kakheti, see *Russian Embassies to the Georgian Kings (1589–1605)*, ed. W. D. Allen, texts trans. Anthony Mango (London: Hakluyt Society, 1970).
2. *Snosheniia Rossii s Kavkazom*, doc. 12, 112.
3. Ibid., doc. 12, 131.
4. Ibid., doc. 10, 80–2; *Kabardino-russkie otnosheniia v 16–18 vv.*, ed. T. Kh. Kumykov and E. N. Kusheva (Moscow: Izdatel'stvo Akademii nauk SSSR, 1957), vol. 1, doc. 38, 62–4.
5. *Snosheniia Rossii s Kavkazom*, doc. 12, 131.
6. Alkas was possibly Alpkaç Bey as mentioned in the relevant Ottoman documents, MD 44, no. 58; Fahrettin Kırzıoğlu, *Osmanlılar'ın Kafkas elleri'ni fethi (1451–1590)* (Ankara: Sevinç Matbaası, 1976), 315.
7. *Snosheniia Rossii s Kavkazom*, doc. 12, 136.
8. This could be Bozok or Buzuk mentioned in the Ottoman sources, MD 41, no. 11.
9. *Snosheniia Rossii s Kavkazom*, doc. 12, 133.
10. Ibid., doc. 12, 134–5.
11. Ibid., doc. 12, 141–3, 145–6.
12. Ibid., doc. 12, 143.
13. See Sean Pollock, '"Thus We Shall Have Their Loyalty and They Our Favor": Diplomatic Hostage-Taking (*amanatstvo*) and Russian Empire in Caucasia', in *Dubitando: Studies in History and Culture in Honor of Donald Ostrowski*, ed. Brian J. Boeck, Russell E. Martin and Daniel Rowland (Bloomington, IN: Slavica, 2012), 139–63.
14. *Kabardino-russkie otnosheniia*, vol. 1, doc. 34, 58–60.
15. *Snosheniia Rossii s Kavkazom*, doc. 12, 128.
16. Ibid., doc. 12, 142–3.
17. Ibid., doc. 12, 143–4; Pollock, '"Thus We Shall Have Their Loyalty"', 152–6.
18. *Snosheniia Rossii s Kavkazom*, doc. 12, 145.
19. Ibid., doc. 12, 148.
20. *Kabardino-russkie otnosheniia*, vol. 1, doc. 35, 60–1.

21. *Snosheniia Rossii s Kavkazom*, doc. 12, 168, 183. '[A]t the time when the prince [Murad Girey] arrives in Astrakhan, they [Murad Girey, the shamkhal, Solokh and Alkas] will unite and bring the Turks to Astrakhan … the prince [Murad Girey] will deliver the city [to the Turks].'
22. Ibid., doc. 12, 181–3.
23. N. A. Smirnov, *Rossiia i Turtsiia v XVI–XVII vv.* (Moscow: Izdatel'stvo Moskovskogo gosudarstvennogo universiteta, 1946), 139; *Pamiatniki diplomaticheskikh i torgovykh snoshenii Moskovskoi Rusi s Persiei*, ed. N. I. Veselovskii (St Petersburg: Iablonskii and Perott, 1890), 1:54; *Pamiatniki diplomaticheskikh snoshenii drevnei Rossii s derzhavami inostrannymi* (St Petersburg: Tipografiia II Otdielenia sobstvennoi E. I. V. Kantseliarii, 1851–71), 1:1011–12.
24. *Pamiatniki diplomaticheskikh i torgovykh snoshenii*, 54.
25. E. N. Kusheva, *Narody Severnogo Kavkaza i ikh sviazi s Rossiei: vtoraia polovina XVI–30-e gody XVII veka* (Moscow: Izdatel'stvo Akademii nauk SSSR, 1958), 276.
26. 'Vash gosudar' takzhe khochet sdelat' kak nad Kazan'iu snachala gorod blizko postavil a potom i Kazan' vzial no Krym ne Kazan' u Kryma mnogo ruk i glaz gosudariu vashemu nadobno budet idti mimo gorodov v seredku.' S. M. Solov'ev, *Istoriia Rossii s drevneishikh vremen* (Moscow: Izdatel'stvo sotsial'no-economicheskoi literatury, 1960), 7:265; its English translation is from C. Max Kortepeter, *Ottoman Imperialism during the Reformation: Europe and the Caucasus* (New York: New York University Press, 1972), 111; Brian L. Davies, *Warfare, State and Society on the Black Sea Steppe, 1500–1700* (Abingdon: Routledge, 2007), 17.
27. *Snosheniia Rossii s Kavkazom*, doc. 12, 145.
28. Ibid., doc. 12, 143–4; Pollock, '"Thus We Shall Have Their Loyalty"', 154.
29. Kusheva, *Narody Severnogo Kavkaza*, 231.
30. Kortepeter, *Ottoman Imperialism*, 91; *Pamiatniki diplomaticheskikh i torgovykh snoshenii*, 106–8.
31. Smirnov, *Rossiia i Turtsiia*, 138.
32. *Kabardino-russkie otnosheniia*, vol. 1, doc. 34, 58–60; *Snosheniia Rossii s Kavkazom*, doc. 12, 112.
33. *Kabardino-russkie otnosheniia*, vol. 1, doc. 34, 58–60.
34. *Snosheniia Rossii s Kavkazom*, doc. 10, 79, doc. 12, 112.
35. Ibid., doc. 12, 203; Michael Khodarkovsky, *Russia's Steppe Frontier: The Making of a Colonial Empire, 1500–1800* (Bloomington: Indiana University Press, 2002), 36.
36. *Snosheniia Rossii s Kavkazom*, doc. 12, 128, 146; *Kabardino-russkie otnosheniia*, vol. 1, doc. 39, 64–5.
37. MD 67, no. 519.
38. Kusheva, *Narody Severnogo Kavkaza*, 278; *Snosheniia Rossii s Kavkazom*, doc. 16, 253–4.
39. *Snosheniia Rossii s Kavkazom*, docs. 16 & 17, 252–9.

40. MD 67, no. 520.
41. MD 69, no. 440.
42. MD 69, no. 447.
43. Ibid.
44. Ibid.
45. Kortepeter, *Ottoman Imperialism*, 112–14.
46. Kusheva, *Narody Severnogo Kavkaza*, 281; *Kabardino-russkie otnosheniia*, vol. 1, doc. 40, 66.
47. MD 72, no 19.
48. RGADA, F. 89, *Turetskie dela*, kniga 3, fol. 227a–228b; *Kabardino-russkie otnosheniia*, vol. 1, doc. 40, 65–6.
49. RGADA, F. 89, *Turetskie dela*, kniga 3, fol. 243a–243b; *Kabardino-russkie otnosheniia*, vol. 1, doc. 40, 66.
50. RGADA, F. 89, *Turetskie dela*, kniga 3, fol. 243a–243b; *Kabardino-russkie otnosheniia*, vol. 1, doc. 40, 66.
51. MD 72, no. 53.
52. RGADA, F. 89, *Turetskie dela*, kniga 3, fol. 272a–275a; *Kabardino-russkie otnosheniia*, vol. 1, doc. 41, 68.
53. RGADA, F. 89, *Turetskie dela*, kniga 3, fol. 259a–260a; *Kabardino-russkie otnosheniia*, vol. 1, doc. 42, 68–9.
54. RGADA, F. 89, *Turetskie dela*, kniga 3, fol. 294a; *Kabardino-russkie otnosheniia*, vol. 1, doc. 43, 71.
55. *Snosheniia Rossii s Kavkazom*, doc. 16, 253–4, 256.
56. *Pamiatniki diplomaticheskikh snoshenii drevnei Rossii*, 1:1286–9.
57. MD 72, no. 53.
58. MD 72, no. 277.
59. Ibid.
60. Order to Cafer Pasha, MD 72, no. 279.
61. Kusheva, *Narody Severnogo Kavkaza*, 273–6.
62. MD 72, no. 279.
63. MD 72, no. 464.
64. MD 72, nos. 279, 513, 851.
65. MD 72, no. 279.
66. MD 72, no. 278.
67. *Snosheniia Rossii s Kavkazom*, doc. 19, 292–3.
68. MD 72, no. 279; PSRL, 14:45–6.
69. MD 72, no. 317.
70. *Snosheniia Rossii s Kavkazom*, doc. 21, 334; *Russian Embassies to the Georgian Kings*, 374.
71. *Kabardino-russkie otnosheniia*, vol. 1, doc. 43, 69–72.
72. *Snosheniia Rossii s Kavkazom*, doc. 19, 292.
73. Isaiah Gruber, 'The Muscovite Embassy of 1599 to the Emperor Rudolf II of the Habsburg', unpublished MA thesis, McGill University, 1999, 74.
74. *Snosheniia Rossii s Kavkazom*, doc. 25, 449.

75. Ibid., doc. 25, 449–50.
76. Ibid., doc. 23, 365–372.
77. Ibid., doc. 23, 365–6. According to the Muscovite sources regarding the arrival of the Kabardinian envoys led by Siunchal Murza Ianglychev, Sultan Mahmud of Daghestan sent two of his people, İbrahim and Derviş, as his representatives.
78. PSRL, 14:57–8; Kusheva, *Narody Severnogo Kavkaza*, 288; M. S. K. Umakhanov, 'Problema beglykh vo vzaimootnosheniiakh dagestanskikh feodalov s tsarskoi administratsiei na Severnom Kavkaze v XVI–XVIII vv.', in *Dagestan v sostave Rossii: Istoricheskie korni druzhby narodov Rossii i Dagestana*, ed. N. A. Magomedov (Makhachkala: Dagestanskii filial Akademii nauk SSSR, 1990), 74–8.
79. The Muscovite sources indicate that the Ottoman governor and his men, including janissaries, came to Tarku to help the Daghestanis. However, the arrival of the governor himself in Tarku cannot be confirmed in the Ottoman documents and could be an exaggeration, perhaps to explain the Muscovite defeat in 1605. Kusheva, *Narody Severnogo Kavkaza*, 288; PSRL, 14:57–8.
80. Kusheva, *Narody Severnogo Kavkaza*, 288; M. Sadık Bilge, *Osmanlı Devleti ve Kafkasya* (Istanbul: Eren, 2005), 86.
81. Kusheva, *Narody Severnogo Kavkaza*, 288; Chantal Lemercier-Quelquejay, 'Cooptation of the Elites of Kabarda and Daghestan in the Sixteenth Century', in *The North Caucasus Barrier: The Russian Advance towards the Muslim World*, ed. Marie Bennigsen Broxup (London: Hurst, 1992), 40.
82. Khodarkovsky, *Russia's Steppe Frontier,* 114.
83. Murat Yaşar, 'The North Caucasus between the Ottoman Empire and the Tsardom of Muscovy: The Beginnings, 1552–1570', *Iran and the Caucasus* 20 (2016): 123–4.

6

Searching for the Milky Way: A Tale of Five Narts

W. E. D. Allen writes, 'A natural desire to ride all the horses at once was characteristic of the North Caucasian chieftains.'[1] Similarly, according to Chantal Lemercier-Quelquejay, the North Caucasian chiefs played one empire off against the other, and in order to maximise their material and political benefits from the imperial rivalry, they readily changed not only their protector but even their religion.[2] They indeed 'rode all the horses', that is to say, they changed their political alliances and religion or sometimes submitted to the Ottoman sultan and Muscovite tsar simultaneously. However, as this chapter argues, while riding all the horses at once, their hands were tied behind their backs.

The arguments and ideas presented here are, to a certain extent, connected with the old question of nomadic 'greedy or needy' theories, common among the historians of Inner Asian Turco-Mongol steppe powers and their relations with their sedentary neighbours.[3] In the case of the North Caucasus, as exemplified above, historians, using either Ottoman or Muscovite sources to examine the history of the region, claim that the North Caucasus rulers – be they Western Circassian, Kabardinian or Daghestani chiefs – tried to gain utmost advantage out of the imperial rivalry over their territories between the Ottomans and Muscovites. They were 'greedy' and persistently sought higher salaries, loftier titles and more gifts from different powers at different times or simultaneously. Pledges of allegiance meant little to these rulers. They broke their promises easily and even changed their religion whenever it promised greater rewards. However, this was certainly not the case from the perspective of the North Caucasus political elite, as the previous chapters explain.

Can it be argued that it was their 'need' to 'ride all the horses' then? The North Caucasus peoples and polities were not fully nomadic except for the Nogay hordes, and most of them in the sixteenth century were, in fact, autarkic. Considering that in the early modern period, the North Caucasus was a source of slaves, renowned ironworks, apiculture products and other desired goods with a location that connected several important trade routes, it is evident that the North Caucasus people and polities were giving their resources to outsiders rather than needing any from outside powers. That means 'needy' was not precisely the case either. It was, however, still a need, not economic but political, that forced the local rulers to play one power off against another. They had to negotiate with external powers and play the imperial game, sometimes for survival and sometimes to retain independence in their own lands.

This chapter analyses policies, strategies and objectives of five rulers who submitted to both the Muscovite tsar and the Ottoman sultan simultaneously or at different times in the second half of the sixteenth century. The local chiefs examined are Kansavuk and Sibok of the Janeys, Solokh of the Kabardinians and Urus of the Greater Nogays. In addition, although his lands were not in the North Caucasus, Alexander II of Kakheti will be mentioned thanks to his role in the North Caucasus borderland and in the imperial rivalry over it. Apart from these individual rulers, the family rivalry between the Kaytuk(ov)s and the Idar(ov)s, which led to the numerous invasions of Kabarda by different powers, is one of the central foci of the Kabardinian section below.

6.1 Kansavuk and Sibok of the Janey Circassians

Kansavuk and his son Sibok, both from the Janeys in the Taman region, are didactic examples of North Caucasus rulers and their intertwined relations with the imperial powers in the Western Circassian lands. Kansavuk was the most potent chief in the immediate vicinity of the Taman Fortress until his death at the hands of the Ottomans in 1559, during one of his attacks on the Ottoman possessions in alliance with the Zaporozhian Cossacks led by Vyshnevetskyi. In 1539, Sultan Süleyman I granted Kansavuk the title of *sancakbeyi* (governor) and salary, a typical aspect of Ottoman 'carrot and stick' policy in the region. This arrangement with the Porte made his lands a province (*sancak*) of the Ottoman Empire – theoretically, an administrative area directly attached to the Porte. However, it would be misleading to consider this as being the same as a regular Ottoman province administrated from the Porte. These titles were a way of rewarding local rulers and cementing their submission to the Ottoman sultan. With titles came imperial status, annuities and support from the Ottoman Empire. Kanvasuk's conversation with Crimean Khan Sahib Girey in 1539, recorded in a chronicle, evinces that in exchange for these favours, he promised to protect Ottoman subjects and possessions close to his realm. He claimed before the Crimean khan that he was able to muster an army of 15,000 men, which was quite a substantial and perhaps a slightly exaggerated number for a local ruler in the early modern North Caucasus.[4]

When he failed to keep his promise towards the sultan, the Crimean khan raided his territories, as the pre-1569 Ottoman policy in the region dictated. Ottoman policy tended to restrict Crimean raids in the Kuban–Taman region, largely thanks to the Porte's intention to turn this strategic area into a centrally administrated region, in which the Porte wanted to impose the Ottoman rule of law. The Kuban–Taman region, especially the Taman Peninsula, was vital for the security of the Black Sea. Despite the Ottoman preference for accommodating the local rulers in this particular region, Kansavuk was targeted more than once by the Crimean Tatars, who often welcomed any chance to raid the Circassian territories for slaves and booty. The Ottoman Porte employed the Crimean Tatars effectively in order to persuade the Western Circassian rulers to submit to the sultan and accept the Ottoman view of the sultanic authority. Kansavuk's case was the same. The Ottomans expected absolute loyalty from Kansavuk after furnishing him with the symbols of investiture, titles and salaries. Their demands, however, were not limited to political submission. The Porte required certain services that could be difficult to carry out such as protecting the nearby Ottoman subjects and possessions. Due to the peculiar structure of the Western Circassian societies, in which each local ruler was virtually independent, he was in no position to control other Circassian tribes or order other chiefs not to attack the Ottomans or Crimeans. Whenever he failed to prevent attacks, the Crimean khan, with the Porte's blessing, raided his lands. This was the pattern of relationship that Kansavuk had to navigate before the rise of Muscovy in the region as a rival to the Porte.

In 1555, Kansavuk's son Sibok came to Moscow along with other representatives of Circassian tribes of the Kuban and Beshtau regions. Kansavuk's experience of the Ottoman 'carrot and stick' policy and the destructive raids of his lands by the Crimean Tatars explains why he sought support from a newly emerging power interested in establishing a sphere of influence in the North Caucasus. The Circassian princes in 1555 petitioned Tsar Ivan IV for protection from the Crimean Tatars, which the tsar gladly accepted.[5] Sibok converted to Orthodox Christianity and took the Christian name Vasilii.[6] He pledged an oath of allegiance (*shert'*) to serve the Muscovite tsar in the name of his people, the Janeys.[7] In return, Ivan IV offered the Janeys military support through Vyshnevetskyi's Cossacks and encouraged them to engage the Crimean Tatars and Ottomans in the Kuban–Taman region by attacking their possessions. While the Janeys and other Western Circassians fought the Crimean and Ottoman forces, the Muscovite officials' preference for establishing their suzerainty in nearby Kabarda did not go unnoticed. Sibok, in these years, realised that

Figure 6.1 Prince Vyshnevetskyi and Prince Sibok in Ivan IV's service, 1560.

Source: *Litsevoi letopisnyi svod XVI veka*, vol. 23, https://runivers.ru/upload/iblock/06d/LLS23.pdf.

the Muscovites took advantage of their submission and would abandon the Janeys and other Western Circassians if there was enough pressure from the Ottoman Porte. Notwithstanding their earlier successes, which enabled effective Muscovite strategies in Kabarda, in the early 1560s, the tide turned against the Cossacks and their allied Circassians, as the Ottoman and Crimean forces began to rout them.

At this point, Sibok and the other chiefs knew that the Crimeans and Ottomans could punish them by raiding their lands because they had allied with Muscovy and the Cossacks. Upon Sibok recognising that the Muscovites had indeed abandoned their Western Circassian allies to the mercy of the Ottomans and Crimeans, he took refuge in territories of the Grand Duchy of Lithuania.[8] Soon after that, most possibly out of the new balance of power in the Western Circassian lands, dominated by the Ottoman Empire and the Crimean Khanate, Sibok entered the service of the Crimean khan. There is no record of Sibok's conversion to Islam when he entered the service of the Crimean khan. He might have served the khan against his former master, the Muscovite tsar, as an Orthodox Christian. What is certain about the strategies of Kansavuk and Sibok is that they did not change their patrons multiple times to maximise their benefits but to survive in their own lands, which were now more intensively targeted by external powers. With a title and a salary from the Porte, Kansavuk had a status within the Ottoman imperial system, but the circumstances beyond his control and the Crimean campaigns caused the devastation of his lands several times in less than a decade. This left him no choice but to look for support against the overwhelming, punitive raids of the Crimean Tatars, which most of the time were supported or sometimes instigated by the Ottoman governors in Kefe and Azak.[9] Muscovy, at that point, promised the much-needed external support to balance the Ottoman and Crimean power. However, the Janeys, just like other inhabitants of this borderland, took the brunt of the imperial competition over their lands. Kansavuk lost his life, and Sibok had to flee, eventually returning to Crimea to serve the khan. In the mid-1560s, the situation for most of the Western chiefs and tribes was the same as before the appearance of Muscovy and their alliance with it between 1552 and 1555 – the Ottomans and Crimeans were the overlords, and Muscovite help was no longer available.

6.2 Solokh of Kabarda

Prince Solokh was from the Tasoltan (Tausaltan) family and related to Temriuk's family of the Idars through Inal, the legendary ancestor of all of the princely Kabardinian families.[10] The Ottoman sources show that, along with Ibak (known as Abak in the Ottoman documents), who was a cousin of Solokh, the Tasoltan family cooperated with the Ottomans and Crimean Tatars in the 1580s and 1590s. Solokh was the eldest of the three sons of Tansaruk and became pshi of his family after Tansaruk died in the first decades of the second half of the sixteenth century.[11] Since Solokh was one of the most prominent rulers in Kabarda in the 1580s, the Muscovites were determined to draw him to their side in this crucial decade for both imperial powers vying for supremacy in the region.

In the 1580s, Solokh received several letters from the Ottoman Porte regarding its North Caucasus supply route. In these letters, often accompanied by gifts, the sultan asked him to help the Ottoman army and messengers going through his lands. For example, the Porte sent him a robe of honour in 1583 with an Ottoman officer who was travelling to Derbend from Kefe.[12] Three years later, Solokh, along with other Kabardinian and Western Circassian chiefs, was instructed to ensure the safety of the treasury sent to Derbend from the Porte as it passed through Kabarda.[13] Solokh's pro-Ottoman/Crimean orientation was further cemented by the marriage of his daughter to the Crimean khan. According to a report sent by Kudenek and Chapalov of Kabarda to the Muscovites, a Crimean prince visited Solokh's settlement and spent a winter there in the late 1580s.[14] The Muscovites were also aware of Solokh's ongoing relationship with the Ottoman Porte.[15]

During this time, Solokh's gentry was not entirely on board with his alliances and his role in the Ottoman/Crimean strategies in Kabarda. The Muscovite sources present an interesting and illustrating conversation between Solokh and his nobles who supported an alliance with the Muscovites rather than the Ottomans and Crimean Tatars. His nobles questioned Solokh: 'The entire Kabardinian land is now serving the sovereign [the Muscovite tsar], and you are still willing to oppose the tsar and the entire Kabardinian land?'[16] One of his nobles even threatened to leave Solokh to serve another prince if Solokh insisted on serving the Crimean khan and the Ottoman sultan.[17] Unfortunately, our source does not specify why Solokh's nobles were trying to convince their prince to join the Muscovite camp. What we know is that, in the late 1580s, Muscovite power in Kabarda was undoubtedly on the rise. By 1588, the Muscovites had achieved a strong position there thanks to the allegiance of the Idar family headed by Kanbulat and Mamstriuk, direct Muscovite military involvement with their troops and Cossacks stationed in Terek Town, and the construction of new fortresses on the Sunzha River. Therefore, the gentry might have thought that offering their allegiance to the Muscovites might be the only way to secure their position in Kabarda. The nobles were most possibly encouraged by Mamstriuk, who visited Solokh's settlements several times to bring him letters from the Muscovite tsar and the governor of Terek. Mamstriuk apparently had some allies among Solokh's gentry.[18] Faced with the opposition of his nobles, Solokh responded that he could not leave the Crimean khan and the shamkhal because his daughters were married to them, and many of his good men were in the Crimean Khanate and Daghestan.[19]

Taking advantage of the international conjecture, the Muscovites were readying for military raids in the late 1580s on the pro-Ottoman/Crimean rulers in Kabarda, including Solokh, Tapshiuk, Aslanbek and Yansokh.[20] The tsar sent an order to the governor of Terek in August 1588, asking him to prepare for a campaign in cooperation with Kanbulat, Mamstriuk, Kudenek and other Muscovite vassals to punish the Kabardinian chiefs who refused to submit to the tsar and 'did not restrain themselves from having relations with the Crimean Tatars and Ottomans'.[21] For this reason, in 1589, Solokh approached the tsar through Crimean Prince Murad Girey, who was still in Muscovy. Solokh probably thought this move would not cause an alarm in the Crimean Khanate or at the Porte because Murad Girey had already sent a letter of submission to the Crimean khan and Ottoman sultan in 1588. As may be remembered, the sultan accepted his submission and pardoned him.[22] In February 1589, Solokh sent his envoys, Bikan and Lana, to Moscow to pledge allegiance to Murad Girey and the tsar. According to the Muscovite records, his envoys petitioned Solokh to be taken 'under the royal hand of the tsar'.[23] Solokh's submission was important for the Muscovites as he was one of the strongest chiefs in Kabarda. For this reason, besides Mamstriuk and Kanbulat, Solokh was the only other Kabardinian chief to whom the tsar sent a letter in July 1589, ordering him to dispatch men to fight for Muscovy against the Swedish Empire.[24]

By submitting to the tsar, Solokh averted a possible military raid on his territories by the Muscovite forces and his rival Kabardinian chiefs. However, this strategy did not last long, and in the autumn of 1589, only a few months after the tsar's letter, Mamstriuk declared Solokh to be the only pro-Ottoman/Crimean chief left in Kabarda.[25] The governor of Terek also reported that Solokh neither gave hostages nor came to Terek Town to pay homage to the tsar and receive his annuity.[26] As their policy dictated, the Muscovites first tried to convince Solokh one more time to part with the Crimean Tatars and Ottomans. The Muscovite envoys to Georgian King Alexander II met with Solokh on their way to Kakheti and gave him a robe of honour, a hat, sables and other gifts with a total value of 82 rubles.[27] The higher value of the gifts sent to him compared to other local rulers shows Solokh's prominence in Kabarda. The contemporary Muscovite sources indicate that other princes in Kabarda feared Solokh's power. When Mamstriuk visited Solokh to bring him a letter from the Muscovites, he and Kudenek preferred out of fear not to enter his settlement but camped a bit further away.[28] In fact, as one of the strongest chiefs, Solokh was a contender for the position of the pshihua after Kanbulat's and Aslanbek's deaths in 1589.

Because of his alliance with the Ottomans and Crimeans, the Idar family and their allies did not favour Solokh for the position of pshihua. Therefore, it must have been clear to Solokh that the Kabardinian chiefs in alliance with Muscovy would fight his bid for this prestigious yet titular position. Following the death of Aslanbek, the pshihua candidate had to receive the support of the pro-Muscovite party as they formed the majority of the Kabardinian chiefs in 1589. Since Mamstriuk, Kudenek and the Muscovites did not trust Solokh, Solokh knew that the only support he could get to strengthen his position in Kabarda could come from the Crimean Tatars and Ottomans. He also knew that even if he accepted Muscovite suzerainty, the Muscovite officials were suspicious of him, and there was a possibility that eventually, Mamstriuk and other rivals could convince the Muscovites to eliminate him.

Yansokh's rapprochement with Muscovy after the death of his brother the Kabardinian pshihua Aslanbek, who worked with the Ottomans in the North Caucasus, can also be explained within the framework of the power struggle among the Kabardinian chiefs. The Muscovites listed Yansokh as one of the Kabardinian chiefs who refused to be taken 'under the royal hand of the tsar'. Besides Aslanbek and Solokh, Yansokh was a target of the military campaigns organised by the Muscovites and pro-Muscovite Kabardinian chiefs in the 1580s.[29] In the autumn of 1589, he switched sides and pledged allegiance to the Muscovite tsar. This was most likely a move made to ensure the support of the Kabardinian chiefs allied with Muscovy for his bid to be the pshihua of Kabarda after Aslanbek in 1589. After all, it was an election, and the support of the pro-Muscovite party was necessary to be elected. His submission to Muscovy also provided him with security against Solokh, who was a contender for the position. By ensuring the support of the Kabardinian chiefs allied with Muscovy, Yansokh secured his position and himself against the ambitions of Solokh. Along with Yansokh, many other princes from his family, who previously assisted the Ottoman operations in the region, submitted to Muscovy in late 1589.

Solokh is the epitome of the inability of local rulers to maintain their independence without relying on an external power in the borderlands.

The same quandary emerged wherever Ottoman/Crimean and Muscovite ambitions collided in the North Caucasus in the sixteenth century. After local rulers of the North Caucasus borderland entered into what they considered to be an alliance with an imperial power, receiving military or financial support, they soon realised the pattern of relationship changed into vassalage and found themselves dependent on one of the imperial powers. Meanwhile, their local and political rivals often appealed to the other imperial power for support, continuing the cycle of dependency and imperial manipulation.

Solokh also represents the flexibility of local and international politics in the North Caucasus borderland. Solokh was able to avoid several attacks on his lands. Because of the growing opposition from his gentry and the imminent threat of a Muscovite military intervention encouraged by Mamstriuk and the new pshihua of Kabarda, Yansokh, Solokh acquiesced to the tsar's authority along with Alkas – one of his allies in Kabarda. He took the oath of allegiance and gave one of his nobles as a hostage to the Muscovite envoys in the autumn of 1589. When he was taking the oath in the presence of the Muscovite envoys, Solokh acknowledged that he had been 'receiving gifts from the Ottoman sultan and Crimean khan but now wished to serve the sovereign tsar and be protected under the tsar's royal hand'. Referring to the local politics, he said to the Muscovite envoys that his rival Kabardinian chiefs must have told them 'many lies about him'.[30]

His submission to the tsar, however, did not save Solokh. Mamstriuk and his allies convinced the Muscovites that Solokh was deceitful, and a punitive force led by the governor of Terek consisting of Muscovite *strel'tsy* and Cossacks and supported by some Kabardinian chiefs raided Solokh's settlements. In the end, Solokh sued for peace by surrendering his son and twenty of his nobles as hostages.[31] Thereby, the pro-Muscovite party in Kabarda pacified Solokh by force. Meanwhile, the Ottoman interests in Daghestan and the possibility of Muscovite intervention in the lands of the shamkhal forced the Porte to direct its resources to Daghestan rather than to support the pro-Ottoman chiefs in Kabarda. In the 1580s and 1590s, Daghestan was much more important to the Ottomans for its strategic location and their newly established administrative units in Derbend, Shirvan and Şemahı. The Ottoman officials might have calculated that Kabarda could be subdued as soon as they secured their hegemony over Daghestan. In fact, this proved to be a well-calculated strategy. When the Muscovites were ousted from Daghestan in the early years of the seventeenth century, they also withdrew from Kabarda. Many Kabardinian chiefs returned to the Ottoman/Crimean camp after the final defeat of the Muscovites in Daghestan in 1605.

Besides, Solokh poses an excellent example of how and why a local ruler in the North Caucasus shifted his loyalty. Solokh did not abandon one overlord for another to maximise his rewards in terms of salaries or gifts. As may be remembered, he refused to meet the Muscovite envoys and receive the gifts sent by the tsar. His daughters were married to the Crimean khan and the shamkhal and many of his men were in the Crimean Khanate and Daghestan. Such arrangements tied his hands, so he trod carefully in his relationships with these external powers. He eventually took the pledge of allegiance to the Muscovite tsar to ensure his survival in the conjecture of the inter-imperial but, more importantly, the domestic political developments of the time. In the end, Solokh succeeded in retaining his power by cleverly navigating the complex situation and power dynamics during and after the Muscovite incursions into Daghestan, eventually becoming the dominant Kabardinian prince at the turn of the century.

Therefore, imperial strategies and local politics were intertwined in Kabarda, as was the case in the entire North Caucasus borderland. If we look at the imperial competition from a Kabardinian viewpoint, what we consider to be the rivalry between the Ottoman Empire and Muscovy in the second half of the sixteenth century can be seen as a power struggle between two princely Kabardinian families – the Kaytuks and the Idars. These princely families were relatives, yet also rivals for power and dominance in Kabarda. Inal's son, Tabuly Mirza, had three sons. The eldest son, Inarmas, was the father of Idar, and Idar was the father of Temriuk and Kanbulat. Thus, Temriuk and his brothers were known as the Idars. The second son of Tabuly Mirza was Yankhot, and from his son Beslen descended Kaytuk, who was the father of Psheapshoko, Arslan and Yansokh, thus forming the Kaytuk family. Yankhot had another son named Tasoltan, whose son was Tansaruk, the father of Solokh.[32]

It was the competition between these two princely families in the first place rather than antagonism towards the Crimean Tatars or the shamkhal that led Temriuk to seek alliance with the Muscovite tsar. Temriuk was the eldest son of Idar, who was the pshihua of Kabarda in the first half of the sixteenth century. With Idar's death, the power struggle in Kabarda intensified; Temriuk then used the opportunity that a rising new power presented, and used it well. He established a military alliance with the Muscovites. However, his Kabardinian rivals were still strong enough to force him to flee to Astrakhan in 1563. Temriuk was able to restore his power in Kabarda only with direct Muscovite military help, consisting of 1,000 *strel'tsy* and Cossacks. Without the Muscovite support, the Kaytuk family, led by Psheapshoko, brother of Aslanbek and Yansokh, could have overwhelmed Temriuk of the Idars. In their struggle against Temriuk and his Muscovite allies, Psheapshoko and Aslanbek of the Kaytuks sought help from the Ottoman sultan and Crimean khan.[33]

With the construction of a Muscovite fortress in the heart of Kabarda in 1567, the Kaytuk family's fortunes further deteriorated. However, the same Muscovite fortress embroiled the Ottoman Empire in North Caucasus affairs and changed the Ottomans' understanding of their northern frontiers. Considering the Muscovite fortress as a threat, the sultan instructed the Crimean khan to raid Kabardinian lands that belonged to the pro-Muscovite chiefs. This raid failed to deter Muscovy, and the tsar refused to abandon the fortress until 1571. He did eventually agree to raze the fortress in order to assuage the Ottoman sultan, following the latter's foundered campaign to take Astrakhan. The real victory for the Kaytuks came in 1570 when the Crimean Tatar forces devastated the lands of Temriuk and other clients of Muscovy. In this campaign, Kazy, son of Psheapshoko, guided the Crimean forces through Kabarda. Kazy was from the Kaytuk family and a nephew of Aslanbek.[34] With the direct military intervention of the Crimean Khanate, the Kaytuk family succeeded in breaking the power and hegemony of the Idars in Kabarda. Temriuk was dead, and his two sons were taken prisoner by the Crimean Tatars.[35]

There is no information in the Ottoman and Muscovite sources about the exact circumstances following Temriuk's death and leading to Kanbulat's election as the pshihua of Kabarda. However, the lack of Muscovite activity until 1577–8, when Kanbulat submitted to the tsar, means that there was a form of peace between the Idar and Kaytuk families. This may also explain how Kanbulat, Temriuk's brother, was successful in attaining this titular position to replace Temriuk despite the great loss of power by the Idars. The chiefs allied with the Ottomans and Crimeans in Kabarda were influential and powerful between 1570 and 1578. As may be remembered, the Ottoman Porte appointed a Kabardinian chief, who had a Muslim name of Mehmed, as the governor of Kabarda in 1573.[36]

The Kabardinian chiefs of the Kaytuk lineage remained loyal to the Ottoman sultan and Crimean khan in the 1580s. The Porte sent orders to Aslanbek, his brothers Yansokh and Tapshiuk, and his nephew Kazy, asking for their assistance for the Ottoman troops passing through their lands.[37] Aslanbek was also a relative of Özdemiroğlu Osman Pasha, and they met in person in Kabarda in 1584. Asafi Dal Mehmed Çelebi, who was with the Ottoman army in the Caucasus at this time, writes in his *Şeca'atname* that Osman Pasha's paternal side was of Egyptian Circassian origin and related to Arslan's family, which implies that Özdemiroğlu Osman Pasha was a member of the Kaytuk clan.[38] Thanks to his Kabardinian lineage and his policy of promoting an active Ottoman presence in the North Caucasus, Osman Pasha had in his retinue some Circassian nobles. He also sent a proposal to the Porte for the construction of fortresses in Kabarda that could facilitate a defined Ottoman control over the region. For their part, as the allies of the Porte, Aslanbek, Gazi and Kaplan of the Kaytuks helped the Ottoman armies and messengers travelling to Kefe from Derbend by building bridges on the rivers and providing them with food and other necessary supplies.[39]

Due to the rising power of the Kaytuks and the support they received from the Ottomans and Crimean Tatars, Kanbulat of the Idars, with the encouragement of Temriuk's son Mamstriuk, decided to seek help from the Muscovites in 1577–8. The Muscovite tsar gladly accepted Kanbulat's petition and began supporting the Idars and their allies in Kabarda against the Kaytuks and the Tasoltans (Solokh's family). With Osman Pasha's departure from the North Caucasus in 1583 and their newly established administrative units in the Caucasus, the Ottomans prioritised Daghestan and the South Caucasus in their policy calculations. As one may remember, another reason for the Ottomans to keep a keen eye on Daghestan at this time was the problem of the fugitive Crimean princes. These new developments paved the way for the Muscovites to solidify their presence in Kabarda. With the help of the Cossacks, the Muscovite tsar provided solid support for his Kabardinian clients and helped them defend their position in Kabarda against the chiefs of the Kaytuk and Tasoltan families.

With Ottoman focus remaining on Daghestan and the construction of a Muscovite fortress at the mouth of the Terek River in 1588, Kabardinian politics underwent yet another change in favour of the Idars. Mamstriuk and Kudenek, son of Kanbulat, signed a *shert'* in Moscow and received guarantees that the tsar would order military operations against their rivals in Kabarda. The Muscovite troops and Cossacks could now support the Idars directly from the Muscovite fortresses in the region. However, the Kaytuks, specifically Aslanbek, were not easy targets. In fact, the Muscovites first tried to draw Aslanbek to their side diplomatically. These efforts did not bear fruit. In the end, he was strong enough to become the pshihua of Kabarda after Kanbulat's death in 1589. This is important because, with his election, the position of pshihua passed from the Idars to the Kaytuks. Despite the palpable Muscovite influence in Kabarda, Aslanbek received this prestigious title while still an ally of the Crimean khan and the Porte, as reported by the Muscovites.[40] However, Aslanbek died shortly after his election in 1589. The Muscovite influence and power in Kabarda reached its high point after his death. In the last decade of the sixteenth century, the Muscovites succeeded in turning the majority of the Kabardinian chiefs into their clients. With Aslanbek out of the picture, they also secured the allegiance of his brother Yansokh, who became the next pshihua of Kabarda. Consequentially, the Kaytuk family split in terms of political alliances with the sultan or the tsar. Yansokh allied with the pro-Muscovite chiefs in Kabarda to keep the title of pshihua and have the upper hand against his main rival, Solokh, but other Kaytuk chiefs were still in contact with the Porte and the Crimean Tatars. In the 1590s, some Kaytuk elite, especially Kazy, were biding their time and watching the developments in Kabarda and other parts of the North Caucasus.

In the end, encouraged by the setbacks suffered by the Muscovites in Daghestan in 1594, Kazy of the Kaytuks planned to get rid of the most fervent supporters of the Muscovites in Kabarda, namely Mamstriuk and Domanuk, both sons of Temriuk. He invited them for a feast in his settlement and put them in chains afterwards, eventually killing them both.[41] With the death of Mamstriuk and Domanuk, the Idars lost their influence in Kabarda. Kazy did not incur punishment from the Muscovites or Yansokh, which indicates that Muscovite power in Kabarda was on the decline, as a result of their overextended resources and defeat in Daghestan. For the Kaytuks and their allies, the Crimean Tatars and Ottomans were preferable to the Muscovites, as they never established fortresses or stationed troops in Kabarda. The Idars, on the other hand, had invested in direct Muscovite support to retain their power and dominance in Kabarda since the time of Temriuk. According to a Muscovite ambassadorial report compiled in 1589, the main reason why Solokh disliked Mamstriuk and Kudenek was that the latter two 'brought the Muscovite soldiers and fortresses into the Kabardinian territories'.[42]

6.3 Urus of the Greater Nogays

Another local ruler caught between the two empires was Urus Mirza (c. 1578,[43] Urus Beg) of the Greater Nogays. The Greater Nogay Horde settled the lands close to the North Caucasus along the lower Volga and Yaik rivers. Urus Mirza's activities had a significant impact on the imperial rivalry in the North Caucasus borderland in the second half of the sixteenth century. In fact, the Greater Nogay Horde was a consequential player in the balance of power in the Pontic–Caspian steppes, the lower Volga and the North Caucasus. The Ottomans appreciated their role and tried to vassalise Urus. If the Greater Nogay Horde allied with the Porte, the Ottomans could encircle the Muscovites not only in the North Caucasus but also in the lower Volga. In the 1570s and 1580s, the allegiance of Urus was also vital for Muscovy, as he was capable of posing a serious danger to the defence of Muscovite cities and people in the south.[44]

Urus was ambitious even when he was only a mirza. Muscovite sources indicate that in 1569, during the Astrakhan campaign, he approached the Ottoman commander Kasım Pasha. He offered to support the Ottoman army during the siege, pointing out that he would only serve the sultan, but not the Crimean khan because of their ancient feud.[45] In 1574, Urus, who was still a mirza, relayed through the governor of Azak his desire to be a vassal of the Ottoman sultan.[46] However, at both these times, the Greater Nogays were clients of the Muscovite tsar under their leaders, İsmail Beg and Tinahmet Beg. According to V. V. Trepavlov, what Urus wanted in these years and after he became the ruler of the Greater Nogay Horde was to reinvigorate his people and revitalise their power along the Volga and Yaik, which had been gradually circumscribed by the Muscovites based in Astrakhan.[47] Urus recognised that if he continued to follow the policies of his predecessors, the independence of the Greater Nogays would be lost completely as their dependence on Muscovy was becoming critical. It meant that the survival of the Nogays in the Pontic–Caspian steppes along the Volga River could soon be a prerogative of the Muscovite tsar. Unlike his father, İsmail Beg, who relied on Muscovy, Urus preferred to multiply his options for alliances and, when strong enough, change the existing pattern of the vassalage relation with Muscovy.

From his perspective, the Ottoman Porte was the only other power that could compete with the rising influence of Muscovy in the lower Volga region. Urus, in both 1569 and 1574, bypassed the Crimean khan, whom he perceived as a rival and enemy, and directly communicated with the Ottoman Porte through its governors in Kefe and Azak. While the Ottoman officials were receptive, they did not want to jeopardise the vassalage of the Crimean Khanate by allying with Urus without Crimean approval. For this reason, in 1574, the Porte instructed the governor of Azak to consult with the Crimean khan about the submission of Urus Mirza of the Greater Nogays.[48] When the Lesser Nogays had settled in the area close to Azak from 1557, there had sometimes been problems of plundering or other unlawful activities until the Ottoman governors succeeded in restraining them.[49] Besides respecting the status of the Crimean khan in the Pontic–Caspian steppes, this initially deleterious experience with the Lesser Nogays could explain the reluctance of the Ottomans to welcome the Greater Nogays with open arms. There are no records of the exact reaction and stance of the Crimean khan vis-à-vis this situation. But no further negotiations about the submission of Urus to the Ottoman sultan took place, which makes it safe to assume that the khan might not have given a positive response in 1574.

The Porte's stance changed in 1578 when the Ottomans welcomed a wide array of allies for its campaign against the Safavid Empire. The sultan and the khan approached Urus and asked for his participation in the Ottoman war effort in the Caucasus, specifically in their operations in Shirvan.[50] Urus welcomed the opportunity for slaves and other spoils of war that could strengthen his position among the Nogays and against the Muscovites. The sultan greatly appreciated the services that Urus Beg rendered during the war. As a reward, he received annuities from the revenues of Azak. Apart from Urus, the Greater Nogay mirzas, who joined the Crimean Tatar army against the Safavids, were granted salaries from the Porte.[51] Unlike their earlier calculations and negotiations, this time the Porte did not consider it necessary to consult with the Crimean khan about registering the Nogay leaders on their payroll. The Ottomans were then determined to secure their hegemony in the Caucasus, and the Greater Nogay cooperation proved to be an effective strategy in the region.

The spoils of war from the raids in Shirvan and the annuities provided by the Porte provided Urus with a means of challenging the Muscovite economic hegemony over the Greater Nogays. Urus also established active diplomatic relations with the Central Asian khanates and received additional annuities from the Khanate of Bukhara.[52] Engaged on its western frontier in the Livonian War, Muscovy was not able to spare any troops to check Urus and his ambitious policies in the lower Volga and Caucasus. Therefore, by taking advantage of the international situation and strategically submitting to multiple patrons, Urus managed to restore the broad autonomy of the Greater Nogays and their bargaining power in the early 1580s. In fact, he was confident enough in 1580 to write to Tsar Ivan IV that the Greater Nogays were now at war with Muscovy. In his letter, he demanded that the Muscovite tsar pay him annuities for Kazan and Astrakhan as well, claiming that these khanates had previously paid annuities to the Nogays. He argued that it was the tsar's responsibility to pay their dues as the current ruler of these former khanates.[53] To add insult to injury, the Greater Nogays raided Muscovite lands in 1580 with the Crimean Tatars and Lesser Nogays. Encouraged by his successes and the Muscovites' inability to react at the time, Urus demanded more from the tsar as the price of peace in the Pontic–Caspian steppes. In 1581, he asked for 500 rubles as an annuity. The tsar eventually accepted the price to contain Urus Beg and his Nogays at this critical time when his armies were suffering defeats in the Livonian War.[54]

With no army to spare against the Nogays in the Pontic–Caspian steppes, the Muscovites began to use their 'wild card', that is, the Cossacks. In the mid-1580s, as was the case in the North Caucasus, Cossack activity along the lower Volga and Yaik rivers intensified with the blessing of the tsar to an extent that it forced Urus Beg to mend his ways with the Muscovites once more. In these years, the Muscovites were also extending their line of defence in the steppes by building new fortresses. Two of these fortresses were designed to control the Greater Nogay Horde. One was Tsaritsyn, between the Don and Volga rivers, and the other was Yaik, at the mouth of the Yaik River.[55] Thanks to these new fortresses and military pressure applied by the Cossacks, Urus Beg had no choice but to appease the Muscovite tsar, while still wanting to keep his options open. In 1586, Urus sent another letter of submission to the Ottoman sultan and petitioned him and the Crimean khan for military assistance against Muscovy.[56] However, the lower Volga was not a priority for the Porte, and the Ottoman armies were busy in the Caucasus. Urus also tried to form an alliance with the Khanate of Bukhara and the Ottoman Empire against the Tsardom of Muscovy by promising the sultan that he would bring the Volga and Yaik rivers and Astrakhan under the sovereignty of the Porte. The Muscovites knew of Urus's plan and promises to the Porte through their officials who were approached by a Nogay mirza, a son of Tinahmet.[57]

Despite his strategies to free the Greater Nogays from the Muscovite control that the tsarist troops and new fortresses brought to bear, Urus had to give in and pledge his allegiance with a *shert'* to the Muscovite tsar in the same year. His *shert'* stipulated that he would not join the military excursions of the Crimean Tatars against the Safavids.[58] Besides, he put his weight behind Crimean Prince Murad Girey in the Crimean succession crisis. As may be remembered, the Muscovites were instrumental in forming an alliance between the fugitive prince and the Nogays. In a letter to Urus, Saadet Girey, Murad's brother, stated that Murad Girey received support from the Muscovite tsar in the form of thousands of *strel'tsy* who were now under his command. Saadet Girey asked Urus to help Murad Girey with his bid for the Crimean throne.[59] The alignment of Urus with the fugitive Crimean princes further distanced him from the Crimean khan and the Ottoman Porte. Urus still hoped to curry favour with the sultan. He sent a letter to the Porte in 1587, in which he justified his actions by saying that he was forced to join the Muscovite camp. Urus wrote that whoever controlled the Volga River and Astrakhan held sway over the Greater Nogays, thus he had no choice but to ally with the Muscovites and Murad Girey for the sake of his people's survival in the steppes.[60] His appeal was essentially true. He certainly had no course but to give in to the Muscovite pressure, as no material support was provided to him by the Ottomans or Crimean Tatars.

However, the letter from Urus to the sultan occasioned discussions about a campaign for Astrakhan among the officials at the Porte. Thus, in the autumn of 1587, the Ottomans were planning another campaign to take the city in order to put an end to Muscovite power in the lower Volga region and the North Caucasus borderland. The Ottomans calculated that Urus Beg could play a substantial role in this undertaking. On 24 September 1587, the sultan sent Urus an imperial letter, asking him to join the Ottoman campaign to 'save Astrakhan from the Muscovite infidels in accordance with the requirements of his submission to the Porte'. The letter was worded as if Urus had always been a loyal vassal of the sultan. The sultan instructed him to consult with Piyale Pasha, the assigned commander of the Ottoman army that would march on Astrakhan.[61] In the end, however, the Porte did not carry out the planned campaign. Following this, Urus Beg fought several battles against the Lesser Nogays, which were prevalent in the steppes between the two Nogay hordes, and in 1590, he was killed in one of them.

If one reads about Urus Beg from the Muscovite sources only, he appears as yet another reptilian nomadic ruler in Muscovy's southern steppes who submitted to the Muscovite tsar, received the tsar's annuity, but always complained about the amount being low and gifts being not enough. Whenever he had the chance or support from a rival power, he did not hesitate to break his promises or even attack the Muscovite possessions. However, such a portrayal of Urus Beg is one-sided and incomplete. The Ottomans, unfortunately, did not keep detailed records about the Greater Nogay Horde, except for their diplomatic correspondences and some references in the sixteenth- and seventeenth-century chronicles. While the Ottoman sources evince that the Porte wanted to employ Urus and the Greater Nogays in its military undertakings in the Caucasus and in its plans to capture Astrakhan, the Ottomans never considered him as a truly loyal subject of the sultan. They knew of the ideological conflicts and power struggles between the Crimean Khanate, the Lesser Nogays and the Greater Nogays. In the end, following their interests and priorities, they always sided with the Crimean Khanate and sometimes with the Lesser Nogays, who were in the vicinity of Azak and, by the 1580s, mostly subdued. The Greater Nogay Horde was far away and outside of the North Caucasus borderland and other targeted northern territories. The Porte turned a blind eye whenever Urus requested direct military assistance against the Muscovites. Such help – especially at a time when the war in the Caucasus against the Safavids was ongoing, and Muscovite activities reached an alarming level with the support of the Cossacks in the North Caucasus and along the Don River – would be futile for the Porte and certainly not very realistic in terms of supply lines and other tactical calculations.

Urus desired to revive Nogay power in the steppes, which had been significantly reduced by Muscovy. As a nomadic people, the Nogays relied on their sedentary neighbours for trade and survival. Muscovy monopolised their trade, annuities and gifts, thus restricting their independence greatly. It was not greed that drove Urus into alliances with or submission to other powers but the notion of revitalising Nogay power and continuing their traditional ways of living in the steppes with or without minimum restrictions. Eventually, Urus died without being able to realise his objectives, except for a brief period of time in the early 1580s when the Greater Nogays acted relatively independently of Muscovy. By the end of the sixteenth century, the Greater Nogays lost their power in the lower Volga and Yaik rivers. Their population was either completely taken under Muscovite control or forced to migrate to the Crimean/Ottoman-controlled areas in the west. At the beginning of the seventeenth century, they were replaced by another nomadic people, the Kalmyks, arriving from the east.

6.4 Alexander II of the Kingdom of Kakheti

Alexander II of the Kingdom of Kakheti (Zegem Hakimi Levendoğlu Aleksander in Ottoman sources) was another local ruler whose policies and alliances affected the balance of power in the North Caucasus borderland. There is abundant information in the primary sources about Kakheti, Alexander II and his sons. For our purposes, this discussion will be restricted to Alexander II's relations with the Ottoman Empire and Muscovy and his simultaneous submission to both empires.

King Alexander II entered the orbit of the Ottoman Porte in 1578 when Ottoman troops invaded the Georgian lands that had been under the rule of the Safavid Empire. Facing a sizeable Ottoman army in 1578, Alexander II considered compliance as the best way to avoid the devastation of his country and sent a letter of submission to Ottoman commander Lala Mustafa Pasha in August 1578. A month later, Alexander II visited the Ottoman commander in a military camp on the way to Shirvan and renewed his submission to the sultan in person.[62] Lala Mustafa Pasha 'granted' Alexander II the Kingdom of Kakheti with the title of governor-general (*beylerbeyi*) and registered his people for taxation, making the kingdom a governor-generalship. He also ordered Alexander II to supply men to the Ottoman army against the Safavids.[63]

Figure 6.2 King Alexander with Lala Mustafa Pasha, 1578.

Source: Asafi Dal Mehmed Çelebi, *Şeca'atname*, Istanbul University Library, TY6043.

Compared to the laxer Safavid rule, Ottoman control was different, as the latter immediately formed administrative districts in the South Caucasus. These activities were early signs for the local rulers such as Alexander II that the Ottomans had come to stay, and their rule was more centralised, which could eventually reduce the power and independence of the local rulers in the Caucasus. The Ottomans also brought with them their formidable tax machine. For example, people of Alexander II's kingdom were already registered for taxation in September 1578, as soon as he submitted. Apart from this, the Porte demanded thirty loads of silk, ten slaves and ten concubines as an annual tribute from the king.[64] While the Ottomans demanded tributes, taxes and soldiers from Kakheti, they did not offer much in return other than an imperial title at the level of a provincial governor and, perhaps more importantly, a chance to survive the Ottoman invasion and to preserve the territories of Kakheti.

As was the case with some North Caucasus rulers, King Alexander II saw in Muscovy a possible source of support. The Muscovites showed an interest in Georgian affairs due to their religious affinity, the strategic position of the Georgian kingdom, connecting Muscovy to the Safavid Empire, and the potential it offered for expansion of the Muscovite sphere of influence. The first recorded envoys to the Muscovite tsar from Alexander II came in 1586 when the Ottoman forces were fighting the Safavids, tension in Europe with the Habsburgs was increasing, and Muscovite power in the North Caucasus borderland was on the rise.[65] In his letter to the Muscovite tsar, Alexander II asked for help against the shamkhal rather than against the Ottomans, perhaps knowing that the Muscovites would not confront the Ottomans or perhaps that the Muscovites would be more of a help in the North Caucasus.[66] Among King Alexander II's regional rivals and foes, the most vexatious one was the shamkhal. The Daghestanis frequently raided Kakheti in the second half of the sixteenth century. In 1588, the Muscovite envoys reached the Kingdom of Kakheti. The king took the pledge of allegiance and agreed to pay an annual tribute to the tsar.[67]

The Muscovite activities in Kakheti alarmed not only the Ottomans but also the Safavids. The Safavid shah enquired about the situation through his envoy in Moscow.[68] However, the Safavid shah was in no position to protest at the submission of Alexander II or the diplomatic relations between Muscovy and their former vassal. The Muscovite envoys revisited Alexander II in 1589–90 when the king, one more time, petitioned the Muscovite tsar to punish the shamkhal. The correspondence between the king and the tsar, as well as the Muscovite ambassadorial reports, indicate that Alexander's objective was to have the shamkhal's power reduced or contained with Muscovite help rather than getting support from the Muscovites against the Ottomans.

From the perspective of the Ottoman Porte, Kakheti was a province granted to its king, who was now an Ottoman vassal. In 1589, the Porte attached the Ottoman fortresses in Kakheti, where the Ottoman soldiers were stationed, to the new governor-generalship of Kutais, administered by a Porte-appointed pasha. The governor-general's authority was limited to the fortresses, and other Kakheti lands were entrusted to Alexander II.[69] Therefore, by 1589, the significant fortresses in the Kingdom of Kakheti were in the hands of the Ottomans. Since there were no raids on Alexander II's territories in these years, he undoubtedly paid his tribute to the Porte despite his claims to the Muscovite envoys that he had been postponing the payment because of the promised Muscovite military assistance.[70]

Alexander II's submission to the Muscovite tsar was a strategic move against the shamkhal and other North Caucasus rulers, which included the Kabardinians, who periodically raided his lands. In this regard, Alexander II was following a policy best suited to protect his lands from invasion by the Ottomans and raids from his unruly neighbours in the North Caucasus. He realised his first objective by submitting to the Ottoman sultan and agreeing to pay a yearly tribute. Alexander II was also successful in containing his northern neighbours through the Muscovite protection, which, in the second half of the 1580s, proved to be effective vis-à-vis the shamkhal and the Kabardinians. Besides, he was able to pursue this flexible policy even in times of crisis, such as the 1594 invasion of the Daghestani lands by the Muscovites. In spite of his promise to send troops to help the Muscovite forces, he opted to stay out of the conflict, mostly due to the letters he received from the Porte in which the Ottoman sultan ordered him to 'help the shamkhal against the Muscovites, as his submission required this sort of service'.[71] In terms of the Ottoman–Muscovite rivalry, Alexander II managed to retain his position in his kingdom by playing one power off against the other. This strategy became unworkable when Shah Abbas I of the Safavid Empire began winning wars in the first years of the seventeenth century against the Ottomans and retaking the Safavid territories and clients that had been lost to the Porte. Shah Abbas I, perhaps rightfully, did not trust Alexander II and instead allied with Alexander II's son Constantine, who, with the shah's blessing, killed his father and became the king of Kakheti as a vassal of the Safavid Empire in 1605.

The local rulers examined above attempted to maintain a form of independence or autonomy in an area targeted by the subject- and territory-making strategies of two major Eurasian imperial powers in the second half of the sixteenth century. At first, the external powers, eager to incorporate these lands into their imperial systems, were a possible source of economic, military and political support for the rulers in the Caucasus against their domestic rivals or neighbouring foes. Eventually, the local rulers were left with no choice but to play one power off against the other to retain their positions or survive in their own lands. Gifts and salaries from the Ottomans and Muscovites mattered little and were not the real reason behind the shifting policies of these rulers vis-à-vis the two rival imperial powers. Moreover, what historians see as an imperial rivalry over a borderland could have different meanings for local rulers and peoples in that borderland. The local rulers in the North Caucasus borderland were not necessarily willing to serve the Muscovite tsar or the Ottoman sultan, but they were rather forced to pick a side. These rulers had certain similarities and differences in their strategies and objectives, but all of them shared one trait: being regarded and treated as *kul* or *kholop* by the officials in Istanbul or Moscow respectively. The North Caucasus local rulers 'rode all the horses' based on an examination of the extant Ottoman and Muscovite sources, but when those horses collided – and they often did – it was naturally the riders that were thrown to the ground.

Notes

1. *Russian Embassies to the Georgian Kings (1589–1605)*, ed. W. D. Allen, texts trans. Anthony Mango (London: Hakluyt Society, 1970), 291.
2. Chantal Lemercier-Quelquejay, 'Cooptation of the Elites of Kabarda and Daghestan in the Sixteenth Century', in *The North Caucasus Barrier: The Russian Advance towards the Muslim World*, ed. Marie Bennigsen Broxup (London: Hurst, 1992), 22.
3. See Nicola Di Cosmo, 'Ancient Inner Asian Nomads: Their Economic Basis and Its Significance in Chinese History', *Journal of Asian Studies* 53 (1994): 1092–1126 for an explanation of these terms. Also see Thomas J. Barfield, *The Perilous Frontier: Nomadic Empires and China* (Cambridge, MA: Blackwell, 1989).
4. Remmal Hoca, *Tarih-i Sahib Giray Han: Histoire de Sahib Giray, khan de Crimée de 1532 à 1551* (with French translation by M. Le Roux), ed. Özalp Gökbilgin (Ankara: Atatürk Üniversitesi Yayınları, 1973), 39.
5. *Kabardino-russkie otnosheniia v 16–18 vv.*, ed. T. Kh. Kumykov and E. N. Kusheva (Moscow: Izdatel'stvo Akademii nauk SSSR, 1957), vol. 1, doc. 1, 4.
6. Ibid., doc. 4, 7.
7. Ibid., doc. 1, 4.
8. E. N. Kusheva, *Narody Severnogo Kavkaza i ikh sviazi s Rossiei: vtoraia polovina XVI–30-e gody XVII veka* (Moscow: Izdatel'stvo Akademii nauk SSSR, 1958), 217.

9. Remmal Hoca, *Tarih-i Sahib Girey Han*, 38–9, 72. For example, in 1542, a letter from the governor of Kefe to the Crimean khan prompted the latter to attack the Janeys. The governor wrote, 'The chief of the Janeys has not delivered the slaves that he promised to give each year and detained four of our men who were sent there to enquire about the slaves. He also captured some herds in the Taman Island and he says, "Let us see what the sultan and khan can do to me." As such he made his intention known…'
10. *Snosheniia Rossii s Kavkazom*, doc. 1, 7.
11. Ibid., doc. 1, 5–7.
12. MD 51, no. 10.
13. MD 61, no. 41.
14. *Snosheniia Rossii s Kavkazom*, doc. 12, 135.
15. Ibid., doc. 12, 130–1.
16. Ibid., doc. 12, 136.
17. Ibid., doc. 12, 136.
18. Ibid., doc. 12, 136. When the horses of several Cossacks, bringing letters from Terek, were seized upon Solokh's orders, Mamstriuk sent the Cossacks back with horses he received from Solokh's nobles, who were on good terms with Mamstriuk.
19. Ibid., doc. 12, 136–7.
20. *Kabardino-russkie otnosheniia*, vol. 1, doc. 30, 54–5.
21. Ibid., doc. 30, 54–5.
22. MD 64, no. 232.
23. *Kabardino-russkie otnosheniia*, vol. 1, doc. 31, 55–6; *Snosheniia Rossii s Kavkazom*, doc. 8, 66.
24. *Snosheniia Rossii s Kavkazom*, doc. 7, 62.
25. Ibid., doc. 12, 140.
26. Ibid., doc. 12, 128.
27. Ibid., doc. 12, 108–9.
28. Ibid., doc. 12, 136.
29. Ibid., doc. 12, 110, 140; *Kabardino-russkie otnosheniia,* vol. 1, doc. 30, 54–5.
30. *Snosheniia Rossii s Kavkazom*, doc. 12, 145.
31. Ibid., doc. 12, 182–3.
32. Ibid., doc. 1, 1–8.
33. PSRL, 13:370–1.
34. *Snosheniia Rossii s Kavkazom*, doc. 1, 5.
35. RGADA, F. 123, *Krymskie dela*, kniga 13, fol. 348a; *Kabardino-russkie otnosheniia*, vol. 1, doc. 14, 26–7.
36. MD 23, no. 130.
37. MD 44, nos 182, 190; MD 51, no. 10.
38. Asafi Dal Mehmed Çelebi, *Şeca'atname*, ed. Abdülkadir Özcan (Istanbul: Çamlıca Basım, 2006), 187–94.
39. Ibid., 379.

40. *Snosheniia Rossii s Kavkazom*, doc. 12, 112.
41. Ibid., 3.
42. Ibid., doc. 12, 136.
43. According to Michael Khodarkovsky, Urus became the *beg* of the Greater Nogays in 1579 (Khodarkovsky, *Russia's Steppe Frontier: The Making of a Colonial Empire, 1500–1800* (Bloomington: Indiana University Press, 2002), 120). V. V. Trepavlov says it was 1578 (Trepavlov, *Istoria Nogaiskoi Ordy* (Kazan: Kazanskaia nedvizhimost', 2016), 319); E. N. Kusheva states that the year was 1580 in her *Narody Severnogo Kavkaza*, 262.
44. Khodarkovsky, *Russia's Steppe Frontier*, 121; Trepavlov, *Istoria Nogaiskoi Ordy*, 331.
45. Report of Simon Maltsev (1569), published in P. A. Sadikov, 'Pokhod tatar i turok na Astrakhan' v 1569 g.', *Istoricheskie zapiski* 22 (1947): 155–6.
46. MD 26, no. 241.
47. Trepavlov, *Istoria Nogaiskoi Ordy*, 319–70.
48. MD 26, no. 241.
49. MD 24, no. 421; MD 28, no. 579.
50. MD 38, no. 98.
51. Ibid.
52. Trepavlov, *Istoria Nogaiskoi Ordy*, 329.
53. Khodarkovsky, *Russia's Steppe Frontier*, 121–122.
54. Ibid., 121; Antonio Possevino, *The Moscovia of Antonio Possevino SJ*, trans. Hugh F. Graham (Pittsburgh: University of Pittsburgh, 1977), 2.
55. Trepavlov, *Istoria Nogaiskoi Ordy*, 333; Khodarkovsky, *Russia's Steppe Frontier*, 123.
56. RGADA, F. 89, *Turetskie dela*, kniga 2, fol. 405b; Trepavlov, *Istoria Nogaiskoi Ordy*, 370.
57. Kusheva, *Narody Severnogo Kavkaza*, 262.
58. Trepavlov, *Istoria Nogaiskoi Ordy*, 337.
59. Kusheva, *Narody Severnogo Kavkaza*, 264.
60. Khodarkovsky, *Russia's Steppe Frontier*, 123; A. A. Novosel'skii, *Bor'ba moskovskogo gosudarstva s tatarami v pervoi polovine XVII veka* (Moscow: Izdatel'stvo Akademii nauk SSSR, 1948), 35.
61. MD 62, no. 231.
62. Gelibolulu Mustafa 'Âli, *Nusret-nâme*, ed. Mustafa Eravcı (Ankara: Türk Tarih Kurumu, 2014), 64–5; Fahrettin Kırzıoğlu, *Osmanlılar'ın Kafkas elleri'ni fethi (1451–1590)* (Ankara: Sevinç Matbaası, 1976), 297.
63. Gelibolulu Mustafa 'Âli, *Nusret-nâme*, 124–5, 148–9.
64. *Gelibolulu Mustafa Ali ve Künhü'l-ahbar'ında II. Selim, III. Murat ve III. Mehmet devirleri*, ed. Faris Çerçi (Kayseri: Erciyes Üniversitesi Yayınları, 2000), 2:293–5.
65. *Snosheniia Rossii s Kavkazom*, doc. 12, 203.
66. Ibid., doc. 12, 203.
67. Ibid., doc. 4, 13–45.

68. Ibid., doc. 25, 563.
69. MD 65, nos. 361, 378.
70. *Snosheniia Rossii s Kavkazom*, doc. 12, 173.
71. MD 72, no. 278.

Conclusion: Imperial Entanglements and Borderlandisation of the North Caucasus

The wars and relationship between the Ottoman and Russian Empires have shaped the history of the Balkans, Eastern Europe and the Caucasus. Historians who ask when and where the rivalry between these two empires began have turned their gaze to the Balkans or other Slavic-speaking parts of Eastern Europe to find an answer. While the more significant wars and conflicts between these two major empires took place in the area between modern-day Ukraine and Turkey, its origin lies further east in the North Caucasus, which, in the mid-sixteenth century, turned into a borderland between the two imperial powers. Similarly, while historians of the Ottoman Empire have examined the Ottoman borderlands, frontiers, vassals and strategies in Eastern and Central Europe in many volumes, its eastern borderlands have only recently gained traction and became a subject of academic research.

This book presents a history and an analysis of the first encounter between the Ottoman Empire and the Tsardom of Muscovy in the second half of the sixteenth century in the North Caucasus, a region until then bypassed by the surrounding imperial powers. The North Caucasus became the first borderland in Eurasia between the Ottomans and the Muscovites, which resulted in its local social and political structures undergoing major alterations and marked its peoples' long-lasting struggle for freedom. The chapters in this book detail the process of borderlandisation of the North Caucasus between the two rival imperial powers that encroached on the region with their own imperial ideologies and objectives.

In the sixteenth century, the Ottoman Porte implemented in the North Caucasus strategies that were devised as a part of its northern policy, whose main objective was maintaining exclusive Ottoman control of the Black Sea. The Ottoman sultans and Crimean khans were content with a nominal claim of sovereignty over the North Caucasus before the rise of Muscovy as a rival imperial power. While the Ottomans recognised the Crimean Khanate's control over the region, they still preferred to establish their rule of law in the territories on the coastal strip of the Taman Peninsula and govern them within the framework of their provincial administration through centrally appointed governors in Azak and Kefe. Perhaps as early as 1552, and undoubtedly following the Muscovite annexation of Astrakhan in 1556, the North Caucasus transformed into a disputed borderland between the Ottoman Empire and the Tsardom of Muscovy. The Muscovite officials appreciated the strategic value of the region for securing their newly annexed territories in the lower Volga on the Caspian shores and providing them with a springboard for further expansion. In the North Caucasus, the Muscovites applied their steppe frontier policy, which consisted of a series of strategies designed to 'tame' Muscovy's southern steppes and put an end to the waves of nomadic hordes raiding their territories. For the Muscovites, the North Caucasus was yet another perilous frontier that needed to be tamed.

When the two empires collided in the North Caucasus for the first time, Ottoman northern and Muscovite steppe frontier policies appeared similar in their form at times, but they were fundamentally different in their methods and applications, and the differences outweighed the similarities. As a new imperial power in the sixteenth century, Muscovy was a contender for the heritage of the Golden Horde and a significant player in Eurasia, and specifically in the Pontic–Caspian steppes, rather than an outsider or intruder.[1] Perhaps for this reason, Muscovite officials proved to be better equipped and more skilled, compared to their Ottoman peers, in their relations with the nomadic and semi-nomadic peoples of the Pontic–Caspian steppes or, at least initially, with the idiosyncratic North Caucasus peoples. The same can also be said about the Muscovite steppe policy, which was more sophisticated and coherent in contrast to the fundamentally laxer Ottoman northern policy. The Ottomans themselves had a steppe and nomadic background and were products of a borderland, but by the sixteenth century, such origins were mere ancient tales.

Both the Ottoman Empire and Muscovy functioned primarily through their vassals, clients and protectorates in the North Caucasus borderland as well as in the contiguous parts of the Pontic–Caspian steppes. While the Crimean Tatars primarily fulfilled this role for the Ottoman Porte, various Cossack hosts did the same for Muscovy in the steppes and the rugged terrain of the North Caucasus where regular armies remained ineffective. Employing vassals in their shared frontier zones, including the North Caucasus borderland, also gave the Ottomans and Muscovites a 'plausible deniability' with respect to responsibility for the assaults perpetuated by those vassals.[2] Battles, raiding and plundering of their clients in the steppes or in the North Caucasus were sometimes protested against but not considered *casus belli*.

Compared to the Cossacks registered for Muscovite service or the Cossack hosts allied with the tsar, the Crimean Khanate was a proper state with its own territorial and ideological ambitions. In fact, the khanate was the most significant component of the broader Ottoman northern policy. Not only was it ruled by the Chinggisid Girey dynasty, but also it possessed a formidable army that regularly invaded Polish and Muscovite territories. The Ottoman Porte recognised the value of the Crimean Girey dynasty in Turco-Mongolian steppe politics, especially in large swathes of Eurasia once ruled by the Golden Horde. As the direct descendants of Chinggis Khan, the Girey family enjoyed the status of lawful and legitimate rulers in the eyes of the Turco-Mongolian nomadic peoples of the Eurasian steppes. Thus, the Ottomans placed the Crimean Khanate under their protection as a client state, allowing it to have a broad autonomy, at times amounting to independence, in the north of the Black Sea, without changing its internal mechanisms and ruling dynasty.[3]

Regardless of the mid-sixteenth-century changes to the Ottoman strategies in their northern frontier zones and borderlands, the Crimean Khanate remained a crucial player in protecting the Ottoman interests and ensuring a balance of power between Muscovy and Poland-Lithuania. Its role was essential for sustaining the Porte's sphere of influence over the Pontic–Caspian steppes and the North Caucasus when the Ottomans could not afford to send their own troops due to their engagements on their eastern and western frontiers against the Safavids and the Habsburgs. Therefore, the Ottoman–Crimean clientage was a reciprocally profitable relationship. The Crimean Khanate provided the Porte with a strong proxy power in the north, allowing the Ottomans to direct their military resources against their major rivals without worrying about their northern frontiers, while the Crimean Tatars benefited from the protection and military support of a major Eurasian empire. It was, at the same time, a reciprocally restrictive relationship. The Ottomans made sure that the Crimean khans never gained too much strength to challenge the authority of the sultan or the imperial ideology of the Porte. The Crimean khans did their best to limit Ottoman control and influence in the north, including the North Caucasus, to protect their broad autonomy or independence.[4]

In the sixteenth century, the Crimean khans employed their own methods of domination in the North Caucasus. They required and regularly received annual tributes and gifts consisting of slaves, birds, horses and sometimes money from numerous North Caucasus rulers and polities. If the local chieftains failed to deliver their tributes, the khans could organise a campaign to punish them. The Crimean khans and nobility also used the institution of *atalyk* as an ideological and practical symbol of their authority over the North Caucasus. As one may remember, the *atalyk* institution was also common among the native peoples of the North Caucasus. As the North Caucasus people understood it, the custom required the overlord to send one of his children to his vassal or client. In terms of the Crimean–North Caucasus relationship, it involved entrusting the children of Crimean khans and nobility, customarily at the age of two or three, to a noble Circassian family until the age of fifteen or sixteen. *Atalyk* children were trained in horse riding, wrestling, swordsmanship and other warrior techniques by their host families, constituting a bond between the Crimean royalty and nobility and the Circassian host families. It created a form of alliance, allegiance and partnership, solidifying the Crimean imperial claims over the region.[5]

Until the second half of the sixteenth century, the Ottomans stayed out of broader North Caucasus affairs, letting the Crimean Tatars keep the region as a source of tribute and slaves, which certainly benefited the Ottoman slave markets in Azak, Kefe and Istanbul.[6] The Porte's only concern when it came to the North Caucasus was the coastal strips of the Black and Azov seas, where the Ottomans strove to establish their rule of law enforced by their fortresses and administrators, as their northern policy dictated. For this reason, the Porte granted imperial titles and salaries to coopt significant local rulers in the Taman and Kuban regions. The Ottoman provinces of Kefe and Azak acted as the headquarters of information gathering and of Ottoman interest in this part of the North Caucasus. It was through these provinces that the Ottomans applied their strategy of *istimalet* (accommodation), the 'carrot' to draw the local rulers to their side by rewarding them with imperial status and salaries. If the policy of *istimalet* did not yield the desired results, the Crimean Khanate was employed as the 'stick' for punishing disobedient local rulers. Therefore, the earlier Ottoman policy in the North Caucasus was a product of the Ottomans' long-term understanding of their northern frontiers and borderlands, in which they prioritised their exclusive control of the Black Sea and allowed the Crimean Khanate to hold sway over the region with broad powers to punish the local populations or exact tributes and slaves from them.[7]

In the shared frontier zones and borderlands between the Crimean Khanate, Muscovy and the Ottoman Empire, the Muscovites effectively employed Cossacks to incorporate the frontier zones into their imperial system and eventually colonise the steppes in the sixteenth to the eighteenth centuries. Muscovy registered a certain number of Cossacks for paid military service and established alliances or clientage relationships with various Cossack hosts in the Pontic–Caspian steppes and in the North

Caucasus borderland. As Charles Halperin states, 'the Cossacks were of, but not in, Muscovite society'.[8] Due to the fluid nature of the Cossack hosts, the relationship between Muscovy and the Cossacks varied over time and was sometimes uneasy. Yet, there was always a special understanding of rights and responsibilities between the allied Cossack hosts and Muscovy. The Cossack hosts in the Pontic–Caspian steppes and the North Caucasus were also militarised settlers, who played a major role in the Slavic colonisation of the Eurasian steppes.[9]

Of the numerous Cossack hosts in Muscovy's southern frontiers and borderlands, the Greben and Terek Cossacks settled in the North Caucasus. With their social structure organised into military fraternities and their contempt for central authority, the Cossacks in the North Caucasus did not have much difficulty integrating themselves into the demographic fabric of the region, as their lifestyle and ideals conformed to those of the North Caucasus societies. However, they were still seen and treated as an extended military arm of the Muscovite state by the local rulers in the region. Evidently, the Cossack hosts could have their own political and military objectives and interests, which did not always align with those of Muscovy. If their interests dictated, they could disobey the Muscovite tsar and officials.[10] However, the benefits of having the Cossacks as clients outweighed the problems they created for Muscovy, which skilfully employed them in the North Caucasus to disturb the Ottoman–Crimean order, vassals and clients, as the chapters above have shown.

While both the Ottomans and Muscovites used their vassals, clients and allies in their subject- and territory-building strategies in the North Caucasus, the Muscovites also relied on their own military when their interests dictated and their military resources allowed it. This strategy of direct intervention with troops was further enhanced by building fortresses filled with musket-bearing *strel'tsy* and Cossacks. Effective usage of clients coupled with direct military intervention and fortress building enabled Muscovy to eventually control and colonise its southern frontier zones and borderlands. Some historians even draw parallels between this Muscovite policy and the European colonisation of the New World.[11]

Of all the strategies, the system of fortresses was the backbone of the Muscovite steppe frontier policy. Initially, the Muscovites built fortresses to protect their subjects from nomadic raids. As Muscovy strengthened its position among the post-Golden Horde polities and began its imperial career, the Muscovite officials realised the value of fortresses for expansion, colonisation and controlling the nomadic and semi-nomadic peoples. In the second half of the sixteenth century, Muscovy steadily enlarged its territorial possessions in Eurasia by relaying on ever-expanding and initially defensive lines of fortresses.[12] As new villages and towns around fortresses were established, the defence lines moved further south. Thus, in the early modern period, the Muscovite frontiers and borderlands showed a trend of southward expansion until their success brought them to the North Caucasus, where their interests collided with those of the Ottomans for the first time.

Besides vassals and clients, both the Ottoman Porte and Muscovy employed their centrally appointed regional governors for information gathering and implementation of their strategies. The Ottoman administrators of Kefe and Azak in the north of the Black Sea were significant players in Ottoman northern policy.[13] These governors facilitated salaries granted to the local rulers in the North Caucasus as well as the Nogay chiefs. Kefe was the Porte's control centre and the main node for information for Crimean and North Caucasus affairs. It was a strategically important location for containing the Crimean Khanate and preventing it from gaining too much strength. In case of turmoil or the rise of an anti-Ottoman party in the khanate, Kefe acted as a safe haven for pro-Ottoman khans and parties. There were also instances of governors sometimes acting independently of the Porte and the Crimean khan and conducting business with the local peoples of the Pontic–Caspian steppes or the North Caucasus.[14]

The governors of Astrakhan and Terek played a similar role on the Muscovite side. After its annexation by Muscovy in 1556, Astrakhan became the centre of operations for North Caucasus and Greater Nogay affairs. The Muscovites built a new stone fortress in Astrakhan where a large number of troops were stationed. Just as Kefe was the commercial hub for the Crimean Khanate and western parts of the North Caucasus, Astrakhan was the main centre of trade for the lower Volga and the eastern parts of the North Caucasus, as well as for the Greater Nogays. Certain local rulers from the North Caucasus and Nogay chiefs were provided with salaries and gifts from this city. It also acted as a safe haven for Muscovite clients and vassals in the North Caucasus who suffered defeats at the hands of their local rivals and foes. In 1588, the Terek Fortress was constructed and, as of 1590, it emerged as another centre for North Caucasus affairs.[15]

Both empires used similar forms of cooptation in the North Caucasus. While the Ottomans initially targeted very specific local rulers in the areas that they cared to control, the Muscovites were more liberal with their cooptation strategies and limits. The Muscovite cooptation method, formulated out of their long-lasting and largely successful practice of dealing with the Khanate of Kazan and the Nogay Horde on their eastern and southern frontiers, was an integral part of their steppe frontier policy.

It helped to incorporate local elites into the Muscovite imperial system, and by doing so, to turn them into loyal clients of the Muscovite tsar. The tsar could provide a certain ruler, a social group or an entire tribe with military and financial privileges and aid, which enabled these rulers or peoples to gain political and economic advantages over their local rivals.[16] There were several tools used by the Muscovite officials within the framework of their cooptation strategy in the sixteenth century. These included obtaining a pledge of allegiance (*shert'*), taking hostages (*amanat*), and gifts and annuities (*pominki* and *zhalovaniia*).[17] Religious conversion, cultural assimilation and even marital ties with the Muscovite elites were also used. Furthermore, the Muscovites preferred to delegate power to one of the local rulers and subdue other local chiefs through him, a practice emanating from the Chinggisid traditions of steppe politics, with which the Muscovite tsars were very familiar. While this strategy engendered favourable outcomes when applied to the former Golden Horde polities and peoples, it failed to produce the same results in the North Caucasus.[18]

A comparison of Ottoman northern policy and Muscovite steppe frontier strategies shows that the Muscovites proved to be better equipped in their shared frontier zones than the Ottomans. The Muscovite strategies generated quicker and more productive results, allowing them to expand in a short time over the territories that once belonged to the Golden Horde at the expense of the Crimean Khanate. This, however, changed when the Muscovite success turned the North Caucasus into a shared borderland with the Ottomans, placing them on a collision course with the Porte's interests in the north of the Black Sea. From the perspective of the Muscovites, establishing a sphere of influence in the North Caucasus to secure their newly acquired territories in the north of the Caspian Sea was a natural outcome of the very strategies that awarded them Astrakhan. From the perspective of the Ottomans, however, the Muscovite annexation of Kazan and Astrakhan and their ambitions to expand further into the Pontic–Caspian steppes, specifically in the North Caucasus, disturbed the balance of power in the north and threatened their possessions on the Black Sea coasts. In response to this challenge, the Ottoman Porte modified its strategies in the North Caucasus to neutralise the Muscovite ambitions over the region and even threaten their recently annexed territories in the lower Volga area.

As soon as the Muscovites began to lay the groundwork for carving a defined sphere of influence in the North Caucasus following their conquest of Astrakhan in 1556, they encountered realities that were different from what they had experienced with the nomadic and semi-nomadic polities in their southern frontier zones. Besides trying to establish a form of suzerainty over the fundamentally diverse political and social structures that existed in the North Caucasus, the Muscovites sought to formulate strategies for confronting the Ottoman challenge to their ideological and territorial expansion for the first time in their imperial career. With the threat of the sultan's wrath looming over them and knowing their own strengths and limitations, the Muscovites implemented a long-lasting strategy of avoiding direct military conflict with the Ottoman Empire. This Muscovite strategy lasted until 1676, when the Ottomans decided to place Ukraine under their rule through their vassal Hetman Petro Doroshenko. Therefore, Muscovy's steppe frontier policy, which was a success over their Turkic neighbours, failed to produce the same results when applied to the North Caucasus. The idiosyncratic socio-political structures as well as the geographical conditions of the region, coupled with the Ottoman interests in it, put a spoke in the wheels of Muscovy's steppe frontier strategies. Although the Muscovites learned a great deal about the region and its complexities through their attempts at establishing a sphere of influence and sovereignty over the North Caucasus, it took more than a century – until the end of the reign of Peter I – for them to alter their strategies in the region.

The Ottomans realised the limits and futility of their traditional northern policy in the North Caucasus when the Muscovites unleashed their Cossack and Circassian clients in the Taman region and initiated their subject- and territory-making process in Kabarda. The challenges to their imperial vision in the North Caucasus, caused by the rise of Muscovy, compelled the Ottomans to modify their northern policy there, taking into account the intricacies and *sui generis* characteristics of this region.[19] One of the influential Ottoman politicians behind this policy change was the experienced Grand Vizier Sokullu Mehmed Pasha, who appreciated the strategic value of the region not only to check the Muscovite ambitions but also to surround the Safavid Empire and connect the Ottomans with the Sunni Central Asian khanates. As of 1569, the Ottomans implemented new strategies in the North Caucasus, aiming to incorporate the region into their imperial system with the eventual aim of taking Astrakhan and controlling the Caspian Sea.

The chapters above have also shown that the arguments frequently made in Turkish and Western historiography about the so-called Ottoman apathy regarding the political developments in the north, including the rise of Muscovy and its annexation of Kazan and Astrakhan, or the fate of the Nogays, are not borne out by the evidence. It is true that following the Ottoman annexations in the northwestern Black Sea region in 1538 and before Muscovy proved itself a power to be reckoned with in the North Caucasus, Ottoman northern policy seemed passive and defensive. The Ottoman Porte focused solely on the security of the Black Sea and the balance of power in the north ensured by their Crimean vassal. Since the Ottomans succeeded in establishing their control over the Black Sea and its hinterland, as much as was possible in the early modern period, they fulfilled their strategic objectives on their northern frontier. Thus, they did not have any impetus to expand further in the north. However, the rising power of Muscovy and its pernicious effects in the North Caucasus, ranging from destructive raids in the Taman region to effective Muscovite control of Kabarda, forced the Ottoman Porte to re-evaluate its policy and confront the new reality in the north, which began with its campaign in 1569 to take Astrakhan. The Astrakhan campaign demonstrated that the North Caucasus was now a borderland that needed to be integrated into the Ottoman imperial system.

Following the Astrakhan campaign, both the Ottomans and the Muscovites continued to rely on the instrument of 'plausible deniability' in the North Caucasus borderland, using their vassals and allies in the North Caucasus when confronting each other. While the Muscovite tsar and officials contended that conflict with the Ottoman Empire could be too precarious, the Ottomans thought that a war in the North Caucasus or Pontic–Caspian steppes was too costly and difficult to organise. Thus, there was no direct Ottoman–Muscovite military confrontation in the second half of the sixteenth century – notwithstanding the Astrakhan campaign of the Ottomans. Even then, the Muscovite tsar did not send troops against the Ottoman army, nor did he demand an explanation from the sultan.

In this new phase of the imperial rivalry over the North Caucasus, the Ottoman strategies of accommodation and integration of local rulers into the Ottoman imperial system accelerated. This time, the Porte did not limit its resources for cooptation in terms of salaries and titles to the Western Circassians, but engaged an array of local rulers from Beshtau to Daghestan. In doing so, the Ottomans paid specific attention to the shamkhal and other Sunni rulers of Daghestan thanks to their strategically located polities and religious affiliation, as well as to the Kabardinian chiefs, to counterbalance the Muscovite influence there. The Porte's vigorous presence with its vast financial and military resources changed the balance of power in the North Caucasus borderland, complicating the already overextended Muscovite ambitions. Despite that, the Muscovite strategies still worked relatively efficiently, at least in Kabarda, allowing them to protect their Kabardinian clients or allies even in the most tumultuous periods of the sixteenth century in the region. Moreover, while these newly rejuvenated Ottoman strategies produced favourable results for the Porte, they caused concern for the Crimean khans, who were worried about the increasing influence and military presence of the Porte in what they considered to be their backyard. Regardless of their colliding interests in the North Caucasus, however, the Muscovite ambitions in the North Caucasus and threat to the Crimean Khanate itself forced the Crimean khans to cooperate with the Ottoman Porte and support the Ottoman priorities in the region, sometimes at the expense of their own imperial ideology and objectives.

The Ottoman Porte planned to kill two birds with one stone by bringing the North Caucasus borderland into its conflict with the Safavids as a supply route and establishing a military presence there. The Ottoman–Safavid War of 1578–90 further boosted the authority of the Ottoman sultan in the region while the competition with Muscovy over Kabarda and later Daghestan intensified. During this period, thanks to their supply route that went through the North Caucasus, Ottoman troops and military activities became a normal part of life in the region. In addition to Sokullu Mehmed Pasha, Ottoman commanders Lala Mustafa Pasha and Özdemiroğlu Osman Pasha promoted active Ottoman strategies over the North Caucasus. In fact, they employed several new strategies, including marital ties, such as the marriage of Özdemiroğlu Osman Pasha to the daughter of the ruler of the Avars, arranged by Lala Mustafa Pasha, and direct military intervention in subduing local rulers in the North Caucasus. Additionally, Özdemiroğlu Osman Pasha lobbied the Porte for the construction of several fortresses in Kabarda to protect the Ottoman interests and allies in the North Caucasus. Overall, the new Ottoman policy over this borderland was more effectual, more diplomatic and as pragmatic as the Muscovite policy in its nature and application. With the application of these energetic strategies, and thanks to its ability to wield sufficiently formidable military power in the North Caucasus, the Ottoman Porte was able to deter Muscovy and thereby establish a palpable sphere of influence in the region.

Meanwhile, renewing their ties with the Kabardinian princes in 1578, the Muscovites continued to pursue their ambitions in the North Caucasus, which, by then, had become more important due to the Ottoman supply route and the possibility that the Ottomans could annex the South Caucasus and turn their gaze to the north of the Caspian Sea. The Muscovite efforts in Kabarda during the Ottoman–Safavid War were fruitful, as they were able to build fortresses and strengthen their vassals. This continued until the Muscovite officials decided to use Kabarda and their Georgian connections as a springboard to control Daghestan and its rulers, which greatly overextended their capabilities at a time when their main armies were engaged in Eastern Europe and the Rurikid dynasty was facing an extinction crisis.

Leaving the various Muscovite and Ottoman strategies in the North Caucasus aside, another essential difference between them was that, despite being better formulated and more functional compared to their earlier laxer policy, Ottoman policy was still negatively affected by the slow and complicated workings of the very apex of the Ottoman state – the Imperial Council. Those Ottoman statesmen who wanted to prioritise and consolidate Ottoman control over the North Caucasus were unable to alter this characteristic of the Porte. Despite his far-sightedness and his intimate knowledge of the region as well as his subsequent appointment as a grand vizier, even the infamous Özdemiroğlu Osman Pasha fell short of obtaining the Porte's permission to construct fortresses in the North Caucasus. In comparison with Muscovite policy, which survived changes of tsars, officials and regional governors, and even dynastic struggles, Ottoman policy was extremely dependent on the personal opinions of influential figures in Istanbul and those of the Crimean khan. The latter was particularly concerned at the prospect of an Ottoman-controlled North Caucasus due to the region's value as a source of slaves and the fact that centralised Ottoman hegemony over this borderland would mean containment of the khanate and the end of its extensive autonomy.

In contrast, the swift decision-making process in their dealings with the local polities and peoples in the North Caucasus was an intrinsic characteristic of Muscovite policy. Their strategies were determined by a close circle of politicians around the Muscovite tsar and left no room for other officials to object. For this reason, the Muscovites were able to make decisions speedily and act resolutely, which enabled them to find eager vassals and erect fortresses in a short time and to compete with the Ottomans and Crimean Tatars at a surprisingly equal level despite their military inferiority in the face of the Ottoman challenge. This continued to be the case even in the last decades of the sixteenth century when the North Caucasus was a crucial supply route for Ottoman armies fighting the Safavids, and Muscovy was facing a series of domestic and international crises.

While the Ottomans and Muscovites were utilising every possible subject- and territory-making strategy in their arsenal in order to establish sovereignty over the North Caucasus, they, in the process, ended up affecting the local political and social structures of the peoples living in this borderland. Their involvement altered the internal dynamics of the polities in the North Caucasus. Each imperial power had its vassals, and through them, they brought about new political forms in the region. Local rulers in the western, Kabardinian or Daghestani parts of the North Caucasus borderland were forced to take sides, as those with no support were unable to defend themselves against the chiefs who received military or material support from one of the imperial contenders in the region. Therefore, as of the second half of the sixteenth century, in order to survive in their own territories, the North Caucasus rulers sought to pledge their allegiance to one of the imperial powers. It is true that salaries, titles and gifts from the sultan or tsar were significant and contributed to the prestige and power of the local rulers. However, those gifts and salaries usually came at a price: loss or restriction of their freedom. When the local rulers – at least some of them—realised this fact, it was too late for them to turn the tide or unite against an empire without the support of another imperial power. Once they took an oath of allegiance to either the sultan or the tsar or both, the local rulers expected to fight for their overlords and support the sultan's or tsar's military enterprises in the North Caucasus borderland or elsewhere – sometimes in Europe against the Swedish, sometimes in Asia against the Safavids. Those who refused to submit suffered invasions and destruction of their lands, and those who submitted risked punishment by the other power.

As this book demonstrates, the imperial rivalry over the North Caucasus allowed its peoples and polities to have broad autonomy, which, for some rulers, reached the level of independence. In addition to playing one empire against the other, the North Caucasus rulers and peoples used the geographical features of their homeland to their advantage. The rough terrain and impregnable mountains allowed them to evade imperial control, whether in the form of taxation, occupation or annexation. However, the parts of the North Caucasus that were adjacent to the nearby imperial provinces or accessible for regular armies were susceptible to imperial exploitation. Thus, the surrounding empires were able to incorporate such areas into their imperial system in the second half of the sixteenth century.

The Ottoman–Muscovite rivalry slowly but surely changed the socio-political and economic patterns of the relationship among the peoples of the North Caucasus borderland, gradually depriving them of their independence, their autonomy, and finally, their lands. However, this relationship was reciprocal. The reciprocity was noticeable in the relationship between the North Caucasus borderland and the imperial centres of Istanbul and Moscow. The Ottoman Porte, for example, changed its administrative structure and units in its northern territories and in the South Caucasus due to the imperial rivalry over the North Caucasus. The elevation of Kefe from a province (*sancak*) to a governor-generalship (*beylerbeyilik*) in 1568 is a good example of how a borderland can affect the centre. Similarly, the establishment of Muscovite cities such as Terek in the North

Caucasus was a product of the same process. Besides, the evolution of the relationship between the Muscovite tsars and the Ottoman sultans, as well as their diplomatic efforts in the sixteenth century, was one of the results of the aforementioned rivalry over the North Caucasus borderland that influenced the imperial centres.

In the end, thanks to their new and robust strategies in the North Caucasus, the Ottomans managed to extend their power and influence to the whole North Caucasus borderland after repulsing two Muscovite offensives aimed at controlling Daghestan at the most inopportune times – in 1594 and 1604–5. During the latter, the Ottomans were at war on their western and eastern frontiers against the Habsburgs and Safavids, respectively. The Muscovite attempt to break Ottoman power in the North Caucasus borderland by establishing their suzerainty over Daghestan failed and resulted in their complete retreat.

However, the real threat to Ottoman hegemony over the North Caucasus, especially in Daghestan, came in the first half of the seventeenth century, not from their new rival but their old foe, the Safavid Empire. Safavid Shah Abbas I, capitalising on the Ottoman engagement in Central Europe and domestic uprisings in Anatolia, organised a major military campaign to expel the Ottomans from the territories in the South Caucasus that had been lost at the end of the Ottoman–Safavid War of 1578–90. Despite losing the territories in the South Caucasus, however, the Ottomans were able to retain their sphere of influence over the North Caucasus, including Daghestan. In the final analysis, if one looks at the outcome of this first round of imperial rivalry in the second half of the sixteenth century from the perspective of the local chiefs and peoples, it was neither the Ottomans nor the Muscovites who lost, but rather the local polities, peoples and rulers of the North Caucasus, who became dependent on the power and strategies of these two empires in the following centuries.

Notes

1. Edward L. Keenan, 'Muscovy and Kazan, 1445–1552: A Study in Steppe Politics', PhD dissertation, Harvard University, 1965; Donald Ostrowski, 'The Mongol Origins of Muscovite Political Institutions', *Slavic Review* 49 (1990): 525–42; George Vernadsky, *The Mongols and Russia* (New Haven, CT: Yale University Press, 1953); Leo de Hartog, *Russia and the Mongol Yoke: The History of the Russian Principalities and the Golden Horde, 1221–1502* (London: British Academic Press, 1996); Charles J. Halperin, *Russia and the Golden Horde: The Mongol Impact on Medieval Russian History* (London: I. B. Tauris, 1987).

2. Brian Boeck, *Imperial Boundaries: Cossack Communities and Empire-Building in the Age of Peter the Great* (New York: Cambridge University Press, 2009), 22–6.
3. Murat Yaşar and Chong Jin Oh, 'The Ottoman Empire and the Crimean Khanate in the North Caucasus: A Case Study of Ottoman–Crimean Relations in the Mid-Sixteenth Century', Turkish Historical Review 9 (2018): 86–103.
4. Ibid., 90; Halil İnalcık, 'Struggle for East-European Empire, 1400–1700', *Turkish Yearbook of International Relations* 21 (1982): 1–16; Halil İnalcık, 'Power Relations between Russia, the Crimea and the Ottoman Empire as Reflected in Titulature', in *Turco-Tatar Past, Soviet Present: Studies Presented to Alexandre Bennigsen*, ed. Ch. Lemercier-Quelquejay, G. Veinstein and E. Wimbush (Paris: École des hautes études en sciences sociales, 1986), 175–215.
5. Ali Barut, 'Kırım Hanlığı ile kuzey-batı Kafkasya ilişkilerinde Atalık müessesesinin yeri', *Emel* 219 (1997): 21–4; Ufuk Tavkul, 'Kırım-Kafkas ilişkilerinde "Atalık" kurumunun kökeni üzerine değerlendirmeler', *Karadeniz Araştırmaları* 51 (2016): 223–32.
6. Yaşar and Oh, 'The Ottoman Empire and the Crimean Khanate', 95.
7. Murat Yaşar, 'The North Caucasus between the Ottoman Empire and the Tsardom of Muscovy: The Beginnings, 1552–1570', *Iran and the Caucasus* 20 (2016): 110–11.
8. Charles J. Halperin, *Ivan the Terrible: Free to Reward and Free to Punish* (Pittsburgh: University of Pittsburgh Press, 2019), 233.
9. Thomas Barrett, *At the Edge of Empire: The Terek Cossacks and the North Caucasus Frontier, 1700–1860* (Boulder, CO: Westview Press, 1999), 3–25; Brian J. Boeck, 'Containment vs. Colonization: Muscovite Approaches to Settling the Steppe', in *Peopling The Russian Periphery: Borderland Colonization in Eurasian History*, ed. Nicholas B. Breyfogle, Abby Schrader and Willard Sunderland (Abingdon: Routledge, 2007), 43; Boeck, *Imperial Boundaries*, 13–27; Willard Sunderland, *Taming the Wild Field: Colonization and Empire on the Russian Steppe* (Ithaca: Cornell University Press, 2004), 23–4; Matthew P. Romaniello, 'Grant, Settle, Negotiate: Military Servitors in the Middle Volga Region', in *Peopling the Russian Periphery: Borderland Colonization in Eurasian History*, ed. Nicholas B. Breyfogle, Abby Schrader and Willard Sunderland (Abingdon: Routledge, 2007), 61–77.
10. Barrett, *At the Edge of Empire*, 19.
11. Michael Khodarkovsky, *Russia's Steppe Frontier: The Making of a Colonial Empire, 1500–1800* (Bloomington: Indiana University Press, 2002), 226–7; Nicholas B. Breyfogle, Abby Schrader and Willard Sunderland, 'Russian Colonizations: An Introduction', in *Peopling the Russian Periphery: Borderland Colonization in Eurasian History*, ed. Nicholas B. Breyfogle, Abby Schrader and Willard Sunderland (Abingdon: Routledge, 2007), 1–19.
12. Brian L. Davies, *Warfare, State and Society on the Black Sea Steppe, 1500–1700* (Abingdon: Routledge, 2007), 40.

13. Yaşar, 'The North Caucasus', 110.
14. For Kefe see Yücel Öztürk, *Osmanlı hakimiyetinde Kefe, 1475–1600* (Ankara: Kültür Bakanlığı Yayınları, 2000); for Azak and 'Azovskie liudi' see A. A. Novosel'skii, *Bor'ba moskovskogo gosudarstva s tatarami v pervoi polovine XVII veka* (Moscow: Izdatel'stvo Akademii nauk SSSR, 1948), 15–43.
15. E. N. Kusheva, *Narody Severnogo Kavkaza i ikh sviazi s Rossiei: vtoraia polovina XVI–30-e gody XVII veka* (Moscow: Izdatel'stvo Akademii nauk SSSR, 1958), 284; N. A. Smirnov, *Rossiia i Turtsiia v XVI–XVII vv.* (Moscow: Izdatel'stvo Moskovskogo gosudarstvennogo universiteta, 1946), 138.
16. Chantal Lemercier-Quelquejay, 'Cooptation of the Elites of Kabarda and Daghestan in the Sixteenth Century', in *The North Caucasus Barrier: The Russian Advance towards the Muslim World*, ed. Marie Bennigsen Broxup (London: Hurst, 1992), 18.
17. Khodarkovsky, *Russia's Steppe Frontier*, 51–68.
18. Yaşar, 'The North Caucasus', 113–14.
19. Ibid., 122–4.

Appendices

Appendix I

Selected Ottoman Documents from *Mühimme* Registers

A. Ottoman version of Selim II's letter to Ivan IV dated 1570. Ahmed Feridun Bey, *Münşa'atü's-Selatin* (Istanbul, 1858–9 (AH 1275)), 460–1.

Facsimile

جواب

عتبهٔ علیهٔ عدالتعنوان وسدهٔ سنیهٔ سعادتنشانمزه که ملجأ سلاطین جهان ومرجع خواقین
دوراندرنام ایلچیکز واسطه سیله نامهٔ مخالصت پیامکز وارد اولوب قدیم الایامدن آباء کرام
واجداد عالی نژاد ذوی الاحترامنز انار الله براهینهم زمان سعادت انجاملرنده سدهٔ سدره
مقاملرینه موالات تام اوزره اولمغین حالا دخی آستانهٔ سعادتعنوانمزه تهنیت وعرض خلوص
ایچون مومی الیه آدمکز کوندریلوب ونواب کامیابمز ایله عساکر نصرت نصابمز حاجی ترخان
جانبلرینه واروب داخل اولدوغن اعلام ایلمشسز هرنه که تحریر اولنوب مومی الیه
آدمکز تقریر ایلمش ایسه پایهٔ سریر عالم مصیرمزه عرض اولنوب علم شریف عالم آرای
ملوکانه مز علی وجه الکمال محیط وشامل اولمشدر ایمدی اعتاب سلطنت مآبمز قدیمدن
اعدا واحبابه دوستلق دشمنلك یوزندن مفتوح الابوابدر کمال اخلاصله انتساب ایدن
سلاطین صداقت نصاب خزاین وممالك تسلیمیله حریم صلحه داخل اولوب عنایات خسروانه
والتفات ملوکانه مز ایله کامران وآستان عالیشانمزه التجا ایدن سایر تاجدارانه مابیننده
محسود الاقران اوله کلمشدر مکتوب مخالصت شعارکزده اشعار ایتدوککز اوزره اکر
سدهٔ سعادت والا رتبتمزه واکر اولیاء دین ودولتمزه خلوص نیت وصفاء طویت ایله
موالاتده ثابت قدم ومصافاتده راسخدم اولورسکز سزدخی اضعاف مضاعف التفات
شاهانه وعنایات پادشاهانه مزه مظهر اولمکز مقرر ومحققدر وحاجی ترخان جانبلرینه که
عسکر نصرت اثرمز کوندرلمش ایدی مرحوم ومغفور له جدم سلطان محمد خان غازی
انار الله برهانه کفه ولایتنی فتح ایدلدنبرو ولایت قریم خانلری وممالك چراکسه بانلری
آستان کیتی ستانمزه اطاعت واظهار عبودیت قیلوب الی هذا الان هر بری نظر فرخنده
اثرمز ایله منظور وکامران واکثری سنجاغ همایونمز ایله تعدیء اعدادن مصون ومأمون
محسود الاقران اولوب فرمان قضا جریانمز صدور ایتدوکی اموردە علی ماهو المأمور
بذل مقدور ایدر بکلر وقوللرمز اولمشلر ایکن ممالك محروسه مزه داخل قبارتای ولایتنده
قدیمی الفت ومحبته مخل قلعه احداث اولندوغندن ماعدا حاجی ترخان جانبلرنده
دشت قپچاق وماوراء النهر مسلمانلری کلوب کچوب بو جانبه مرور وکذر ایتدکلری
یوللری آدملرکز سد ایلدکلرین اول اول جانبلرك امراء وسلاطینی عموما درکاه عالم پناهمزه
اعلام وانها قیلوب استدعای عون وعنایت والتماس حمایت وصیانت ایلمکین اولجانبده

﴿ ٤٦١ ﴾

اولان قلاع و بقاع احوالنه وسایر اموره وقوف واطلاع نیتنه جناب اما رتمآب ایالتنصاب
قریم خانی دامت معالیه یه بعض امراء ذوی الاقتدار قوللرمدن بر مقدار عسکر جرار
دشمن شکار ارسالنه باعث اولمش ایدی مقدما وحالیا دخی مشار الیه قریم خانی دامت
معالیه اوجانبه وران ایلچیسی درت بش ییلدنبرو ولایتکزده عوق اولنوب کیرو عودته
رخصت ویرلدوکی موالات قدیمه ومصافات مستدیمه یه مخل وضع ایکن عسکر نصرت
اثر ظفر نمونمز ایله اوجانبه آقین مراد ایتدکجه رخصت واجازت همایون ویرلمیوب محضا
بوجانبه خلوص وموالاتکز شایع اولمغین نیجه دفعه منع ودفع اولنمق واقع اولمشدر وبالجمله
سرحدمزده ایکی ییللق سفرتمدارکی مقرر ایکن مجرد اولطرفك احوال واموردینه وقوف
وشعور ایله اکتفا اولنوب عسکر ظفر اثر سعادتمندمز طرفندن ولایتکزدن هیچ برمحله
خلوص وموالاته مخل ضرر وکزند واقع اولمامشدر بناء علیه مومی الیه آدمکز اداب رسالت
وارکان سفارتی کماینبغی ادا ورعایت ایلدکدنصکره کیرو اوجانبه عودت ایتدیرلمشدر
کرکدرکه نامهٔ همایونمز وصول بولدقده مکتوب مخالصت مصحوبکز ایله عرض اولندوغی
اوزره قواعد وداد مشید ومبانیٔ اتحاد مؤید اولوب حاجی ترخان یولنی اچوب وموالات
قدیمه یی اخلاله باعث ماینده قبارتای ایچنده حادث قلعه یی رفع ایلیوب اولدیاردن مرور
وعبور ایدن رهروان احسن واسان وجهله امین وسالم کذران ایدوب ممالك محروسه مزه
کچوب ومشار الیه قریم خانی دامت معالیه نك ذکر اولنان ایلچیسنه اجازت ویریلوب
کیرو مملکت وولایتنه عودت ایتدیریلوب طرفیندن اولان مخالصت قوی البنیان وبنیان
موالفت سدید الارکان ممهد واستوار وبوقاعدهٔ مرضیه نسلا بعد نسل محکم پایدار اولوب
فراغ بال وجمهور رعایا ورفاهیت حال عامهٔ برایا بر نوعله منتظم اوله که انك قواعد وضوابطنه
انقطاع دوران وانقراض زمانه دکین احتمال خلل وفتور ونقض وقصور یول بولمیه والسلام

Text

ʿAtabe-i ʿulya-i adālet-ünvān ve südde-i seniyye-i saʿādet-nişānımuza ki melce'-i selatīn-i cihān ve merceʿ-i ḫevākin-deverāndır … nām ilçiniz vāsıṭasıyla nāme-i muḫālasat peyāmınuz vārid olub kadīmü'l-eyyāmdan ābā'-i kirām ve ecdād-ı ʿālī nijād-ü'l-iḥtirāmımuz enara'llah berahinihüm zamān-ı saʿādet-encāmlarından südde-i sidre maḳāmlarına muvalāt-ı tāmm üzere olmagın ḥālā dāḫi āsitāne-i saʿādet ʿünvānımuza teḥniyet ve ʿarż-ı ḫuluṣ içün mümaileyh adamıñuz gönderilüb ve nuvvāb-ı kāmyābımız ile ʿasākir-i nuṣret-neṣābımuz Ḥācı-Tarḫan cāniblerine varub dāḫil oldugun ʿilām itmişsiz her ne taḥrir olunub mümaileyh adamıñuz takrīr itmiş ise pāye-i serīr-i ʿālem-masīremize ʿarż olunub ʿalem-i şerīf ʿālem-i ārāy-ı mülūkhanemüze ʿala vechü'l-kāmil muḥīt ve şāmil olmuşdur imdī ʿitāb-ı salṭanat-me'abımıza kadīmden āʿdā ve aḥibbāya dostluk düşmanlıḳ yüzünden meftūḥü'l-ebvābdır kemāl-i iḫlāṣla intisāb iden selaṭeyn-i ṣadāḳat-nisāb ḫezā'in u memālik teslīmiyle harīm-i ṣulha dāḫil olub ʿināyet-i ḫüsrevāne ve iltifāt-ı mülūkanemüz ile kāmrān ve āsitān-ı ʿālīşānımıza iltica iden sā'ir tācdārān mābeyninde maḥsudu'l-aḳrān ola gelmüşdür mektūb-ı muḫālaṣat şiʿārınızda işʿār itdügüñüz üzere eger südde-i sa'ādet ve alā rütbetimüze ve eger ulyā'-i dīn ve devletimüze ḫulūs-u niyet ve ṣafā'-i ṭaviyyet ile muvālatda s̱abit-ḳadem ve muṣāfatda rasiḫdem olursanız siz daḫi iẓ'āf-ı müzā'if iltifāt-ı şāhāne ve 'ināyet-i pādişāhānemize maẓhar olmanuz muḳarrer ve muhaḳḳaḳdır ve Ḥacı Tarḫān cāniblerine ki 'asker-i nuṣret-eserimiz gönderilmiş idi merḥum ve maġfūrlu ceddüm sulṭan Meḥmed Ḫān Ġāzi enāra illahi berhanihu Kefe vilāyetini feth idildinberü vilāyet-i Ḳırım ḫānları ve memālik-i Çerākise bānları āsitān-ı gitī-setānımıza iṭā'at ve iẓhār-ı 'ubūdiyyet ḳılub ala' haża elān her biri nıẓār-ı ferḫunde es̱erimiz ile manẓur ve kāmrān ve ekseri sancaġ-ı hümayūnumuz ile ta'addi-i 'ādādan maṣūn ve me'mūn ve maḥsūdü'l-aḳrān olub fermān-ı ḳazā ceryānımuz ṣudūr itdigi umūrda 'ala māhuve'l-ma'mūr beẕl-i maḳdūr ider begler ve ḳūllarımuz olmuşlar iken memālik-i maḥrūsamıza dāḫil Ḳabartay vilāyetinde ḳadīmi ulfet ve muḥabbete muḫil ḳal'a iḥdās olduġundan mā'adā Ḥācı Tarḫān cāniblerinden Deşt-i Ḳıpçāk ve Maverā'ün-nehr müslümānları gelüb geçüb bu cānibe murūr ve güẕārān itdükleri yolları adamlarıñuz sedd itdüklerin ol cāniblerin ümarā'-i selātini 'umumen dergāh-ı 'ālem-penāhımıza 'ilām ve inhā ḳılub istid'ā-i 'avn ve 'ināyet ve iltimās-ı ḥimāyet ve ṣıyānet iylemegin ol cāniblerde olan ḳala' ve bıḳā' ahvāline ve sāir umūra vuḳūf ve ıṭlā' niyetine cenāb-ı emāret-me'ab eyālet-niṣāb Kırım Ḥānı dāme me'ālihuya ba'żı umerā'-i ẕü'l-iḳtidār ḳullarımdan bir miḳdār 'asker-i cerrar düşman-şikār irsāline ba'is̱ olmuş idi muḳaddeman ve ḥāliya daḫi müşarüileyh Ḳırım Ḫānı dāme me'ālihu ol cānibe varan ilçisi dört beş yıldan berü vilāyetinizde 'avḳ olunub gerü 'avdete ruḫṣat verilmedügü muvālāt-ı ḳadīme ve muṣāfat-ı müstedīmeye muḫil vaż' iken 'asker-i nuṣret-eser ẓafer-numunemüz ile olcānibe aḳın murād itdükce ruḫṣat ve icāzet-i hümayūn virülmeyüb maḥża bu cānibe ḫūluṣ ve muvālātınuz şāyi' olmaġın nice def'a men' ve def' olunmaḳ vāḳi' olmuşdur ve bi'l-cümle serḥaddimüzde iki yıllık sefer tedāriki muḳarrer iken mücerred ol ṭarafın aḥvāl ve umūruna vuḳūf ve şu'ūr ile iktifā olunub 'asker-i ẓafer-eser-i sa'ādet-mendemiz ṭarafından vilāyetinizden hiç bir maḥale ḫulūṣ ve muvālāta muḫil żarar ve gezend vāḳi' olmamışdır binā'an 'aliyye mümaileyh adamıñuz ādāb-ı risālet ve erkān-ı sefāreti kemāyenbaġı edā ve ri'āyet iyledikdensonra gerü ol-cānibe 'avdet itdürülmişdir gerekdir ki nāme-i hümayūnum vusūl bulduḳda mektūb-ı muḫālaṣat-maḥsūbuñuz ile 'arż olunduġu üzere ḳavā'id ve dād-ı müşeyyed ve mübāni' ittiḥād mü'eyyid olub Ḥācı Tarḫān yolunu açub ve muvālāt-ı kadīmiyyeyi iḫlāle bā'is̱ mābeynde Ḳābartāy içinde ḥādis̱ ḳal'ayı ref' iyleyüb oldiyārdan murūr ve 'ubūr iden rāh-ı revān isān ve āsān vechle e'mīn ve sālim güẕārān idüb memālik-i maḥrūsamuza geçüb ve müşarileyh Ḳırım Ḥānı dāme me'āliyuehunuñ ẕikr olunan ilçisine icāzet virülüb gerü memleket ve vilāyetine 'avdet itdürülüb ṭarafından olan muḫalaṣat-ı ḳuvva-i bünyān ve bünyān-ı mu'ālefe-i sedīdü'l-erkān-ı mümehhed ve ustuvar ve bu ḳa'ide'-i marżiyye naslen ba'ad-i nesl muḥkem ve pāyidār olub ferāġ-ı bāl ve cumhūr-u re'āyā ve refāhiyyet-i ḥāl 'āmme-i berāyā ber nev'ale müntezim ola ki anuñ kavā'id ve ẓavābaṭına inḳiṭaġ-ı devrān ve inḳırāż-ı zamāna degin iḥtimāl ḫalel ve futūr ve naḳż ve ḳuṣūr yol bulmaya ve's-selam.

Translation

Your letter with your truthful message to our threshold known with the highest justice and to our Porte of felicity, which is the refuge for the world's kings and the house of the *ḫaḳans*, arrived with your ambassador named [Novosiltsev]. [In this letter] you say that you sent the aforementioned man of yours to inform our threshold renowned with its felicity of your congratulatory greetings and your petition of cordiality in accordance with [the fact] that from the ancient times and from the auspicious times of our illustrious fathers and our venerated ancestors of noble lineage – may God illuminate their manifestations – you have been ready to offer your complete support to [our] offices of the exalted Porte. You have also informed [us] that [with God's help] our victorious representatives and soldiers reached [the direction of] Astrakhan. Whatever was written [by you] and repeated by your aforementioned man has been known to the foot of our throne, the abode of the world, and has been, in a complete manner, understood by our noble royalty adorned by the world. Now, from the old times, those loyal kings who submit with a mature sincerity to our benevolent court [of refuge] which is an open door to enemies and beloved friends for enmity and friendship are adjoined to those who attain the state of peace that is restricted to the selected ones with the granting of treasures and countries [by the Porte] and to those who become prosperous through blessing and favour of our royalty and to those who are adorned [thanks to] their virtue of being among other kings who find refuge at our exalted threshold. In accordance with what your truthful letter conveys [in writing], if you are to be at the front line of being ready to support and be unwavering in your amity with your earnest desire and clear affectionate devotion to our threshold of the highest felicity and to our noble religion and state, it has been determined and is certain that you too will be honoured with our constantly increasing magnificent blessings and our royal grace. And our victorious soldiers were sent in the direction of Astrakhan. Since my late and already forgiven [by God for his sins] ancestor Sultan Mehmed Han Gazi – may God illuminate his proof – conquered the province of Kefe, the country of the Crimean khans and Circassian lands has submitted and has displayed subservience to our threshold of the world.

After this, and presently, each of them, [thanks to] our worldly wisdom of felicity, is prosperous, and most of them are protected from and are fearless against enemy attacks [by carrying] our imperial banner, [and as such they are] envied by their peers. And in accordance with our decrees, while they have been lords and our slaves [*ḳullarımız*], and they are prosperous with much power granted to them; your construction of a fortress in the province of Kabarda – a part of our well-protected domains – violated the ancient terms and fraternity. Moreover, that your men have blocked the roads through which the Muslims of Desht-i Kipchak and Transoxiana used to reach this side [through Astrakhan] has been brought by all the rulers of those lands to the attention of our Porte, which is the refuge of the world. Their petition for help and our favour of protection caused [us] to send his honourable excellency of proper governing Crimean khan – may his court endure – who knew well the fortresses and buildings [the whole territory] in those areas with some of our powerful lords and with a number of devastating and enemy-hunting soldiers. And despite that previously and presently the envoy of the aforementioned Crimean khan – may his court endure – has been detained in your country and not been given permission to return in an act that is not in conformity with the old amity and perpetual devotion, and he [the Crimean khan] desires to raid those [Muscovite] lands with our soldiers who are the embodiment of victory; he has not been given permission or an imperial diploma. And [the khan's request for permission to raid] has been refused and stopped many times, only because your devotion and amity to us is well known. And having campaign materiel stocked for two years on all our frontiers and knowing the situation and conditions of those directions [lands] well, our victorious soldiers of our felicity did not bring any destruction or harm, adverse to sincerity and amity, to any parts of your country. Consequently, the aforementioned man of yours observed the rules of his duty and formalities of the embassy, as good as it may be, and following this he has been sent back to your side. It is necessary that upon the arrival of my imperial letter, in line with what your sincere letter conveyed, by corroborating to strengthen and act in conformity with the given principles and amity, you should open the Astrakhan road and demolish the fortress in Kabarda which is a breach of the ancient fraternity and, by being benevolent and easing, allow those travellers who pass through those lands to our well-protected domains in safety. And you should give permission to the aforementioned envoy of the Crimean khan – may his court endure – and return him [back to] his country. You should keep your amity [to us] strong and in its orderly and proper place and be constant and firm, generation after generation, to observe these well-liked principles. And as such, you will attain easement [from anxiety] and your mass of flocks [*re'āyā*] and your whole nation's [state of] welfare will be absolute. These principles and norms are not to be harmed or disrupted by weakness and shortcomings or failure until the demolition of the world and the end of time.

B. Letters and orders from the Porte regarding plans for construction of two fortresses in the North Caucasus, Mühimme Defteri (MD) 43, nos. 193, 206, 247, 480.

1. MD 43, no. 193, 14 Cemāẕiü'l-evvel 988/27 June 1580

Facsimile

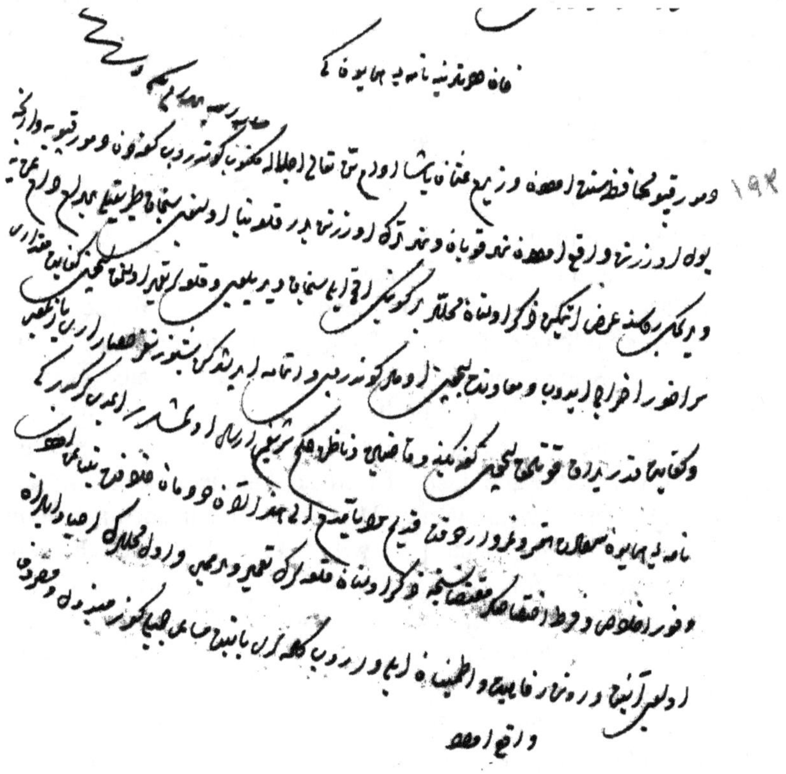

Text

Müşarileyh Behrām Bege virüldü.

[1] Ḫān ḥażretlerine nāme-i hümāyun ki [2] Demür ḳapu muḥāfaẓasında olan vezīrim ʻOsmān Paşa adamallahu teʻāla iclālihu mektūb gönderüb Kefeden Demürkapuya varınca [3] yol üzerinde vāki‘ olan nehr-i Kubān ve nehr-i Terek üzerine birer ḳala‘ binā olunub sancāḳ ṭarīkiyle Behrām dāme ʻizzihuya [4] verülmek ricāsına ʻarż itmegin ẕikr olunan mahāller iki [yüz] bin akçe ile sancāḳ virülüb ve ḳala‘lar taʻmir olunmaḳ içün kifāyet miḳdāri [5] serāḫor iḫrāc idüb ve muʻāvenet içün adamlar gönderüb ve itmāma irişdükte beş-yüz nefer ḥiṣār eri yazulub [6] ve kifāyet miḳdār yarāḳ ḳonulmaḳ içün Kefe beyine ve każısına ve nāẓırına ḥükm-ü şerīf irsāl olunmuşdur imdī gerekdir ki [7] nāme-i hümāyūn saʻādet makrūnumuz varduḳda ḳadīmü'l-eyyāmdan ila hazā'l-an dudmān-ı ṣaltanat-penāhımıza olan [8] vufūr-ı iḫlās ve farṭ-ı iḥtiṣaṣınız muḳteżasınca ẓikr olınan ḳala‘ların taʻmir ve termīmi ve ol maḥāllerüñ iḥyā ve irā [9] olub āniye rūzane-i refāhiyyet ve iṭmīnān ile varub gelmeleri bābında mesā‘i-i cemīlenuz mebzūl ve meṣrūf [10] vāḳi‘ ola.

Translation

Given to the aforementioned Behrām Beg.

Imperial letter to the [Crimean] khan

Osman Pasha – may exalted God endure his magnificence – who is assigned to the defence of Derbend sent a letter to petition that two fortresses on the Kuban and Terek rivers which are located on the route between Kefe and Derbend be built and given to Behram – may his glory endure – as a *sancak* (province). Our exalted orders have been dispatched to the governor, judge and *nazır* of Kefe so that the aforementioned lands will be granted as a *sancak* with 200,000 *akçe*, and an adequate number of workers and troops to protect them will be sent. And when the construction is finished, 500 fortress troops will be registered for service and an adequate number of weapons will be stationed. Now, it is necessary that when our felicitous imperial letter arrives, in accordance with your sincere devotion and loyalty to our imperial dynasty since the ancient times, you should bring forth pleasing effort for the repair of the aforementioned fortresses and making those lands flourish and for their [materiel and men] arrival with salaries and in security.

2. MD 43, no. 206, 20 Cemāẕiü'l-evvel 988/3 July 1580

Facsimile

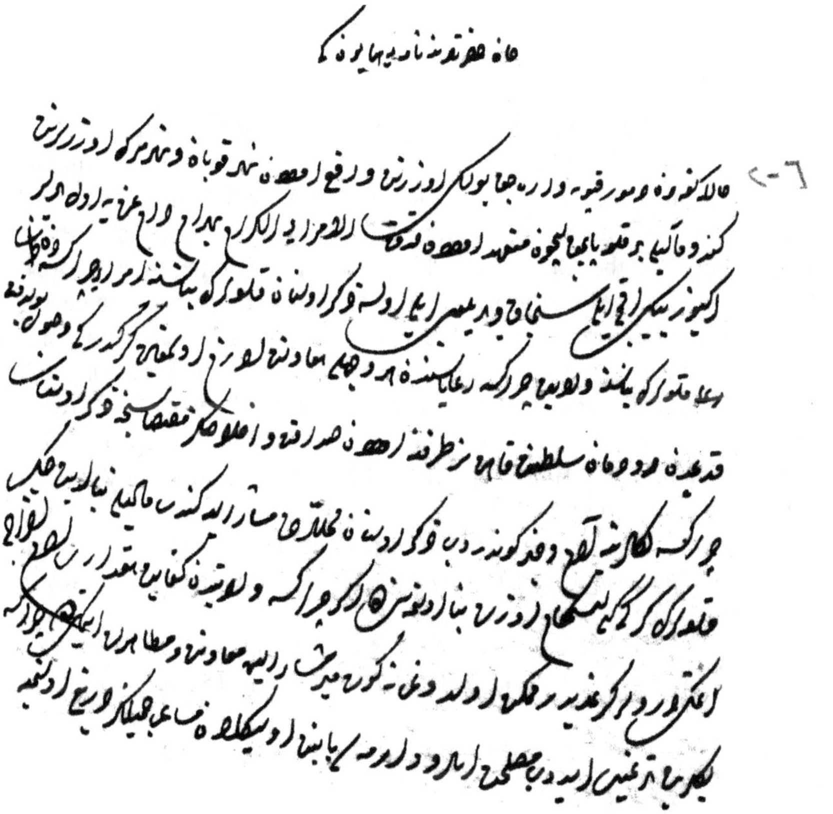

Text

[1] Ḫān ḥażretlerine nāme-i hümāyun ki [2] ḥālā Kefeden Demür ḳapuya varacak yolun üzerinde vāḳi' olan nehr-i Ḳubān ve nehr-i Terek üzerleründe [3] kendü mālīyle bir ḳala' yapmaḳ içün müte'ahhid olan ḳıdvetü'l-ümerāü'l-kerām Behrām dāme 'izzuhuya ol yerler [4] iki yüz biñ aḳçe ile sancāḳ virülüb öyle olsa ẕikr olunan ḳala'ların bināsına ümerā-i Çerākiseden ṬB [5] ḥālā kāla'ların bināsına vilāyet-i Çerākise re'āyāsından her vechle mu'āvenet lāzım olmağın gerekdir ki vusūl buldukta [6] ḳadīmden dudmān-ı salṭanat-ı fāhiremüz ṭarafına olan ṣadaḳat ve iḫlāsunuz mukteżasınca ẕikr olunan [7] Çerākise beglerine ilām ve ḫaber gönderüb ẕikr olunan mahāllerde müşarileyh kendü mālīyla binā idecek [8] ḳala'ların geregi gibi istihkām üzere binā olunmasında eger

Çerākise vilāyetinden kifāyet miḳdāri adam iḫrāc [9] itmekdür ve eger ġazir mümkün olduġuna göre mīr-i müşarileyhe mu'āvanet ve maṭahirle itmekde Çerākise [10] beylerine terġib idüb muṣalahat itdürülmesü bābında olagelen mesā'-i cemīlenüz zāī' olunmaya.

Translation

Imperial letter to the [Crimean] Khan

The lands on the Kuban and Terek rivers have been granted as a *sancak* with [a revenue of] 200,000 *akçe* to the noblest of the noble commanders Behram – may his glory endure – so that he will build a fortress [one on each river] with his own money and resources. As this is the case, the request* of the Circassian chiefs for the aforementioned fortresses and all sorts of help from the people of the Circassian province for the aforementioned fortresses are necessary. As such, I have commanded in accordance with your loyalty and sincerity to our glorious imperial dynasty since the ancient times that you are to send news to the aforementioned Circassian chiefs for the proper construction of the fortresses that the aforementioned [Behram] will build with his own money in the said lands, by evaluating whether it is necessary to recruit an adequate number of men from the Circassian province or whether it is abundant. You should bring forth pleasing effort to assist the aforementioned and to encourage the Circassian chiefs to agree on this.

3. MD 43, no. 247, 7 C[emāẕiü'l-aḫīr] 988/20 July 1580

Facsimile

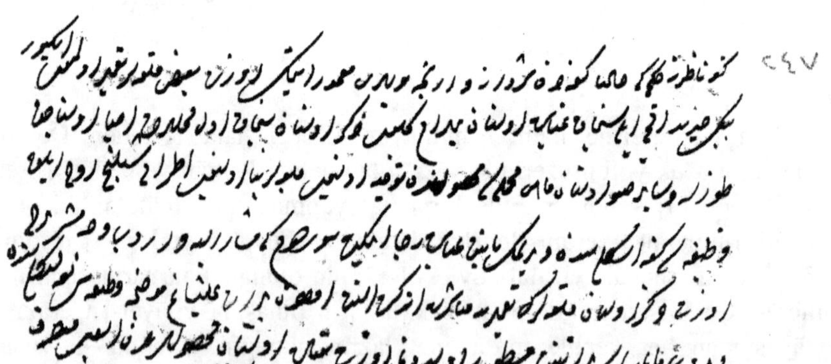

* The original text is unclear. The legible letters are T and B, which may represent *taleb*, meaning 'request'.

Text

[1] Kefe nāẓırına ḥükm ki ṣābıkan Kefeden Şirvāna varunca yolları ma'mūr itmek üzere ba'ẓı ḳala'lar ta'mir olunub iki yüz biñ [2] aḳçe-i harīr ile sancāḳ 'ināyet olunan Behrām gelüb ẕikr olunan sancāḳ ol maḥāllerde iḥyā olunacak [3] tuzla ve sāir ṣu olunan māhī maḥallesi maḥṣulunden tevżi' olunub ḳala'lar binā olunub eṭrafı şenliḥ[k] üç aylık [4] vaẓifesi Kefe iskelesinden virülmek bābında 'ināyet ricā itmegin buyurdum ki müşarileyh varub vech-i meşrūḥ [5] üzere ẕikr olunan ḳala'ların ta'mirine mübāşeret itdükte elinde olan berāt-ı 'alişānım mucebince vaẓifesin Kefe iskelesinden [6] verüb ma'dā berātında mastūr olduğu üzere ta'ayyur olunan maḥṣullerinden alunub maṣraf [7] ola.

Translation

Order to the *nazır* of Kefe

Behram, who has been granted a *sancak* with an a salary of 200,000 *akçe* with the condition that some fortresses would be repaired in order to make the roads between Kefe and Shirvan prosperous, came forth to petition our benevolence that until the fortresses are built and prosper with their revenues of saltworks and yields of other water bodies, his salary for three months be given from the [revenue] of the port of Kefe. I have commanded that in accordance with my exalted diploma [*berāt*] that he holds, his salary be given from the [revenue] of the port of Kefe and then be registered as an expense to be received from the allocated products.

4. MD 43, no. 480, 27 Şa'bān 988/7 October 1580

Facsimile

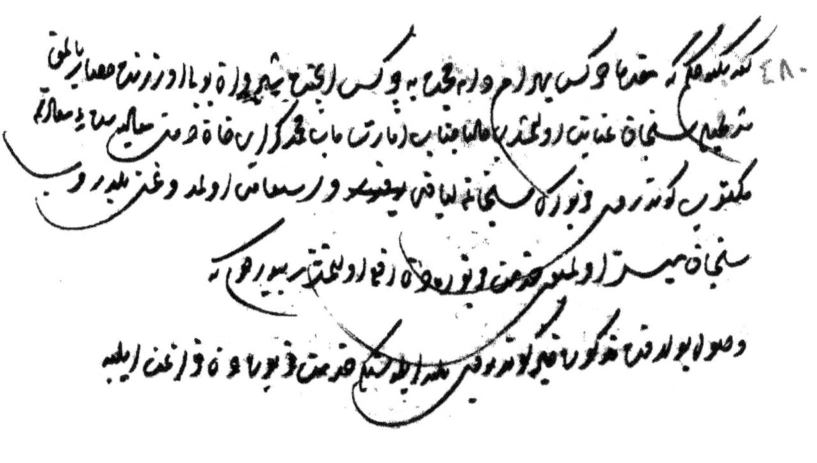

Text

[1] Kefe begine ḥükm ki muḳaddemān Çerkes Behrām dāme mecduhuya Çerkes içinde Şirvān yolu üzerinde ḥisār yapmak [2] şarṭıyla sancāḳ ʻināyet olmuşidi ṣabıkān cenāb-ı imāret-me'ab Mehmed Giray H̱ān dāme meʻāliyehu südde-i saʻādetime [3] mektūb gönderüb mezbūrun sancāḳa liyāḳati ve istiḳāḳı olmaduġun bildirüb [4] sancāḳ müyesser olmayub ḫiẕmet-i mezbūreden refʻ olunmuşdur buyurdum ki [5] vusūl buldukta mezkūra ḫaber gönderüb bildiresün ki hiẕmet-i mezbūreden ferāġat iyleye.

Translation

Order to the Governor of Kefe

Previously Çerkes Behram – may his fortune endure – was granted a *sancak* with the condition of building fortress[es] in the Circassian [lands] on the route to Shirvan. Previously his honourable excellency of proper governing Mehmed Girey Khan – may his court endure – sent a letter to my threshold of felicity informing that the aforementioned [Behram] was not worthy of [being granted] a *sancak*. As being granted a *sancak* is not [his] lot, he has been released from this service. I have commanded that when it arrives, you are to send the news and inform [him] so that he [Behram] will quit the aforementioned service.

C. Imperial Letter to the Shamkhal of Daghestan dated 7 Şaʻbān 1002/28 April 1594, MD 72, no. 277.

Facsimile

Text

[1] Cenāb-ı imāret-me‘ab eyālet-nişāb devlet iktisāb el-muḫtaṣṣ-ı bī-mezīd ‘ināyetü’l-melikü’l-müte‘al Ṭaġıṣtān Ḥākimi Şamhāl dāme me‘āliyuhuya ḥükm ki [2] hālā Şirvān eyāletine mutaṣarrıf olan destūr-u mükerrem

müşir-i mufahham niẓāmü'l-'ālem vezirim Ca'fer Paşa adāmu illahi te'āla iclālehu [3] dergāh-ı 'izzet destgāhımıza mektūb gönderüb rūs-u menḫūs keferesi yigirmi biñ miḳdārı tüfeng-endāz melā'in-i ḥāsirīn ile [4] senüñ ülkene gelüb iki yerde ḳala' yapub içlerine beş altı biñden ziyāde tüfeng-endāz kāfir komağla [5] senin içün ülkesinde iḳāmete ḳādir olmayub ṣa'b sengistān yerlere çıkub aḥvāli mukadder olmuşdur deyü [6] 'arż ve 'ilām eyledü imdī sen ve baban abā-i kirām ve'l-ecdād-i 'azām enāruillahi berahinihum zamān-ı şerīflerinden ḥusūsan eyālet-i Şirvān fetḥünden berü [7] südde-i seniyye-i sıpıhrasta[n] ve 'atabe-i 'aliyye-i felek-fersamıza 'arz-ı ṣadaḳat ve iḫlāsdan ḫāli olmaduğunuz ecilden [8] mutaṣarrıf olduğunuz eyāletin memālik-i mahrūsam mużafat-ı masubesinde olub ḥıfz u ḥırāseti her vecḥle ẕimmet-i mütme'il-i 'aliyye-i mülūkanum lāzım-i vecḥ olmağın [9] melā'in-i ḫāsirīnin ülkenüzde binā iyledükleri ḳala'ları 'ināyet-i ḥakla beraber hadm olunmak bābında fermān-ı 'alişānım ṣādır olub [10] bu bābda müşarileyh Ca'fer Paşaya lāzım olduğu ḳadar 'asakir ve ol ḳala'leri yıḳmak içün [11] 'arabalarıyla ṭopçular irsāl olunmuşdur ve sen yüce āsitānemize dāi'ma ḫulus-u mu'ād ile itā'at ve isnād üzere [12] olduğun ecilden ḥaḳḳında mezīd-i 'avātıf-ı 'aliyye şahāne ve mersa-i 'avārif-i seniyye-i pādişāhānem ẓuhūra getürüb [13] ḫila'-ı fāḫiremden bir sevb ḫil'at-ı mūrisü'l-behçet ve isyaf-ı fāhimü'l-eknāfımdan bir ḳabża şimşir tığımız tāsīr-i 'ināyet [14] idüb buyurdum ki vusūl bulduḳda 'ināyet olunan [15] ḫil'at-ı fāḫire ve kısmet bāhiremizi envā'-i ta'ẓīm ve'l-ikrām ile giyüb ve tığ-ı ḫun-ı işāmımızı dāḫi īżāẕü'l-ikrām (?) ve iḥtirām ile [16] kuşanub daḫi mümaileyh vezirim Ca'fer Paşa adāmallahi te'āla iclalihu ile yekdil ve yekciḥet olub [17] ve sen dāḫi Ṭağısṭān 'askeriyle mümaileyh vezirimin vecḥ-i münāsib gördügü üzere ḥüsn-ü ittifaḳ ve ictihād ile melā'in-i haksarīn üzerlerine [18] yürüyüb bi-izni'l-lahü'l-melikü't-teāli yapdukları ḳala'ları ḥaḳla beraber hadm idüb ve rūs-u menḫūsu [19] 'ulf-u yerr ve ṭa'me-i şemşir iyleyüb envā'i yüzaḳlıḳları taḥṣiline mesa'-i cemīl iyleyesüz ve 'asākiri menṣūreme [20] żaḫire tedārik itdürüb bir nesneye müżayeke çıkardurmayub ğānimet ve sālimle gerü Şirvāna 'avdet ve mürāca'at itdürmege ḥüsn-ü ihtimām iyleyesün.

Translation

Order to his honourable excellency, proper governing ruler of his state, Shamkhal, the ruler of Daghestan, chosen for prosperity and auspiciousness by the blessing of the highest God, may his court endure. My most noble vizier and illustrious marshal order of the world Cafer Pasha – may God endure his magnificence – sent a letter to our exalted palace, informing us that the ill-fated Rus' [Muscovites] infidels came to your country with 20,000 musket-bearing cursed mischievous soldiers and built fortresses in two places and stationed more than 5,000–6,000 musket-bearing infidels inside these fortresses and that you are not capable of protecting your country and retreated to the arduous mountains as your destiny revealed. Now, because you and your father have never forsaken your loyalty and pure devotion to our very high threshold, exalted as the spheres, since the honourable times of our illustrious fathers and noble ancestors – may God illuminate their manifestations – and specifically since the conquest of the province of Shirvan and because your country is a part of our well-protected domains, defence and protection of the country you possess is by all means a duty of my powerful and lofty sovereignty. As such, my exalted order was sent to demolish – with God's help – the fortresses built in your country by the cursed enemies. For this reason, an adequate number of soldiers and gunners with their carts in order to destroy those fortresses have been dispatched to the aforementioned Cafer Pasha. And your constant devotion, loyalty and leaning towards our exalted Porte brought about many magnificent gifts and harbouring of my majestic favours. I convey my favour [to you] by the present of a splendid robe of honour from among my glorious robes to cause delight and a sword from among the sides of conquerors. I have commanded when they arrive, you are to wear the splendid robe of honour with every sign of respect and esteem, to gird our bloodthirsty sword with respect and veneration, and to have one voice and direction with my aforementioned vizier Cafer Pasha – may God endure his magnificence. And you should attack the cursed enemies with Daghestani soldiers as my aforementioned vizier commands and in unity of thought and with God's help and permission, demolish the fortresses that they built. And by razing the ill-fated Rus' [Muscovites] to the ground and putting them to the sword, you should make glorious effort to bring forth all kinds of honourable acts and provide my victorious soldiers with grains and not allow any hardship to fall on them and pay careful attention to ensure their safe return with booty to Shirvan.

Appendix II

Selected Muscovite Documents from *Posol'skii Prikaz* Records

A. Posol'skii Prikaz translation of Selim II's letter to Ivan IV dated 1570. Rossiiskii gosudarstvennyi arkhiv drevnikh aktov, F. 89, *Turetskie dela*, kniga 2, fol. 56b–59a.

Facsimile

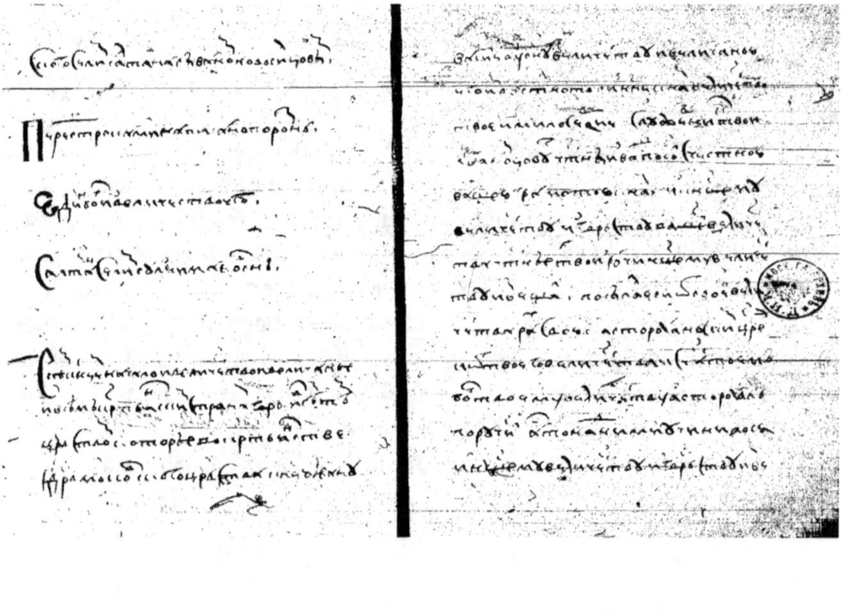

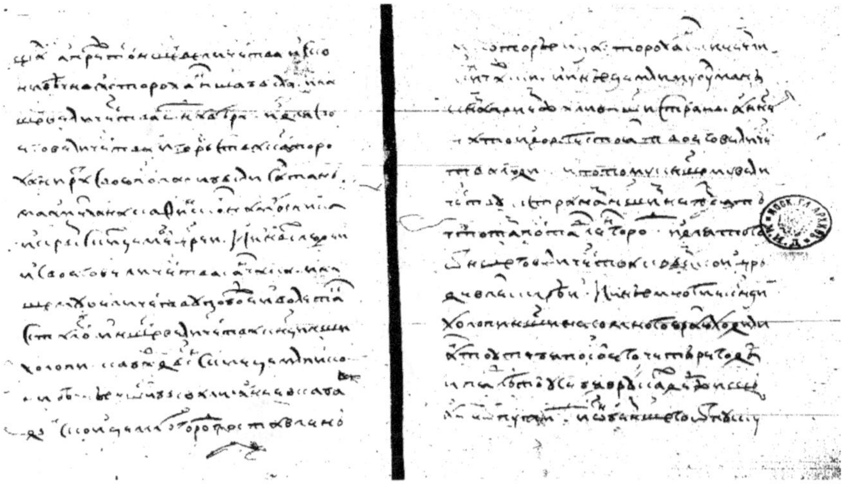

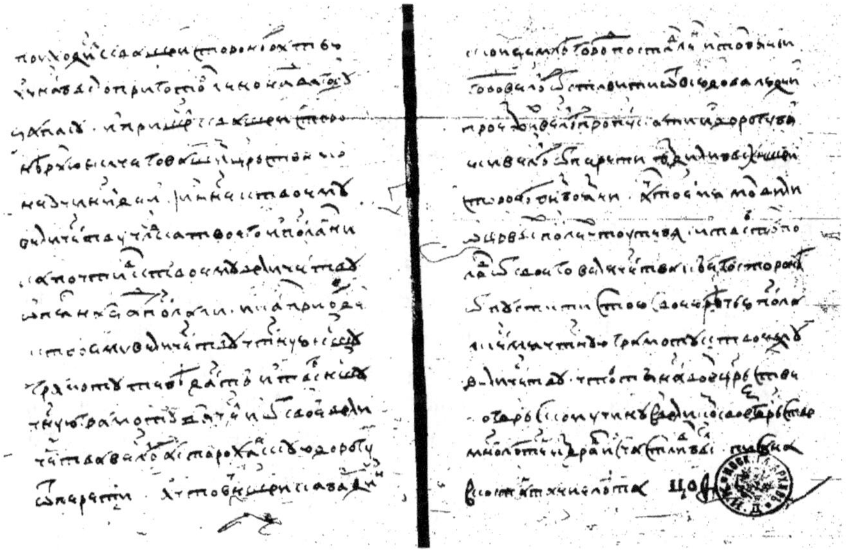

Text

[fol. 56a] A se gramota ko tsariu i velikomu kniaziu tur-[fol. 56b]skogo Selim Saltana s Ivanom Novosil'tsovym.

Pered strokami napisano porozn':

Edin bog i velichestvo ego.

Saltan Selim Suleimanov syn.

Vsiem kniazem nachalo i velichestvo i velichan'e, i vsiem krest'ianskim stranam gosudar' i vsiem tiem tsar'stvom, kotorye vo krest'ianstve, gosudar', Moskovskogo tsar'stva kniaziu Ivanu [fol. 57a] Vasil'evu synu velichestvu i velichan'iu ego izviestno, to i nyne k nam velichestvo tvoe i miloserdie, sluzhebnik tvoi, Ivanom zovut, chestnyi vash posol s chestnoiu vasheiu gramotoiu k nam i k nashemu velichestvu i gosudar'stvu vashego velichestva chestnye tvoi riechi nashemu velichestvu izveshchal. Posylal esi ot svoego velichestva rat' svoiu [k] Astorokhan'skim tsarem, i ot tvoego velichestva i schast'em bog tvoemu velichestvu Astorokhan' poruchil, a chto nad nimi uchinilosia, i nashemu velichestvu i gosudar'stvu izve-[fol. 57b]shchal. A prezh togo nashego velichestva iskoni viechno Astorokhan' nasha byla, i nashego velichestva odna viera, i dlia svoego velichestva i gosudar'stva k Astorokhani rat' svoiu poslali byli: Saltan Maamet khana, Kafinskogo namiesnika, i krymskikh zemel' tsarei i inykh liudei, i svoego velichestva sanchaka. I nashemu velichestvu po bozhei vole tak sstalos'. I nashego velichestva kniazi nashi kholopi Kabardynskie zemli iskoni viechnye nashi byvali, a nyne v Kabardynskoi zemlie gorod postavlen, [fol. 58a] i kotorye iz Astorokhanskie zemli, kipchazhskie i inye zemli musul'many k nam priezzhali v nashi strany, a nyne na toi doroge stoiat tvoego velichestva liudi, i potomu k nashemu velichestvu k stranam nashim ne iezdiat, chto tam postavlen gorod. I dlia togo ot nashego velichestva krymskoi tsar' Devlet Kiriei i inye mnogie kniazi, kholopi nashi, ne so mnogoiu rat'iu khodili. A chto u tebia posol ego, chetyre gody i piat' liet u sebia v rukakh derzhish, a ne otpustish. I on bez nashego otpusku [fol. 58b] prikhodil k vashei storonie rat'iu, a u nas bylo prigotovleno na dva godu zapasu. I prishel k vashei storonie rat'iu, nichego vashim tsar'stvam ne uchinil, dei. I nyne k tvoemu velichestvu cheloveka tvoego i poslannika pochtiv k tvoemu velichestvu opiat' nazad poslali. I kak priiedet k tvoemu velichestvu, chestnuiu nashu gramotu tebie dast, i ty b nashu chestnuiu gramotu vychel i ot svoego velichestva veliel Astorokhanskuiu dorogu otpereti. A chto v nashei Kabardin-[fol. 59a]skoi zemlie gorod postavlen, i tot by esi gorod veliel otstaviti, otvsiudova liudei proezzhikh veliel propuskati i dorogu by esi veliel otpereti, iezdili by k nashei storonie bez boiazni. A chto esmia molvili o tsarevykh poslekh, chto u tebia, i ty b tiekh poslov ot svoego velichestva k ego storonie otpustiti [veliel]. S toiu svoeiu riech'iu poslali esmia chestnuiu gramotu k tvoemu velichestvu, chtob ty na svoem tsar'stve [p]o gosudar'skomu chinu v velikom svoem gosudar'stve mnogolieten i zdrav i schastliv byl. Pisana v Kostantanie lieta 979-go.

Translation

And this is the letter of the Turkish Sultan Selim [sent] with Ivan Novosiltsov to the Tsar and Grand Prince.

Above the text is written:

God is one, his majesty.

Sultan Selim, son of Süleyman.

It is known to the head and majesty and glory of all princes, the ruler of all Christian countries, the sovereign of all those tsardoms that belong to Christianity, his majesty and glory Prince Ivan, son of Vasilii, of the Muscovite Tsardom, that presently [from] your majesty and grace there [has come] to us your servitor by the name of Ivan, your honourable envoy, with your sincere letter to us, our majesty and crown, [and] communicated the sincere words of your majesty to our majesty. From your majesty's side, you sent your army to the khans [*sic*] of Astrakhan, and owing to your majesty and good fortune, God entrusted Astrakhan to your majesty, and what happened to them [that is, the people of Astrakhan], [you] informed our majesty and crown. But prior to that, from time immemorial Astrakhan had been our majesty's, of the same faith with our majesty, and for the sake of our majesty and crown we sent to Astrakhan our army: Sultan Mehmed Khan; governor of Kefe; khans [*sic*] and other men of the Crimean lands; and a *sancak* [*bey*] of our majesty's. And through God's will, so it happened to our majesty. From time immemorial, the princes of the Kabardinian land have been our majesty's slaves, but now a fortress has been built in the Kabardinian land. And as for those Muslims from the Astrakhan lands [and] Kipchak and other lands, that used to come to us, to our countries, now on the route [they used to take] are stationed your majesty's people, and because of the town built there they [Muslims] do not come to our majesty, to our countries. And for this reason, from our majesty's side, Crimean Khan Devlet Girey and other princes, our slaves, campaigned with not many troops. As to his [the khan's] envoy, you have detained him for four or five years and refused to grant him leave. And it was without our permission that he [the khan] came to your country with an army, whereas we had two years' worth of supplies prepared. And he said that he came to your country with an army, he did not cause your tsardoms any harm. And now we have sent your majesty's envoy, having honoured him, back to your majesty. And as he comes to your majesty and delivers to you our sincere letter, would you read our sincere letter and order from your majesty's side that the Astrakhan route be opened. As to the fact that a fortress has been erected in our Kabardinian land, would you order that fortress be demolished, travellers from everywhere be allowed to pass, the route be opened, so that they would come to our country without fear. As to what we have said about the khan's envoys that are with you, would you grant leave to those envoys from your majesty to his country. With these words of ours we have sent a sincere letter to your majesty [wishing] that you may remain on your royal throne as a sovereign in your great dominion for many years in health and happiness.

Written in Constantinople in the year 979 [1571].

B. Sokullu Mehmed Pasha's discussion with Muscovite envoy Ivan Novosiltsev regarding the route that the envoy took in order to go to Istanbul from Moscow and the status of Astrakhan, 1570. Rossiiskii Gosudarstvennyi Arkhiv Drevnikh Aktov, F. 89, *Turetskie dela*, kniga 2, fol. 88b–89b.

Facsimile

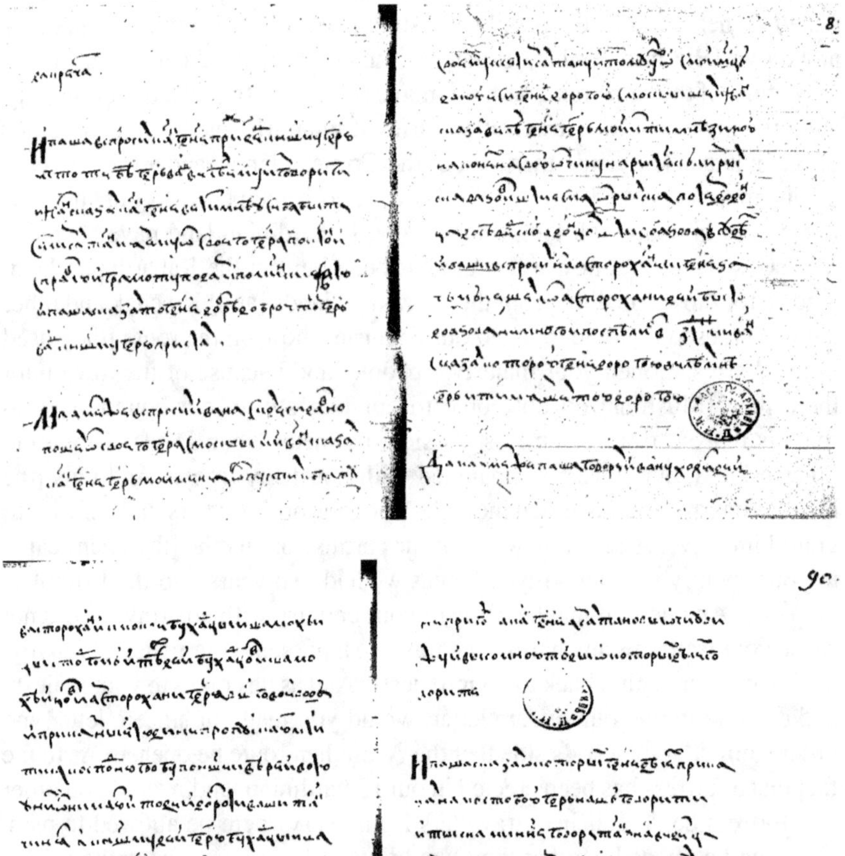

Text

[fol. 88b] Maamet zhe vsprosil Ivana: skol' esi davno poshel ot svoego gosudaria s Moskvy? I Ivan skazal: kak, gospodine, gosudar' moi menia otpustil k bratu [fol. 89a] svoemu k Selim saltanu, i tomu uzh osmoi mesiats. Da koiu esi, gospodine, dorogoiu s Moskvy shel? I Ivan skazal: veliel, gospodine, gosudar' moi itti mnie zimoiu na konekh na svoiu otchinu na Rylesk, a iz Ryl'ska v Azov, i shli esmia ot Ryl'ska polem do Dontsa do Sieverskogo, a Dontsom shli do Azova v sudiekh. I pashi vsprosili: na Astorokhan' esi, gospodine, zachiem ne shel? A ot Astorokhani, dei, bylo do Azova nemnogo i pospieli b v 17 dnei. I Ivan skazal: kotoroiu, gospodine, dorogoiu veliel mnie gosudar' itti, i iaz shel toiu dorogoiu.

Da Maamet zhe pasha govoril Ivanu: khodiat, dei, [fol. 89b] v Astorokhan' i k Moskve bukhartsy i shamokhieitsy s torgom, i tiekh, dei, bukhartsov i shamokhieitsov iz Astorokhani gosudaria vashego voevody i prikaznye liudi ne propuskaiut molitisia k Ospodniu grobu po nashei viere i voliu u nikh otnimaiut, i to, dei, dobro li vashi tak chiniat? A k nashemu, dei, gosudariu bukhartsy i shamokhieitsy o tom prikhodili biti chelom, koe ikh iz Astorokhani k Ospodniu grobu ne propuskaiut.

Translation

[Sokullu] Mehmed [Pasha] also asked Ivan [Novosiltsev], 'How long ago did you depart from your sovereign in Moscow?' And Ivan said, 'It is now the eighth month, sir, since my sovereign sent me to his brother Sultan Selim.' 'And by which road, sir, did you travel from Moscow?' And Ivan said, 'My sovereign ordered me, sir, to travel in winter on horseback to his patrimony, to Ryl'sk, and from Ryl'sk to Azov, and so we went from Ryl'sk by steppe to the Severskii Donets [River], and by the Donets we travelled in boats to Azov.' And the pashas asked, 'Why did not you, sir, go through Astrakhan? For [the distance] from Astrakhan to Azov is not large and you could have made it in 17 days.' And Ivan said, 'Whichever road, sir, my sovereign ordered me to take, I took that road.'

And Mehmed Pasha then told Ivan, 'People of Bukhara and Şemahı [*sic*, perhaps Samarkand is meant] go to Astrakhan and to Moscow to trade, and your sovereign's *voevoda*s and *prikaz* officials do not allow those people of Bukhara and Şemahı to go from Astrakhan to pray at the Lord's Tomb [Mecca], in accordance with our faith, and detain them – is it right for your people to do that? And the people of Bukhara and Şemahı came to our sovereign to complain that they were not allowed to go from Astrakhan to the Lord's Tomb.'

C. *Shert'* signed in 1588 by Kabardinian Mamstriuk Kniaz, Kudenek Mirza and others, *Snosheniia Rossii s Kavkazom: Materialy izvlechennye iz Moskovskago glavnago arkhiva Ministerstva Inostrannykh diel, 1578–1613 gg.*, ed. S. L. Belokurov (Moscow: Universitetskaia tipografiia, 1889), 47–8; *Kabardino-russkie otnosheniia v 16–18 vv.* (Moscow: Izdatel'stvo Akademii nauk SSSR, 1957), 1:50–1.

Запис шертная как приведены черкасы Мамстрюкъ князь да Худенекъ мурза Канбулатов сын Черкаской и черкасы Елбуздук с товарыщи.

Даю шерть по своей вѣре, по мусулманскому закону, г. ц. и в. к. Ѳ. И. в. Р. и его дѣтем, которых ему Бог дасть вперед, на том, что приезжалі есмя биті челом г. ц. и в. к. Ѳ. И. в. Р. ото князя Канбулата князя и ото всѣх Кабардинскихъ черкас, чтоб государь нас пожаловал, взял под свою царскою руку потому ж, какъ ихъ держал в своем жалованье отецъ государя нашего ц. и в. к. Ив. Вас. в. Р. И нас Канбулата князя и меня Мамстрюка князя и Куденека мурзу и всѣхъ братью нашу и племянников ц. и в. к. Ѳ. И. в. Р. пожаловал, взял нас под свою царскую руку и во оборону ото всяких нашихъ недругов; и нам Канбулату князю и братье нашей Думануку князю и всей братье нашей и дѣтем нашим и племянником и всѣм нашим лутчим людем со всею Кабардою Черкасскою г. ц. и в. к. Ѳ. И. в. Р. служиті и от г. ц. и в. к. быті нам всѣм неотступным и до своего живота и х Турскому и х Крымскому и к Шевкалскому и к иным государевым недругом ни х кому не приставаті. А хто будет г. ц. и в. к. Ѳ. И. в. Р. друг, тот и нам будет другъ; а хто будет г. ц. и в. к. Ѳ. И. в. Р. недруг, тот и нам будет недруг и на того нам со государевымі воеводамі с Астараханскимі и с Терскимі воеводамі с ратнымі людмі ходиті и приводіті во государеву волю. И житі Канбулату князю и мнѣ Мамстрюку князю и Очикану князю и Куденеку мурзѣ и братье моей Дамануку да Избулдуку князю да Анзаруку да Сингалѣю князю Канглычевым да князю Бітемрюку и всей братье нашей племянником и дѣтем и лутчим нашим людем, переменяясь, житі в государеве в Терском городе со государевымі воеводамі и государю служити и стояті нам всею землею Черкасскою с Терскимі воеводамі на государева недруга на всякого заодин. А хто будет г. ц. и в. к. Ѳ. И. в. Р. его государским воеводам Астараханским и

Терскым воеводам непослушен будет и к Терскому городу не пристанет и в государеве жалованье с нами быти не похочет, Шевкалской князь или Тюменской князь или горские князи или Кумыки или Иверские князи или из нашего роду которой Черкаской князь от государева жалованья отстаті похочет, также которые Черкаские князи с своимі улусы Тоилостанов род Шолох князь Ташбарувовъ з братьею и с племянникі и з детмі да Кантуков род Пашнук княз да Ослонбек да Жансох служат Крымскому и Шевкалскому,—и нам с Канбулатом князем и з братьею своею и со всею Черкаскою землею на тѣх на всѣх на государевых непослушников вмѣсте з государевыми воеводами ходиті ратью и ко государеву волю их ко государеве вотчине к Асторахани и к Терскому городу в государеву волю их приводіті и заклады у них поиматі и стояті нам всѣм Черкаским князем и мурзам з государевымі воеводы заодин на всякого недруга и на них ходіти ратью и государю пряміті о всем потому, как в сей шертной записі написано. Также которые недругі Терского рат и Крымской или иные которые недругі поидут ко государеве вотчіне в Астарахани или к Терскому городу,—и нам, будучі в Терском городе, со государевымі воеводамі за город стояті и битись с нимі до смерти и государевых воевод не выдаті и хитрості и оману над государевымі воеводамі и над ратнымі людмі и над городом хитрості никоторые не учініті. Также коли г. ц. и в. к. Ѳ. И. в. Р. велит нам итті на которого своего недруга на Литовского или в Нѣмцы,—и нам и нашім братьям и дѣтем итті на государеву службу, колким колі государь велит итті на свою государеву службу. И о всем нам со всею Черкаскою землею государю служіті и пряміті и к недругом государевым ни х кому не прíставаті,—о всем потому, как в сей шертной запісі писано.

Июля въ 25 день по сей записи прíведены шерті Мастрюк княз да Куденек мурза да черкасы лутчіе іх люді Илбуздукъ с товарыщі.

Text

Zapis' shertnaia, kak privedeny cherkasy Mamstriuk kniaz', da Khudenek murza Kanbulatov syn Cherkaskoi i cherkasy Elbuzduk s tovaryshchi.

Daiu shert' po svoei viere, po musul'manskomu zakony, gosudariu tsariu i velikomu kniaziu Feodoru Ivanovichu vsea Rusii i ego dietem, kotorykh emu bog dast vpered, na tom, chto priezzhali esmia biti chelom gosudariu tsariu i velikomu kniaziu Feodoru Ivanovichu vsea Rusii oto kniazia Kanbulata kniazia i oto vsiekh kabardinskikh cherkas, chtob gosudar' nas pozhaloval, vzial pod svoiu tsarskuiu ruku po tomu zh, kak ikh derzhal v svoem zhalovan'e otets gosudaria nashego, tsar' i velikii kniaz' Ivan Vasil'evich vsea Rusii. I nas, Kanbulata kniazia, i menia,

Mamstriuka kniazia, i Kudeneka murzu, i vsiekh brat'iu nashu i plemiannikov tsar' i velikii kniaz' Feodor Ivanovich vsea Rusii pozhaloval, vzial nas pod svoiu tsarskuiu ruku i vo oboronu oto vsiakikh nashikh nedrugov. I nam, Kanbulatu kniaziu, i brat'e nashei Dumanuku kniaziu, i vsei brat'e nashei, i dietem nashim, i plemiannikom, i vsiem nashim lutchim liudem so vseiu Kabardoiu cherkasskoiu gosudariu tsariu i velikomu kniaziu Feodoru Ivanovichu vsea Rusii sluzhiti, i ot gosudaria tsaria i velikogo kniazia byti nam vsiem neotstupnym i do svoego zhivota i kh Turskomu, i kh Krymskomu, i k Shevkal'skomu i k inym gosudarevym nedrugom ni kh komu ne pristavati. A khto budet gosudariu tsariu i velikomu kniaziu Feodoru Ivanovichu vsea Rusii drug, tot i nam budet drug; a khto budet gosudariu tsariu i velikomu kniaziu Feodoru Ivanovichu vsea Rusii nedrug, tot i nam budet nedrug, i na togo nam so gosudarevymi veovodami s astarakhanskimi i s terskimi voevodami s ratnymi liud'mi khoditi i privoditi vo gosudarevu voliu. I zhiti Kanbulatu kniaziu, i mne, Mamstriuku kniaziu, i Ochikanu kniaziu, i Kudeneku murzie, i brat'e moei Damanuku, da Izbulduku kniaziu, da Anzaruku, da Singalieiu kniaziu Kanglychevym, da kniaziu Bitemriuku, i vsei brat'e nashei, plemiannikom, i detiem i lutchim nashim liudem, peremeniaias', zhiti v gosudareve v Terskom gorode so gosudarevymi veovodami, i gosudariu sluzhiti i stoiati nam vseiu zemleiu Cherkaskoiu s terskimi voevodami na gosudareva nedruga na vsiakogo zaodin. A khto budet gosudaria tsaria i velikogo kniazia Feodora Ivanovicha vsea Rusii ego gosudarskim voevodam astarakhanskim i terskim voevodam neposlushen budet, i k Terskomu gorodu ne pristanet, i v gosudareve zhalovan'e s nami byti ne pokhochet – shevkal'skoi kniaz', ili tiumenskoi kniaz', ili gorskie kniazi, ili kumyki, ili iverskie kniazi, ili iz nashego rodu kotoroi cherkaskoi kniaz' ot gosudareva zhalovan'ia otstati pokhochet, takzhe kotorye cherkaskie kniazi s svoimi ulusy, Toilostanov rod: Sholokh kniaz Tashbzarukov z brat'eiu, i s plemianniki, i z det'mi da Kaitukov rod: Papshnuk kniaz', da Oslonbek, da Zhansokh, sluzhat Krymskomu i Shevkal'skomu – i nam s Kanbulatom kniazem, i z brat'eiu svoeiu, i so vseiu Cherkaskoiu zemleiu na tiekh na vsiekh na gosudarevykh neposlushnikov vmieste z gosudarevymi voevodami khoditi rat'iu, i ko[1] [*sic*] gosudarevu voliu ikh ko gosudareve votchine k Astorakhani i k Terskomu gorodu v gosudarevu voliu ikh privoditi, i zaklady u nikh poimati, i stoiati nam vsiem cherkaskim kniazem i murzam z gosudarevymi voevody zaodin na vsiakogo nedruga, i na nikh khoditi rat'iu i gosudariu priamiti o vsem po tomu, kak v sei shertnoi zapisi napisano. Takzhe kotorye nedrugi, Terskogo[2] [*sic*] rat' i Krymskoi ili inye kotorye nedrugi, poidut ko gosudareve votchine k Astarakhani ili k Terskomu gorodu – i nam, buduchi v Terskom gorode, so gosudarevymi voevodami za gorod stoiati, i bitis' s nimi do smerti, i gosudarevykh voevod ne vydati, i khitrosti i omanu nad gosudarevymi voevodami, i nad ratnymi liud'mi i nad gorodom khitrosti nikotorye ne uchiniti. Takzhe koli gosudar' tsar' i velikii kniaz' Feodor Ivanovich vsea Rusii velit nam itti na kotorogo svoego nedruga, na Litovskogo ili v Niemtsy, i nam, i nashim brat'iam, i dietem itti na gosudarevu sluzhbu, kol'kim koli gosudar' velit itti na svoiu gosudarevu sluzhbu. I o vsem nam so vseiu Cherkaskoiu zemleiu gosudariu sluzhiti i priamiti i k nedrugom gosudarevym ni kh komu ne pristavati – o vsem po tomu, kak v sei shertnoi zapisi pisano.

Iiulia v 25 den' no sei zapisi privedeny [k] sherti Mastriuk kniaz' da Kudenek murza da cherkasy lutchie ikh liudi Ilbuzduk s tovaryshchi.

Translation

Record of the pledge of allegiance (*shert'*) given by the Circassian Prince Mamstriuk; Kudenek Mirza, son of [Prince] Kanbulat Cherkaskoi; and Circassians Elbuzduk and others.

In accordance with my faith, under Muslim law, I give the pledge of allegiance to the Sovereign Tsar and Grand Prince Feodor Ivanovich of all Rus' and to his children whom God may give him in the future. Thereupon, we have come from Prince Kanbulat and from all Kabardinian Circassians in order to petition humbly the Sovereign Tsar and Grand Prince Feodor Ivanovich of all Rus' to be granted favour and be taken under his royal hand according to the same conditions as our sovereign's father, the Tsar and Grand Prince Ivan Vasil'evich of all Rus', granted them his favour. And the Tsar and Grand Prince Feodor Ivanovich of all Rus' has [also] granted favour to us, Prince Kanbulat and myself, Prince Mamstriuk, and Kudenek Mirza, and all our brothers and nephews, [and] has taken us under his royal hand to be protected from our various enemies. And we, Prince Kanbulat and our brother Prince Dumanuk and all our brothers and children, and nephews, and all our better men with all Circassian Kabarda, will serve the Sovereign Tsar and Grand Prince Feodor Ivanovich of all Rus', and for the rest of our lives we all will never quit [serving] the Sovereign Tsar and Grand Prince, nor will we ally with the Turkish [sultan], the Crimean [khan], the shamkhal or any other enemies of the sovereign. And whoever is a friend to the Sovereign Tsar and Grand Prince Feodor Ivanovich of all Rus', he will be our friend too; and whoever is an enemy to the Sovereign Tsar and Grand Prince Feodor Ivanovich of all Rus', he will be our enemy as well, and together with the sovereign's governors of Astrakhan and Terek [Town] and soldiers we will wage war against him and bring him into submission to the sovereign's will. And Prince Kanbulat and myself, Prince Mamstriuk, and Prince Ochikan and Kudenek

Mirza and my brothers Prince Dumanuk and Prince Izbulduk and Anzaruk, and Prince Sunchalei, sons of Kanglych, and Prince Bitemriuk and all of our brothers and nephews and children, and better men will live by turns in the sovereign's Terek Town with the sovereign's governors and serve the sovereign, and, together with the entire Circassian land, stand against every enemy of the sovereign with the governors of Terek [Town] as one. And whoever disobeys the Astrakhan and Terek [Town] governors of the Sovereign Tsar and Grand Prince Feodor Ivanovich of all Rus' and does not come to Terek Town, and refuses to accept the sovereign's favour along with us – be they the shamkhal or the prince of Tiumen or mountain princes or Kumyks or Iberian princes, or any Circassian prince from our family, who would wish to forsake the sovereign's favour, also any Circassian princes with their *uluses*, [such as] the Toilastanov family: Prince Sholokh [Solokh], son of Tashbzaruk, with his brothers and nephews and children; and the Kaitukov family: Prince Papshunuk and Oslonbek [Aslanbek], and Jansokh [Yansokh] [who] serve the Crimean [khan] and the shamkhal. And with Prince Kanbulat and our brothers, and with the entire Circassian land we will, together with the sovereign's governors, wage war against all those who disobey the sovereign and bring them into submission to the sovereign's will, to the sovereign's patrimony, to Astrakhan and Terek Town, and obtain hostages from them. And we, all the Circassian princes and mirzas, will stand as one with the sovereign's governors against every enemy and campaign against them, and act faithfully towards the sovereign in everything as recorded in this pledge of allegiance. Also, should any enemies, [be they] the army of the Turkish [sultan], or the Crimean khan, or any other enemies, attack the sovereign's patrimony of Astrakhan or Terek Town, we too, stationed in Terek Town, will defend the fortress together with the sovereign's governors and fight them [the enemies] to the death and not surrender the sovereign's governors and not trick or deceive the sovereign's governors and soldiers, and not commit anything devious against the fortress. Also, should the Sovereign Tsar and Grand Prince Feodor Ivanovich of all Rus' order us to campaign against some enemy of his – be that the Lithuanian [prince] or the Germans[3] – and when [this happens] we and our brothers and children will go to the sovereign's service, as many [of us] as the sovereign orders to go to his royal service. And in every way we, with the entire Circassian land, will serve the sovereign and be faithful [to him], and not ally with any of the sovereign's enemies, according to what is recorded in this pledge of allegiance.

On 25 July, Prince Mamstriuk and Kudanek Mirza and their better men Circassians Ilbuzduk and others swore a pledge of allegiance in accordance with this record.

Notes

1. It should read 'vo gosudarevu voliu'.
2. It should read 'Turskogo rat'.
3. 'The Germans' in this context refers not to ethnic Germans but to the Swedes.

Appendix III

Glossary of Terms

aamista see *aamistadi*
aamistadi (or *aamista/tawad*) nobility among the Abazas
ah see *akha*
ahipshi serfs among the Abazas
akçe main currency in the Ottoman Empire
akha (or *ah*) an Abaza chief
amanat a hostage requested from local rulers by the Muscovites as security
anyayoutskia (or *tefekashou*) land-owning peasants among the Abazas
atalyk foster-father tradition among the Circassians
aul a mountain village in Daghestan
azat a slave among the Kabardinians
bey once a ruler, then a prince, and in the sixteenth century denoting a governor
beylerbeyi a governor-general in the Ottoman Empire
beylerbeyilik a governor-generalship in the Ottoman Empire
burg a fortress-like stronghold made of stones in the North Caucasus
cagar (or *rayat*) peasants upon whom forced labour was imposed in Daghestan
cema'at a rural commune in Daghestan
cerahor a worker in the Ottoman Empire
chanka son of a prince born to a commoner woman in Daghestan
defterdar a book-keeper, finance official in the Ottoman Empire
dezhenugo a title denoting a less noble person among the Kabardinians
dizdar a castellan in the Ottoman Empire
emirü'l-umera a supreme commander in Islamic parlance used by the Ottomans
gramota an imperial order written by the Muscovite tsar
haraç payment made to the Crimeans by Muscovy, Poland-Lithuania
hil'at a robe of honour
hisar erleri resident soldiers of an Ottoman fortress
hükm an Ottoman imperial order
istimalet Ottoman policy of reconciliation
kabak an estate belonging to Kabardinian or Western Circassian nobility

kekovat (or *keykuvat*) third-in-rank to the succession in the Greater Nogay Horde
kethüda a representative in the Crimean Khanate
keykuvat see *kekovat*
kholop a slave, servant among the Muscovites
kniaz a prince in Muscovite parlance
krym-shamkhal see *yarım-shamkhal*
kul a slave or servant among the Ottomans; see also *yasir*
loganapit see *og*
ma'sum (or *tabarasan shah*) a ruler of the Tabarasan Principality in Daghestan
mirza (or *murza)* originally from Persian *emir-zade*, a prince; a title used for North Caucasus elites by the Muscovites and Ottomans
mühimme defteri register of imperial orders written by the Ottoman sultan or the Imperial Council
murza see *mirza*
mutasarrıf an Ottoman provincial official
nişancı a chief-scribe in the Ottoman Empire
nureddin a heir-apparent of the Greater Nogay Horde and second in line to succession to the Crimean throne
nutsal a ruler of the Avars of Daghestan
og (or *loganapit*) peasants upon whom forced labour was imposed among the Kabardinians
oprichnina a period of political oppression and terror against the boyars and public to reduce the power of the former and increase the autocratic powers of the Muscovite tsar
'öşr tithe tax in the Ottoman Empire
özden see *uzden*
palanka a redoubt
pominki gifts given to the Crimean khan or local rulers by the Muscovite tsar
posol'skaia kniga an ambassadorial book prepared for each embassy dispatched to a foreign ruler
pshi a prince among the Kabardinians and Western Circassians
pshihua (or *pshim yapsh*) a grand prince or prince of the princes in Kabarda
pshim yapsh see *pshihua*
pshitle peasants upon whom forced labour was imposed among the Western Circassians
rayat see *cagar*
resm-i çift annual tax on farmlands in the Ottoman Empire

sala uzden nobility who were granted the best lands in the Shamkhalate of Daghestan
sancak an Ottoman province. It also refers to annuities granted to officials and local rulers from a *sancak*
sancakbeyi an Ottoman governor
serdar an Ottoman commander
shamkhal a ruler of the Shamkhalate of Daghestan
shert' a written pledge given by local rulers to the Muscovite tsar
silahdar a weapon master in the Ottoman Empire
stateinye spiski reports written by Muscovite envoys
strel'tsy Muscovite military unit armed with firearms
tabarasan shah see *ma'sum*
tawad see *aamistadi*
tefekashou see *anyayoutskia*
tekhoqotle land-owning peasants among the Western Circassians
timar a land grant
tlakotlesh a title denoting a more noble person among the Kabardinians
tlfekotl land-owning peasants among the Kabardinians
unatle slaves among the Western Circassians
unavi slaves among the Abazas
uork see *work*
usmi (or *ustmii*) a ruler of the Daghestani Kaytaks
ustmii see *usmi*
uzden noble agricultural lords, vassals of the Daghestani Shamkhal; (or *özden*) noble class among the Western Circassians
voivode a ruler of Moldavia or Wallachia under the Ottomans
vol'nost' notion of freedom among the Cossacks
werk see *work*
work (or *werk, uork*) nobility among the Kabardinians
yarım-shamkhal (or *krym-shamkhal*) a heir apparent in the Shamkhalate of Daghestan
yasir (or *kul*) a slave among the Daghestanis
zeuche an assembly of gentry among the Kabardinians
zhalovanie annuity paid to local rulers by the Muscovite tsar

Appendix IV

Chronology

1453 Mehmed II takes Constantinople. End of the Byzantine Empire.
1461 Trebizond falls to the Ottomans.
1472 Ivan III of Muscovy marries a Byzantine princess, Sofia Paleologue, a niece of the last emperor.
1475 Gedik Ahmed Pasha captures Caffa (Ottoman Kefe). The Crimean Khanate reduced to Ottoman vassalage.
1480 Standoff on the Ugra between the Great Horde and Muscovy.
1481 Mehmed II dies. Beyazid II enthroned.
1500 Ivan III defeats Lithuania at the battle of Vedrosha. Muscovy annexes Novgorod, Chernigov and Starodub.
1501 Safavid dynasty takes over Iran and Azerbaijan.
1502 Mengli Girey razes Saray and puts an end to the Great Horde.
1505 Ivan III dies. Vasilii III enthroned.
1510 Muscovy annexes Pskov.
1512 Beyazıd II dies. Selim I enthroned.
1514 Muscovy annexes Smolensk. Selim I defeats Shah İsmail I of the Safavids at the Battle of Chaldiran; East Anatolia under Ottoman control.
1515 Mengli Girey dies. Mehmed Girey I becomes khan in the Crimea.
1519 Ottomans construct forts in the Kuban region.
1520 The reign of Süleyman I begins.
1521 Muscovy annexes Ryazan. Sahib Girey becomes the khan of Kazan.
1523 Filofei, a monk in Pskov, articulates idea of 'Third Rome'.
1526 Battle of Mohács: Süleyman I defeats Louis II of Hungary and Bohemia.
1532 Vasilii III installs his candidate Canali as the khan of Kazan. Sahib Girey becomes the khan of the Crimean Khanate.
1533 Vasilii III dies. Ivan IV enthroned.
1538 Battle of Preveza: Ottomans gain control of the Mediterranean Sea.
1539 Sahib Girey raids the Janeys in the Taman Peninsula.
1541 Süleyman I conquers Buda in Hungary.
1542 Sahib Girey organises a campaign against the Janeys.
1544 Sahib Girey attacks Kabarda.

1546 Lesser Nogays attack the Crimean Khanate and are annihilated by the Crimeans.
1547 Ivan IV crowned, takes title of 'tsar'.
1549 Sahib Giray occupies Astrakhan. Sefa Girey of Kazan deposed.
1550 Ivan IV enacts a new code of law and reforms the army.
1551 Sahib Girey raids Kabarda. Deposed by the Ottomans.
1552 Muscovy annexes the Khanate of Kazan. Western Circassians dispatch envoys to the tsar. Safavids establish diplomatic relations with Muscovy.
1555 Treaty of Amasya between the Ottoman Empire and Safavid Iran.
1556 Ivan IV annexes the Khanate of Astrakhan. Dmytro Vyshnevetskyi pledges allegiance to Ivan IV. Zaporozhian Cossacks under Vyshnevetskyi and their Circassian allies begin raiding Ottoman/Crimean possessions in the north of the Black Sea.
1557 Kabardinian Chief Temriuk sends envoys to the tsar.
1558 Ivan IV attacks the Livonian Order. The Livonian War begins. The Stroganovs hire Cossacks to subdue the Tatars of Siberia.
1563 Muscovy annexes the territory of the Livonian Order. Vyshnevetskyi is captured and killed by the Ottomans.
1565 Ivan IV initiates the *oprichnina*, reign of terror.
1566 Süleyman I dies. Selim II enthroned.
1567 Muscovites build Sunzha Fortress in Kabarda.
1569 Ottomans organise a campaign to capture Astrakhan. Union of Lublin: formal political union of Poland and Lithuania. Muscovy offers an anti-Ottoman alliance to Shah Tahmasp I of the Safavids.
1570 Conquest of Cyprus by Piyale Pasha of the Ottoman Empire.
1571 The Crimean Tatars reach Moscow. Suburbs of Moscow burned. Tsar Ivan IV has to leave the city.
1572 The *oprichnina* in Muscovy ends.
1576 Shah Tahmasp I dies. İsmail II enthroned.
1577 Kabardinians send envoys to the tsar.
1578 Ottoman–Safavid War begins. Muscovites erect a fortress in Kabarda.
1579 Stroganov expedition against the Khanate of Siberia.
1581 Ivan IV kills his own son and heir.
1582 Muscovy signs the Treaty of Jam Zapolski and renounces its claims to Livonia and Polotsk. The Stroganov army conquers the Khanate of Siberia.
1583 Muscovy cedes its Baltic lands to Sweden with the Treaty of Plussa. End of the Livonian Wars.
1584 Ivan IV dies. His son Feodor enthroned.

Chronology

1586 Muscovite–Georgian negotiations begin.

1587 Muscovite envoys visit King Alexander II of Kakheti. Ottoman officials decide to undertake a campaign to capture Astrakhan. Abbas I becomes shah of Safavid Iran.

1588 Muscovites construct Terek Fortress at the mouth of the Terek River.

1589 Patriarchate of Moscow created. Metropolitan Iova becomes patriarch.

1590 Treaty of Istanbul between Ottoman Empire and Safavid Iran; Georgia, Azerbaijan, Armenia and North Caucasus under Ottoman rule. Muscovite–Swedish War commences.

1591 Crimean Tatars raid Muscovy.

1591 Feodor's brother and only male heir to Muscovite throne, Dmitrii, assassinated in Uglich.

1592 Governor of Terek, Alexander Zasekin, attacks Daghestani lands.

1593 Zasekin captures Tarku, capital of the shamkhalate. Habsburg–Ottoman War begins.

1594 Daghestanis with the help of the Ottomans expel the Muscovite troops.

1595 Muscovy acquires Baltic territories from Sweden.

1598 Feodor, the last Rurikid tsar, dies. Boris Godunov becomes tsar. The Time of Troubles begins.

1601 Famine kills more than one million people in Muscovy.

1603 Safavid–Ottoman War begins.

1604 Boris Godunov orders invasion of Daghestan.

1605 Boris Godunov dies suddenly. His son Feodor Godunov enthroned. Muscovite troops in Daghestan annihilated by Daghestani and Ottoman forces. End of Muscovite influence in North Caucasus.

1606 First False Dmitrii deposes Feodor Godunov.

1612 Ottomans and Safavids sign Treaty of Nasuh Pasha.

1613 Mikhail Romanov elected tsar by the *Zemskii sobor* (parliament).

Bibliography

Primary Sources

I. Archival Sources

Turkish Presidency State Archives, Department of Ottoman Archives, Istanbul

Mühimme defterleri (MD)

MD 8, 1569–70.
MD 9, 1569–70.
MD 12, 1570–1.
MD 14, 1571.
MD 14–2, 1570.
MD 16, 1571.
MD 23, 1573–4.
MD 24, 1573–4.
MD 25, 1573–4.
MD 26, 1574.
MD 28, 1576.
MD 29, 1576–7.
MD 32, 1577–8.
MD 37, 1578–9
MD 38, 1579–80.
MD 40, 1579.
MD 41, 1579–80
MD 42, 1579–81.
MD 43, 1580.
MD 48, 1582–3.
MD 58, 1585.
MD 60, 1585.
MD 61, 1585–6.
MD 62, 1586–7.
MD 64, 1587
MD 65, 1588–9.
MD 67, 1589–91.
MD 68, 1589–90.

MD 69, 1591–2.
MD 71, 1592–3.
MD 72, 1593–4.
MD 73, 1594–5.
MD 74, 1595–6.

Rossiiskii gosudarstvennyi arkhiv drevnikh aktov (Russian State Archive of Ancient Acts), Moscow

F. 89, *Turetskie dela*, kniga 2.
F. 89, *Turetskie dela*, kniga 3.
F. 123, *Krymskie dela*, kniga 9.
F. 123, *Krymskie dela*, kniga 13.

II. Published Documentary Sources

3 numaralı mühimme defteri, 966–968/1558–1560. Edited by Nezihi Aykut et al. Ankara: Türkiye Cumhuriyeti Başbakanlık, Devlet Arşivleri Genel Müdürlüğü, 1993.

5 numaralı mühimme defteri, 973/1565. Edited by Hacı Osman Yıldırım et al. Ankara: Türkiye Cumhuriyeti Başbakanlık, Devlet Arşivleri Genel Müdürlüğü, 1994.

6 numaralı mühimme defteri, 972/1564–1565. Edited by Hacı Osman Yıldırım et al. Ankara: Türkiye Cumhuriyeti Başbakanlık, Devlet Arşivleri Genel Müdürlüğü, 1995.

7 numaralı mühimme defteri 975–976/1567–1569. Edited by Hacı Osman Yıldırım et al. Ankara: Türkiye Cumhuriyeti Başbakanlık, Devlet Arşivleri Genel Müdürlüğü, 1997.

12 numaralı mühimme defteri, 978–979/1570–1572. Edited by Hacı Osman Yıldırım et al. Ankara: Başbakanlık, Devlet Arşivleri Genel Müdürlüğü, 1996.

82 numaralı mühimme defteri, 1026–1027/1617–1618. Edited by Hacı Osman Yıldırım et al. Ankara: Başbakanlık, Devlet Arşivleri Genel Müdürlüğü, 2000.

83 numaralı mühimme defteri, 1036–1037/1626–1628. Edited by Hacı Osman Yıldırım et al. Ankara: Başbakanlık, Devlet Arşivleri Genel Müdürlüğü, 2001.

85 numaralı mühimme defteri, 1040–1041/1630–1631. Edited by Hacı Osman Yıldırım et al. Ankara: Başbakanlık, Devlet Arşivleri Genel Müdürlüğü, 2002.

91 numaralı mühimme defteri, 1056/1646–1647. Edited by Murat Cebecioğlu et al. Ankara: Başbakanlık, Devlet Arşivleri Genel Müdürlüğü, 2015.

Ahmed Feridun Bey. *Münşa'atü's-selatin*. Istanbul, 1858–9 (AH 1275).

Başbakanlık Osmanlı Arşivi rehberi. Edited by Hacı Osman Yıldırım, Nazım Yılmaz and Yusuf İhsan Genç. Istanbul: Başbakanlık Devlet Arşivleri Genel Müdürlüğü Osmanlı Arşivi Daire Başkanlığı, 2000.

Bennigsen, Alexandre et al. *Le Khanat de Crimée dans les archives de Musée du palais de Topkapi*. Paris: Mouton, 1978.

Ishin, V. V. and I. V. Toropitsyn, eds. *Astrakhanskii krai v istorii Rossii XVI–XXI vv.* Astrakhan: Astrakhanskii universitet, 2007.

Kabardino-russkie otnosheniia v 16–8 vv. 2 vols. Edited by T. Kh. Kumykov and E. N. Kusheva. Moscow: Izdatel'stvo Akademii nauk SSSR, 1957.

Kurat, Akdes Nimet, ed. *Topkapı Sarayı müzesi arşivindeki Altın Ordu, Kırım ve Türkistan hanlarına ait yarlık ve bitikler*. Istanbul: Burhaneddin Matbaası, 1940.

Mühimme defteri 44. Edited by M. A. Ünal. Izmir: Akademi Kitabevi, 1995.

Osmanlı Devleti ile Azerbaycan Türk hanlıkları arasındaki münasebetlere dair arşiv belgeleri. Ankara: Türkiye Cumhuriyeti Başbakanlık Devlet Arşivleri Genel Müdürlüğü, 1992.

Pamiatniki diplomaticheskikh i torgovykh snoshenii Moskovskoi Rusi s Persiei. 3 vols. Edited by N. I. Veselovskii. St Petersburg: Iablonskii and Perott, 1890–8.

Pamiatniki diplomaticheskikh snoshenii drevnei Rossii s derzhavami inostrannymi. Part 1. 10 vols. St Petersburg: Tipografii II Otdielenia sobstvennoi E. I. V. Kantseliarii, 1851–71.

Pamiatniki diplomaticheskikh snoshenii Krymskago khanstva s Moskovskim gosudarstvom v XVI–XVII v.v., khraniashchiesia v Moskovskom Glavnom Arkhivie Ministerstva Inostrannykh Diel. Edited by F. Lashkov. Simferopol: Tipografiia gazety 'Krym', 1891.

Posol'skaia kniga po sviaziam Rossii s Nogaiskoi Ordoi (1576 g.). Edited by V. V. Trepavlov. Moscow: Institut rossiiskoi istorii RAN, 2003.

Posol'skie knigi po sviaziam Rossii s Nogaiskoi Ordoi (1551–1561 gg). Edited by D. A. Mustafalina and V. V. Trepavlov. Kazan: Tatarskoe knizhnoe izdatel'stvo, 2006.

Prodolzhenie drevnei rossiiskoi vivliofiki. 11 vols. St Petersburg: Imperatorskaia akademiia nauk, 1793. Reprint, The Hague: Mouton, 1970.

Puteshestviia russkikh poslov XVI–XVII vv.: Stateinye spiski. Moscow: Izdatel'stvo Akademii nauk, 1954.

Russian Embassies to the Georgian Kings (1589–1605). 2 vols. Edited by W. E. D. Allen. Texts translated by Anthony Mango. Cambridge: Hakluyt Society, 1970.

Snosheniia Rossii s Kavkazom: Materialy izvlechennye iz Moskovskago glavnago arkhiva Ministerstva inostrannykh diel, 1578–1613 gg. Edited by S. L. Belokurov. Moscow: Universitetskaia tipografiia, 1889.

Sultanın emir defteri: 51 numaralı mühimme defteri. Edited by Hikmet Ülker. Istanbul: Tarih ve Tabiat Vakfı Yayınları, 2003.

Topkapı Sarayı Arşivi H.951–952 tarihli ve E-12321 numaralı mühimme defteri. Edited by Halil Sahillioğlu. Istanbul: IRCICA, 2002.

III. Published Narrative Sources

Asafi Dal Mehmed Çelebi. *Şeca'atname*. Edited by Abdülkadir Özcan. Istanbul: Çamlıca Basım, 2006.

Bibliography

Aşık Mehmed. *Menazirü'l-avalim*. Edited by Mahmut Ak. Ankara: Türk Tarih Kurumu, 2007.

Evliya Çelebi. *Evliya Çelebi seyahatnamesi*. 9 vols. Edited by Yücel Dağlı, Seyit Ali Kahraman and Robert Dankoff. Istanbul: Yapı Kredi Yayınları, 2003.

Gelibolulu Mustafa 'Âli, *Nusret-nâme*. Edited by Mustafa Eravcı. Ankara: Türk Tarih Kurumu, 2014.

Gelibolulu Mustafa Ali ve Künhü'l-ahbar'ında II. Selim, III. Murat ve III. Mehmet devirleri. 3 vols. Edited by Faris Çerçi. Kayseri: Erciyes Üniversitesi Yayınları, 2000.

Gelibolulu Mustafa Ali ve Meva'idü'n-nefais fi-kava'idi'l-mecalis. Edited by Mehmet Şeker. Ankara: Türk Tarih Kurumu Basımevi, 1997.

Hakluyt, Richard. *The Principal Navigations, Voyages, Traffiques & Discoveries of the English Nation Made by Sea or Over-land to the Remote and Farthest Distant Quarters of the Earth at Any Time within the Compasse of These 1600 Years*. 12 vols. Glasgow: J. MacLehose, [1589] 1903–5.

Herberstein, Sigmund F. *Notes upon Russia: A Translation of the Earliest Account of That Country, Entitled Rerum Moscoviticarum Commentarii*. Edited and translated by R. H. Major. London: Hakluyt Society, 1851.

Hezarfen Hüseyin Efendi. *Telhisü'l-beyan fi kavanin-i al-i Osman*. Edited by Dr Sevim İlgürel. Ankara: Türk Tarih Kurumu, 1998.

'Istoriia o prikhode turetskago i tatarskogo voinstva pod Astrakhan' v lieto ot Rozhdetsva Khristova 1677'. Translated by N. N. Murzakevich. *Zapiski Odesskago obshchestva istorii i drevnostei* 8 (1872): 479–88.

Katip Çelebi. *Cihan-nüma*. Istanbul, 1732.

Kefeli İbrahim bin Ali. *Tevarih-i Tatarhan ve Dağıstan ve Moskov ve Deşt-i Kıpçak ülkelerinindir*. Edited by Cafer Seyid Ahmet Kırımer. Pazardzhik, 1933.

Kırımi, Abdülgaffar ibn Hasan. *Umdetü't-tevarih*. Istanbul: Matbaa-i Amire, 1924.

Naima, Mustafa. *Naima tarihi*. Edited by Zuhuri Danışman. Istanbul: Zuhuri Danışman Yayınevi, 1967.

Peçevi, İbrahim. *Peçevi Tarihi*. 2 vols. Edited by Fahri Derin and Vahit Çabuk. Istanbul: Enderun, 1980.

Polnoe sobranie russkikh lietopisei. Vol. 13. *Lietopisnii sbornik, imenuemyi Patriarshei ili Nikonovskoi lietopis*. St Petersburg, 1904. Reprint, Moscow: Nauka, 1965.

Polnoe sobranie russkikh lietopisei. Vol. 14. *Novyi lietopisets*. St Petersburg, 1910. Reprint, Moscow: Nauka, 1965.

Possevino, Antonio. *The Moscovia of Antonio Possevino, SJ*. Translated by Hugh F. Graham. Pittsburgh: University of Pittsburgh, 1977.

Remmal Hoca. *Tarih-i Sahib Giray Han*: *Histoire de Sahib Giray, Khan de Crimée de 1532 à 1551*. With French translation by M. Le Roux. Edited by Özalp Gökbilgin. Ankara: Atatürk Üniversitesi Yayınları, 1973.

Selaniki, Mustafa Efendi. *Tarih-i Selaniki*. Edited by Mehmet İpşirli. Istanbul: Edebiyat Fakültesi Yayınları, 1999.
Silahdar, Fındıklılı Mehmed Aga. *Silahdar Tarihi*. Edited by Ahmed Refik. Istanbul: Devlet Matbaası, 1928.
Tarih-i Osman Paşa. Edited by Yunus Zeyrek. Ankara: Kültür Bakanlığı Yayınları, 2001.

Secondary Sources

Abaza, R. 'The Abazinians'. *Caucasian Review* 8 (1959): 34–40.
Ágoston, Gábor. 'A Flexible Empire: Authority and Its Limits on the Ottoman Frontiers'. In *Ottoman Borderlands: Issues, Personalities and Political Change*, edited by Kemal H. Karpat and Robert W. Zens, 15–33. Madison: University of Wisconsin Press, 2003.
Ahmed Cevded Paşa, *Tezakir*. Edited by Cavid Baysun. Ankara: Türk Tarih Kurumu, 1953.
Ahmed Refik. 'Bahr-i Hazar – Karadeniz Kanalı ve Ejderhan Seferi'. *Tarih-i Osmani Encümeni mecmuası* 43 (1917): 1–14.
Aliev, B. G. and M. S. K. Umakhanov. *Dagestan v XV–XVI vv.: Voprosy istoricheskoi geografii*. Makhachkala: Institut istorii, arkheologii i etnografii dagestanskogo nauchnogo tsentra RAN, 2004.
Aliev, B. G. and M. S. K. Umakhanov. *Istoricheskaia geografiia Dagestana, XVII–nach. XIX v*. Makhachkala: Institut istorii, arkheologii i etnografii dagestanskogo nauchnogo tsentra RAN, 2001.
Allen, W. E. D. *Problems of Turkish Power in the Sixteenth Century*. London: Central Asian Research Centre, 1963.
Allen, W. E. D. and Paul Muratoff. *Caucasian Battlefields: A History of the Wars on the Turco-Caucasian Border, 1828–1921*. Cambridge: Cambridge University Press, 1953.
Anderson, James and Liam O'Dowd. 'Borders, Border Regions and Territoriality: Contradictory Meanings, Changing Significance'. *Regional Studies* 33 (1999): 593–604.
Arslan, Hüseyin. *16. yy Osmanlı toplumunda yönetim, nüfus, iskan, göç ve sürgün*. Istanbul: Kaknüs, 2001.
Asiwaju, A. I. 'Borderlands in Africa: A Comparative Research Perspective with Particular Reference to Western Europe'. *Journal of Borderland Studies* 8 (1993): 1–12.
Ataev, D. M. et al. *Istoriia Dagestana*. Vol. 1. Moscow: Glavnaia redaktsiia vostochnoi literatury, 1967.
Ateş, Sabri. *The Ottoman–Iranian Borderlands: Making a Boundary, 1843–1914*. New York: Cambridge University Press, 2013.
Atkin, Muriel. 'Russian Expansion in the Caucasus to 1813'. In *Russian Colonial Expansion to 1917*, edited by Michael Rywkin, 139–87. London: Mansell, 1988.

Baddeley, John F. *The Rugged Flanks of Caucasus*. 2 vols. London: Oxford University Press, 1940.

Baddeley, J. F. *The Russian Conquest of the Caucasus*. London: Longmans, Green, 1908.

Barfield, Thomas J. *The Perilous Frontier: Nomadic Empires and China*. Cambridge, MA: Blackwell, 1989.

Barkan, Ömer Lütfi. 'Osmanlı İmparatorluğunda bir iskan ve kolonizasyon metodu olarak sürgünler'. *İstanbul Üniversitesi İktisat Fakültesi Mecmuası* 11 (1949–50): 524–69; 13 (1951–2): 56–78; 15 (1953–4): 209–37.

Barrett, Thomas M. *At the Edge of Empire: The Terek Cossacks and the North Caucasus Frontier, 1700–1860*. Boulder, CO: Westview Press, 1999.

Barthold, W. and A. Bennigsen, 'Dāghistān'. In *Encyclopaedia of Islam*, 2nd ed., ed. P. Bearman et al., 2:86–7. Leiden: Brill, 1998–2009.

Bartov, Omer and Eric D. Weitz. 'Introduction: Coexistence and Violence in the German, Habsburg, Russian, and Ottoman Borderlands'. In *Shatterzone of Empires: Coexistence and Violence in the German, Habsburg, Russian, and Ottoman Borderlands*, edited by Omer Bartov and Eric Weitz, 1–22. Bloomington: Indiana University Press, 2013.

Barut, Ali. 'Kırım Hanlığı ile Kuzey-Batı Kafkasya ilişkilerinde atalık müessesesinin yeri'. *Emel Dergisi* 219 (1997): 21–4.

Baud, Michiel and Van Schendel, Willem. 'Towards a Comparative History of Borderlands'. *Journal of World History* 8 (1997): 211–42.

Beituganov, S. N. *Kabarda: Istoriia i familii*. Nal'chik: El'brus, 2007.

Bennigsen, Alexandre. 'L'expédition turque contre Astrakhan en 1569, d'après les Registres des "Affaires importantes" des Archives ottomanes'. *Cahiers du monde russe et soviétique* 8 (1967): 427–46.

Berkok, İsmet. *Tarihte Kafkasya*. Istanbul: İstanbul Matbaası, 1958.

Bilge, M. Sadık. *Osmanlı Devleti ve Kafkasya*. Istanbul: Eren, 2005.

Boeck, Brian J. 'Containment vs Colonization: Muscovite Approaches to Settling the Steppe'. In *Peopling the Russian Periphery: Borderland Colonization in Eurasian History*, edited by Nicholas B. Breyfogle, Abby Schrader and Willard Sunderland, 41–60. Abingdon: Routledge, 2007.

Boeck, Brian. *Imperial Boundaries: Cossack Communities and Empire-Building in the Age of Peter the Great*. New York: Cambridge University Press, 2009.

Bronevskii, Semen. *Noveishiia geograficheskiia i istoricheskiia izvestiia o Kavkaze*. Vol. 1. Moscow: S. Selivanovskii, 1823.

Broxup, Marie Bennigsen. 'Introduction: Russia and the North Caucasus'. In *The North Caucasus Barrier: The Russian Advance towards the Muslim World*, edited by Marie Bennigsen Broxup, 1–18. London: Hurst, 1992.

Broxup, Marie Bennigsen (ed.). *The North Caucasus Barrier: The Russian Advance towards the Muslim World*. London: Hurst, 1992.

Budak, Mustafa. 'The Caucasus and the Ottoman Empire (16th–20th Centuries)'. In *The Great Ottoman-Turkish Civilization*, edited by Kemal Çiçek et al., 1:350–70. Ankara: Yeni Türkiye, 2000.

Bushev, P. P. *Istoriia posol'stv i diplomaticheskikh otnoshenii russkogo i iranskogo gosudarstv v 1586–1612 gg*. Moscow: Nauka, 1976.

Bushkovitch, Paul. 'Princes Cherkasskii or Circassian Murzas: The Kabardians in the Russian Boyar Elite, 1560–1700'. *Cahiers du monde russe* 45 (2004): 9–30.

Carrère d'Encausse, H. and A. Bennigsen. 'Avars'. In *Encyclopaedia of Islam*, 2nd ed., ed. P. Bearman et al., 1:755–6. Leiden: Brill, 1998–2009.

Colarusso, John. *A Grammar of the Kabardian Language*. Calgary, AB: University of Calgary Press, 1992.

Colarusso, John. *Nart Sagas from the Caucasus: Myths and Legends from the Circassians, Abazas, Abkhaz, and Ubykhs*. Princeton, NJ: Princeton University Press, 2002.

Colarusso, John. *The Nart Sagas of the Circassians*. Princeton, NJ: Princeton University Press, 1998.

Croskey, Robert M. 'The Diplomatic Forms of Ivan III's Relationship with the Crimean Khan'. *Slavic Review* 43 (1984): 257–69.

Croskey, Robert M. *Muscovite Diplomatic Practice in the Reign of Ivan III*. New York: Garland, 1987.

Davies, Brian L. *Warfare, State and Society on the Black Sea Steppe, 1500–1700*. Abingdon: Routledge, 2007.

de Waal, Thomas. *The Caucasus: An Introduction*. New York: Oxford University Press, 2010.

Di Cosmo, Nicola. 'Ancient Inner Asian Nomads: Their Economic Basis and Its Significance in Chinese History'. *Journal of Asian Studies* 53 (1994): 1092–1126.

Dzamikhov, K. F. *Adygi v politike Rossii na Kavkaze: 1550-e–nachalo 1770-kh gg*. Nal'chik: El'-Fa, 2001.

Elliott, Mark. 'Frontier Stories: Periphery as Center in Qing History'. *Frontiers of History in China* 9 (2014): 336–60.

Farzaliev, Akif. *Yuzhnyi Kavkaz v kontse XVI v.: Osmano-sefevidskoe sopernichestvo*. St Petersburg: Izdatel'stvo Sankt-Peterburgskogo universiteta, 2002.

Fisher, Alan. 'Azov in the Sixteenth and Seventeenth Centuries'. *Jahrbücher für Geschichte Osteuropas* 21 (1973): 161–74.

Fisher, Alan. 'Chattel Slavery in the Ottoman Empire'. *Slavery and Abolition* 1 (1980): 25–45.

Fisher, Alan. *The Crimean Tatars*. Stanford, CA: Hoover Institution Press, 1978.

Fisher, Alan W. 'Muscovite–Ottoman Relations in the Sixteenth and Seventeenth Centuries'. *Humanoria Islamica* 1 (1973): 207–17.

Fisher, Alan. 'The Ottoman Crimea in the Sixteenth Century'. *Harvard Ukrainian Studies* 5 (1981): 135–70.

Floria, B. N. 'Proekt antituretskoi koalitsii serediny XVI v.'. In *Rossiia, Pol'sha i Prichernomor'e v XV–XVIII vv.*, edited by B. A. Rybakov, 71–86. Moscow: Nauka, 1979.

Forsyth, James. *The Caucasus: A History*. Cambridge: Cambridge University Press, 2013.

Freshfield, Douglas W. *The Exploration of the Caucasus*. 2 vols. London: Edward Arnold, 1896.

Frost, Robert I. *The Northern Wars: War, State and Society in Northeastern Europe, 1558–1721*. Abingdon: Routledge, 2014.

Gadzhiev, M. G., O. M. Davudov and A. P. Shikhsaidov. *Istoriia Dagestana s drevneishikh vremen do kontsa XV v*. Makhachkala: DNTs RAN, 1996.

Glagoleva, Olga E. *Working with Russian Archival Documents*. Toronto: Centre for Russian and East European Studies, 1998.

Grimsted, Patricia Kennedy. *Archives and Manuscript Repositories in the USSR: Moscow and Leningrad*. Princeton, NJ: Princeton University Press, 1972.

Gruber, Isaiah. 'The Muscovite Embassy of 1599 to the Emperor Rudolf II of the Habsburg'. MA thesis, McGill University, 1999.

Gökbilgin, Özalp. *1532–1577 yılları arasında Kırım Hanlığı'nın siyasi durumu*. Ankara: Sevinç Matbaası, 1973.

Gökbilgin, M. Tayyip. 'Bazı arşiv belgelerine göre XVI. yüzyılda Osmanlı-Rus ticareti ve İstanbul-Moskova güzergahı'. *Araştırma dergisi* 5 (1974): 171–83.

Gökbilgin, Tayyib. 'L'expédition ottomane contre Astrakhan en 1569'. *Cahiers du monde russe et soviétique* 11 (1970): 118–23.

Gökçe, Cemal. *Kafkasya ve Osmanlı İmparatorluğunun Kafkasya siyaseti*. Istanbul: Has Kutulmuş Matbaası, 1979.

Halperin, Charles J. *Ivan the Terrible: Free to Reward and Free to Punish*. Pittsburgh: University of Pittsburgh Press, 2019.

Halperin, Charles J. *Russia and the Golden Horde: The Mongol Impact on Medieval Russian History*. London: I. B. Tauris, 1987.

Halperin, Charles J. 'Russia between East and West: Diplomatic Records during the Reign of Ivan IV'. In *Saluting Aron Gurevich: Essays in History, Literature and Other Related Subjects*, edited by Yelena Mazour-Matusevič and Alexandra S. Korros, 81–104. Leiden: Brill, 2010.

Hartog, Leo de. *Russia and the Mongol Yoke: The History of the Russian Principalities and the Golden Horde, 1221–1502*. London: British Academic Press, 1996.

Heyd, Uriel. *Ottoman Documents on Palestine, 1552–1615: A Study of the Firman According to the Mühimme Defteri*. Oxford: Clarendon Press, 1960.

Hosking, Geoffrey. *Russia: People and Empire, 1552–1917*. Cambridge, MA: Harvard University Press, 1997.

Hrushevsky, Mykhailo. *History of Ukraine-Rus'*. Vol. 7. *The Cossack Age to 1625*. Translated by Bohdan Struminski. Edited by Serhii Plokhy and Frank E. Sysyn. Toronto: Canadian Institute of Ukrainian Studies Press, 1999.

İnalcık, Halil. 'The Khan and the Tribal Aristocracy: The Crimean Khanate under Sahib Giray I'. *Harvard Ukrainian Studies* 3/4 (1979–80): 444–66.

İnalcık, Halil. 'The Origin of the Ottoman–Russian Rivalry and the Don–Volga Canal (1569)'. *Annales de l'Université d'Ankara* 1 (1947): 47–110.

İnalcık, Halil. 'Osmanlı-Rus rekabetinin menşei ve Don-Volga Kanalı teşebbüsü (1569)'. *Belleten* 12 (1948): 349–402.

İnalcık, Halil. 'Ottoman Methods of Conquest'. *Studia Islamica* 2 (1954): 103–29.

İnalcık, Halil. 'Power Relations between Russia, the Crimea and the Ottoman Empire as Reflected in Titulature'. In *Turco-Tatar Past, Soviet Present: Studies Presented to Alexandre Bennigsen*, edited by Ch. Lemercier-Quelquejay, G. Veinstein, and E. Wimbush, 175–215. Paris: École des hautes études en sciences sociales, 1986.

İnalcık, Halil. 'The Question of the Closing of the Black Sea under the Ottomans'. *Archeion Pontou* 35 (1979): 74–110.

İnalcık, Halil. 'Struggle for East-European Empire, 1400–1700'. *Turkish Yearbook of International Relations* 21 (1982): 1–16.

İnalcık, Halil. 'Yeni vesikalara göre Kırım hanlığının Osmanlı tabiliğine girmesi ve ahidname meselesi'. *Belleten* 8 (1944): 185–229.

Ivanics, Mária. 'Enslavement, Slave Labour and the Treatment of Captives in the Crimean Khanate'. In *Ransom Slavery along the Ottoman Borders*, edited by Géza Dávid and Pál Fodor, 193–221. Leiden: Brill, 2007.

Jackson, Peter and Laurence Lockhart (eds). *The Cambridge History of Iran*. Vol. 6. *The Timurid and Safavid Periods*. Cambridge: Cambridge University Press, 1986.

Jaimoukha, Amjad. *The Circassians: A Handbook*. New York: Palgrave, 2001.

Kaflı, Kadircan. *Şimali Kafkasya*. Istanbul: Vakit, 1942.

Kamalov, İlyas. *Moğollar'ın Kafkasya politikası*. Istanbul: Kaknüs, 2003.

Kamalov, İlyas. *Rus elçi raporlarında Astrahan seferi*. Ankara: Türk Tarih Kurumu, 2011.

Kanbolat, Yahya. *1864'e kadar Kuzey Kafkasya kabilelerinde din ve toplumsal düzen*. Ankara: Bayır Yayınları, 1989.

Kargalov, V. V. *Na granitsakh stoiat' krepko! Velikaia Rus' i Dikoe Pole – protivostoianie XIII–XVIII*. Moscow: Russkaia panorama, 1998.

Kazemzadeh, Firuz. 'Russian Penetration of the Caucasus'. In *Russian Imperialism from Ivan the Great to the Revolution*, edited by Taras Hunczak, 239–63. New Brunswick, NJ: Rutgers University Press, 1974.

Keenan, Edward Louis, Jr. 'Muscovy and Kazan: Some Introductory Remarks on the Patterns of Steppe Diplomacy'. *Slavic Review* 26 (1967): 548–58.

Keenan, Edward L. 'Muscovy and Kazan, 1445–1552: A Study in Steppe Politics'. PhD dissertation, Harvard University, 1965.

Kemper, Michael. *Herrschaft, Recht und Islam in Daghestan: Von den Khanaten und Gemeindebünden zum Ǧihad-Staat*. Wiesbaden: Reichert, 2005.

Khan-Girey. *Zapiski o Cherkesii*. St Petersburg, 1836. Reprint, edited by V. K. Gardanova and G. Kh. Mambetova. Nal'chik: El'-Fa, 2008.

Khodarkovsky, Michael. *Bitter Choices: Loyalty and Betrayal in the Russian Conquest of the North Caucasus*. Ithaca, NY: Cornell University Press, 2011.

Khodarkovsky, Michael. 'Colonial Frontiers in Eighteenth Century Russia: From the North Caucasus to Central Asia'. In *Extending the Borders of Russian History*, edited by Marsha Siefert, 127–43. New York: Central European University Press, 2003.

Khodarkovsky, Michael. '"Ignoble Savages and Unfaithful Subjects": Constructing Non-Christian Identities in Early Modern Russia'. In *Russia's Orient: Imperial Borderlands and Peoples, 1700–1917*, edited by Daniel R. Brower and Edward J. Lazzerini. 9–27. Bloomington: Indiana University Press, 1997.

Khodarkovsky, Michael. 'Of Christianity, Enlightenment, and Colonialism: Russia in the North Caucasus, 1550–1800' *Journal of Modern History* 71 (1999): 394–430.

Khodarkovsky, Michael. *Russia's Steppe Frontier: The Making of a Colonial Empire, 1500–1800*. Bloomington: Indiana University Press, 2002.

Khotko, S. Kh. 'Matrimonial'nye soiuzy i sistema priemnogo rodstva kak instrumenty vneshnei politiki cherkesskikh kniazhestv (XIII–XVII vv.)'. *Nauchnaia mysl' Kavkaza* 2 (2016): 76–86.

Khotko, S. Kh. 'Protivostoianie voenno-politicheskikh koalitsii v Cherkesii: Na osnove soobshchenii Elizara Rzhevskogo (1578 g.)'. *Klio* 7 (2019): 77–83.

King, Charles. *The Ghost of Freedom: A History of the Caucasus*. New York: Oxford University Press, 2008.

Kırzıoğlu, Fahrettin. *Osmanlılar'ın Kafkas elleri'ni fethi (1451–1590)*. Ankara: Sevinç Matbaası, 1976.

Kochekaev, B. B. *Nogaisko-russkie otnosheniia v XV–XVIII vv*. Alma-Ata: Nauka kazakhskoi SSR, 1988.

Kołodziejczyk, Dariusz. 'Inner Lake or Frontier: The Ottoman Black Sea in the Sixteenth and Seventeenth Centuries'. In *Enjeux politiques, économiques et militaires en Mer Noire, XIVe–XXIe siècles: études à la mémoire de Mihail Guboglu*, edited by Faruk Bilici, Ionel Cândea and Anca Popescu, 125–39. Braïla: Musée de Braïla, 2007.

Kołodziejczyk, Dariusz. *Ottoman–Polish Diplomatic Relations (15th–18th Century): An Annotated Edition of 'Ahdnames and Other Documents*. Leiden: Brill, 2000.

Koretskii, V. I. *Formirovanie krepostnogo prava i pervaia krest'ianskaia voina v Rossii*. Moscow: Nauka, 1975.

Korpela, Jukka. *Slaves from the North: Finns and Karelians in the Eastern European Slave Trade, 900–1600*. Leiden: Brill, 2019.

Kortepeter, Carl Max. 'Complex Goals of the Ottomans, Persians, and Muscovites in the Caucasus, 1578–1640'. In *New Perspectives on Safavid Iran: Empire and Society*, edited by Colin P. Mitchell, 59–84. Abingdon: Routledge, 2011.

Kortepeter, C. Max. *Ottoman Imperialism during the Reformation: Europe and the Caucasus*. New York: New York University Press, 1972.

Kozlov, S. A. *Kavkaz v sud'bakh kazachestva, XVI–XVIII vv*. St Petersburg: Kol'na, 1996.

Kunt, Metin. '17. yüzyılda Osmanlı kuzey politikası üzerine bir yorum'. *Boğazici Üniversitesi dergisi* 4–5 (1976–7): 111–15.

Kunt, Metin. 'Ottomans and Safavids: States, Statecraft, and Societies, 1500–1800'. In *A Companion to the History of the Middle East*, edited by Youssef M. Choueiri, 191–207. Malden, MA: Blackwell, 2005.

Kudriavtsev, A. A. 'Spetsifika formirovaniia i istoricheskaiia rol' grebenskogo i terskogo Kazachestva na rannem etape razvitiia'. *Gumanitarnye i iuridicheskiie issledovaniia* 4 (2015): 82–8.

Kurat, Akdes Nimet. *IV–XVIII. yüzyıllarda Karadeniz kuzeyindeki Türk kavimleri ve devletleri*. Ankara: Murat Kitabevi Yayınları, 1992.

Kurat, Akdes Nimet. 'The Turkish Expedition to Astrakhan in 1569 and the Problem of the Don–Volga Canal'. *Slavonic and East European Review* 40 (1961): 7–23.

Kurat, Akdes Nimet. *Türkiye ve İdil Boyu.* Ankara: Türk Tarih Kurumu, 1966.

Kusheva, E. N. *Narody Severnogo Kavkaza i ikh sviazi s Rossiei: Vtoraia polovina XVI–30-e gody XVII veka.* Moscow: Izdatel'stvo Akademii nauk SSSR, 1963.

Kusheva, E. N. 'Politika russkogo gosudartsva na Severnom Kavkaze v 1552–1572 gg.'. *Istoricheskie zapiski* 34 (1950): 236–87.

Kütükoğlu, Bekir. *Osmanlı-İran siyasi münasebetleri.* Istanbul: Edebiyat Fakültesi Matbaası, 1962.

Ladyzhenskii, Aleksandr. *Adaty gortsev Severnogo Kavkaza.* Rostov on Don: SKNTs VSh, 2003.

Lane, George. *Early Mongol Rule in Thirteenth-Century Iran: A Persian Renaissance.* London: RoutledgeCurzon, 2003.

Lattimore, Owen. *Studies in Frontier History: Collected Papers, 1928–1958.* London: Oxford University Press, 1962.

LeDonne, John P. *The Grand Strategy of the Russian Empire, 1650–1831.* New York: Oxford University Press, 2003.

Lemercier-Quelquejay, Chantal. 'Cooptation of the Elites of Kabarda and Dagestan in the Sixteenth Century'. In *The North Caucasus Barrier: The Russian Advance towards the Muslim World*, edited by Marie Bennigsen Broxup, 18–45. London: Hurst, 1992.

Lemercier-Quelquejay, Chantal. 'Les expéditions de Devlet Girây contre Moscou en 1571 et 1572, d'après les documents des Archives ottomanes'. *Cahiers du monde russe et soviétique* 13 (1972): 555–9.

Lemercier-Quelquejay, Chantal. 'Une source inédite pour l'histoire de la Russie au XVIe siècle: Les registres des "Mühimme Defterleri" des Archives du Baş-Vekâlet'. *Cahiers du monde russe et soviétique* 8 (1967): 335–43.

Lemercier-Quelquejay, Chantal. 'La structure sociale, politique et religieuse du Caucase du nord au XVIe siècle'. *Cahiers du monde russe et soviétique* 25 (1984): 125–48.

Leontovich, Fedor I. *Adaty Kavkazkikh gortsev: Materialy po obychnomu pravu Severnogo i Vostochnogo Kavkaza.* Odessa: P. A. Zelenyi, 1883.

Lermontov, Mikhail. *Major Poetical Works*, translated by Anatoly Liberman. Minneapolis: University of Minnesota Press, 1983.

Lermontov, Mikhail. *Sobranie sochinenii v chetyrekh tomakh*. Vol. 1. Moscow: Izdatel'stvo Akademii nauk SSSR, 1961.

Liubavskii, M. K. *Obzor istorii russkoi kolonizatsii s drevneishikh vremen do XX veka*. Moscow: Izdatel'stvo Moskovskogo universiteta, 1996.

Martin, Janet. 'Muscovite Relations with the Khanates of Kazan' and the Crimea (1460s to 1521)'. *Canadian-American Slavic Studies* 17 (1983): 435–453.

Martin, Janet. 'The Novokshcheny of Novgorod: Assimilation in the 16th Century'. *Central Asian Survey* 9/2 (1990): 13–38.

Matthee, Rudi. 'Anti-Ottoman Concerns and Caucasian Interests: Diplomatic Relations between Iran and Russia, 1587–1639'. In *Safavid Iran and Her Neighbors*, edited by Michel Mazzaoui, 101–128. Salt Lake City: University of Utah Press, 2003.

Matthee, Rudi. 'The Safavid–Ottoman Frontier: Iraq-i Arab as Seen by the Safavids'. *Journal of Turkish Studies* 9 (2003): 157–73.

Mitchell, Colin P. (ed.), *New Perspectives on Safavid Iran: Empire and Society* (Abingdon: Routledge, 2011).

Mitchell, Colin P. *The Practice of Politics in Safavid Iran: Power, Religion and Rhetoric*. New York: Palgrave Macmillan, 2009.

Namitok, Aytek. 'The "Voluntary" Adherence of Kabarda (Eastern Circassia) to Russia'. *Caucasian Review* 2 (1956): 17–28.

Newman, Andrew J. *Safavid Iran: Rebirth of a Persian Empire*. London: I. B. Tauris, 2006.

Novosel'skii, A. A. *Bor'ba moskovskogo gosudarstva s tatarami v pervoi polovine 17 v*. Moscow: Izdatel'stvo Akademii nauk SSSR, 1948.

Ostapchuk, Victor. 'Cossack Ukraine In and Out of Ottoman Orbit, 1648–1681'. In *The European Tributary States of the Ottoman Empire in the Sixteenth and Seventeenth Centuries*, edited by Gábor Kármán and Lovro Kunčević, 123–54. Leiden and Boston: Brill, 2013.

Ostapchuk, Victor. 'Crimean Tatar Long-Range Campaigns: The View from Remmal Khoja's *The History of Sahib Gerey Khan*'. In *Warfare in Eastern Europe, 1500–1800*, edited by Brian L. Davies, 147–72. Leiden: Brill, 2012.

Ostapchuk, Victor. 'The Human Landscape of the Ottoman Black Sea in the Face of the Cossack Naval Raids'. *Oriente Moderno* 81 (2001): 23–95.

Ostrowski, Donald. 'The Mongol Origins of Muscovite Political Institutions'. *Slavic Review* 49 (1990): 525–42.

Öztürk, Yücel. *Osmanlı hakimiyetinde Kefe, 1475–1600*. Ankara: Kültür Bakanlığı Yayınları, 2000.

Panaite, Viorel. *The Ottoman Law of War and Peace: The Ottoman Empire and Tribute Payers*. Boulder, CO: East European Monographs, 2000.

Panaite, Viorel. 'The Voivodes of the Danubian Principalities as Haracgüzarlar of the Ottoman Sultans'. In *Ottoman Borderlands: Issues, Personalities, and Political Changes*, edited by Kemal H. Karpat and Robert W. Zens, 59–79. Madison: University of Wisconsin Press, 2003.

Panesh, R. A. 'Sotsial'no-ekonomicheskoe i politicheskoe razvitie zapadnoadygskogo sotsiuma v poslednei chetverti XV–pervoi polovine XVI vv.'. *Vestnik Adygeiskogo gosudarstvennogo universiteta* 135 (2014): 68–77.

Pelenski, Jaroslaw. 'Muscovite Imperial Claims to the Kazan Khanate'. *Slavic Review* 26 (1967): 559–76.

Pelenski, Jaroslaw. *Russia and Kazan: Conquest and Imperial Ideology (1438–1560s)*. The Hague: Mouton, 1974.

Pienaru, Nagy. 'The Black Sea and the Ottomans: The Pontic Policy of Beyazid the Thunderbolt'. In *Ottoman Borderlands: Issues, Personalities, and Political Changes*, edited by Kemal H. Karpat and Robert W. Zens, 33–59. Madison: University of Wisconsin Press, 2003.

Piotrovskii, B. B. and A. L. Narochnitskii (eds). *Istoriia narodov Severnogo Kavkaza s drevneishikh vremen do kontsa XVIII v.* Moscow: Nauka, 1988.

Platonov, S. F. *Ivan the Terrible*. Edited and translated by Joseph L. Wieczynski. Gulf Breeze, FL: Academic International Press, 1986.

Platonov, S. F. *The Time of Troubles: A Historical Study of the Internal Crises and Social Struggle in Sixteenth- and Seventeenth-Century Muscovy*. Translated by John T. Alexander. Lawrence: University Press of Kansas, 1970.

Pollock, Sean. '"Thus We Shall Have Their Loyalty and They Our Favor": Diplomatic Hostage-Taking (*amanatstvo*) and Russian Empire in Caucasia'. In *Dubitando: Studies in History and Culture in Honor of Donald Ostrowski*, edited by Brian J. Boeck, Russell E. Martin and Daniel Rowland, 139–63. Bloomington, IN: Slavica, 2012.

Popko, I. *Terskie kazaki s starodavnikh vremen*. St Petersburg: Tipografiia Departamenta udielov, 1880.

Potto, V. A. *Dva veka terskogo kazachestva (1577–1801)*. 2 vols. Vladikavkaz: Tipografii Terskago oblastnogo pravleniia, 1912.

Power, Daniel and Naomi Standen. 'Introduction'. In *Frontiers in Question: Eurasian Borderlands, 700–1700*, edited by Daniel Power and Naomi Standen, 1–31. New York: St Martin's Press, 1999.

Richmond, Walter. *The Circassian Genocide*. New Brunswick, NJ, and London: Rutgers University Press, 2013.

Richmond, Walter. *The Northwest Caucasus: Past, Present, Future*. Abingdon: Routledge, 2008.

Rieber, Alfred. *The Struggle for the Eurasian Borderlands: From the Rise of Early Modern Empires to the End of the First World War*. Cambridge: Cambridge University Press, 2014.

Rogozhin, N. M. *Posol'skie knigi Rossii kontsa XV–nachala XVII vv.* Moscow: Institut rossiiskoi istorii, 1994.

Rogozhin, N. M. *Posol'skii prikaz: Kolybel' rossiiskoi diplomatii*. Moscow: Mezhdunarodnye otnosheniia, 2003.

Romaniello, Matthew P. 'Grant, Settle, Negotiate: Military Servitors in the Middle Volga Region'. In *Peopling the Russian Periphery: Borderland Colonization in Eurasian History*, edited by Nicholas B. Breyfogle, Abby Schrader and Willard Sunderland, 61–77. Abingdon: Routledge, 2007.

Rothman, E. Natalie, *Brokering Empire: Trans-Imperial Subjects between Venice and Istanbul*. Ithaca, NY: Cornell University Press, 2012.

Sadikov, P. A. 'Pokhod tatar i turok na Astrakhan' v 1569 g.'. *Istoricheskie zapiski* 22 (1947): 153–64.

Safvet. 'Hazar denizinde Osmanlı sancağı'. *Tarih-i Osmani encümeni mecmuası* 3 (1912): 857–61.

Şakul, Kahraman. 'Siege Warfare in Verse and Prose: the Ottoman Conquest of Kamianets-Podilsky (Kamaniçe), 1672'. In *The World of the Siege: Representations of Early Modern Positional Warfare*, edited by Anke Fischer-Kattner and Jamel Ostwald, 205–41. Leiden: Brill, 2019.

Savory, Roger. *Iran under the Safavids*. Cambridge: Cambridge University Press, 1980.

Schuster-Walser, Sibylla. *Das safawidische Persien im Spiegel europäischer Reiseberichte (1502–1722): Untersuchungen zur Wirtschafts- und Handelspolitik*. Baden-Baden: B. Grimm, 1970.

Sergeev, F. P. *Formirovanie russkogo diplomaticheskogo iazyka*. Lviv: Vyshcha shkola, 1978.

Smirnov, N. A. (ed.). *Istoriia Kabardy: S drevneishikh vremen do nashikh dnei*. Moscow: Izdatel'stvo Akademii nauk, 1957.

Smirnov, N. A. *Kabardinskii vopros v russko-turetskikh otnosheniiakh XVI–XVIII vv*. Nal'chik: Kabardinskoe gosudarstvennoe izdatel'stvo, 1948.

Smirnov, N. A. *Politika Rossii na Kavkaze v XVI–XIX vekakh*. Moscow: Izdatel'stvo sotsial'no-economicheskoi literatury, 1958.

Smirnov, N. A. *Rossiia i Turtsiia v XVI–XVII vv*. Moscow: Izdatel'stvo Moskovskogo gosudarstvennogo universiteta, 1946.

Smirnov, V. D. *Krymskoe khanstvo pod verkhovenstvom Otomanskoi Porti do nachala XVIII vieka*. 2 vols. St Petersburg, 1887. Reprint, edited by Svetlana F. Oreshkova. Moscow: Rubezhi XXI, 2005.

Solov'ev, S. M. *Istoriia Rossii s drevneishikh vremen*. 15 vols. Moscow: Izdatel'stvo sotsial'no-economicheskoi literatury, 1959–66.

Spuler, Bertold. *Die Goldene Horde: Die Mongolen in Rußland, 1223–1502*. Leipzig: Otto Harrassowitz, 1943.

Stanislavskii, L. *Grazhdanskaia voina v Rossii XVII v.: Kazachestvo na perelome istorii*. Moscow: Mysl', 1990.

Subtelny, Maria E. 'The Binding Pledge (*möchälgä*): A Chinggisid Practice and Its Survival in Safavid Iran'. In *New Perspectives on Safavid Iran: Empire and Society*, edited by Colin P. Mitchell, 9–30. Abingdon: Routledge, 2011.

Sunderland, Willard. *Taming the Wild Field: Colonization and Empire on the Russian Steppe*. Ithaca, NY: Cornell University Press, 2004.

Tatlok, T. 'The Ubykhs'. *Caucasian Review* 7 (1958): 100–9.

Tavkul, Ufuk. 'Kırım-Kafkas ilişkilerinde "Atalık" kurumunun kökeni üzerine değerlendirmeler'. *Karadeniz Araştırmaları* 51 (2016): 223–32.

Terim, Şerafettin. *Kafkas tarihinde Abazalar ve Çerkeslik mefhumu*. Istanbul: Murat Matbaacılık, 1976.

Togan, A. Zeki Velidi. *Bugünkü Türkili Türkistan ve yakın tarihi*. Istanbul: Güven Basımevi, 1947.

Trepavlov, V. V. *Istoriia Nogaiskoi Ordy*. Kazan: Kazan'skaia nedvizhimost', 2006.

Tucker, Ernest S. *Nadir Shah's Quest for Legitimacy in Post-Safavid Iran*. Gainesville: University Press of Florida, 2006.

Tymoczko, Maria and Edwin Gentzler, eds. *Translation and Power*. Amherst: University of Massachusetts Press, 2002.

Uğur, Ahmet. 'Yavuz Sultan Selim ile Kırım Hanı Mengli Giray ve oğlu Muhammed Giray arasında geçen iki konuşma'. *Ankara Üniversitesi İlahiyat Fakültesi dergisi* 21 (1963): 357–61.

Umakhanov, M. S. K. 'Problema beglykh vo vzaimootnosheniiakh dagestanskikh feodalov s tsarskoi administratsiei na Severnom Kavkaze v XVI–XVIII vv.'. In *Dagestan v sostave Rossii: Istoricheskie korni druzhby narodov Rossii i Dagestana*, edited by N. A. Magomedov, 74–8. Makhachkala: Dagestanskii filial Akademii nauk SSSR, 1990.

Unezhev, K. Kh. *Istoriia Kabardy i Balkarii*. Nal'chik: El-Fa, 2005.

Vernadsky, George. *The Mongols and Russia*. New Haven, CT: Yale University Press, 1953.

Vynar, Liubomyr. *Kniaz Dmytro Vyshnevets'kyi*. Munich: Ukrainian Free Academy of Arts and Sciences, 1964.

White, Sam. *The Climate of Rebellion in the Early Modern Ottoman Empire*. New York: Cambridge University Press, 2011.

Yakubovskii, A. Yu. *Altın Ordu ve Çöküşü*. Translated by Hasan Eren. Ankara: Türk Tarih Kurumu, 1992.

Yaşar, Murat. 'Evliya Çelebi in the Circassian Lands: Vampires, Tree Worshippers, and Pseudo-Muslims'. *Acta Orientalia Academiae Scientiarum Hungaricae* 67 (2014): 75–96.

Yaşar, Murat. 'Ivan Petrovich Novosiltsev'. In *Christian–Muslim Relations: A Bibliographical History*. Vol. 7. *Central and Eastern Europe, Asia, Africa and South America, 1500–1600*, edited by David Thomas and John Chesworth, 426–9. Leiden: Brill, 2015.

Yaşar, Murat. 'The North Caucasus between the Ottoman Empire and the Tsardom of Muscovy: The Beginnings, 1552–1570'. *Iran and the Caucasus* 20 (2016): 105–25.

Yaşar, Murat and Chong Jin Oh. 'The Ottoman Empire and the Crimean Khanate in the North Caucasus: A Case Study of Ottoman–Crimean Relations in the Mid-Sixteenth Century'. *Turkish Historical Review* 9 (2018): 86–103.

Yerasimos, Stefanos. 'Türklerin Kafkasları: egzotizmle jeopolitik arasında-II'. *Toplumsal Tarih* 37 (1997): 7–13.

Zaitsev, I. V. *Astrakhanskoe khanstvo*. Moscow: Vostochnaia literatura, 2004.
Zasedateleva, L. B. *Terskie kazaki: Seredina XVI–nachalo XX v*. Moskva: Izdatel'stvo Moskovskogo universiteta, 1974.
Zelkina, Anna. *In Quest for God and Freedom: The Sufi Response to the Russian Advance in the North Caucasus*. New York: New York University Press, 2000.

Index

aamista see *aamistadi*
aamistadi, 30
Abadzehs, 30
Abak, 135, 182
Abazas, 29, 30, 44
Abdullah Khan, 42
Abkhazis, 29, 30
adat, 24, 31, 43, 146
Adil Girey (Crimean prince), 106, 117–18, 126–7, 129
Adil Girey (Daghestani prince), 168, 170
Adyghe, 23
ah see *akha*
ahipshi, 30
Ahmed Çavuş, 96, 112
Ahmed (Janey chief), 92, 136
Ahtı, 128, 150
akha, 30
Akkerman, 68, 121
Alacahisar, 68
Aleppo, 52, 66
Alexander II, 14, 133, 142, 150, 155, 158, 163–4, 166–8, 178, 183, 194–7
Ali Bey, 112, 143
Alkas, 135, 156–8, 160, 173–4, 185
Altynchach, 71
amanat, 58, 157–8, 208
Amasya, 91
Ambassadorial Office *see Posol'skii Prikaz*
Anapa, 37
Anastasia Romanovna, 69
Anatolia, 4, 39, 80, 89, 90, 119, 127, 169, 172, 214
Anderi, 170
Andi, 169
Andrei Khvorostinin, 146–7, 166
Andrei Kuzminskii, 6, 107–8
Antonio Possevino, 84, 103, 112
anyayoutskia, 30
Araghi Valley, 21
Armenia, 22, 37, 39
Asafi Dal Mehmed Çelebi, 129, 151–2, 187
Aslanbek, 8, 71, 73, 75, 106, 114, 116, 121, 134–5, 145, 155–6, 183–4, 186–9
Assyrians, 33
Astrakhan, 3, 11, 13, 26, 35–6, 40–2, 49, 55–7, 59, 63–9, 71, 73–6, 78, 82, 86–109, 117–24, 135, 138, 141–7, 158, 160, 162–6, 174, 186–7, 190–3, 203, 207–10
atalık see *atalyk*
atalyk, 24–5, 157, 204–5
Atsymguk, 62, 66
aul, 31
Avars, 21, 24, 31–2, 125, 126, 128–9, 146, 150, 211
Azak, 8, 35, 37, 51, 59, 65, 67, 68, 80–1, 83, 89, 90–1, 93, 100–1, 115, 121–5, 135–7, 144, 165, 181, 190–1, 193, 203, 205, 207
azat, 27
Azerbaijan, 22, 37
Azlov, 156
Azov Sea, 19–20, 83, 89, 205

Babylonians, 33
Bahçesaray, 67, 99
Balkans, 80, 91, 202
Balkars, 23, 36, 126
Behram Bey, 134
Bekbulat, 71
Berduk, 136
Beşir, 136
Beslen, 186

Besleneys, 26, 29, 30–1, 54, 66, 92, 135–6
Bestau, 26–7, 29–30, 54, 62–3, 67, 92, 96, 130, 136, 179, 210
beylerbeyi, 90, 194
beylerbeyilik, 12, 90, 213
Bibikov, 160
Black Sea, 13, 20–1, 25, 28–30, 37, 40, 49–51, 53–5, 60, 65, 67–8, 89–90, 98, 102, 124, 137, 165, 171, 179, 202, 204–5, 207–10
Boğazcık Fortress, 137
Bolayıkoğlu, 136
Boris Blagovo, 6, 140–1
Boris Godunov, 169–71
Bozok, 135, 156, 173
Bozokoğlu Mehmed, 121
burg, 26–7
Burgun, 126
Buzuruk Murza *see* Bozok
Byzantine Empire, 28, 37

Cafer Bey (governor of Kefe), 89
Cafer Pasha (Ottoman commander/governor in the Caucasus), 130, 133, 142, 166–7
Caffa *see* Kefe
cagar, 32
Cane Fortress, 37, 51
Canik, 91
Caspian Sea, 19–21, 26, 39, 42, 49, 60, 88–9, 101, 118, 120, 125, 127, 129, 141, 162, 203, 208–9, 211
Catholicisation, 65
çavuş, 139, 146
cema'at, 30, 32
Central Asia, 26, 88–9, 100–1, 105, 141, 191, 209
Çermik, 126
Cezeri Kasım Pasha, 37
chanka, 32
Chechens, 36
Chechnya, 3
China, 89
Chinggis Khan, 204
Chinggisid, 35–6, 50, 55, 57–8, 64, 124, 140–1, 204, 208
Chopolov, 156, 158
Çıldır, 127
Circassians, 23–4, 26, 28–31, 37, 39, 51–3, 56, 59, 62, 66–7, 73–4, 76, 80, 83–4, 90, 95, 101, 106, 120, 122–3, 127, 130, 135–6, 149, 158, 165, 168, 178–81, 210
Circassian genocide, 3
Çirmen, 68
Constantine, 197
Çorum, 90–1
Cossacks, 24, 33–4, 52, 60–2, 65, 67–8, 73, 74–6, 80–1, 83, 92, 107, 123, 124–5, 137, 139–41, 143, 146–7, 156, 158, 160, 162, 165, 167, 178–9, 181–2, 185–6, 188, 192, 194, 199, 204–6
Crimean Khanate, 6, 9, 13, 29, 35–7, 39–42, 49–51, 54–5, 60, 63, 65–7, 69, 71, 76, 77, 81, 88, 92, 93, 95, 97, 98, 100, 103, 105–6, 108–9, 118, 123–4, 126, 128, 137, 139–141, 143, 145, 147, 156, 172, 181, 183, 186, 187, 190, 193, 202, 204–5, 207–8, 211
Crimean Tatars, 25, 30–1, 34, 36, 39–41, 50–3, 56, 59–62, 66–7, 69, 71, 73, 75–6, 82, 86, 106, 108, 112, 115–16, 118, 121, 133, 137, 139, 141, 144–6, 155–6, 166, 172, 179, 181–9, 191–3, 203–5, 212
Cyprus, 97, 101, 105, 108

Daghestan, 13, 20–4, 26, 31–3, 37, 39, 53, 54, 56, 63, 69, 73–6, 93, 95, 97, 101, 122, 125–140, 142, 146–7, 149, 150, 155, 158, 162–72, 176, 177, 183, 185–6, 189, 196–7, 210–14
Danilo Adashev, 68
darü'l-islam, 64
Daryal Pass, 20–1, 26, 69
Davud Khan (Georgian king), 126–7
Davud (Janey chief), 136
Derbend, 21, 32–3, 89, 120, 129, 130, 133–6, 139, 142, 146, 150, 159, 162–3, 165–8, 170, 172–3, 182, 185, 188
Devlet Girey I, 6, 64, 76, 88, 89, 93, 96–9, 106, 108, 143
dezhenugo, 27
dirliksüz, 68
Diyarbakır, 111, 119, 167
Dmytro Vyshnevetskyi, 13, 31, 34, 52, 65–9, 82, 86, 178
Dnieper River, 34, 68

Don Cossacks, 34, 141, 165
Don River, 34, 123–5, 160, 194
Don-Volga Canal, 90, 95, 111
Dutahferuk, 136

Eltyuk, 157
Emir Mirza, 125, 149
Erzurum, 119
Evliya Çelebi, 2, 128, 151
Ezbozluk, 62–3

Feodor I, 140–2, 155, 159, 165, 168
Ferhad Kethüda, 133, 135

Gazi Girey II, 137, 143, 160
Gazi Salih, 33, 125, 128
Gazi-Kumuk, 31
Gedik Ahmed Pasha, 37
Gelibolulu Mustafa Ali, 126, 129–30
Gence, 167
Golden Horde, 25, 35–40, 46, 50, 54–7, 106, 108, 203–4, 206, 208
Goria, 39, 127
Grand Duchy of Lithuania, 181
Great Horde, 36, 40
Greater Caucasus Mountains, 19–21, 26, 28, 53, 129
Greater Nogay Horde, 14, 35, 42, 71, 73, 92, 123–4, 137–8, 142, 144–5, 160, 178, 189–94, 207
Greben Cossacks, 33–4, 61, 206
Grebentsy see Greben Cossacks
Grigorii Nashchokin, 165–6
Grigorii Zasekin, 164

Habsburgs, 159, 165–6, 168–9
Halil Bey, 52
haraç, 136, 152
Hasan Pasha, 164
Hatukhays, 24, 30
Hezarfen Hüseyin (chronicler), 53
Hoşab, 167
Hunzah, 32
Hüseyin (envoy of the *shamkhal*), 126

Ibak *see* Abak
Ibero-Caucasian, 31–3
İbrahim Peçevi, 88, 130
Idars, 14, 29, 107, 115, 155, 178, 181–2, 184, 186–9
Ignatii Veshniakov, 68
Ilkhanid Empire, 36
İmam Kulı Khan, 133
Imereti, 39
Inal, 26, 29, 181
İnebahtı, 68
İslam Girey, 138–40, 143
İslam-Kerman, 67
Islamisation, 33, 53, 127, 136
İsmail Beg, 35, 42, 54, 71, 89, 123, 190
Istanbul, 12, 25, 28, 41, 52, 67, 68, 89, 97, 99, 101, 106, 107, 120–1, 123, 125, 133, 134–6, 138, 141, 165, 169, 171, 198, 205, 212–13
istimalet, 51, 53, 78, 205
Ivan Baturlin, 170–1
Ivan Dashkov, 73–4
Ivan IV, 6, 41, 56, 62–5, 67–9, 71–4, 82, 84, 87, 98–9, 101–4, 106–8, 112, 114–19, 122, 139–40, 145, 157, 162, 165, 168, 171, 179, 191
Ivan Novosiltsev, 6, 98–108, 111

Janeys, 14, 26, 29, 39, 52–4, 66, 74, 120, 135–6, 178–9, 181, 199
Joasaph II, 103

kabak, 27
Kabarda, 7–8, 14, 21, 23, 26–31, 39, 49, 54, 63–9, 71, 73–6, 86, 93, 96, 98, 100–2, 105–8, 115–19, 121–2, 124, 134–5, 139, 142–7, 155–65, 168–9, 171–2, 178–9, 181–9, 209–11
Kabardinians, 14, 21, 23–4, 26–30, 39, 54, 56, 66–7, 76, 84, 96, 116, 122, 144, 145–6, 151, 155, 160, 166, 168, 170, 178, 197
Kakheti, 14, 39, 133, 142, 150, 155–6, 163–4, 167–9, 178, 183, 194–7
Kanbulat, 107, 115–17, 122, 144–7, 155–7, 182–4, 186–8
Kanoke, 29
Kansavuk, 14, 66–7, 178–9, 181
Kansutrak, 136
Kanuko, 66
Kara Koysu River, 32

Kara-Budak, 170
Karachai, 23, 36
Kartli, 39
Kasım Mirza (of Shirvan), 150
Kasım Pasha (Ottoman commander), 88, 90–2, 95–100, 122, 124, 190
Kastamonu, 140
Kastok, 136
Kaytaks, 24, 31–2, 126, 129–30, 167
Kaytuks, 14, 71, 73, 75, 106, 116, 155–6, 178, 186–9
Kazan, 35–6, 40–2, 54–7, 59, 62–4, 76, 88–9, 92, 98, 101–3, 108, 123, 160, 162, 191, 207–9
Kazy (Lesser Nogay leader), 71, 84, 115, 123
Kazy (Kabardinian prince), 106, 135, 169, 187, 189
Kefe, 8, 11–12, 37, 51–3, 59, 67–8, 83, 88–91, 96–8, 101, 105, 119–23, 127, 130, 133–42, 144, 172, 181–2, 188, 190, 199, 203, 205, 207, 213
kekovat, 35
Kemirgoys, 29–31, 54, 130, 136–7
Kerç, 90, 130
keykuvat see *kekovat*
Khanate of Bukhara, 141, 191–2
Khanate of Sibir, 36
Khoroshai (baptised as Boris), 117
Khotov, 147, 156
Kipchak, 31
Kirkan, 136
Kızıltaş, 37, 51
kniaz, 26–7, 63, 75
Koba, 37
konak, 25
Köstendil, 91, 130
Koysu, 170
Koysu Andi River, 32
Koysu Avar River, 32
Koysu River, 166, 170
krym-shamkhal, 32, 45, 166
Kuban region, 21, 23–4, 27, 29–30, 35, 71, 136
Kuban River, 19–20, 29, 37, 50, 130, 134
Kuban–Taman region, 53, 62, 66, 69, 86, 92, 120–1, 123, 179, 205
Kuchenei (baptised as Maria), 28, 69, 71, 84
Kudadik (baptised as Alexander), 62–3
Kudenek, 144–7
Kulgun Mirza, 74
Kuma River, 20, 26
Kuma-Manych Depression, 19, 21
Kumyks, 21, 24, 31–2, 101, 146, 158, 166
Kura River, 32, 120

Laba River, 130
Laks, 21, 24, 31
Lala Mustafa Pasha, 125–8, 194, 211
Lesser Nogay Horde, 35, 71, 73, 84, 93, 115–16, 123, 137, 142, 190–1, 193
Levant, 89
Lezgins, 33
Livny, 159–60
Livonian War, 56, 107, 118, 191
loganapit, 27
Lori, 167
Luka Novosiltsev, 117–18

ma'sum, 33, 126, 167
Maashuk, 62
Malkhurub, 71
Mamstriuk, 28, 107, 115–18, 144–7, 156–8, 182–5, 188–9, 199
Maykop, 90
Mazandaran, 173
Mecca, 64, 88, 100
Mehmed Çelebi (Ottoman merchant), 100
Mehmed Girey I, 41
Mehmed Girey II, 118, 138–40
Mehmed II (Ottoman sultan), 37, 101, 105
Mehmed (Western Circassian chief), 136–7
Mehmed (Besleney chief), 136
Mehmed (Ottoman-appointed governor of Kabarda), 116, 121, 134–5
Mengli Girey, 40, 143
Mesih Pasha, 141
Metropolitan Makarii, 103
Mingrelia, 39, 127
Moldavia, 68, 82, 91
Moscow, 6–7, 12, 28, 31, 54, 58, 62–3, 69, 71, 84, 99–101, 103, 107–8, 115–17, 138, 140, 144, 155, 157–8, 166, 168–9, 179, 183, 188, 196, 198, 213

Mount Elbrus, 20
Mount Kazbek 20
Mübarek Girey, 166
mühimme, 4–5, 7–8, 121
Murad Girey, 65, 138, 140–3, 147, 153, 158, 163, 165–6, 174, 183, 192
Murad III, 125–6, 141, 151, 165–6
Mustafa (Western Circassian chief), 52, 92, 120
mutasarrıf, 88

Nadir Shah, 37
Niğbolu, 91, 130
Nikonian Chronicle, 67, 75
nişancı, 4
Nogays, 14, 22–4, 34–6, 39–42, 54–5, 57, 59, 64, 71, 73, 80, 84, 91, 98, 115, 120, 123–5, 137–8, 140–2, 144–5, 158, 160, 178, 189–94, 207, 209
Novorossiisk, 137
Nurdevlet Girey, 40
nureddin, 35, 143
nutsal, 32

og see *loganapit*
oprichnina, 69, 108
Osmanovskii shliakh see Ottoman road
Ossetians, 36
Ottoman Imperial Council, 4, 88–9, 100, 125, 142, 212
Ottoman road, 139
Özdemiroğlu Osman Pasha, 13, 120, 128–9, 133–5, 139–41, 151–2, 162–3, 187–8, 211–12
özden see *uzden*
Özi, 66

palanka, 123
Pannonia, 32
Papacy, 146
Peter I, 41, 209
Petro Doroshenko, 209
Piyale Pasha, 142, 193
plausible deniability, 62, 81, 203, 210
Poland-Lithuania, 34, 40, 42, 49–50, 60–1, 92, 95–6, 98–9, 103, 114, 145, 204
pominki, 58–9, 208
Pontic–Caspian steppes, 8, 20, 37, 49, 55, 60–1, 67, 81, 88, 97, 123–4, 197, 159, 171–2, 189–92, 203–8, 210
posol'skia kniga, 4–6
Posol'skii Prikaz, 5–8, 99, 103–5, 107, 163
Prince Beyazıd, 92, 111
Psheapshoko, 71, 73, 75, 84, 106, 116, 135, 186–7
pshi, 26–7, 29–30, 144–5, 182
pshihua, 27, 71, 107, 115–16, 134, 144–5, 147, 155–6, 158–9, 184–9
pshim yapsh see *pshihua*
pshitle, 29

rayat see *cagar*
Remmal Hoca, 55, 64
Revan, 167
Roma, 91
Romanov dynasty, 173
Rudolf II, 159, 166
Rumelia, 4, 169

Saadet Girey, 138, 140, 192
Safavid Empire, 13–14, 21–2, 36–7, 39, 55–6, 58, 63–5, 69, 88, 92, 96, 99, 115, 117–29, 133–43, 146, 156, 159, 162–3, 166–72, 191–7, 204, 209, 211–14
Sahib Girey I, 39, 41–2, 50, 54–5, 64, 66
sala uzden, 32
Saltankul (baptised as Mikhail Temriukovich Cherkasskii), 28, 69, 157
sancak, 12, 76, 121, 137, 213
sancakbeyi, 51–2, 66, 78, 116, 121, 134, 178
Saraichuk, 35
Şeca'atname, 187
Sefa Girey (khan of Kazan), 41
Sefa Girey (Crimean prince), 138, 140, 143
Selanik, 68
Selim I, 37, 43
Selim II, 89, 97–105, 107–8, 140
Şemahı, 129, 150, 169–70, 185
Semen Zvenigorodskii, 156–7
Seyyid Ahmed, 40
Shafi'i, 33
Shah Abbas I, 159, 166, 169–70, 197, 214
shamkhal, 31–3, 53, 56, 63, 73–6, 95, 101, 122, 125–6, 128–30, 135, 142,

146, 149–50, 157–8, 162–70, 174, 183, 185–6, 196–7, 210
shamkhalate, 31–2, 75, 126, 163, 166
Shapshugs, 24, 30
shert', 58, 117, 144–7, 156, 169, 179, 188, 192, 208
Shi'ite, 33, 37
Shirvan, 22, 117, 120, 126–9, 133, 136, 139, 150, 164, 166–9, 185, 191, 194
Shumunuk, 156
Sibok (baptized as Vasilii), 14, 62, 66, 74, 178–81
Sigismund II, 65, 69, 82
Silistre, 68, 84, 91, 130
Simon Maltsev, 124
Sinan Pasha (governor of Silistre), 68
Sinan Pasha (Ottoman vizier), 165
Şirin tribe, 143
Sivas, 126
Sochi, 3
Soğucak, 136–7
Sokullu Mehmed Pasha, 88–90, 97, 100–1, 119–20, 209, 211
Solokh, 14, 135, 145, 147, 155–60, 169, 174, 178, 181–9, 199
South Caucasus, 14, 21–2, 39, 63, 69, 115, 117, 119, 125–7, 129, 143, 147, 155–6, 159, 162, 171–2, 188, 196, 211, 213–14
Sozomuko, 136
stateinye spiski, 5
strel'tsy, 74–5, 107, 139, 143, 147, 158, 160, 185, 192, 206
Sulak River, 32, 130, 164
Süleyman I, 39, 41, 54–5, 64, 89, 92, 99, 119, 123, 178
Sultan Mahmud (Daghestani prince), 169–70
Sunni, 33, 35, 37, 64, 88, 120, 122, 126, 150, 209–10
Sunzha River, 33–4, 75, 117, 139, 156, 159–60, 164–5, 182
Sweden, 145, 146, 183

Tabarasan, 32–3, 125–6, 128–9
Tabarasan shah see *ma'sum*
Tabriz, 37, 89
Tabuly Mirza, 186
Tahmasp I, 39, 119
Taman, 19, 21–2, 29–31, 37, 50–3, 62, 65–7, 69, 86, 90–2, 96, 109, 120–1, 123, 127, 130, 135–6, 138, 178–9, 199, 202, 205, 209–10
Tana *see* Azak
Tanashuk, 62
Tansaruk, 182
Tapshiuk, 147, 183, 187
Tarku, 31–2, 75, 126, 166, 168, 170, 176
Tasoltan, 181–2, 186, 188
tawad see *aamistadi*
Tausaltan *see* Tasoltan
Tazriut, 63
Tbilisi, 120, 126–7
tefekashou see *anyayoutskia*
tekhoqotle, 29
Temriuk, 8, 28, 63, 69, 71, 73–6, 83–4, 86, 93, 98, 101, 106–7, 111, 115–16, 121, 134–5, 140, 144, 155, 157, 162, 165, 186–7, 189
Temrük, 37, 51, 65, 67, 130, 137
Terek Cossacks, 34, 61, 67, 141, 206
Terek Fortress, 74, 144–7, 155–9, 162, 163–4, 166, 170, 182–3, 185, 199, 207, 213
Terek hakimi, 93
Terek River, 20, 26, 33–4, 36, 75–6, 86, 93, 101, 107, 117–18, 124, 130, 134, 139–40, 142, 144, 146, 150, 160, 162, 164–5, 188
Terek Valley, 21
Terek Town *see* Terek Fortress
Third Rome, 58
Tiflis see Tbilisi
timar, 52, 66, 78, 87
timariot, 68, 91, 93, 130
Timurid Empire, 36
Tinahmet Beg, 71, 190, 192
tlakotlesh, 27
tlfekotl, 27
Tokhtamysh, 36
Topkapı Palace, 5, 101
Torkh Antonov, 156–7
Trabzon, 37
Trebizond Empire, 37
Treaty of Amasya, 39
Treaty of Istanbul, 162, 169
Tsaritsyn, 144, 159–60, 192

Tsurak, 31
Tuchalav Burhaneddin, 125, 128–9
tukhum, 32
tuma, 27
Turco-Mongoalian, 57, 172, 177, 204
Turkey, 202
Tutaryk (baptised as Ivan), 63

Ubykhs, 30
Ukraine, 61, 65, 80, 202, 209
unatle, 29
unavi, 30
Urup River, 130
Urus Beg, 14, 123–4, 137–8, 142, 178, 189–94, 200
Urus Mirza *see* Urus Beg
usmi, 32–3, 126, 129–30, 167
usmiate, 32, 129
ustmii see *usmi*
uzden, 27, 29, 32, 78, 163

Vainaks, 23
Van, 119, 167
Venice, 97
Vidin, 68
voevoda (Muscovite governor), 68, 74
voivode (ruler of Wallachia and Moldavia), 68
Volga River, 13, 34–6, 42, 49, 59–61, 71, 76, 88–91, 95, 100, 109, 111, 119–20, 123, 144, 159–60, 162, 171, 189–94, 203, 207–8
Vulçitrin, 68

Wallachia, 68, 91
Western Circassians, 8, 23, 26, 29–31, 51, 56, 62, 66–7, 73, 95, 120, 122, 127, 135–6, 165, 179, 181, 210
werk see *work*
work, 27

Yağmurcu, 41, 64
Yahşi Saat Mirza, 138
Yaik River, 35, 59, 160, 189–90, 192, 194
Yankhot, 186
Yansokh, 134–5, 155–6, 158–9, 183–7, 189
yarım-shamkhal see *krym-shamkhal*
yasir, 32
Yerevan, 169
yurt, 31, 35
Yusuf Mirza, 54, 89

Zaporozhian Cossacks, 31, 34, 52, 65, 67, 80–1, 178
zeuche, 27
zhalovaniia, 58–9, 208